11.25

P9-ASN-270

CINEMA BOOKLIST

Supplement One

by

George Rehrauer

The Scarecrow Press, Inc.
Metuchen, N.J.   1974

Library of Congress Cataloging in Publication Data

    Rehrauer, George.
      Cinema booklist.

    -- ---Supplement one.
      1. Moving-pictures--Bibliography. I. Title.
    Z5784.M9R42 Suppl.   016.79143   70-188378
    ISBN 0-8108-0696-7

To Allie
the lady who carried
me into my first movie

CONTENTS

FOREWORD

In the 1970's, authorship of any material pertinent to the cinema is a challenge because of the knowledge, interests, and reactions of the potential readership. During the last decade the publication of film literature has increased many times over and the appetite for information about all aspects of films appears still to be growing enormously.

There was no single guide to this deluge of material, and the publication of Cinema Booklist in 1972 was an attempt to fill that gap.

This volume continues that effort. Using mostly books published from 1971 to 1973 that were concerned with film or filmmaking, the author has gathered more than 900 entries. Possibilities for inclusion were sought out, read, examined, described, and/or evaluated. Certain limitations prevent the volume from being as comprehensive or as detailed as the author wished it to be. Revision, addition, enlargement, and correction will take place in any subsequent editions that may occur. Reader comment is encouraged and will be most gratefully received.

George Rehrauer
Rutgers University
July, 1973

INTRODUCTION

This volume is not intended to be a work of scholarly research or a collection of clever book reviews; it is meant to be an aid for the large general audience that is interested in reading about the cinema for one reason or another. Its major purpose is to assist the librarian and the interested reader in the search for books on film topics, and in building film-related collections.

Arrangement

The arrangement of the material was dictated by one criterion: ease and simplicity of use. If the reader is aware of a few patterns, the book can be used more quickly and efficiently.

1. Books are listed in alphabetical order using the dictionary method--letter by letter (i.e., regardless of word breaks).

2. Every word except initial "a," "an," and "the" is taken into account with one exception: when a real person's full name appears in a title, the first name is ignored. So, The Cinema of Stanley Kubrick would appear before The Cinema of Orson Welles since neither Stanley nor Orson is considered. The rationale for this departure from usual practice is that current usage refers to many directors and personalities by last name--Fellini, Lubitsch, Gable, Monroe, Dietrich, etc.

3. The publisher indicated is the one responsible for the edition examined. Most of the volumes included are available in paperback or soft cover format. Conversely, it is a growing practice for libraries to rebind paperback originals in hard cover. Dates given in parentheses (e.g., for Arno reprints) are the original publication dates and the work has not been revised since. If the reader wishes more information on a particular volume, he is directed to his library, his bookstore, or to:

A. Books in Print. New York: R. R. Bowker Company.
B. Paperbound Books in Print. New York: R. R. Bowker Company.

Selection

The stream of books on film is so copious that the reader will find it difficult to keep informed about what is being published. Topics have become so specialized that the appearance of The Films of J. Carroll Naish is a distinct possibility. Cinema bookstores have trouble in keeping their catalogs up-to-date and reviews found in most professional journals represent only a very small sampling. With the forthcoming video-cassette and other newer technologies, the increased use of films by libraries, and the multiplicity of film courses appearing in our schools and colleges, the interest in film topics can only increase, and publication of books will follow in direct proportion. The most positive aspect of this publishing bonanza is that many of the books are of very high quality--in fact, they are more entertaining and satisfying than many of today's films.

An attempt was made to sample this entire spectrum of books on film, ranging from the trashy original paperback through the souvenir program book to the commercialized doctoral dissertation. In searching for the books to be included, the writer used his own collection as a base. In addition, the library of the Museum of Modern Art and the Library for the Performing Arts at Lincoln Center were bountiful sources. Small public libraries in New York and New Jersey provided older books of interest. Finally, some publishers were kind enough to furnish copies of their books for review.

Using these sources, any book which could be related to any aspect of film was included in the final grouping. Omitted were all fictional novels having Hollywood or film themes (The Carpetbaggers, The Magic Lantern, The Trojans, etc.), and all novels derived from film scripts (Bonnie and Clyde, The Misfits, etc.). Several out-of-print books were considered, either because of their easy availability in the used-book stores or because of their potential for republication. Any book of quality written about film in the past 70 years is a candidate for resurrection by publishers.

Availability, cutoff dates, and deadlines dictated which books could be accorded detailed consideration and which could not. The shorter descriptions of certain books will be enlarged in future editions.

A very small number of the books listed have not been published at this writing. In all cases, the publishers were contacted and assurances were received about their appearance in the near future. Information on certain other volumes was obtained from secondary sources. In all these cases, more than one source was consulted if possible. Any inaccuracies brought to the writer's attention will be appreciated and corrected in later editions.

Scripts

The word "script" is used throughout this book and is meant to apply to screenplays, treatments, shooting scripts, scenarios, photoplays, etc. While the differences in the various forms are acknowledged, any attempt at labeling the many volumes in this category would only cause confusion for the reader.

Filmmaking

This important word is usually spelled in three ways --film making, film-making, and filmmaking. In reference to individual books, the spelling preferred by the author of that book is used. In all other cases, filmmaking is used.

Film Scripts

A selected listing of published scripts follows the last entry, number 2909. Both modern and classic are combined in the single listing. It should be noted that excerpts, fictionalized or novelized scripts, and picture books from scripts are not considered. Only complete scripts are included.

Souvenir Books

More than 100 of the entries in this volume are for souvenir books or, as they are sometimes called, program books. Published usually for the more expensive or road-show film, they are sold to patrons as they enter and leave the theatre. Once the film has completed its reserved-seat run, the books are usually remaindered and picked up by discount or specialty bookstores.

The decision to include them was reinforced by several

factors. First, they get an original distribution and audience exposure equivalent to that received by many other film books. In addition, the quality of both production and content found in some is more than comparable to many independently produced books about specific films. Finally, as a matter of record or historical interest, their inclusion may further some film studies yet to be undertaken.

The reader should be aware of several characteristics of the souvenir books. More often than not, authorship or editorial credit is not acknowledged. This is also true of publisher information in a few cases. The books are always positive about the film they describe and tend to offer information--not criticism. Photographs take up the major portion of the pages and include stills from the film, portraits of the stars and leading production personnel, and candid shots made during the filming. All contain cast and production credits and most single out the leading actors, the director and the producer for individual attention.

Nearly all of the souvenir books examined for this volume are part of a collection belonging to William Kaiser, who has been collecting them since his pre-teen years. His cooperation with the author is most appreciated.

Interviews

The interview book is a relatively new form in publishing. It exists in many variations from the complete single interview (The Cinema of Otto Preminger, 2129) to the collection (Encountering Directors, 2216) or the interview used to supplement a film script (CISCO PIKE, 2143). A newer use is the oral history (The Magic Factory, 2506) which combines several interviews into a unified statement. At times the interview is called a conversation or a dialogue, and certain artists have been known to have a conversation with themselves in print (Cinema Yesterday and Today, 2139).

The subjects of these interviews have, for the most part, been directors or actors. Interviews with other craftsmen and artisans such as cameramen, musicians, editors, etc. have been appearing with greater frequency lately.

In order to isolate this form from the multiple subject listings and to indicate some interviews not included in the subject index, a list of selected interviews is given in this volume.

Author Index

A straightforward index of authors and co-authors of works cited in this volume and in Cinema Booklist follows. It also includes directors of all motion pictures entered in both books as filmscripts. This is, then, a cumulative index covering both volumes. Numbers 1 to 1505 refer to titles in Cinema Booklist while all 2000 numbers (2001 to 2909) are entries in this volume.

Subject Index

The subject index is selective and not meant to be comprehensive. Obviously, consideration of the contents of more than 2400 volumes prohibited total indexing. For example: Mary Pickford is mentioned in more than 100 of the books; the subject index lists, in this case, the nine sources that the author believes to be most important. Readers should not feel limited by this index but may find it useful as a starting point for any investigation.

The subject index is also cumulative and covers both Cinema Booklist and this volume. Numbers 1 to 1505 refer to Cinema Booklist while all 2000 numbers (2001 to 2909) are entries in this volume.

2001.   Academy Players Directory, edited by James R.
         Roberts. 2 vols. 735, 826 p. (paperback) illus.
         Los Angeles: Academy of Motion Picture Arts and
         Sciences, 1972.
         This set consists of two volumes, the first for
women and children (735 pages), and the second for men
(826 pages). Published annually as a guide to those actors
who are currently available for parts in films, the books
list credits, addresses or phone numbers, and usually a
portrait of the player. Acceptable for all collections.

2002.   ACCIDENT. A script of the 1967 film, by Harold
         Pinter (director: Joseph Losey). 367 p. London:
         Methuen & Co., Ltd., 1971.
         Found in Five Screenplays by Harold Pinter (2291).

2003.   Action! Camera! Super 8 Cassette Film Making
         for Beginners, by Rich Carrier and David Carroll.
         78 p. illus. New York: Charles Scribner's Sons,
         1972.
         A most helpful aid for beginning filmmakers. By
considering only super 8mm cassette film, the authors cover
their topic with clarity and economy. An explanation of the
camera is followed by a discussion of filming techniques--
pan, tilt, dissolve, etc. Film qualities such as type and
ASA rating are defined and some suggestions are offered
about editing, storage, and cleaning films.
         Four short films are presented as models for ini-
tiation or inspiration. Final sections deal with screening
films, and the preparation and planning of future films.
         The text is strongly supported by many illustrations
and diagrams which are well reproduced. No index is necessary as the table of contents provides sufficient location
data for the various topics.
         Because of its basic understandable approach to
beginning filmmaking, this book will aid and satisfy many
readers. It will be very popular with school libraries but
is by no means limited to a youth audience. Highly recommended for all collections.

2004.   Actors Guide: What You Should Know about Contracts
          You Sign, by D. Farber.   272 p.   (paperback) New
          York: Drama Book Shop, 1972.
          Although there is some information about film con-
tracts, the emphasis is overwhelmingly on theatrical-stage
matters.   Samples, information and advice are included.
Acceptable for all collections.

2005.   ADAM'S RIB.   A script of the 1949 film, by Ruth
          Gordon and Garson Kanin (director: George Cukor).
          118 p.   (paperback)   illus.   New York: Viking
          Press, 1972.
          Contains cast credits and production credits.

2006.   The Adventures of Antoine Doinel: 4 Autobiograph-
          ical Screen Plays, by Francois Truffaut.   320 p.
          illus.   New York: Simon and Schuster, 1971.
          Contains the following: 1) "Who is Antoine Doinel?"
by Francois Truffaut; 2) THE 400 BLOWS (1959)--First
treatment (not the script--see 564), Description of the Characters, The Session with the Psychologist; 3) LOVE AT
TWENTY (1962)--First Treatment, Final Screenplay (not
the script for LOVE AT TWENTY but only the sequence
directed by Truffaut entitled ANTOINE AND COLETTE);
4) STOLEN KISSES (1968)--Work Notes, First Treatment,
Final Screenplay; 5) BED AND BOARD (1970)--Outline,
Work Notes, Final Screenplay.

2007.   THE ADVENTURES OF MARCO POLO.   A script
          of the 1938 film, by Robert E. Sherwood (director:
          Archie Mayo).   365 p.   New York: Covici-Friede,
          1937.
          Found in How to Write and Sell Film Stories, by
Frances Marion (2410).

2008.   African Film Bibliography 1965, arranged by War-
          ren D. Stevens.   31 p.   (paperback)   Bloomington,
          Ind.:   African Studies Association, 1966.
          The Committee of Fine Arts and the Humanities of
the African Studies Association, with financial support from
the Ford Foundation, is responsible for this survey of commercially issued films devoted to African subjects.   Using
the Educational Media Index as a source, most entries have
the following information: title, source, year of production,
gauge, sound or silent, running time, audience level, color
or black and white, rental prices, and film guide availability.
A short annotation follows.
          The subject headings appear comprehensive and the

16

annotations are acceptable but one wishes they were both evaluative and descriptive rather than only the latter. Distributor addresses and an alphabetical title list complete the book.

Much of this material is dated and probably some of the films are no longer available, but it is a starting point, and there is little reason why this film bibliography cannot be called a filmography and be brought up to date. Acceptable given the date limitations.

2009. The Age of the American Novel, by Claude-Edmonde Magny. 239 p. New York: Frederick Ungar, 1972.
An unusual book that is intellectually satisfying without the obfuscation and murkiness one expects with such works. Written in France during the late 1940s, this is the first English translation to appear. The intent of the author is to show how films inspired a new literary form. She points out examples of literary equivalents to cutting, elipsis, close-ups, long shots, in-depth focus, etc. Much of her argument supports the auteur theory of filmmaking. The subtitle indicates the parameters of her study: "The Film Aesthetic of Fiction Between the Two Wars." Among the authors whose works are analyzed are Hemingway, Dos Passos, Faulkner, and Steinbeck.

There need be no hesitancy in accepting this book as a future classic. Its importance and influence on cinema literature will be measurable and continuing. Occasionally one may be dismayed at some sentence which time has proved to be in error, but the totality of this work makes such imperfections a negligible matter. The reader will leave the book with two impressions: the validity of the statement and the clarity with which it is expressed. An essential volume for all film collections.

2010. THE AGONY AND THE ECSTASY, by Howard Liebling. 40 p. (paperback) illus. New York: National Publishers, 1965.
An historical approach is used in this souvenir book. The background of the story is established by maps of Rome, the Vatican areas, and Florence. The ceiling plan for the Sistine Chapel is also shown. Charlton Heston, Rex Harrison, and director Carol Reed are each given one page of attention. The supporting cast, the artists, and other production credits are also noted.

2011. THE ALAMO, edited by Thomas J. Kane. 36 p. illus. Hollywood: Sovereign Publications, 1960.
This souvenir booklet resembles the dull film it

salutes; it is a run-of-the-mill assembly-line product which
lacks any individuality. John Wayne, as producer, director,
and star, obviously gets the most attention. Other leading
members of the cast are shown on individual pages as the
characters they portray in the film: Richard Widmark as
Colonel James Bowie, Laurence Harvey as Colonel William
Travis, Richard Boone as General Sam Houston, etc. Many
stills from the film are included but with only a quotation or
descriptive sentence provided for explanation. Cast and production credits are noted and some background information
is provided for behind-the-scenes personnel--Dimitri Tiomkin
and others.

2012. Robert Aldrich, edited by Bruce Henstell. 27 p.
(paperback) Washington, D.C.: American Film
Institute, 1972.
  In November 1972 Robert Aldrich visited the AFI
Center in Beverly Hills to discuss his film, THE DIRTY
DOZEN. The first section concentrates on the film, another
discusses general topics in filmmaking. A bibliography and
a filmography are included. Acceptable for all collections.

2013. Algerie-Cinema, by Younes Dadci. Paris: DAC,
1972.
  A study of the growing pains of the film industry in
Algeria, this book indicates the successes and the failures up
to the seventies. Poor planning, a lack of trained personnel,
and passive audiences are a few of the problems discussed.

2014. THE ALL-AMERICAN BOY. A script of the 1973
film, by Charles Eastman (director: Charles Eastman). 184 p. (paperback) illus. New York:
Farrar, Straus & Giroux, 1973.
Contains cast and production credits.

2015. All the Bright Young Men and Women, by Josef
Skvorecky. 280 p. illus. Toronto: Peter Martin
Associates, 1971.
  This book was written as a personal memoir, yet it
is much more. Using his own experiences, various research
sources and several Czech film magazines, the author has
created a critical history of Czech cinema, with a strong
emphasis on the later years--those of his participation. Many
familiar names appear--Hedy Lamarr, Hugh Haas, George
Voskovec, Milos Forman, Jiri Menzel, Ivan Passer, etc.
While the Czech film is not well known here, the coverage
supplied by both text and visuals makes it seem more familiar. Most outstanding is his account of the Czech "New

Wave," a dramatic, informative, and ironic story. Certainly
the visuals selected here provide an introduction or review
that equals anything else about Czech films in print. The
text is chatty, sympathetic, informal and personalized, all
adding to the book's readability. Typical of the author's sensitive approach is the chronological listing of films which he
calls simply "The More Interesting." The list covers the individual years from 1898 to 1970. The director for each
film is mentioned, as is the total number of films produced
during that year. A detailed index concludes the book.

Four other recent volumes on Czech cinema have
appeared recently (334, 483, 1076, 1086), but not one has the
overall impact of this one. What it may lack in historical
structure, emphasis, or inclusion, it makes up for in style,
selection, and warmth. Highly recommended for colleges
and for larger collections. Other libraries wishing a representative volume on Czech film won't go wrong in choosing
this one.

2016. ALL THE KING'S MEN. A script of the 1949 film,
by Robert Rossen (director: Robert Rossen). 274 p.
(paperback) illus. New York: Doubleday, 1972.
Found in Three Screenplays (2806).

2017. American Film Criticism, edited by Stanley Kauffmann. 443 p. New York: Liveright, 1972.
This fine anthology is subtitled, "From the Beginnings to CITIZEN KANE," and deals only with reviews of
important films at the time they first appeared. No retro-
spective or current evaluations are used.

The forty-five year period is divided into three
unequal parts. Some fifty pages of reviews are devoted to
the beginnings: that early period of short films which lasted
up to 1911. The next section of approximately 150 pages addresses itself to the longer silent films and includes reviews
on such late twenties classics as THE CIRCUS and THE
CROWD.

The largest section deals with sound film reviews
and takes the reader up to the early forties. The aim of the
editor was to document the pre-Agee period of film reviewing, purportedly a wasteland in which no one was writing anything that could be considered serious criticism. The arrangement of the reviews is chronological by film, not by
author. In certain cases--INTOLERANCE, METROPOLIS,
LITTLE CAESAR, etc.--more than one review is offered.
Notes, a selected bibliography, and a long detailed index
complete the book.

Writers represented include both familiar and

unknown critics; it is in this selection that the editor has
served the reader well. While some argument might be
made about individual films--both those included ones and
those missing--none can be made about the quality of the articles chosen for this entertaining, informative collection.
Highly recommended for all libraries.

2018.   The American Film Heritage, by Kathleen Karr.
         184 p.   illus.   Washington, D.C.:   Acropolis Books,
         1972.
         Although the subtitle, "Impressions From the Amer-
ican Film Institute Archives," is appropriate, a more descriptive one might be "The American Film Institute Reader."
The book is a collection of original articles which are con-
nected in some way with the AFI collection, concern, or
operation. "Lost" films which the AFI has rediscovered or
reconstructed are described--e.g., THE MYSTERY OF THE
WAX MUSEUM, THE EMPEROR JONES.
         The work of neglected American directors--Michael
Curtiz, William Beaudine, etc., is noted. Sections on film
history relate accounts of early color attempts, the first animation films, comedy shorts, the "B" western, and vintage
films from 1907-1914. Writers include Tom Shales, William
Everson, Kevin Brownlow and others. In most instances the
text is both factual and critical, attempting to give an honest
evaluation of the importance of the subject at hand.
         More outstanding than the text are the visuals. Near-
ly 200 are supplied, and selection and reproduction are outstanding. The book is indexed. It has a certain reference
value. This beautifully produced volume succeeds in all de-
partments--text, visuals, format, subject matter, etc. One
can find little fault with it and yet one expects a sturdier
product from AFI. This is a sampling--and one to be ad-
mired--but AFI should be encouraging, producing, and facili-
tating major works in all areas of film literature rather than
a pseudo-souvenir book like this one. This is more a criticism of AFI than of this volume since its excellence is acknowledged. In any event, this book will please many readers
and will delight anyone interested in film history. It is recommended for all collections.

2019.   The American Film Institute Report, 1967-1971,
         edited by Sali Ann Kriegsman.   80 p.   (paperback)
         illus.   Washington, D.C.:   The American Film In-
         stitute, 1972.
         This report of the first four years of the American
Film Institute gives the reader some idea of the scope of the

20

Institute's activities, from film preservation to publications, grants, and research. As with all reports, this one is self-congratulatory and some of the material sounds inflated beyond its actual importance; it is never dull, however.

Since the Institute is a controversial matter in many minds, this report may serve as an informational resource. It is nicely illustrated, and appropriate for all collections.

Another example of an AFI publication is Tribute to Mary Pickford, by Robert B. Cushman. It consists of an introductory essay about her career which is both factual and critical, an account of her short films made at Biograph, and film notes on nine of her feature films. A complete filmography of 141 short films and 52 features concludes the tribute. The 16 pages in this paperback book are used efficiently to present a portrait of Pickford that is not available elsewhere. Illustrations are fine and the content is excellent. Recommended for all collections.

2020. The American Newsreel, 1911-1967, by Raymond Fielding. 392 p. illus. Norman, Okla.: University of Oklahoma Press, 1972.

Buried in the bibliography of this book is the information that Fielding wrote his Ph.D. thesis in 1961 on "A History of the American Motion Picture Newsreel," and in 1956 he wrote a Master's thesis on "The March of Time, 1935-42." Probably both studies were blended to form this volume, a detailed study of the rise and decline of the American newsreel.

Some interesting statements made by the author give an idea of the book's coverage--for example: many of the early newsreels used false restagings of events; newsreels did not deliver the news; newsreels were more entertainment than education or information; newsreels affected film booking to a large extent during the block-booking era; The March of Time, which was more a documentary than a newsreel, indicated some of the potential value of the form; Newsreels failed because of a domination by newspapermen rather than filmmakers, and an inability or refusal to compete with television and newspapers.

These arguments and many more are woven into the factual history that Fielding has written from so much data. The notes, bibliography and index take up about 20 per cent of the book. Some pictures are included but they are often too small and most are poorly reproduced.

As a detailed scholarly history of an extinct film form, this volume is impressive. The text is readable, and the author is not afraid to use gossip, emotion, opinion, and affection in telling his story. Recommended for all collections.

2021.   The Americans, by David Frost.   250 p.   New York:
         Stein & Day, 1970.
         A collection of transcripts of David Frost's television
programs.   It is noted here since it contains interviews with
Orson Welles, Jon Voight, Raquel Welch, Peter Fonda and
Dennis Hopper.

2022.   American Theatrical Arts: A Guide to Manuscripts
         and Special Collections in the U.S. and Canada, by
         William C. Young.   168 p.   Chicago: American Li-
         brary Association, 1971.
         A survey of 138 Theatrical Arts collections, this is
also useful for locating film items.   The book lists the collections alphabetically by state, and then by the symbol used
in the National Union Catalog.   The second portion lists subjects and personalities covered by the various collections.
A good reference tool, acceptable for all collections.

2023.   Amphoto Books--Cinematography.   (some paperback).
         illus.   New York: Amphoto, 1965 to 1973.
         Amphoto is a publishing house which specializes in
books on various aspects of photography, including cinematography.   Some current titles are:
    Better 8mm Home Movie Guide (Murray Duitz)
    Better Electric Eye Movies (Myron Matzkin)
    Better Super 8 Movie Making (Myron Matzkin)
    Camera Techniques for the Color Movie Maker (Dick Ham)
    Electric Eye Movie Manual (Ira B. Current)
    Family Movie Fun for All (Myron Matzkin)
    How to Animate Cut-Outs (C.H. Barton)
    How to Choose Music (F. Rawlings)
    How to Direct Your Own Home Movies (Tony Rose)
    How to Do Sound Films (D.M. Neale)
    How to Edit Your Own Home Movies (H. Baddeley)
    How to Film (G. Wain)
    How to Make 8mm Movies (N. Bau)
    How to Title Your Own Home Movies (L.F. Minter)
    Lens Techniques for Color Movie Magic (Glen H. Turner)
    Making Movies (Carlton Wallace)
    Movie and Videotape Special Effects (Emil Brodbeck)
    Photographer's Guide to Movie Making (Edwin Gilmout)
    Photographic Make-up for Still and Movie (Vincent J.R.
        Kehoe)
    Scenarios, Scenarios, Scenarios (Donald Horn)
    Sound for Your Color Movies (G.W. Cushman)
    Titling Your Color Movies (James W. Moore)
         The above represent a sampling of titles.   They
are included here since they deal with cinematography, but

also because some of the titles offer inexpensive alternatives for certain areas of film information.

2024.   The Animated Cartoon Film in Belgium, by R. Maelstaf. 100 p. (paperback) illus. Brussels: Ministry of Foreign Affairs, 1970.
Although cartoon films were being produced in Belgium prior to World War I, no written record or history was kept. This publication attempts to remedy that neglect for the period since that time. A very short section notes the pioneers who were active in the twenties and thirties. The animated cartoon made in Belgium after 1940 is the major concern of the text. Biographical notes on 12 Belgian animators, along with descriptions of their films, are followed by detailed annotations of four full length cartoons: PINOCCHIO IN SPACE, ASTERIX THE GAUL, ASTERIX AND CLEOPATRA, and TINTIN AND THE TEMPLE OF THE SUN. Some film companies, a few film animation training schools, and a list of the Belgian animated films made since 1958 are given next. The closing section is devoted to the technique of the animated film from the idea to the production.
This is very specialized material that certainly belongs in large film collections. It will be of moderate interest to most readers but it is a support item rather than an essential.

2025.   ANNE OF THE THOUSAND DAYS. 24 p. (paperback) illus. Hollywood: Universal Studios, 1970.
This small publication resembles a souvenir booklet but it was never sold at theatres. It was probably prepared for critics, reviewers, and publicists. The background of the film is given along with two letters--one written by Henry to Anne, and the second by Anne to Henry. Individual pages are devoted to Richard Burton, Genevieve Bujold, producer Hal Wallis and director Charles Jarrott. Supporting cast and technical credits are included.

2026.   Annotated Bibliography of Films in Automation, Data Processing, and Computer Science, by Martin B. Solomon, Jr. and Nora G. Lovan. 38 p. (paperback) Lexington, Ky.: University of Kentucky Press, 1967.
This short older paperback is noted here because of the difficulty in finding suitable films on automation, data processing, and computer science and because of its impressive arrangement of film information. How effective the book is can only be determined by teachers or specialists using it in the three areas.

An alphabetical list of the film titles is followed by a
subject index to the films. In the next section each entry
lists the film code, the year of production, the suggested
audiences, and the film title. An annotation follows which is
mostly descriptive rather than critical or evaluative.

Film data--time, sound/silent, color/black and white,
and film gauge-size--are listed, and the entry concludes with
purchasing or rental information, along with the name of the
organization distributing the film. A detailed directory of
these distributors appears at the end of the book.

The need for frequent revision of such filmographies
is dictated by changes in certain data (price, rental, distrib-
utorship) and the production of many new films in these three
areas. Five years is a bit long to wait for revision of such
a guide. A specialized reference whose value can only be
determined after use by a computer specialist, this book
should still be regarded as a model for other filmographies.

2027.   ANTOINE AND COLETTE. A script of the 1962
         film, by Francois Truffaut (director: Francois
         Truffaut). 320 p. illus. New York: Simon and
         Schuster, 1971.
         Found in The Adventures of Antoine Doinel (2006).
This is one episode from the international sketch film called
LOVE AT TWENTY. The first treatment and the final
screenplay of the Truffaut episode are given.

2028.   THE APARTMENT. A script of the 1960 film, by
         Billy Wilder and I. A. L. Diamond (director: Billy
         Wilder). 618 p. (paperback) New York: Appleton-
         Century-Crofts, 1972.
         Found in Film Scripts Three (2269).

2029.   The Apu Trilogy, by Robin Wood. 96 p. illus.
         New York: Praeger, 1971.
         As the title indicates, this short book concentrates
exclusively on the films which form Satyajit Ray's Apu trilogy: PATHER PANCHALI, APARAJITO, and THE WORLD
OF APU, each of which is given a separate chapter, following an introductory section which explores the overall qualities of the trilogy. The closing pages contain picture credits,
a list of Ray's other films, and a selected bibliography.
There are fewer illustrations than usual in this Praeger volume and their quality is no better than acceptable. The book
is not indexed. The acceptance or success of this volume
will depend upon the reader's enthusiasm for Ray's work,
and that appears to be minimal in America. Although Robin
Wood tries to create admiration for Ray and his work, his

task is somewhat akin to selling Little Women to readers of The Godfather. A specialized book, suitable for larger collections.

2030.   Are You Now or Have You Ever Been?, edited by
        Eric Bentley. 160 p. (paperback) illus. New
        York: Harper & Row, 1973.
        Words and pictures recreate some moments from
the long investigation of show business by the House Committee on Un-American Activities (HUAC). The period covered here is 1947 to 1958 and there are 18 witnesses plus some familiar names from the HUAC such as Richard Nixon and J. Parnell Thomas. Film personalities include Sterling Hayden, Larry Parks, Lionel Stander, Elia Kazan, Edward Dmytryk, Sam Wood and Ring Lardner, Jr. Acceptable for all collections.

2031.   ARIZONA: The Winning of a Mighty Empire Inspires
        the Making of a Great Picture. 36 p. illus. Holly-
        wood: Columbia Pictures, 1940.
        This impressive, oversized book has much to recommend it. The black and white illustrations, large in size and reproduced with great clarity, are outstanding. Twelve pages are devoted to a portion of the script which is illustrated directly. Some attention is paid to Director Wesley Ruggles, the writers, the cast, and other studio personnel. Statistics about the film are also offered. This book was not sold at theatres but was probably issued as a studio campaign book or souvenir.

2032.   Art in Movement: New Directions in Animation, by
        John Halas with Roger Manvell. 192 p. illus.
        New York: Hastings House, 1970.
        The two major sections in this excellent book are outstanding. The first, dealing with new techniques in animation and visual effects, covers film stock, stop-motion camera, combined media, split screen, freeze frame, etc. The second surveys the animated film in the contemporary international scene. The book is generous in providing many excellent stills to accompany the informative and understandable text. An index is provided. Written and produced with care and expertise, this book belongs in all collections.

2033.   The Art of the Cinema: Selected Essays. New York:
        Arno, 1972.
        This original compilation consists of several well-known articles on film. Included are: a. The Ambivalence of Realism by George Amberg; b. An Anagram of Ideas on

25

Art, Form and Film by Maya Deren; c. Cinematography: The Creative Use of Reality by Maya Deren; d. Psychology of Film Experience by Hugo Mauerhofer; e. Towards a Film Aesthetic by Herbert Read; f. The Witness Point: Definitions of Film Art by Vernon Young. A foreword by George Amberg introduces the essays which direct attention to the acceptance of film as an art form. Acceptable for large collections.

2034.   ASHES AND DIAMONDS. A script of the 1958 film, by Andrzej Wajda and Jerzy Andrzejewski (director: Andrzej Wajda). 239 p. (paperback) illus. New York: Simon & Schuster, 1972.
Found in The Wajda Trilogy (2861).

2035.   Richard Attenborough, edited by Rochelle Reed. 24 p. (paperback) illus. Washington, D.C.: American Film Institute, 1973.
Richard Attenborough was on a publicity tour for YOUNG WINSTON when this discussion took place in November, 1972. Most of the interview pertains to the new film, with occasional references to OH, WHAT A LOVELY WAR, his other directorial attempt. He talks of films in which he has acted and of people with whom he has worked. One of the better books in this series. Acceptable for all collections.

2036.   Audio Visual Man, edited by Pierre Babin. 218 p. (paperback) illus. Dayton, Ohio: Pflaum, 1970.
Media and religious education is the major theme of this volume, which has three parts. The first deals with audio visual language and faith. Learning a new language is the second heading, while projects and projections make up the final part. The understanding of visuals is emphasized and although film is not singled out, it is an essential part of this discussion. The plea for visual literacy is persuasively stated. Much of the argument can be applied to any visual medium--film, television, posters, slides, etc. The many visuals used are noteworthy and the entire production is exemplary. The book was written originally in French.
Of primary interest to religious educators, this volume has much pertinence for others--training directors, teachers, media designers, etc. Recommended for all collections.

2037.   Audio Visual Resource Guide, edited by Nick Abrams. 477 p. (paperback) New York: Friendship Press, 1972.

The ninth edition of this excellent reference book up-
dates and replaces previous editions, the last of which appeared in 1966 (82). Some of the previous evaluations reap-
pear here but there are many new materials listed. Selection is made on the basis of pertinence to religious education
but that does not limit the use of many of the materials in
other fields. In addition to films, many slides, audio tapes,
recordings, and other non-print materials are listed. The
structure of the evaluations is consistent: divided into thirds,
each considers biographical data, a summary of the content,
and an evaluation--either highly recommended, recommended,
acceptable, or limited.

A subject area index along with an alphabetical guide
to those areas will assist users searching for materials in
general rather than for specific titles. The hundreds of evaluations which follow are arranged alphabetically by title.
Suggestions for appropriate audiences are also given. The
films considered in the main body of the guide are the short
ones but a closing section does give attention to a large selection of feature films. The distributors of the materials
listed in the guide are given, as are some recommended publications on media resources. In this latest edition, the publishers have improved on established excellence. The selection, evaluations, coverage and format of this volume make
it an essential reference for all collections.

2038. The Australian Cinema, by John Baxter. 118 p.
(paperback) illus. Sydney: Pacific Books, 1970.
The purpose of this small volume is to acquaint
readers with the Australian cinema via a bit of history, some
discussion of the artists concerned, and a very partial survey
of the films. Because of an initial lack of interest in the
Australian native cinema, the reconstruction is sketchy and
piecemeal. As a beginning step in the recording of a country's cinema, the book is admirable. While major names
are not treated in depth, they are recognized, and a basis
for further exploration is established. The photographs are
provocative and a sturdy index is provided.

Worth the price of the book alone is the notation of
two films which offer a sampling of Australian films and are
available from Australian Consulates the world over. Recommended especially for larger collections.

2039. Authors on Film, edited by Harry M. Geduld. 303 p.
Bloomington: Indiana Univ. Press, 1972.
An anthology designed to indicate the diverse interests
and involvements of well-known writers in film. Five general categories indicate the organization of the material:

1) From Silence to Sound--Gorky, Tolstoy, Sandburg, Gide, Brecht, Hardy, etc.; 2) The Medium and its Messages-- Woolf, Mencken, G. B. Shaw, Mann, etc.; 3) Authors on Screenwriting--T. S. Eliot, W. S. Maugham, Capote, etc.; 4) The Hollywood Experience--Dreiser, F. Scott Fitzgerald, Faulkner; 5) Of Mice and Movie Stars--Cocteau, Dos Passos, Hemingway, Baldwin, etc.

Thirty-five authors are represented and all the articles offer interesting and worthwhile content. The selection, arrangement, and editing by Geduld are commendable, as is the original conception for the book. The interest evidenced by the appearance of several recent books about the relationship between literature and film is served well here. Some short notes on the authors are provided and there is an index--a thoughtful addition not usually found in books of this genre. Recommended highly for all larger collections and for college libraries. Other libraries will find it to be a valid addition to their collections.

2040.   An Autobiography, by Margaret Rutherford. 230 p.
         illus. London: H. W. Allen, 1972.
         This autobiography, as told to Gwen Robyns, is
about what you might expect from Dame Rutherford. She is
frank, open, and amusing when she discusses herself. When
speaking of her co-workers, she is kind, courteous, and always the lady. Her life was not without its deep sorrows,
and she was rather late in reaching celebrity status. The
sex-change of her adopted son must have caused her considerable anguish when the story was picked up by the press
and published around the world, yet she handles this subject
with dignity and sensitivity. Anyone who has enjoyed Margaret Rutherford on the screen will be pleased with this volume. Recommended for large collections; acceptable for
other libraries.

2041.   The Autobiography of Will Rogers, edited by Donald
         Day. 410 p. illus. Boston: Houghton Mifflin,
         1949.
         A selection of Rogers' writing taken mostly from
pieces written between 1922 and 1935. Editing, arrangement,
and linking narratives are by Donald Day, who has also written a separate biography (2690). Unfortunately, because of
the source material there is little about films here; in fact,
only two humorous articles about the industry. Persons looking for information about Rogers' film career are advised
to look elsewhere (2690, 2691, 2692). Not pertinent for film
collections.

2042. Awards, Honors, and Prizes, edited by Paul Wasser-
       man. 579 p. Detroit, Mich.: Gale Research, 1972.
       Anyone searching for a directory of motion picture
awards and their donors is advised to consult this volume.
Divided into three sections, the material deals not only with
motion picture awards, but also with art, business, government, literature, fashion, medicine, and other categories,
professions, or industries in which awards are given.
       The first section is a main listing arranged alpha-
betically by sponsoring organization. Here each award that
the organization gives is noted (even discontinued ones) along
with a full description that includes data such as purpose of
the award, terms of eligibility, form of award, frequency,
etc. Entries are quite thorough and explain the awards most
satisfactorily. For example:
       American Association of University Professors
       Education Writers Award
       "To recognize outstanding interpretive reporting of
       issues in higher education in the following media:
       radio, tv, film, or print. To the author. Cer-
       tificate. Awarded annually. Established 1969."
       A second section is an alphabetical arrangement of
the individual awards by specific or distinctive name; for
example, Jean Hersholt Humanitarian Award, Emily Award,
Ralph H. Landes Award.
       A subject index which contains headings for music,
theatre, entertainment and television as well as motion pictures comprises the final section of the book. For ease of
use, comprehensiveness and readability, this volume is excellent and belongs in most reference collections.

2043. BARABBAS. 20 p. (paperback) illus. New York:
       Program Publishing Co., 1962.
       Attention is given first to the novel by Pär Lagerkvist
on which the film was based and then to the actual production.
Later, the final film story is outlined in detail. A single
page is devoted to Anthony Quinn and some cast and production credits are indicated. Six paintings of Barrabas which
were commissioned for the film are reproduced nicely.

2044. Bardot: Eternal Sex Goddess, by Peter Evans.
       186 p. illus. London: Lester Frewin, 1972.
       This recent biography of Bardot has more pertinence
for European audiences than for Americans since Bardot never enjoyed a great popularity here. The usual and well-
known factual material is here along with photographs, a filmography, and an index. Acceptable for all collections.

2045.   THE BASEMENT, by Harold Pinter (director:
        Charles Jarrott).   112 p.   New York: Grove Press,
        1967.
        Found in a collection entitled The Lover, Tea Party,
The Basement.   Notes accompanying the film script indicate
that it was first shown on B.B.C. Television in 1967.

2046.   Basic Books in the Mass Media, by Eleanor Blum.
        252 p.   Urbana, Ill.:   University of Illinois Press,
        1972.
        The subtitle describes the general content of this
reference book: "An Annotated, Selected Booklist (665 titles)
Covering General Communications (104), Book Publishing
(70), Broadcasting (124), Film (109), Magazines (33), Newspapers (99), Advertising (64), Indexes (13), and Scholarly and
Professional Periodicals (49)."   For obvious reasons, the film
section was the one chosen for evaluation here.   It is assumed that it is a representative sample.
        The books are listed alphabetically by author, then
title, location, publisher and date.   No mention is made of
paperback formats; illustrations and the presence of an index
in several of the books are not noted, i.e., The Film Till
Now, Movie Comedy Teams, etc.   The name of the author
of this latter book is Maltin--not Malton as listed.
        Blum states that her choices are subjective.   Fine,
but when a book uses the word "basic" in its title, there is
a responsibility to exercise care in selection.   Some of the
inclusions are pleasant volumes but certainly not basic: e.g.,
Baxter's The Gangster Film, the Camerons' Dames and The
Heavies, Lahue's Clown Princes and Court Jesters, Walker's
Stardom: The Hollywood Phenomena.   Where are the Blum
volumes? Powdermaker? Bluestone? Arnheim? Bazin?
Many other excellent books which are now basic staples of
any film collection could be named.
        Placement of the titles may be questionable.   Should
Stedman's The Serials, which deals with magazines, comic
strips, films, radio and television, be listed in the film section?   Especially since the film portion occupies about one-
third of the text to the two-thirds assigned to Radio and TV?
Some of the annotations are incorrect--Variety does not review underground or commercial films.   The articles in AV
Communication Review are not experimental.
        No evaluations are offered, only descriptive annota-
tion.   However, the inclusion of a title in this "Basic" listing would indicate approval or endorsement.   What could have
been an outstanding reference book, is only an average one
because of poor selection criteria, lack of evaluations, faulty
descriptions, misspellings, and inaccuracies.   If used with

care and with an understanding of its weaknesses and limitations, it can be an aid to librarians.

2047.   Basic Color Photography, by Andreas Feininger.
128 p.   illus.   Englewood Cliffs, N.J.:   Prentice-Hall, 1972.
Although the text addresses itself to still photography, there is much that is pertinent for the cinematographer. Specifically, it is the latter two sections, dealing with techniques of color photography and the art of color photography, which are most applicable.   The rationale for the last section is stated succinctly by the author: "It is an indisputable fact that successful color photography is impossible unless the know-how is guided by the know-why." Acceptable for all collections.

2048.   Basic Titling and Animation for Motion Pictures, by Eastman Kodak.   (paperback) illus.   New York: Amphoto, 1970.
This Kodak book is designed for the amateur rather than the skilled professional.   It describes techniques for titling and animation that are appropriate for the small-scale producer--the teacher, the media specialist, the librarian, etc.

2049.   THE BATTLE OF BRITAIN, edited by Peter Tipthorp.
32 p.   (paperback) illus.   London: Sackville Publishing Ltd., 1967.
In this souvenir book, a foreword by the Duke of Edinburgh and an introduction by Lord Dowding are followed by the historical data and quotations that provide the basis for the film.   In addition to the film story, there are biographical data on director Guy Hamilton and producers Harry Saltzman and Ben Fisz.   Cast and production credits follow a long description of how the film was made.   The concluding section is a tribute to the aces of the Battle in the form of a Roll of Honor.

2050.   BATTLE OF THE BULGE.   28 p.   (paperback) illus.   Hollywood: Warner Brothers, 1966.
The usual format is followed in this souvenir book: the story and production are discussed first, followed by page portraits of Henry Fonda, Robert Shaw, Robert Ryan and Dana Andrews.   A map of the battle area precedes a plug for Jack Warner and William R. Forman of Cinerama.   The director, Ken Annakin, and producers Milton Sperling and Philip Yordan get the largest share of attention in the supporting cast-and-credits section.

2051.   Cecil Beaton: Memoirs of the 40's, by Cecil Beaton.
         310 p. illus. New York: McGraw-Hill, 1972.
         In his memoir of the forties, Beaton divides the text
geographically. London, Paris, New York and California are
the settings against which he recalls his interactions with the
famous and near-famous. Names, places, events, and comments are the substance of the book. Cocteau, Picasso,
Churchill and, of course, Garbo are featured prominently and
other film names of the period are given lesser attention. A
look from on high at the beautiful people of the forties by an
author who wears a very specialized kind of eyeglass. Not
essential, but acceptable for all film collections.

2052.   BEAUTY AND THE BEAST. A script of the 1946
         film, by Jean Cocteau (director: Jean Cocteau).
         250 p. (paperback) illus. New York: Grossman,
         1972.
         Found in Jean Cocteau--Three Screenplays (2157).
Contains cast credits.

2053.   BECKET. 32 p. (paperback) illus. New York:
         National Publishers, 1964.
         A section entitled "Footnotes to History," which de-
tails the story of Thomas Becket opens this souvenir book.
Two pages are given to each of the stars, Richard Burton
and Peter O'Toole, while producer Hal Wallis and director
Peter Glenville get a page. The rest of the cast and production crew members receive some small mention. An article
by Stephen Watts entitled "The Mood of Becket" is followed
by a section about the various stage versions of Jean Anouilh's
play, "Becket," upon which the film was based.

2054.   BED AND BOARD. A script of the 1970 film, by
         Francois Truffaut (director: Francois Truffaut).
         320 p. illus. New York: Simon and Schuster, 1971.
         Found in The Adventures of Antoine Doinel (2006).
Contains an outline, work notes, and final screenplay.

2055.   Behind the Camera, by Leonard Maltin. 240 p.
         (paperback) illus. New York: New American Li-
         brary, 1971.
         A volume about the artists behind the camera which
contains a long introductory essay by Maltin and five interviews with noted American cameramen. Arthur C. Miller,
Hal Mohr, Hal Rosson, Lucien Ballard, and Conrad Hall are
representative of almost all the periods of American film
history. After each interview, a listing of the films that
each shot is given. The nominees for Academy Awards in

32

cinematography are noted, with the winners indicated by an asterisk. The book is illustrated and indexed.

The Maltin essay is a historical survey and evaluation of the contribution that the cameraman has made to films. The article is well-researched and serves as a tribute to the neglected artist whose work can be crucial to the success or failure of a film. The interviews are interesting and indicate a sort of pioneer individuality in the subjects.

This is an unusual illuminating volume that may need a little help in gaining reader attention. In this case, the effort is most worthwhile. Recommended for all collections.

2056.   BELLE DE JOUR. A script of the 1967 film, by Luis Buñuel and Jean-Claude Carriére (director: Luis Buñuel). 168 p. (paperback) illus. New York: Simon and Schuster, 1971.
Contains: Two interviews with Buñuel; an article by Andrew Sarris; and cast and production credits.

2057.   Ingmar Bergman Directs, by John Simon. 315 p. illus. New York: Harcourt Brace Jovanovich, 1972.
A lengthy interview begins this latest Simon venture into film literature. In the short introduction which follows, he disposes of fellow critics Andrew Sarris, Richard Schickel, and Parker Tyler in short order and goes on to assess the work and artistry of Bergman. To prove his point that Bergman is the greatest filmmaker in the world today, he examines four films in detail: THE CLOWN'S EVENING (NAKED NIGHT), SMILES OF A SUMMER NIGHT, WINTER LIGHT and PERSONA. The filmography at the book's end gives cast and production credits for only this quartet of films.

The analyses of the films, which deal with themes, symbols, relationships, are in depth, --with Simon's faults as a critic-writer less apparent than usual. As expected, he writes with style, discrimination and intellect. His appreciation of Bergman and his efforts seems sincere and almost affectionate. Absent are the Simon smugness, self-satisfaction and intolerance that appear in other writings.

The visuals, attributed to Halcyon Enterprises, are an asset to the book. They provide an analysis which attempts to run concurrently with the Simon narrative, and most of them appear to be taken directly from the films. Their reproduction is much better than usual for this type of photograph.

The fact that Simon treats only four Bergman films may disappoint those who have personal favorites. Incidentally, one might suspect, on the basis of the interview, that these four would be Bergman's choices also. The sampling offered does give enough evidence of Bergman's style, recurrent themes, artistic growth, and overall virtuosity to satisfy most readers.

The book belongs in all college libraries and in other large film collections. Its place in smaller libraries will be determined by the number of Bergman titles already owned. The few films treated here may limit its value for these institutions, which may opt for the fuller coverage of Steene's Ingmar Bergman (114), Wood's Ingmar Bergman (115), Young's Cinema Borealis (214), Gibson's The Silence of God (1241), or Donner's The Personal Vision of Ingmar Bergman (1090).

2058.   Bergman: PERSONA and SHAME, by Ingmar Bergman. 191 p. (paperback) illus. New York: Grossman, 1972.
Contains: An introduction, "Snakeskin," by Ingmar Bergman; and cast and production credits for PERSONA, 1966 (2640) and SHAME, 1968 (2729).

2059.   Sarah Bernhardt; The Art within the Legend, by Gerda Taranow. 287 p. illus. Princeton, N.J.: Princeton University Press, 1972.
It is the art of Sarah Bernhardt that the author is concerned with here rather than the biography. Divided into sections which treat voice, pantomime, gesture, spectacle, roles and repertoire, the book offers as appendices a filmography, an audiography, and a bibliography. It is because of the filmography that the book is noted here.

2060.   THE BEST MAN. A script of the 1964 film, by Gore Vidal (director: Franklin Schaffner). 500 p. (paperback) New York: Appleton-Century-Crofts, 1973.
Found in Film Scripts Four (2270).

2061.   Between the Acts, by Eddie Cantor. 115 p. New York: Simon and Schuster, 1930.
This small book is noted here because it contains one article called "talkies." Not much, but someone may re-assess Cantor's talent as a film performer one of these days and the information may help. For the record only.

2062.   BETWEEN TWO MOONS. An Unfilmed Screenplay, by Raymond Mungo and Richard Bartlett. 223 p. (paperback) illus. Boston, Mass.: Beacon Press, 1972.

Using the screenplay form, this unique paperback
has a text, many drawings and lots of murky symbolism. It
is included here as an example of the influence of film on
current literature. A case of the medium being far more
important than the message.

2063.   THE BIBLE, by Howard Liebling and Herb Lubalin.
        44 p. (paperback) illus. New York: Alsid Dis-
        tributors, 1966.
        Beginning with some quotations from the screenplay
by Christopher Fry, this souvenir book tells of the attempts
of producer Dino De Laurentis and director John Huston to
preserve fidelity to the text of the Bible. Using large illustrations by Ernst Haas, the cameraman who is probably better known for his still photography than for his motion picture work, the book gives evidence of an attempt to make a
film on a grand scale. Only the last few pages are devoted
to cast and production credits. An impressive effort that
causes the reader to wonder what went wrong in making the
film.

2064.   Bibliography of Film Librarianship, by Sam Kula.
        68 p. (paperback) London: The Library Associa-
        tion, 1967.
        Using works published in English, this bibliography
goes up to 1965. It employs the following subject headings:
Bibliographies--General, Evolution of Library Film Services,
Training for Film Librarianship, Administration of Film
Services (Public), Administration of Film Services (College,
University), Administration of Film Services (Special Libraries), Administration of Film Services (Television Libraries),
Cooperative Library Film Services, Stock Material Libraries,
Film Archives (Film as History), Film Archives (Administra-
tive), Cataloging Rules, Cataloging and Classification, Storage
and Presentation, Copyright, Glossaries of Film Terms. A
combined author and title index completes this small but valuable book which is somewhat dated but still of value to any
library that deals in film service.

2065.   The Big Love, by Florence Aadland and Tedd Thomey.
        158 p. (paperback) New York: Lancer Books, 1961.
        More trash from the past. The opening sentence
gives a preview of what is to follow: "There's one thing I
want to make clear right off: my baby was a virgin the day
she met Errol Flynn." This account of Beverly Aadland's
relationship with Errol Flynn as interpreted by Beverly's
mother is obviously suspect. An investigation of murder and
prostitution several years after Flynn's death put Beverly in

juvenile hall for a period. Mother Aadland was held on five charges of contributing to Beverly's delinquency. The book is dedicated to "The Swashbuckler, himself, with all our love." Depressing, sad, and an example of what many would consider obscene in publishing. Not recommended, but noted for the record.

2066.   THE BIG SLEEP. A script of the 1946 film, by William Faulkner, Leigh Brackett and Jules Furthman (director: Howard Hawks). 544 p. (paperback) New York: Century-Appleton-Crofts, 1971. Included in Film Scripts One (2267).

2067.   Biograph Bulletins 1896-1908, by Kemp R. Niver. 464 p. illus. Los Angeles, Calif.: Locare Research, 1971.
    This very specialized reference work is typical of Niver's continuing contribution to film history and literature. Using the Biograph Bulletins, those handbills which described individual films produced by the company, he provides reproductions of original source materials that may be used in many ways. The period covered is 1896 to 1908, when D. W. Griffith became a full time director at Biograph. Some of the bulletins contain capsule annotations and reminders of other Biograph films in addition to the one being featured.
    As an introduction, selected newspaper accounts of audience reaction to Biograph projectors, programs and films are reprinted. Niver supports all this material by personal notes where necessary, an alphabetical filmography with cameraman, filming date, copyright date, and page number reference, and finally a chronological filmography for each of Biograph's major cameramen.
    Niver has once more created an example of research that should be studied by other historians and scholars. It is informative, entertaining, and above all, arranged for easy reference. Uses for the material seem unlimited and the volume has a curiosity-nostalgia quality that will appeal to many audiences. The volume is highly recommended for all college, university and large public collections. Smaller libraries will also find it a valuable acquisition.

2068.   Biograph Bulletins 1908-1912. 471 p. illus. New York: Octagon Books, 1973.
    This volume contains Biograph Bulletins issued from 1908 to 1912, when they were discontinued. This period coincides with the early part of D. W. Griffith's tenure at the studio and the book begins with his first film, THE AD-

VENTURES OF DOLLY. Many of his other short films are included, but the bulletins also contain the work of other directors of the period.

Each bulletin describes the film, has one or more stills, and gives some other data. This set has an introduction by Eileen Bowser and some of the bulletins have annotations by Billy Bitzer, who worked at the Museum of Modern Art during the thirties. It is the Museum's collection which is reproduced here.

The preservation of the bulletins in this edition and the earlier one (2067) is a commendable project. Material of interest to students, researchers, and historians has become accessible. The book belongs in all large film collections, and is recommended for libraries in schools and colleges that support film studies.

2069.   THE BIRTH OF A NATION. A script of the 1914 film, by Theodore Huff and D. W. Griffith (director: D. W. Griffith). 69 p. (paperback) illus. New York: The Museum of Modern Art, 1961.
A shot-by-shot analysis of D. W. Griffith's THE BIRTH OF A NATION.

2070.   Focus on THE BIRTH OF A NATION, edited by Fred Silva. 184 p. (paperback) illus. Englewood Cliffs, N.J.: Prentice-Hall, 1971.
The content of this "Focus on" volume is divided among D. W. Griffith, the film, and its effect. Introductory chapters on the director and his film are followed by six original reviews. The commentaries address themselves to the making of the film, newspaper editorials and replies, and several articles by Griffith. Writers like Sarris, Jacobs and Noble try to assess the impact of the film, its effect on the Black struggle for equality, and its importance in film and national history. The usual plot synopsis and outline are given, as are a Griffith filmography, a bibliography and an index. A few illustrations are not impressive. This collection of articles covers both the immediate (1915) response to the film, and some later assessments which are cooler and more objective. It is important to note that the selections in the book indicate a wide range of opinion. This is another fine contribution from this consistently excellent series. Highly recommended for all collections.

2071.   Billy Bitzer: His Story, by G. W. Bitzer. 266 p. illus. New York: Farrar Straus & Giroux, 1973.
What a satisfying autobiography this is! Although it was written around 1944, and covers only the period up to

1920, it does not have the flavor of memorabilia. For the
most part it is an honest, unpretentious account of the early
and middle career of the most widely known cameraman in
motion picture history. His images often had a simple beauty
to them; that can be seen by the samples used in this book.
His text has that same quality. In his descriptions of the
personalities with whom he worked, he is generous, sensitive,
and affectionate. His love of his profession is evident throughout.

Since he was inseparable from D. W. Griffith for so
many years, it is not surprising that Griffith gets as much
attention here as he did in Lillian Gish's autobiography (990).
He co-stars once again.

As indicated above, the visuals provide pure pleasure
and the publishers have watched their reproduction carefully.
A Bitzer filmography--probably the first complete one--and
an index complete the book. Excellent on all counts and a
fine contribution to American film history. Highly recommended.

2072.   BLOW-UP. A script of the 1966 film, by Michel-
         angelo Antonioni and Tonino Guerra (director:
         Michelangelo Antonioni). 119 p. (paperback) illus.
         New York: Simon and Schuster, 1971.
         Contains: one interview with Antonioni; three articles
written by Antonioni; cast and production credits; notes.

2073.   Focus on BLOW-UP, edited by Roy Huss. 171 p.
         (paperback) illus. Englewood Cliffs, N.J.: Pren-
         tice-Hall, 1971.
         There are three introductory pieces about Antonioni
and BLOW-UP that provide a base for the material that follows. Six original reviews are followed by seven essays
which interpret, evaluate, and discuss this controversial film.
A synopsis and outline, a shot analysis of three important
sequences, a filmography and a bibliography complete the
book. In the appendix one finds the short story by Julio
Cortazar upon which the film was based and an article telling
of its adaptation. There is one center section containing a
few stills which are nicely reproduced.

Since BLOW-UP received a mixed critical reaction
on its first appearance, it is not surprising to find some of
the contributors here addressing themselves to the topic of
critical responsibility. Other aspects of the film, its reception, its importance and its director are treated. Selection
of the articles is fine and the format of this series applies
beautifully to this particular film. Highly recommended for
all collections.

2074.   THE BLUE MAX, by Howard Liebling.   32 p.   (paperback) illus.   New York: Souvenir Programs, Inc., 1966.

As background for the reader of this souvenir book, there is a picture gallery of famous flyers, medals, and airplanes from World War I.   Film stills used tend to resemble actual photographs of the period.   The cast and technical credits are given and the final section deals with the making of the film.

2075.   The Bluffer's Guide to Cinema, by Ken Wlaschin.   64 p.   (paperback) New York: Crown, 1971.

This is one of those inexpensive novelty books designed to give to a friend in order to indicate your own sophistication.   While it is meant to be sharp, devasting, and oh-so-clever, the material defeats the purpose.   Much of it is too close to the truth to be either satire or humor and, therefore, will be read for information instead.   For example:

"Stanley Kubrick: It's OK to call Kubrick the best American director in some circles and 2001: A SPACE ODYSSEY has made science-fiction respectable (the hippies loved it).   PATHS OF GLORY is perhaps his best."

The author is not David Frost, whose name appears in large letters on the cover.   The inside title page indicates the author to be Ken Wlaschin and the American editor to be Leslie Elliott.   Mr. Frost's rather small contribution is a page and a half introduction.

The major theme of the book is cults--those for directors, actors, supporting players, films, and genres. Sections on critics and on cinema jargon complete the book. This is a mixture that does not blend well.   It may amuse and entertain the more knowledgeable reader but others may have some difficulty in differentiating valid information from some rather strained attempts at humor.

2076.   "B" Movies, by Don Miller.   350 p.   (paperback) illus.   New York: Curtis Books, 1973.

The first thing some will want to do with this book is to rip out the objectionable advertising bound into it. After that the book is certain to please and impress you.   In a detailed narrative, the author provides a history of the "B" film from the early thirties until the close of World War II. The "B" product of the major studios, the independent studios, the poverty row group--Republic, Monogram, PRC--and others is described.   A small collection of illustrations appears in the book's center.   An almost necessary table of contents

and an introduction are missing but there is a lengthy index
to compensate in part for these omissions.

The author's style is informal, yet serious and respectful of his material. In a way this modest volume provides in textual material what other more expensive volumes
provide only partially in visuals--i.e., A Thousand and One
Delights (2804) or The Thrill of It All (2807). This is another fine entry in a new paperback series that can be recommended for inclusion in all collections.

2077.   Humphrey Bogart, by Alan G. Barbour. 160 p.
         (paperback) illus. New York: Pyramid, 1973.
         This is one of a quartet of initial releases in a se-
ries entitled "Pyramid Illustrated History of the Movies."
Congratulations seem to be in order on all counts--writing,
selection, production and value.

The book is logically arranged--an opening section on
Bogart's personal and professional life is followed by a de-
tailed discussion of his films. A final evaluation, a filmog-
raphy, bibliography and an index complete the book. The
films are divided into appropriate periods: The Early Years,
The Warner Repertory Company, The Peak Years (THE
MALTESE FALCON to THE AFRICAN QUEEN), and The Final
Films.

Although Bogart has been more than adequately covered in the literature, this small volume combines the best
elements of the older, more expensive books. It is decidedly
visual, with many stills, all clearly reproduced. It is a
well arranged reference tool, with the filmography and index
as supports to the film chronology. Finally, it covers in a
most acceptable prose style all of the elements that make up
the Bogart legend, without resorting to innuendo or gossip.
The films are not only described but also evaluated. In summary, this seems to be the basic volume on Bogart and is
recommended for inclusion in all collections.

2078.   BONNIE AND CLYDE. A script of the 1967 film,
         by David Newman and Robert Benton (director:
         Arthur Penn). 223 p. illus. New York: Simon
         and Schuster, 1972.
         Found in The BONNIE AND CLYDE Book (2080).

2079.   Focus on BONNIE AND CLYDE, edited by John G.
         Cawelti. 176 p. (paperback) illus. Englewood
         Cliffs, N.J.: Prentice-Hall, 1973.
         This anthology has more to recommend it than does
the higher priced The Bonnie and Clyde Book (2080). It in-

40

cludes an interview with director Arthur Penn, original reviews, essays, some original articles by the real life participants, a script extract, and some changes and revisions
of the original script. Supporting these elements are a
Penn filmography, a bibliography, an index and a few illustrations.

While all the materials are worthy of inclusion, the
outstanding article is the analysis by the author entitled "The
Artistic Power of BONNIE AND CLYDE." Since he had access to Penn's script and obviously studied it in detail, his
understanding and interpretation of the film is impressive.
The section on changes and revisions is a result of access
to the script. This volume on BONNIE AND CLYDE is the
superior and less expensive one, and is highly recommended
for all libraries serving mature adults.

2080.   The BONNIE AND CLYDE Book, edited by Sandra
         Wake and Nicola Hayden.   223 p.   illus.   New York:
         Simon and Schuster, 1972.
         In this departure from the Modern and Classic Film
Script series, the publishers have placed in hardcover material similar to that found in the series.   In addition to the
script which occupies more than one half of the book, there
are several interviews with director Arthur Penn and Warren
Beatty, some articles by the script writers, the consultant,
and Pauline Kael, and finally a sampling of the critical reaction to the film.

With the exception of the script, all the material has
appeared earlier elsewhere.   The potential popularity of the
script, its cost to the publisher and the hardcover format
probably dictated the publication of this script outside the
Modern and Classic series.   The ultimate value of that decision is questionable.   Certainly the acclaim and reputation of
the paperback series is such that it seems discriminatory to
exclude one fine script and roadshow it.   The book is, of
course, acceptable for all collections, and will be very popular with a wide audience.   Whether its minor differences
merit individual and separate treatment is a question librarians will have to decide.

2081.   A Bookless Curriculum, by Roland G. Brown. 136 p.
         (paperback) illus. Dayton, Ohio: Pflaum, 1972.
         This is an account of an educational experiment con-
ducted by the author, a senior high school teacher.   An attempt was made to create a media-based curriculum for use
with those high school students who cannot or will not read--
the potential dropouts, failures, school-haters, etc.   The
initial design procedures, the objectives, the testing instru-

ments and the curriculum--which consisted of film units, discussion units and project units--are all given, along with a final evaluation of the project. The appendix contains sample questionnaires, statistical analyses, student evaluations of the films, a bibliography and a film list with distributors' names and individual film rental costs. (Total cost was about $1,000.)

Brown's account has several values. As an educational experiment, it has pertinence for curriculum change in the humanities. In addition, the plan can serve as a stimulus or model for other exploration, experimentation, study and research in changing curriculum. Finally, the study guide type units can be most helpful to teachers using any of the individual films. The book is highly recommended for all secondary school collections and for libraries in those colleges which prepare educators, librarians, or media specialists.

2082.   Stan Brakhage, Ed Emshwiller, edited by Rochelle
         Reed.   24 p.   (paperback) illus.   Washington, D.C.:
         American Film Institute, 1973.
         Stan Brakhage took part in a 1972 summer seminar
at the AFI Center in Beverly Hills; Ed Emshwiller preceded
him by a year in a similar session.   Edited transcripts of
both discussions are given here.   Acceptable for all collections.

2083.   The Brakhage Lectures, by Stan Brakhage.   106 p.
         illus.   Chicago: The Good Lion, 1972.
         The author gave these four lectures at the School
of Art Institute of Chicago in the winter of 1970-71.   Each
is devoted to a director-legend: Melies, Griffith, Dreyer,
and Eisenstein.   Brakhage's writing style is unusual--at times
non-linear, then narrative, followed by a stream of consciousness featuring digressions involving history, politics, semantics, etc.   As with Brakhage's films, the patron should expect the unexpected.   Each lecture is preceded by a small
gallery of illustrations and portraits of the subject.   They
are from the collection of the Museum of Modern Art and
their reproduction here is adequate.

For the reader familiar with the life and work of
the four directors, the book will provide a new perspective
on rather familiar material.   The novice will find both the
style and the content quite baffling.   (It should be noted that
the original presentation of this material was supplemented
by showings of many of the directors' films.)   Recommended
generally for larger collections and specifically for college
libraries.

2084.   Brando, by Gary Carey.   279 p.   (paperback)   illus.
        New York: Pocket Books, 1973.
        This is still another surprisingly good paperback
original and, along with the Robert Taylor biography (2479),
suggests a possible trend in publishing.   All of the well-
known Brando stories, incidents, films and newspaper noto-
riety are related.   His rebel image, STREETCAR, the marriages to oriental women, MUTINY ON THE BOUNTY, the
career decline, THE GODFATHER and LAST TANGO IN
PARIS are all here, as is his April 1973 rejection of the
Academy Award.
        The book is mostly pro-Brando but occasionally the
author presents a contrasting view.   The text is both descriptive and critical when speaking of his screen performances.
The off-screen personality is a bit harder to examine and
evaluate.   His TANGO co-star's assertion about Brando's bi-
sexuality, in a New York Times interview, is carefully
avoided, as is any in-depth examination of his off-screen
behavior.   Missing, too, is a final evaluation of his contribution to screen acting and film art.   Many people regard
Brando as a major force in bringing film to its wide acceptance as an art form today.
        There is a collection of illustrations at the book's
center but no index or filmography--serious omissions.
        This biography provides a full portrait of the profes-
sional side of Brando and a limited one of the personal.
Much better than the Offen attempt (2085), it is highly recommended for all collections.

2085.   Brando, by Ron Offen.   222 p.   illus.   Chicago:
        Henry Regnery Co., 1973.
        Brando is what you would expect to appear at this
time.   Apparently designed to capitalize on his GODFATHER
comeback and a second Academy Award, the book has a deadline quality that allows for little more than a researching of
the periodical literature and film references.   Probably the
best chapter is the concluding one in which Offen summarizes
Brando's contributions to and effects on film acting and muses
a bit about his professional future.   Most of the preceding
material is a chronological arrangement of previously printed
material.   The author has apparently never met Brando.
        There are numerous omissions and errors, i.e.,
Joan Tetzel is listed as Joan Teizel, Robert Keith is identified
as J. C. Flippen, Vivien Leigh's Academy Award for STREET-
CAR is not mentioned, nor is Brando's non-participation in
World War II.   Many sources claim Brando named his first
son for his friend, Christian Marquand, but Offen makes no
comment on this.

Some interesting visuals are gathered in a center arrangement and, although the book is not indexed, a filmography with cast listings is appended.

The final portrait that the book projects is that of a loner who has tried to be true to himself in all ways. In doing so, he has not sought public affection and there is little in this derivative account to make him a likeable person. While one can admire his performances and his dedication to causes, Brando does not seem, from the material in this book, to be a person you would like to know. The validity of this reaction can only be proven when Brando cooperates in a biographical venture.

For the immediate present, this volume will appease the curious and please most non-discriminating readers. Its economy in recapping Brando's career makes it easy, non-controversial reading. A popular addition to all collections.

2086.   Brando: The Unauthorized Biography, by Joe Morella and Edward Z. Epstein.   248 p.   illus.   New York: Crown, 1973.

It is surprising to find how much of the material in this biography is identical with that in Gary Carey's (2084). The reason is that both are unauthorized and depend on secondary sources. This one is not as detailed and leans more toward the anecdote or the short moment. As an example, compare the treatment in both books of the 1947 Brando-Bankhead collision.

The first portion is the biography up to the release of LAST TANGO IN PARIS but it does not relate the Academy Award embarrassment. The account is rather straightforward and, for the most part, avoids the not-so-subtle innuendo that blemished the authors' Lana (2465). The reader will not learn much that is new about Brando for he has been the recipient of wide media coverage. The authors' attempt is to tie it all together in the hope that some defineable portrait emerges; unfortunately, it doesn't.

A definite plus for this volume is the second section called "Brando--His Careers to Date." Resembling a mini-version of the typical Citadel Picture book, this could easily be called, "The Films of Marlon Brando." Not surprisingly, a book with that exact title, written by Tony Thomas, has just appeared (2282). Here some attention is given to his theatre appearances but the major focus is his films. Cast and production credits, a few stills and some review excerpts are given for each. In this section the illustrations are fine but some of those used earlier (see Shelley Winters, page 44) are simply bad.

Since this volume is not as detailed as Carey's and cannot compete with the 400 photos promised in the Thomas book, its only potential is as a compromise book, if only one on Brando can be considered. Otherwise libraries are directed to the inexpensive paperback and advised to preview the Thomas book.

2087.　Breaking Through, Selling Out, Dropping Dead and Other Notes on Filmmaking, by William Bayer. 227 p. New York: Macmillan, 1971.

"In theory an agent is someone who admires your talent, gives you love, warmth, and protection, and develops your career. In practice you will find that the amount of admiration and love you receive is directly proportional to your income." The two sentences above introduce a much longer section, "Agents," which appears between "AFI" and "Audiences." Many other pertinent topics on filmmaking appear in this cynical, witty, and abrasive book. The alphabetical arrangement is arbitrary, since titles such as "Paying One's Dues," "Ego Trips," "Juggling," and "Hustling," are more entertaining than referential. It is the writing that counts here--a style and a statement that indicates wisdom, experience, and a survival instinct in the difficult field of filmmaking.

Since the book is really advice to the student, the novice, or the beginning director, some of it may have a cliché sound to the more mature reader. But even familiar topics are treated with honesty, candor and clarity. The result is a book that is intelligent, valuable and entertaining. This unusual volume is highly recommended for college libraries which service film courses. All other collections will find it to be a popular addition.

2088.　BRIAN'S SONG. A script of the 1972 film, by William Blinn (director: Buzz Kulick). 119 p. (paperback) illus. New York: Bantam, 1972.

This is a film made for television but eventually shown elsewhere. Includes production and cast credits, and a list of awards the film received.

2089.　THE BRIDGE ON THE RIVER KWAI. 16 p. (paperback) illus. New York: Progressive Lithographers, Inc., 1957.

This short souvenir booklet has one section on making the film, full page photographs of William Holden, Jack Hawkins, and Alec Guinness, some misprinted color shots from the film, a few black and white scenes (which are better), and one half-page devoted to director David Lean.

2090.   The British National Film Catalog, edited by Michael
         Moulds. London: British Industrial and Scientific
         Film Assoc., annual.
         Provides full information about all short films re-
leased in Great Britain. It is published in quarterly issues,
followed by a bound annual cumulated volume. The non-fiction films are arranged in subject order with full subject indexing. Titles, companies, and individuals associated with
the films are also indexed.

2091.   Richard Burton: Very Close Up, by John Cottrell
         and Fergus Cashin. 385 p. illus. Englewood
         Cliffs, N.J.: Prentice-Hall, 1971.
         This unofficial biography is arranged as a predictable
trilogy--Richie Jenkins, Richard Burton, and Richard and
Elizabeth. Its outstanding quality is its detail. Using sources
ranging from some close gushing friends to critical newspaper reviews, the authors have reconstructed Burton's career
from South Wales to London and Hollywood, and from Philip
Burton to Sybil to Elizabeth. (It is the last lady to whom the
authors seem devoted.) Conversations, quotes, facts, and
opinions are all blended into an interesting portrait which
surpasses Waterbury's fan magazine biography written in the
sixties (167).
         One tends to forget Burton's long involvement with
both stage and films. His pre-CLEOPATRA films are numerous and, as a group, show the same inconsistent performer that the later films do. The text is disproportionate
in its attention to individual films; WHO'S AFRAID OF VIR-
GINIA WOOLF? gets a short two pages which tell nothing of
the filmmaking, while THE VIPs and THE NIGHT OF THE
IGUANA get whole chapters. A final section attempts to
separate Burton, the man, from Burton, the myth, and to
assess his work as an actor in several media. Burton's contribution to this biography was apparently minimal.
         A picture gallery presented in the book's center is
merely adequate. More photographs should have been selected
and with greater care. Many of Burton's career highlights
are missing: "The Lady's Not For Burning," "Time Remem-
bered," LOOK BACK IN ANGER, ANNE OF THE THOUSAND
DAYS, THE ROBE, etc. The greatest lack is an index.
There are certainly sufficient names and titles in the text to
warrant one. A filmography, a discography and a listing of
the plays and television appearances would also enhance the
book.
         In summary, Burton's life is related in a detailed,
documented fashion that is rather flat and devoid of emotion
--a style that seems to be a contrast and an ultimate dis-

service to the man. The book will please readers who want a reminder of the well-publicized facts and can read between the lines of this rather formal presentation. A few additions --more pictures, an index, etc.--could make this merely acceptable book one that could be recommended.

2092.   The Business Man in the Amusement World: A
        Volume of Progress in the Field of the Theatre, by
        Robert Grau. 362 p. illus. New York: Ozer,
        1972 (1910).
        A reprint of the 1910 book originally published by
the Broadway Publishing Company, this was one of the first
volumes to note the rise of motion pictures as both entertainment and social force. Written by a booking agent, the text
records the growth of the nickelodeons, the use of films with
vaudeville, and the commercial importance of this early curiosity. Comment on theatre is intermingled with the information on motion pictures. This interesting look at the commercial side of motion pictures is suitable for large collections.

2093.   CABARET. 24 p. (paperback) illus. New York:
        Souvenir Book Publishers, 1972.
        The emphasis in this souvenir book is on performers.
Star Liza Minnelli receives six pages of attention via some
general shots from the film. Joel Grey, Michael York, and
supporting cast members, Helmut Griem and Marisa Beren-
son, are also spotlighted. The story, other cast members
and technical credits are given, and there are longer profiles
of producer Cy Feuer and director Bob Fosse.

2094.   Cable Television, edited by Bruce Henstell. 26 p.
        (paperback) Washington, D.C.: American Film In-
        stitute, 1972.
        This discussion about CATV is only peripheral to
film literature at this point but promises to become an important topic. The showing of films over cable TV is a
major concern, mentioned only briefly here. Most attention
is given to a description of cable TV and its ultimate effects.
A bibliography is included. Acceptable for all collections.

2095.   Cagney, by Ron Offen. 217 p. illus. Chicago:
        Henry Regnery, 1972.
        Using a fan magazine approach that includes "re-
created" conversations, this unauthorized biography is not
much of a compliment to Cagney. While it gives the ex-
ternal facts of his life and covers his films fairly compre-
hensively, it remains a restatement of what has already

been published. Errors are made with names, studios and in the general text. The illustrations are average and the filmography is anemic. Forget this one and look at The Films of James Cagney (2282), which has some production faults but a much better coverage of the subject.

2096.   CAMELOT, by Carl Combs. 48 p. (paperback) illus. New York: National Publishers, 1968.
Some small, unfocused, fuzzy photographs spoil this otherwise attractive souvenir book. Starting with the Arthurian legend, the text and photos describe the actors, costumes, sets, artifacts, armor, animals, makeup, and hairstyles. Richard Harris, Vanessa Redgrave, Franco Nero and David Hemmings receive individual attention, as do composers Alan Jay Lerner and Frederick Loewe, conductor Alfred Newman, director Joshua Logan and producer Jack Warner. Supporting cast and technical credits are also noted.

2097.   Cameras West, by Frank Manchel. 150 p. illus. Englewood Cliffs, N.J.: Prentice-Hall, 1971.
The history of the western film, from THE GREAT TRAIN ROBBERY (1903) to TRUE GRIT (1969), is covered in this most welcome book. Aimed at a high school audience, the volume has many attractive features. The text is factual, evaluative, and critical, with many films being described as "overlooked" or "underrated,"--for example, "one week later another low-budget screen masterpiece appeared and with just as little recognition as Peckinpah's RIDE THE HIGH COUNTRY: David Miller's LONELY ARE THE BRAVE." The author justifies his opinion in the paragraph that follows.
Many film stills and some actual photographs--Doc Holliday, Wyatt Earp, The Long Branch Saloon in Dodge City, etc.--add interest and clarity. Unfortunately, since the visuals are presented in six groupings, they do not always coincide with the narrative, but this is a minor matter. A bibliography and an index complete the book. With nearly twice the number of pages of his previous books, the author has been able to develop his theme in a most satisfactory way. Treatment, selection, and total coverage are commendable. A highly recommended book for all school libraries.

2098.   Canadian Feature Films, Part I (1913-1940), edited by Peter Morris. Ottawa: Canadian Film Institute, 1970.
Some 60 Canadian films are arranged in chronological order, and 19 foreign films which were shot in Canada are listed. Volume II, covering the period from 1941 to 1969, has been announced.

2099.   Frank Capra: One Man-One Film, edited by James
          R. Silke. 27 p. (paperback) illus. Washington,
          D.C.: The American Film Institute, 1971.
          The discussion published here was held in May 1971
at the AFI Center in Beverly Hills. Capra's autobiography
(173) had just been published and there was a renewal of interest in the man and his films. In addition to the interview
there is a filmography, a bibliography and an index to the
topics covered in the discussion. A few illustrations are
also included. Acceptable for all collections and recommended for the larger ones.

2100.   Caravan of Love and Money, by Thomas King
          Forcade. 128 p. (paperback) illus. New York:
          New American Library, 1972.
          Warner Brothers decided to make a rock movie, a
kind of sequel to WOODSTOCK. They put together a caravan
of far-out characters, hippies, freaks, a French director and
some rock performers. This group was sent on a cross-
country tour and eventually landed in England. The author
accompanied much of the tour and describes the activities
in this volume. Sex, music and drugs are given the most
attention. The final film was to be called MEDICINE BALL
CARAVAN or CARAVAN OF LOVE. Rumor has it that the
crew was so high on drugs that no suitable footage was obtained. A finished film was shown for a very short period
and was quickly withdrawn by Warners.
          The book details some unattractive excesses of in-
dividuals, groups and institutions. Far from being a joyous
experience, the trip reads like a come-together of some very
sad human beings looking for the impossible. It's a real
bummer. The language is coarse, the visuals are suggestive, and the personnel need washing. Acceptable for mature
collections if they are interested enough to order it.

2101.   THE CARDINAL, by Beverly Quint. 48 p. (paper-
          back) illus. New York: Mar-King Publishing Corp.,
          1963.
          Director Otto Preminger is really the star of this
souvenir book. The story of the film is interwoven with an
account of the making of the film. Cast and technical credits
are given in the centerfold. Several fuzzy photographs are
distracting.

2102.   CARNAL KNOWLEDGE. A script of the 1971 film,
          by Jules Feiffer (director: Mike Nichols). 118 p.
          illus. New York: Farrar, Straus, and Giroux,
          1971.

Contains cast and credits.

2103.   CASABLANCA. A script of the 1942 film, by Julius
         Epstein, Philip Epstein and Howard Koch (director:
         Michael Curtiz). 223 p. illus. Woodstock, N.Y.:
         Overlook Press, 1973.
         Found in CASABLANCA: Script and Legend, by
Howard Koch (2104).

2104.   CASABLANCA: Script and Legend, by Howard Koch.
         223 p. illus. Woodstock, N.Y.: The Overlook
         Press, 1973.
         In addition to the full script by Julius J. Epstein,
Philip G. Epstein and Howard Koch, this volume contains
some interesting background that is already causing controversy. In an article called, "The Making of CASABLANCA,"
author Koch suggests, not so subtly, that he was most responsible for the final script. This has been quickly refuted
by Julius Epstein, who, with his brother, claims the major
contribution. Be that as it may, the script reads almost as
beautifully as the film plays; perhaps because of the film's
familiarity, the reader's mind can envision each scene and
almost hear the dialogue being recited. There are some
original reviews, a few critical analyses of the film and a
closing comment by Koch to complete the volume. The book
is illustrated but not indexed.
         For about three decades, CASABLANCA has been a
most popular film and this volume can only help to solidify
its position as a classic. Recommended for inclusion in all
collections. For most readers, finding it on a library shelf
will be like rediscovering an old friend.

2105.   John Cassavetes, Peter Falk, edited by Bruce
         Henstell. 23 p. (paperback) Washington, D.C.:
         American Film Institute, 1972.
         In January 1971 this interview with Cassavetes and
Falk was held at the AFI Center in Beverly Hills. Both had
worked together in HUSBANDS and Cassavetes had just completed MINNIE AND MOSKOWITZ. A bibliography and a
filmography for Cassavetes is included. Acceptable for all
collections.

2106.   The Celluloid Curriculum, by Richard A. Maynard.
         276 p. illus. New York: Hayden Book Co., 1971.
         This is a book about using films in the classroom
that should be a continual source of ideas and suggestions for
teachers. It is composed of units which depend upon film
for their execution. Unit subjects include Power and Revolu-

tion, Black America, Crime and Punishment, Marriage, Sex
Education, Responsibility, Ethics, Social Problems, and Literature. In a second section, movies are used as reflections
of a time, era, or stereotype; included here are the West,
War, Africa, The Black in Films, The Depression, Mc-
Carthyism, History, and Violence. Annotations on films are
plentiful, as are suggestions on how to use them. A filmography, bibliography, and a title index are supportive elements to the units.

Not only should this volume be a part of every school
library, but it would seem basic for the teacher's personal
collection. It is an essential resource for the modern teach-
er--at all levels.

2107.   The Celluloid Love Feast, by Martin A. Grove and
        William S. Ruben. 174 p. (paperback) illus. New
        York: Lancer Books, 1971.
        This paperback is quite a mixture: a reasonable
text combined with erotic photographs that are probably included to capture the browser's dollar. The subtitle, "The
Story of Erotic Movies," is a valid one, since the book considers the history, directors, (Osco, De Renzy, Metzger,
Meyer), censorship, the content, the audience, and a sampling
of films. In addition, the attitudes of various nations towards
pornographic films are explored and the landmark films, I
AM CURIOUS YELLOW and CENSORSHIP IN DENMARK, receive detailed treatment. An interview with Saul Shiffrin, a
distributor of erotic films, and a prediction of the effect of
video-cassettes and cable television on the viewing of these
films concludes the book.

Throughout, there are stills from the various films
which are reproduced well enough to give pause as to the
acquisition and subsequent treatment of this volume in libraries. An extended bibliography is given. For anyone interested in the erotic film the book does present an overall
survey that seems rather complete. The text is unexpectedly
literate and elements of basic research are evident. The
only other similar volume is the recent Contemporary Erotic
Cinema (2169). This book may be considered by all libraries
that serve mature audiences. The visuals may determine the
pattern of circulation for the book.

2108.   The Celluloid Weapon, by David M. White and
        Richard Averson. 271 p. illus. Boston: Beacon
        Press, 1972.
        The feature-length commercial film which contains
a "message" or looks at a problem is the concern of this

oversized book. Sometimes called "films of social consciousness," they indicate the potential of the motion picture
to go beyond the entertainment function. Some of these
films were obvious propaganda, others were more subtle versions of the celluloid weapon. The concern of the authors
is to put forth a history of these films rather than a critical
analysis.

With emphasis on the Griffith era, social comment
made in silent films is covered in two early chapters.
Themes found in the thirties films include prison reform,
depression problems, war, criminals, mob action, corrup-
tion in politics. The forties added topics such as migrant
workers, the Nazi threat, alcoholism, racial prejudice, the
shame of our mental institutions, and anti-Communism. The
fifties and sixties added films which reflected the social concerns of those decades. Some notes, additional bibliographic
sources and two detailed indexes complete the book.

Richard Averson has selected many attractive stills
which are reproduced with a consistent clarity. The type
face (Melior) and the special paper used are pleasing to the
eye. The scope of the work is so large that it limits the
authors to a descriptive rather than an evaluative or analytical approach. Since an historical account, however, is their
stated goal, the book is most successful in fulfilling it. It
is carefully researched; it fills an obvious void in film literature and it is written and produced with excellence. Highly
recommended.

2109.   Censorship: For and Against, edited by H. H. Hart.
         255 p. illus. New York: Hart Publishing, 1972.
         This original anthology includes twelve essays by
critics, lawyers, and publicists arguing for or against censorship. Critics Hollis Alpert and Judith Crist focus their
contributions on film, while others consider books, magazines,
the stage, and government data as targets of censorship.
The book is noted here for its concise summary of all aspects of censorship.

2110.   (Selected Articles on) Censorship of the Theater
         and Moving Pictures, compiled by Lamar T. Beman.
         385 p. New York: Ozer, 1971 (1931).
         This reprint of a 1931 volume, originally published
by H. W. Wilson Company and now published as part of the
series, "Moving Pictures--Their Impact on Society," deals
with both film and the theater. The film portion resembles
a printed debate; a brief with affirmative and negative arguments is presented first. It is followed by a general bibliog-

raphy and then separate references for the affirmative and negative sides.

A general discussion consisting of articles from Scientific Monthly, New York Times, and Educational Screen is followed by an affirmative discussion section (World's Work, Bookman, etc.) and the negative section (Review of Reviews, Cleveland Plain Dealer, etc.) Of interest to scholars, researchers, and historians, this volume belongs only in the larger film collections.

2111.   Champagne Before Breakfast, by Hy Gardner.   304 p. New York: Henry Holt, 1954.

Throughout this compilation of anecdotes, column paragraphs and longer personality pieces, enough film personalities are mentioned to warrant its inclusion here. One chapter is entitled "So This Is Hollywood."

Most of the material is press agentry designed for a fan magazine audience. The accuracy of some of it is questionable: for example, on page 210--"W. C. Fields' feud with Ed Wynn was tame compared with the one he had around 1924 with a scene stealer then known as Baby LeRoy. Though highly publicized and good for a thousand laughs the feud was really on the level." Baby LeRoy was a gurgling infant who appeared in several films with Fields about 1934.

The book is not indexed, so it has no reference value, and scholars will have to wade through a lot of nonsense to find anything worthwhile. Noted here for the record.

2112.   A Change of Hearts, by Kenneth Koch.   257 p.   (paperback) illus.   New York: Vintage, 1973.

A collection of plays, films, and other dramatic works by Kenneth Koch from 1951 to 1971. Included on pages 195-197 are ten suggested film scripts: 1. Because; 2. The Color Game; 3. Mountains and Electricity; 4. Sheep Harbor; 5. Oval Gold; 6. Moby Dick; 7. L'Ecole normale; 8. The Cemetery; 9. The Scotty Dog; 10. The Apple. Not essential in any way.

2113.   Focus on Chaplin, edited by Donald W. McCaffrey. 174 p.   (paperback) illus.   Englewood Cliffs, N.J.: Prentice-Hall, 1971.

After a short introduction, the editor divides his selections into four groups: Career, Working Method, Essays, and Reviews. Five articles in the Career-Method sections are by Chaplin himself. The reviews range from the early films to the mini-features, THE KID, THE PILGRIM, and to the classic features, THE GOLD RUSH, THE CIRCUS,

CITY LIGHTS, MODERN TIMES, THE GREAT DICTATOR,
MONSIEUR VERDOUX, and LIMELIGHT. Short excerpts
from THE KID, SHOULDER ARMS, and MODERN TIMES are
included, with a Chaplin filmography, a bibliography and an
index. The illustrations used in the centerfold are familiar
and not reproduced well.
    Since there is so much material available on Chaplin,
any new volume must offer something not easily available
elsewhere. By its inclusion of the reviews, the original
Chaplin articles, and the script excerpts, this book merits
attention. Recommended for inclusion in all collections.

2114.   CHARADE. A script of the 1963 film, by Marc
         Behm and Peter Stone (director: Stanley Donen).
         618 p. (paperback) New York: Appleton-Century-
         Crofts, 1973.
         Found in Film Scripts Three (2269).

2115.   THE CHARGE OF THE LIGHT BRIGADE. 28 p.
         (paperback) illus. New York: United Artists, 1968.
    Each of the major characters in the film is given an
individual page in this oversized souvenir book. Attention is
also paid to such topics as Victorian aristocracy, historical
research, maps and diagrams of the charge, etc. The book
includes many interesting photographs of varying size, along
with cast and technical credits.

2116.   Children and Movies, by Alice Miller Mitchell.
         181 p. New York: Jerome S. Ozer, 1971 (1929).
    Published originally by the University of Chicago in
1929, this study of children and movies appeared prior to the
Payne Fund Studies, which treated some of the same topics.
Supported by the Wiebolt Foundation, Ms. Mitchell examined
the movie experience of 10,000 children--from public schools,
from juvenile correction institutions, and from the Boy Scouts
and Girl Scouts of America. The study investigated frequency
and time of attendance, movie companions, reasons for choice
of films, and a comparison with other recreational forms.
There is a fascinating comparison of film attendance and book
reading. Many tables support the text of the study and the
conclusions are interesting. The book is indexed.
    Although this pioneer study is dated, and certain of
its conclusions are questionable today, it can still serve as
a guide and model for present day studies. For that reason
it is recommended for all university libraries. It is acceptable, too, for all other large collections.

2117.   CHITTY CHITTY BANG BANG, by Jeffrey Newman.
         48 p. (paperback) illus. New York: National Pub-
         lishers, Inc., 1968.
         An example of one of the better souvenir books.   The
text relates the synopsis of the film in a correlation with the
songs.   A second section deals with Dick Van Dyke, Sally
Ann Howes and Lionel Jeffries in detail, and with the others
in the cast to a lesser degree.   Some behind-the-camera
credits are given, with special attention to the production design.   Photographs throughout are quite clear, a rarity for
this kind of book.

2118.   Church and Cinema: A Way of Viewing Film, by
         James M. Wall.   135 p.   illus.   Grand Rapids:
         William B. Eerdmans Publishing Co., 1971.
         Author Wall, who is also the editor of The Christian
Advocate, presents suggestions for viewing films designed to
help the print-oriented person discover film as film.
         After a treatment of the relationships of film and the
church from both an historical and current perspective, an
attempt is made to persuade the film viewer to abandon the
plot pattern (What is it about?) in favor of the film-as-film
approach (What is it trying to say?).   Using many well-cho-
sen examples, the author expands his argument in chapters
dealing with blacks in film and with sex in cinema.   Concluding sections contain a history of censorhsip and some film
reviews taken from The Christian Advocate.
         Although the book seems to promise much more than
it eventually delivers, its arguments/examples are so intel-
ligently presented that the reader becomes absorbed despite
the rather familiar territory.   The author's stretching of a
long article into a book can be forgiven because of his per-
suasiveness and sensitivity.   Illustrations are rather good
and the book is indexed.   A provocative book recommended
for all collections.

2119.   The Cinema, by Stanley Reed.   122 p.   illus.   Lon-
         don: The Educational Supply Association, Ltd.,
         1952.
         This nicely illustrated history of the cinema empha-
sizes the early years.   Written by the Secretary of the British Film Institute, the book is aimed at the elementary
school student and, in this context, is excellent.   Not only
is the text suitable but the supporting illustrations and suggestions are fine.   For example, there are diagrams on
how to make a thaumatrope, a flip book, and a phenakisti-
scope.   Actual photographs are well selected but the reproduction is overly dark.   The book is indexed.   This volume

is certainly worth revising, with some improvement in picture
reproduction.   It would find a warm welcome from many
younger readers.   Recommended for school libraries.

2120.   Cinemabilia: Catalogue of Film Literature.   264 p.
          (paperback) illus.   New York: Cinemabilia, 1972.
          This catalogue lists some 3500 entries, alphabetized
by author, under 17 headings.   There is no appreciable annotation and absolutely no evaluation.   An index lists names
of authors and selected personalities.
          While this volume can be used with efficiency by
persons familiar with film literature, the general reader
and even the librarian will find the going a bit rough if they
are looking for something which is rare, unusual, or unique.
It is necessary to guess the subject category or to know the
author.   A reference book with limited potential, this is acceptable for all collections.

2121.   Cinema in Britain, by Ivan Butler.   307 p.   illus.
          New York: Barnes, 1973.
          This is the long needed British equivalent to the
American Blum-Mayer-Griffith books.   Using a chronological
format, beginning with 1895 and ending with 1971, the author
selects a few important films for each year, usually notes
the credits for same, and gives an historical-critical rationale for their inclusion.   A few "Facts of Interest" close each
yearly section.
          Because of unfamiliarity and a lack of any memorable
achievement in silent films, the book comes alive in 1925
when Hitchcock directed PLEASURE GARDEN.   Probably the
most discernible fact about the films prior to that time is the
early use of subject matter dear to the hearts of British filmmakers: ROMEO AND JULIET (1908), HENRY VIII (1911),
SCOTT'S ANTARCTIC EXPEDITION (1911), HAMLET (1913),
60 YEARS A QUEEN (Victoria, 1913).   The films from the
next four decades are mostly familiar, although titles are
listed that one does not usually think of as being British
films: THE AFRICAN QUEEN, MOBY DICK, SUDDENLY
LAST SUMMER, THE HAUNTING, REPULSION, etc.   Another
apparent fact is that not all worthwhile British films find their
way to American screens: PEEPING TOM (1960), and HOFF-
MAN, a 1970 Peter Sellers' vehicle, have not received any
perceptible attention in the U.S., yet Butler endorses them
as fine films.
          The text is informed, readable, and objective in its
evaluations.   Picture reproduction is quite good and the selection of illustrations is outstanding, with rare stills taking
priority over the frequently used ones.   Up to this time, the

reader had to look at many different books to survey the
British film: Low (675), Larsen (1270), Balcon, et al. (1388),
Powell (527), Manvell (1027), Gifford (157) and others. Butler
has performed a service in creating a book that is excellent
as entertainment, history, or reference. Highly recommended
for all collections.

2122. The Cinema in Denmark, by Morten Peetz-Schou.
35 p. (paperback) Copenhagen: The Danish Gov't.
Film Foundation, 1970.
The role that can be played by government in foster-
ing, nurturing and encouraging the art of film is documented
in this short, provocative book. In May 1964 a new law was
passed that placed a 15 per cent tax on every admission tick-
et and a sliding scale tax on the profits made by licensed
films. These revenues were allocated to a film foundation
whose purpose is "to promote the art of the film." Grants
are made to scriptwriters, loans, festivals, workshops, a
film school, production guarantees, and awards. A film museum and books on film are also the responsibility of the
foundation. Short films as well as feature films are considered.
The clear, logical explanation offered by this book
should serve as a stimulus to similar efforts by other countries. A longer book which would examine and evaluate the
law and the foundation, and their effect on Danish film, would
be most valuable. Meanwhile, this short outline is a good
addition to all collections.

2123. The Cinema in the Arab Countries, edited by Georges
Sadoul. Beirut, Arab Cine/TV Center.
Based on reports given between 1962 and 1965 at
round table meetings held in Alexandria and Beirut, this survey of film activities in 17 Arab countries is quite unusual.
Statistical data are given as to films produced, number of
theatres, traveling units, imported films, etc. A good reference for large film collections.

2124. Cinema in the U.A.R., by Farid El-Mazzaoui.
Ministry of Culture, 1972.
Combines a history of the Egyptian cinema and a
survey of the creative artists involved.

2125. The Cinema of Luis Buñuel, by Freddy Buache.
207 p. (paperback) illus. New York: A. S.
Barnes, 1973.
From UN CHIEN ANDALOU to TRISTANA, the author
explores and examines all of Buñuel's films except the recent

THE DISCREET CHARM OF THE BOURGEOISIE. The individuality and often sacrilegious views that characterize
Buñuel's films, and the varied audience reactions to them,
are noted.

The book was translated from the French by Peter
Graham and has acceptable illustrations and a complete filmography. An index is also provided. A good addition to all
film collections.

2126. The Cinema of John Ford, by John Baxter. 176 p.
(paperback) illus. New York: Barnes, 1971.

In this tribute to John Ford, the opening chapter considers certain factors which help to interpret Ford's success
as a director. History, style, writers, Catholicism and the
Ford hero are discussed. Selected films are used to illustrate recurring themes, consistency of style, and Ford's ex-
pansive artistry. For example, THE INFORMER uses much
of Ford's Irish background and heritage, while THE FUGITIVE
and MARY OF SCOTLAND indicate Catholic themes and influence. STAGECOACH, FORT APACHE, and SHE WORE A
YELLOW RIBBON show his use of natural settings (Monument
Valley, especially) as symbols which could be linked with
dramatic situations. The family as the basic strength of society is examplified in THE GRAPES OF WRATH, MY DARLING
CLEMENTINE, and HOW GREEN WAS MY VALLEY. Other
sections deal with the sea, war, pilgrims, and the aging hero.
A total Ford filmography from 1917-1966 and a very short
bibliography complete the book. Illustrations tend to be somewhat dark and the poor contrast values diminish their effectiveness.

Earlier interviews (553, 770) have considered some
of the same Ford materials. Even so, the selection of films
and the discussion-analysis of them here is different and
quite admirable. Many of the arguments proposed by Baxter
are extreme in their subjectivity, others illuminate areas
formerly taken for granted or ignored. Baxter's work here
is of the same high quality as in his previous books. This
is a welcome addition to any collection.

2127. The Cinema of Gene Kelly, by Richard Griffith.
16 p. (paperback) illus. New York: Museum of
Modern Art, 1962.

A three-page biography, some stills and a filmography take Kelly's career from FOR ME AND MY GAL
(1942) to GIGOT (1962), which he directed. Dance numbers
from the films are listed. Acceptable for all collections.

2128.   The Cinema of Stanley Kubrick, by Norman Kagan.
         204 p. illus. New York: Holt, Rinehart and
         Winston, 1972.
         Kagan's study of Kubrick's films employs a structured
approach.   For each film he gives a visual summary and also
notes lines, plots, sound effects, music, etc.   Kubrick's
comments, if any, are quoted and there is a summarization
of critical reaction.   Kagan then offers his own analysis and
evaluation of the film.   All of the above procedure is explained in an introduction and there is one summary chapter
on problems and prospects.   Some notes and a filmography
appear at the book's end.
         Kagan's attempt to familiarize the reader with the
film before discussing it critically is sound.   Unfortunately,
at times, the description takes up more space than the criticism.   Acceptable for all collections.

2129.   The Cinema of Otto Preminger, by Gerald Pratley.
         190 p. (paperback) illus. New York: Barnes,
         1971.
         The first section of this book considers films made
while Preminger was a contract director for various studios
(1931-1952); films made by him as an independent filmmaker
are examined in the second section (1953-1971).   A large portion of the book is taken from interviews, press releases,
and articles--all written by Preminger.   Supporting the many
Preminger statements are cast credits and a short synopsis
for each of the films.
         While Preminger does not remember every film,
there is more than enough comment to give the reader a good
idea of Preminger as a director-producer.   His ideas and
methods are colorful, opinionated and stimulating.   Pratley's
task in preparing this volume seems to be primarily in selection, arrangement, and editing of Preminger's prose.   This
he has done with economy and style.
         The illustrations are small but reproduction is better
and sharper than usual in these books.   A final section offers
data on Preminger's stage productions both here and in Europe.   The format of the book, together with Preminger's
open prose, will please most readers.   Recommended for
all collections.

2130.   The Cinema of Edward G. Robinson, by James Robert
         Parish and Alvin H. Marill.   270 p. illus. New
         York: Barnes, 1972.
         This volume resembles the Citadel series in size,
format, title and style.   An introductory biographical essay

is followed by a list of Robinson's stage appearances and a few selected photographs of him in various theatrical roles. The major section on his films begins with THE BRIGHT SHAWL (1923) and ends with SONG OF NORWAY (1970). For most, cast and production credits, a synopsis, and a few selected critical excerpts are given. Brief sections on radio, television and short film appearances complete the book.

Fortunately, the picture quality in this volume is much improved over certain earlier Barnes' efforts--Swanson (1306), DeMille (286), James Stewart (520)--but there are still a few which are badly reproduced. While the opening essay is critical to a degree, it would have been a greater service to the reader to place the pertinent author comments with the individual films and enlarge them. Selecting excerpts is no substitute for a well organized total critique. The lack of an index is a major omission and seriously limits the book's reference value. Although this volume is an improvement over some earlier Barnes' efforts, it still has some flaws. Acceptable for all collections.

2131.   Cinema of the Fantastic, by Chris Steinbrunner and Burt Goldblatt. 282 p. illus. New York: Saturday Review Press, 1972.

In this collection of fifteen extended film reviews, some attempt is made to create a developmental history of the fantasy film by using a chronological arrangement: A TRIP TO THE MOON, 1902; METROPOLIS, 1927; FREAKS, 1932; KING KONG, 1933; THE BLACK CAT, 1934; THE BRIDE OF FRANKENSTEIN, 1935; MAD LOVE, 1935; FLASH GORDON, 1936; THINGS TO COME, 1936; THE THIEF OF BAGDAD, 1940; BEAUTY AND THE BEAST, 1946; THE THING, 1951; 20,000 LEAGUES UNDER THE SEA, 1954; INVASION OF THE BODY SNATCHERS, 1956; FORBIDDEN PLANET, 1956.

Each film is described by cast and credit data, some introductory narrative, a lengthy plot description, and a few concluding statements. The illustrations accompanying each include stills and enlarged frames from the films. Reproduction is simply bad in several cases and in no case is it ever better than acceptable. The authors' selection is mixed: a few films have not been considered in earlier books--MAD LOVE, FREAKS, THE BLACK CAT--while several others have been overly analyzed--KING KONG, FLASH GORDON, BEAUTY AND THE BEAST. The narrative is average and seems more at ease in description than in evaluation and criticism. What would have been a pleasant paperback original has been produced as an expensive hard cover edition. Acceptable for devotees of the genre and for larger collections.

2132.   The Cinema of Josef von Sternberg, by John Baxter.
         192 p. (paperback) illus. New York: Barnes,
         1971.
         Another excellent Baxter book, this adds interpreta-
tion, critical comment, and personal reminiscence to some
familiar material. Production quality of the volume is outstanding. A fine collection of visuals, a bibliography and
a filmography add greatly to the readable text, which is
footnoted. The enigma and charisma of von Sternberg are
explored and his films are described and evaluated. The
analysis of I, CLAUDIUS is noteworthy. Recommended for
all collections.

2133.   The Cinema of Andrzej Wajda, by Bolislaw Michalek.
         (paperback) illus. New York: Barnes, 1973.
         Announced as a monograph on Andrzej Wajda, the
director of GENERATION, ASHES AND DIAMONDS, KANAL,
EVERYTHING FOR SALE, and LANDSCAPE AFTER THE
BATTLE. Written by one of Poland's most prominent critics, the volume will include a full filmography and other
reference material.

2134.   The Cinematic Imagination, by Edward Murray.
         330 p. New York: Frederick Ungar, 1972.
         A specialized, scholarly exploration of the effect
that film has had upon writers and their product. The works
of modern playwrights are examined with a view toward discovering cinematic techniques--montage, parallel editing,
dissolves, etc.--in the writings of O'Neill, Brecht, Tennessee Williams, Gertrude Stein, Arthur Miller and others.
A second section attempts a similar study of novelists, including Dreiser, Joyce, Woolf, Dos Passos, Hemingway,
Steinbeck and others.
         Interrelationships between film and the two literary
forms are suggested and a few large concepts are stated,
such as: "The literary history of our times has to a large
extent been that of the development of the cinematic imagination," and "Literary works based on cinematic technique
often lose power when transferred to the screen."
         The explorations of the novels and plays sometimes
seem verbose and digressive. The analyses offered are
likely to be at variance with those of the informed reader.
The author rarely considers alternative interpretations,
usually opting for the one that suits his argument. The
book is documented, however, by copious footnotes and

references. For a full appreciation of this work, the reader must come to it with a wide experience in playgoing, film-viewing and novel-reading. A willingness to wade through a long and demanding argument is also required. The reader with these qualifications will be rewarded with a provocative, stimulating look at film's effect on other media.

Somewhat similar material appears in Richardson's Literature and Film (857) and in Van Nostrand's The Denatured Novel (287).

College libraries should welcome this book enthusiastically. Other libraries will want to consider it carefully because of its specialized quality and limited appeal.

2135. Cinematographic Annual, 1930-1931, edited by Hal Hall. 606, 425 p. New York: Arno, 1972.

These yearbooks, published originally by The American Society of Cinematographers, contain over 70 articles. Among the titles in the 1930 volume (606 pages) are: "Cinematography As An Art Form"; "Motion Pictures in Natural Color"; "Architectural Acoustics"; "Cinemachinery For the Personal Movie."

The 1931 volume (425 pages) includes: "Making Matte Shots"; "Projection Arcs"; "The Larger Screen"; "Motion Pictures Must Move."

The range of subjects is broad, but they will be primarily of interest to researchers and historians. Acceptable for large collections.

2136. Cinematographic Techniques in Biology and Medicine, edited by Alexis L. Burton. 512 p. illus. New York: Academic Press, 1971.

A collection of chapters by different authors about the techniques and equipment necessary for producing films in biology and medicine. An opening section deals with film--its properties, storage, processing, and handling. The next section deals with the hardware, cameras and projectors. Filmmaking is covered with special chapters on time-lapse, X-ray and high speed cinematography, as well as on animation, microscope filming and oscilloscope cameras. Sections on editing and projection are provided, and the book closes with four chapters on television, the TV camera, the film chain and the videotape machine.

The qualities found in the book are uniformly high: the text, visuals, charts, diagrams, plates, index, etc. all contribute to the book's excellence. Certain sections are technical and demand background in mathematics and science for full comprehension. The book may be useful as a model for future volumes dealing with filmmaking in other specific disciplines--chemistry, physics, dance, etc. It is comprehensive, thorough and structured.

With the growing interest of medical libraries in nonprint materials, this book is a natural for such institutions. It has much value, too, in colleges and universities for its valuable suggestions on making teaching films in biology and medicine. It is highly recommended for both types of libraries.

2137. Cinematography: A Guide for Film Makers and Film Teachers, by J. Kris Malkiewicz and Robert E. Rogers. 216 p. illus. New York: Van Nostrand Reinhold, 1973.

An attractive volume intended for the person with some experience in filmmaking. It covers the same topics as many others in the field--cameras, filters, lights, techniques, etc.--but the production of this book is outstanding. Good visuals predominate, and both a bibliography and index are included. Acceptable for all collections with major use probably in the academic libraries.

2138. Cinema Verité, by M. Ali Issari. 208 p. illus. East Lansing: Michigan State University Press, 1971.

After presenting many conflicting statements about it, the first portion of this volume attempts to define Cinema Verité. The author then covers the history of Cinema Verité, the French (Jean Rouch) versus the American school (Richard Leacock), some brief biographies of Cinema Verité filmmakers--Mario Ruspoli, Jacques Rozier, Chris Marker, Albert Maysles, William C. Jersey, Jr., Frederick Wiseman--and the recent technological developments that facilitate Cinema Verité. Extended bio-filmographies of Dziga Vertov and Robert Flaherty are included in the appendices.

The book is indexed and a multi-language bibliography is included. Illustrations are few for a book of this type and the selection is not impressive. Since this is one of the first books devoted to Cinema Verité, it deserves consideration by most libraries. However, it seems to be more a "paste-up collection" of quotation data and opinions than an original work, and may leave the reader a bit disappointed.

2139. Cinema Yesterday and Today, by René Clair. 260 p. (paperback) illus. New York: Dover Books, 1972. Clair has written a revision of his earlier book,

"Reflections on the Cinema (1158), adding material and comment reflecting a 1970 viewpoint. Thus, three periods predominate: the earlier two, when the Clair of 1950 "conversed" with the Clair of 1930, and now, the modern seventies. Clair's comments are wise, well-stated and of lasting pertinence. His range of topics is very wide, and all are handled with professional ease. The device of three "Clairs" who can exchange opinions works well; the resulting total statement is remarkably unified and evidences Clair's passionate involvement with film.

The translation by Stanley Appelbaum is graceful, and there is a short, appropriate introduction by R. C. Dale. Illustrations, and separate indexes for films and persons, have been supplied for this American edition. This is a welcome revision of an important early work with, now, an extra dimension. Recommended for all collections.

2140.   Cine Photography All the Year Round, by Carlton Wallace. (paperback) illus. New York: Amphoto, 1965.
A basic book on cinematography that considers the problem of varied weather. Discusses techniques and the processing of film.

2141.   CINERAMA HOLIDAY. 20 p. (paperback) illus. New York: Cinerama Publishers, 1954.
This early Cinerama effort was the work of producer Louis de Rochemont and pictured the experiences of two couples as they visited various foreign locales. The production and the story are described, the musical numbers by Morton Gould are listed, and there is a diagram of the three-projector system of Cinerama. Photographic work is very poor and the booklet appears to have been assembled in haste.

2142.   CIRCUS WORLD. 32 p. (paperback) illus. New York: National Publishers, 1964.
This souvenir book is divided into two parts: (1) The World of the Circus, and (2) An Inside View. Stars John Wayne, Claudia Cardinale, and Rita Hayworth receive full page attention along with producer Samuel Bronston and director Henry Hathaway. Other cast and production credits are indicated.

2143.   CISCO PIKE. A script of the 1971 film, by Bill L. Norton (director: Bill L. Norton). 165 p. (paperback) illus. New York: Bantam Books, 1971.

Contains cast credits and four articles: 1) CISCO
PIKE and Its Parts (Gerald Ayres); 2) The Cycle Becomes a
Maze (Jacoba Atlas); 3) Kris Kristofferson: Lonely Sound
From Nashville (Edwin Miller); 4) "Did You Enjoy Working
with the Actors?" "Oh, Yeah. Especially the Nonactors,"
an interview with Bill Norton conducted by Norma Whittaker.

2144.   CITIZEN KANE. A script of the 1941 film, by Her-
        man J. Mankiewicz and Orson Welles (director:
        Orson Welles). 440 p. illus. Boston: Little,
        Brown, 1971.
        Found in The CITIZEN KANE Book (234, 2145).

2145.   The CITIZEN KANE Book, by Pauline Kael. 440 p.
        illus. Boston: Little, Brown, 1971.
        This is one of the most popular and widely-known
film books to appear in recent years. It combines Pauline
Kael's brilliant long piece, "Raising Kane," with the shooting
script of CITIZEN KANE by Herman J. Mankiewicz and Orson Welles. The cutting continuity, which is a record of
the final film, is also included. Kael's position is that
Mankiewicz is responsible for much of KANE, and has not
received appropriate acknowledgement; accordingly, she offers a listing of his screenwriting credits, from THE ROAD
TO MANDALAY in 1929 to THE PRIDE OF ST. LOUIS in
1952. An index to "Raising Kane" is also provided. In all
her writing Kael combines scholarship, research, intelligence,
wit and ability. "Raising Kane" is already recognized as a
classic article.
        The book has been produced in an oversized format
with large type and sufficient space for the many frame enlargements from the film. Kael's contribution, added to the
scripts of the film that many think is the greatest ever created, makes this volume an essential for every film collection. Hopefully it will be a model for future books.

2146.   CLAIRE'S KNEE. A script of the 1972 film, by
        Eric Rohmer (director: Eric Rohmer). (paperback)
        illus. London: Lorrimer, 1972.
        Found in Eric Rohmer (2694). Announced for pub-
lication by Simon and Schuster.

2147.   The Classic Cinema, by Stanley J. Solomon. 354 p.
        (paperback) illus. New York: Harcourt, Brace,
        Jovanovich, 1973.
        The fourteen films chosen for study in this volume
are not "The Top 14," nor are they always examples of the
best work of a specific director--e.g., Hitchcock's VERTIGO.

What they do try to represent is a varied sampling of great
films that exemplify historical and stylistic developments in
the narrative film.

The films are: INTOLERANCE, THE CABINET OF
DR. CALIGARI, POTEMKIN, THE GOLD RUSH, THE PAS-
SION OF JOAN OF ARC, M, RULES OF THE GAME, CIT-
IZEN KANE, THE BICYCLE THIEF, THE SEVENTH SEAL,
VERTIGO, THE RED DESERT, BELLE DE JOUR, and
SATYRICON.   For each, cast and production credits are
given, plus an introductory statement and several critical
articles.   For VERTIGO, the following articles are offered:
"Narrative Viewpoint in VERTIGO," by David Thompson;
"Thematic Structure in VERTIGO," by Robin Wood; and "VER-
TIGO: The Cure is Worse Than the Dis-Ease," by Donald
M. Spoto.   A single still is used as a title page for each
film.   Filmographies and selected bibliographies are supplied
for the 14 directors, and the book has an index.

Of all the recent books designed to support introductory courses in film study or appreciation, this one seems
most suitable.   It treats the silent films that are usually
shown and considers directors--if not the films--representing
the sound era.   No book will ever satisfy all teachers; some
may prefer a Ford western, a Kelly-Donen musical, or a
Truffaut, Godard or Resnais to certain of the directors represented here.   The book's greatest potential is as a supporting text.

2148.   CLEOPATRA.   48 p.   (paperback)   illus.   New
         York: National Publishers, Inc., 1963.
         "Cleopatra, Queen of Egypt, History and Legend"
is the title of the introductory article in this souvenir book.
How the final screen story was taken from historical accounts and then filmed is related in the next section.   Double pages are given to each of the stars, Elizabeth Taylor,
Richard Burton and Rex Harrison, and to director Joseph
Mankiewicz.   Other cast members and technical credits are
noted.   Unusual features include a section on the battles,
and a chronology of the lives of Cleopatra, Caesar and
Anthony.

2149.   (Stanley Kubrick's) A CLOCKWORK ORANGE.   A
         script of the 1971 film, by Stanley Kubrick (direc-
         tor: Stanley Kubrick).   (paperback)   illus.   New
         York: Ballantine Books, 1972.
         This visualized script of the film is best described
by Kubrick's introductory statement: "I have always won-
dered if there might be a more meaningful way to present

a book about a film. To make, as it were, a complete, graphic representation of the film, cut by cut, with the dialogue printed in the proper place in relation to the cuts, so that within the limits of still photographs and words, an accurate (and I hope interesting) record of a film might be available." Right on. A most successful and fascinating screenplay book that belongs in all college and university collections. The inclusion of the material which earned the film an X rating may bother some school and public libraries.

2150.   CLOSELY WATCHED TRAINS. A script of the 1967 film, by Bohumil Hrabal and Jiri Menzel (director: Jiri Menzel). 144 p. (paperback) illus. New York: Simon and Schuster, 1971.
Contains: An Introduction by Bohumil Hrabal; "Jiri Menzel" by Jan Zalman; "A Track All Its Own" by John Simon; cast and credits.

2151.   Close Up: (a series), edited by Kenneth MacPherson and Winifred Bryher. illus. New York: Arno, 1973.
One of the first magazines devoted to the history, aesthetics, theory, and criticism of film, Close Up is reprinted in the following volumes: Vol. I, 1927; Vol. II and III, 1928; Vol. IV and V, 1929; Vol. VI and VII, 1930; Vol. VIII, 1931; Vol. IX, 1932; Vol. X, 1933.
An introduction to the series was written by Herman Weinberg and there is a new three-part index in Volume X. One of the outstanding features of this magazine was its use of many stills. Acceptable for large collections.

2152.   Close-Up: A Critical Perspective on Films, by Marsha Kinder and Beverle Houston. 395 p. (paperback) illus. New York: Harcourt, 1972.
An attempt to establish an aesthetic for the evaluation of films. This is not the usual pedantic, philosophical discourse but an excellent book which examines, in depth and detail, films which are accepted examples of the aesthetic being considered. For example, the qualities in the silent film that indicated film as an art form are noted in BIRTH OF A NATION, POTEMKIN, CALIGARI, THE LAST LAUGH, THE LOVE OF JEANNE NEY, BALLET MECANIQUE, UN CHIEN ANDALOU and THE PASSION OF JOAN OF ARC.
A second section examines sound, depth focus, advanced technology (2001: SPACE ODYSSEY), and a few underground films. Three large categories of documentary films--

ethnic, war, and rock--are treated next, and there are chapters on neo-realism, the French New Wave, American humanistic realism, myth in movies, and politics in film.

As indicated, the scope is wide, but the material is presented in a sequential, hierarchical order that aids comprehension. Some of the discussions are engrossing. The authors have brought thought, intelligence and effort to a difficult task in film criticism and have succeeded admirably. Illustrations are fine, and are placed appropriately throughout the book. The films discussed in the text are listed along with distributor addresses and there is a most helpful index. Impressive as a college text, the book also has enough literary merit to qualify for a place in most collections. Highly recommended for all libraries.

2153. Cocteau, by Francis Steegmuller. 583 p. illus. Boston: Little, Brown, 1970.

This biography covers Cocteau's creative life from about 1914 to the immediate post-World War II years. Heavy documentation gives the volume the appearance of a dissertation. Many papers and letters are quoted at great length and, while they add dimension to the characterizations, they slow up the pace of the narrative. Since Cocteau had so many interactions with famous names of the period, the biographical line gets a bit lost from time to time.

All the major films except THE TESTAMENT OF ORPHEUS receive attention but the reader will sense no great enthusiasm for this facet of Cocteau's art.

The book is supported by illustrations, an index, notes, a bibliography, and many appendices. This is a scholarly achievement in biography that will appeal to a small minority audience. It is suitable for all film collections that serve a mature audience.

2154. Cocteau on the Film, by Jean Cocteau. 141 p. (paperback) illus. New York: Dover Publications, 1972.

An updating of the original 1954 English edition (244). Conversations between Cocteau and Andre Fraigneau were recorded by the latter and translated into English by Vera Traill. Cocteau talks about his films, the role of a poet, the nature of film, his actors, and many other topics. For this edition the publishers have added 30 stills from the films, most of which are adequately reproduced. A Cocteau filmography completes the book. Highly recommended.

2155. Jean Cocteau: The History of a Poet's Age, by

Wallace Fowlie. 181 p. illus. Bloomington, Ind.:
Indiana University Press, 1968.
Considers various aspects of Cocteau's artistry in
individual chapters on his novels, plays, art, films, and
other writings. Three very spare biographical chapters open
the book.

The interest here is in the work rather than the person. Cocteau's exotic, flamboyant life is related only when
and if it helps to explain the many examples of his poetic
genius. The chapter on films is very good, and mention is
made of his films in several other parts of the book. Illustrations are few and unimpressive, but a chronology, a bibliography, and an index add to the book. Acceptable for all
collections serving mature adults.

2156. Jean Cocteau: The Man and the Mirror, by Eliza-
beth Sprigge and Jean-Jacques Kihm. 286 p. illus.
New York: Coward-McCann, 1968.
Enough attention is given to Cocteau's films in this
complex biography to warrant its inclusion here. Starting
with a 16mm amateur film called JEAN COCTEAU TAIT DU
CINEMA, the text describes Cocteau's contribution to BLOOD
OF A POET, THE ETERNAL RETURN, BEAUTY AND THE
BEAST, THE HUMAN VOICE, RUY BLAS, THE EAGLE
WITH TWO HEADS, LES PARENTS TERRIBLES, ORPHEUS,
LES ENFANTS TERRIBLES, THE TESTAMENT OF ORPHEUS,
among other films.

Cocteau's life is heavily punctuated by interactions
with the creative artists of his period and this volume tries
to mention them all; as a result, everything gets a rather
short description rather than the scholarly detail supplied by
Francis Steegmuller in his Cocteau biography (2153).

The book is illustrated, indexed, and includes a
chronological bibliography. A fascinating subject is given
a quality biography here. The book should please the more
sophisticated, and is recommended for all collections which
serve mature readers.

2157. Jean Cocteau: Three Screenplays, by Jean Cocteau.
250 p. (paperback) illus. New York: Grossman,
1972.
Contains scripts and cast credits for: THE ETER-
NAL RETURN (1943); BEAUTY AND THE BEAST (1946);
ORPHEUS (1950).

2157a. LA COLLECTIONEUSE. A script of the 1968 film,
by Eric Rohmer (director: Eric Rohmer). (paperback) illus. London: Lorrimer, 1972.

Found in Eric Rohmer (2694). Announced for publication by Simon and Schuster.

2158. The College Film Library Collection, edited by
Emily Jones. 154 p. (paperback) Williamsport,
Pa.: Bro-Dart, 1971.
A listing of films by subject area, with entries
quite similar to the EFLA evaluations with which Ms. Jones
worked for so many years. They offer data, description,
and evaluation. One section contains a listing of feature
films that are described as classics; the final section lists
film distributors. The subject index appears at the back
(an unfortunate decision). Recommended for all collections.

2159. The Comic Mind: Comedy and the Movies, by
Gerald Mast. 288 p. illus. Indianapolis, Ind.:
Bobbs-Merrill, 1973.
Mast begins this study with some basic definitions
and then analyzes many comedy films. The first section
deals with the silent film and illuminates those qualities
which were unique to its comedy form. Sound films are
treated in the latter portion and the differences between
them and the silents are described. The book treats international film, is illustrated, indexed and has a bibliography.
Mast's previous book (1233) indicated that he could
write with style, economy and quality; this volume confirms
that opinion. It is somewhat similar to but much better
than Comedy Films by John Montgomery (247). Highly recommended for all collections.

2160. The Community and the Motion Picture, by 1929
National Conference on Motion Pictures. 96 p.
New York: Jerome S. Ozer, 1971 (1929).
This report of the National Conference on Motion
Pictures held in New York City in 1929 was originally published by the Motion Picture Producers and Distributors of
America. Representatives from 21 states met for four days
to discuss motion picture production, distribution and exhibition. Speaker statements, questions, answers and comments make up the report. Three pages of motion picture
definitions will cause the reader to smile--for example,
"triangle" is defined as "two men and a woman story"--an
interpretation not necessarily accurate today. The report
is indexed.
As an example of the interaction between interested
lay persons and the industry, this book has interest for the
historian or researcher; suitable for large collections only.

2160a. Community Media Handbook, by A. C. Lynn Zelmer. 241 p. Metuchen, N.J.: Scarecrow Press, 1973.

Film is only one of many types of media discussed in this provocative volume, but the importance of the total concept makes it worth noting. Zelmer is concerned with a new-breed institution--the Community Media Center, which offers a service to community groups and persons who cannot use professionals or experts, for whatever reason. He suggests simple and inexpensive ideas on media basics, low budget films, TV, photography, simulations, street theatre, cable TV and other community communication topics.

The question that should occur to librarians is to what extent they wish to provide the services suggested here. For other readers, the information has relevance in its suggestions of simple and economical media methods. Strongly recommended for all public libraries. School libraries will also find the book most useful in a variety of ways.

2161. A Companion to the Movies, by Roy Pickard. 286 p. illus. London: Lutterworth Press, 1972.

This volume calls itself "a guide to the leading players, directors, screenwriters, composers, cameramen and other artists who have worked in the English-speaking cinema over the last 70 years." Using a genre approach, the author further divides each genre chapter into a chronology of the famous films, and then a listing of personalities associated with the films. He has included several other bonus check-lists and the entire effort is a very good reference book. Recommended for all collections.

2162. The Compleat Guide to Film Study, edited by G. Howard Poteet. 242 p. (paperback) illus. Urbana, Illinois: The National Council of English Teachers, 1972.

The stated purpose of this anthology is "to help teachers and students learn how to explore the art form of film and to help them derive some bases for understanding it." Using a traditional approach, the book considers rationale for teaching film, some past history, film language, film as literature, film composition, film and the curriculum, and the future of film study. Supporting these sections are a filmography about films and filmmaking, with rental sources, a list of published screenplays, a short selected bibliography and an index. The book is nicely illustrated with many stills from the films mentioned in the narrative. One puzzling characteristic of the book is its shape--six inches high and nine inches wide--which may create some problems in both handling and storage.

Since many of the articles have appeared previously in periodicals (Media and Methods, etc.) and brochures (Films About Movies, by Kodak), the quality is almost built-in. However, the editor's contribution in selection and arrangement is commendable: the book does provide a "compleat" guide to film study. Recommended for all schools and colleges.

2163. The Compleat Sinatra, by Albert I. Lonstein and Vito R. Marino. 388 p. illus. Monroe, N.Y.: Library Research Association, 1970.

This unusual reference book deals with the many show business careers of Frank Sinatra. A discography, filmography, TV, radio, film, concert and stage appearances are all noted. From his first short in 1935, MAJOR BOWES AMATEUR HOUR, to DIRTY DINGUS MAGEE in 1970, his films are noted. In each case, title, studio, release date, color or black and white, cast, production credits, running time and a synopsis are given. Cameos, guest appearances and unbilled walk-ons are noted, too.

The photographs used throughout the book are well reproduced, and include numerous candids and publicity shots in addition to movie stills. Many of the recordings are of movie songs and they are so indicated in the recording section.

This specialized reference book is admirable on many counts--content, photos, arrangement--and is an ideal supplement to the articles and books listed in a selected bibliography, and to the recent Citadel book, The Films of Frank Sinatra (2288).

2164. The Complete Book of Amateur Film Making, by Phillip Grosset. illus. New York: Amphoto, 1967.

The author discusses the problems he has encountered in making films, and offers much practical advice. Topics include equipment, techniques, and other aspects of compiling a film.

2165. The Complete Book of 8mm Movie Making, by Jerry Yulsman. 224 p. illus. New York: Coward, McCann & Geoghegan, 1972.

The text of this valuable aid is divided into four major sections: Equipment, Film Making, In the Can, and Sound. Each provides a rather complete overview; for example, the first introduces the 8mm filmmaking world, then considers lenses, and finally suggests some 25 guidelines or criteria for the purchase of an 8mm camera. The other sections are equally comprehensive and include many correlated pictures and charts. Eleven appendices range from tables on running times to comparisons of footage on audio cassettes and 8mm film which may aid synchronization. A lengthy index is provided.

The author's style is practical-pedantic; the information is presented in a clear, straightforward manner and is arranged in a hierarchical fashion. For older students and adults, the book can provide valuable direction and insight into 8mm filmmaking. It is recommended for inclusion in all collections which serve mature audiences.

2166.   The Complete Book of Movie Making, by Tony Rose.
        109 p.   illus.   New York: Morgan and Morgan,
        1971.
        This attractive book by the editor of Movie Maker Magazine deals with both 16mm and 8mm filmmaking.   In 17 chapters, the basic elements such as camera, lens, lighting, editing, sound, etc. are presented in progressive fashion.   Since the author is concerned with both the mechanics and the creativity of filming, several chapters are devoted to film language and aesthetics.   The sections are brief but comprehensive, and each contains visuals which help explain and expand the text.   Diagrams, script extracts, and some tables of data on gate sizes, running times, etc. are also helpful.   The production qualities contained here are both unique and attractive.   Arrangement of the material is quite pleasing, and the full color film frames on the cover will catch the reader's eye.

"Complete" is a word to use with caution, but in this case it is almost justified by the text.   Rose's blending of mechanics and aesthetics succeeds very nicely.   Recommended for all collections serving older students and adults.

2167.   The Complete GREED of Erich von Stroheim, by
        Herman G. Weinberg.   illus.   New York: Arno,
        1972.
        This oversized memorial to von Stroheim and his classic film is a very special publishing venture.   With the careful reproduction of 348 stills and 52 production stills, Herman Weinberg has tried to reconstruct the original GREED.   Using the full script, he arranges the pictures in sequential order, and gives some dialogue or continuity. The concluding page of the novel and of the screenplay are reproduced.   This beautiful book will appeal to anyone who knows the von Stroheim-GREED legend.   Recommended for large collections and certainly acceptable for others, though the high price may be prohibitive for some libraries.

2168.   The Complete Works of Akira Kurosawa, by Akira
         Kurosawa. illus. Tokyo: Kinema Jumpo Sho Com-
         pany, 1971-72.
         The scripts of Kurosawa's major films are printed
in what has been announced as a twelve-volume set. Printed
in a bilingual format, with Japanese and English columns
set side by side, the scripts are generously illustrated.
There has been no American distribution of these volumes
as yet and they are obtainable only from the Japanese publisher.

2169.   Contemporary Erotic Cinema, by William Rotsler.
         280 p. (paperback) illus. New York: Ballantine,
         1973.
         The first of three major parts gives definitions,
background, legal attitudes and critics' reactions, and reviews filmmaking activity on both coasts. Interviews with
actors, actresses, producers, directors and distributors
form the second section. The final portion offers interviews
and articles about the standard ingredients of the erotic
films. An appendix presents what the author calls "The
Erotic Cinema Checklist." Films are evaluated on criteria
such as: XXX - Hardcore, XX - Simulation, X - Relatively
Cool. The author is looking for erotic content and reaction
rather than artistic merit, and awards stars on that basis.
Thus BEHIND THE GREEN DOOR, DEEP THROAT, and
HIGH RISE all get four stars and 3 Xs which means they
are erotic hardcore. A section of soft core illustrations is
included.
         The subject matter, the interview dialogue, and the
topic itself may be offensive to certain readers. Acquisition
should be considered only by those libraries which serve a
mature audience.

2170.   Contemporary Film and the New Generation, edited
         by Louis M. Savary and J. Paul Carrico. 160 p.
         (paperback) illus. New York: Association Press,
         1971.
         A selection of stills, script excerpts, and comments
from film personalities. The first section deals with the
audience and the reasons they attend films. Some concerns
about contemporary films, such as violence, insiders, out-
siders, social change, religion, heroes--are stated, and
predictions are made about directors, financing films, experimental films, and the film of the future.
         The book was designed to appeal to the under-30's
and it puts into words and reinforces what they already know
or feel. Visuals are quite good and the selective format

works nicely. The potential danger of a volume like this is that it may be accepted as gospel rather than as a basis for further discussion. Acceptable for all collections.

2171. CROMWELL, by Dr. Maurice Ashley. 40 p. (paperback) illus. London: Juvenile Group, IPC Magazines, 1970.
A biography of Cromwell opens this souvenir book. Other names from the same period are noted and there is a historical essay entitled "The Man From Huntingdonshire." A diagram of the Battle of Naseby follows. The remainder of the book deals with the making of the film and with its stars, Richard Harris and Alec Guinness. Other cast and technical credits include director Ken Hughes.

2172. Current Film Periodicals in English, compiled by Adam Reilly. 25 p. (paperback) New York: Educational Film Library Association, 1972.
A revised edition of Reilly's original work which has been impossible to obtain for several years. For each periodical, he gives subscription data, a description including size, content, themes, recent article titles, etc., and the policy of the periodical in publishing submitted manuscripts.
A back page has a statistical breakdown of the periodicals by place of origin, along with two recommended lists of periodicals--one for large libraries (25 titles) and a second for the small library (7 titles). An editorial slip seems to have placed the lists in the wrong position. "All of the above" apparently refers to the titles in the closing small library list.
The information, its arrangement, and the ease of use make this an outstanding reference work. It is not only a selection tool, but will serve as a guide to aspiring film critics and writers in search of a market for their efforts. Essential for all large film collections, though one drawback is the paperback format, which seems too fragile for the probable use.

2173. CUSTER OF THE WEST. 20 p. (paperback) illus. 1966.
This brief souvenir book contains mostly historical background on George Armstrong Custer along with shots from the film. Cast credits are noted in the centerfold and only star Robert Shaw receives extra attention throughout. Neither author nor publisher would own up to this one.

2174.   "Cut! Print!," by Tony Miller and Patricia George
         Miller.   188 p.   (paperback) illus.   Los Angeles,
         Calif.:   Ohara, 1972.
         Subtitled "The Language and Structure of Filmmak-
ing," this book is for the most part an illustrated glossary
of film terms supported by some peripheral material on the
studio complex, its departments, personnel, procedures, and
budgets.   A Film Industry Directory (for the west coast only)
completes the book.
         All of the elements, with the possible exception of
the limited directory, are just fine.   The glossary seems
complete, non-technical, tinged with some humor (e.g., for
One-liner, see Zinger), and is nicely illustrated with many
line drawings.   Film production procedures are shown in
some of the best flow charts to be found in any volume.
         Far superior to a similar volume (605), this excel-
lent reference is highly recommended for every film collection.

2175.   [No entry]

2176.   Dale: My Personal Picture Album, by Dale Evans
         Rogers.   127 p.   illus.   Old Tappan, N.J.:   Flem-
         ing H. Revell Co., 1971.
         The same material covered in Woman at the Well
(2895) is visualized in this autobiography-picture book.   Some
of the illustrations are of the professional appearances of the
author and her husband but most are of family members, including about 14 grandchildren.   The text is brief, and with
much less religious sermonizing than in the Woman at the
Well.   Much of the text is a verbatim duplication of the
earlier book.   Picture reproduction is average.
         The book has little pertinence for film collections.
Admirers of Roy and Dale and their religious philosophy will
enjoy this version of the Rogers-Evans saga.   Others will
only look and wonder.

2177.   Dance and Its Creators: Choreographers At Work,
         by Kathrine Sorley Walker.   214 p.   illus.   New
         York: John Day Co., 1972.
         One extremely short section is devoted to dance in
films; this book is otherwise concerned almost exclusively
with classical ballet, though modern dance gets some slight
acknowledgment.   A selected filmography lists mostly short
films, along with three feature films: THE GOLDWYN FOL-
LIES, OKLAHOMA, and THE RED SHOES.   Even within the
narrow definition of dance used here, the topic of ballet in

films--e.g., THE TALES OF HOFFMAN, THE GLASS
SLIPPER, HANS CHRISTIAN ANDERSEN, LIMELIGHT, THE
UNFINISHED DANCE, THE KING AND I, ON YOUR TOES,
BLACK TIGHTS, the Gene Kelly or Fred Astaire films--
deserves more than just a passing mention of WEST SIDE
STORY and OLIVER.

It may be petty to carp about this omission, since
the author is obviously not concerned with any form other
than the live classical ballet performance. But a more appropriate title is needed--this one is misleading.

2178.　Dorothy Dandridge: A Portrait in Black, by Earl
　　　　Mills. 250 p. (paperback) illus. Los Angeles,
　　　　Cal.: Holloway House, 1970.

A biography by the personal manager of Dorothy
Dandridge. Readers familiar with her autobiography (376)
will find this modest paperback an interesting supplement.
Some may be a bit shocked by the rawness and the compromise that characterized her life.

An outstanding element of this book is the number
of beautifully reproduced photographs, probably, one would
guess, from the author's collection.

This is a portrait of a black entertainer as envi-
sioned by a personal friend and business associate. It is
a modest, rewarding book, acceptable for all collections
and recommended for large public libraries.

2179.　DARLING. A script of the 1965 film, by Frederic
　　　　Raphael (director: John Schlesinger). 500 p.
　　　　(paperback) New York: Appleton-Century-Crofts,
　　　　1973.
　　　　Found in Film Scripts Four (2270).

2180.　DARLING LILI. 26 p. (paperback) illus. Lon-
　　　　don: National Publishers, 1971.

The story of this underrated film is told via a
collection of sepia-tinted photographs in this souvenir book.
One specific section is devoted to "The German Ace" and
attention is paid to historical background, the cars, and
The Windsors' House. Cast and production credits are
noted, with individual pages given to Julie Andrews, Rock
Hudson, and director Blake Edwards.

2181.　Marion Davies, by Fred Lawrence Guiles. 419 p.
　　　　illus. New York: McGraw-Hill, 1972.

Not only was Marion Davies a movie performer for
a long period of time but, in the minds of many people,

she also served as the inspiration for the character of
Susan Alexander in CITIZEN KANE. Author Guiles documents the first association and disproves the second.
Marion Davies had few of the personal qualities ascribed
to Susan Alexander and was a talented performer to boot.
In this detailed and well researched biography, the author
traces Davies' rise from Follies girl in 1916 to film actress of reknown in the late twenties and early thirties.
During this time and for many years after (a total of some
35 years), she was William Randolph Hearst's mistress.

The experiences with filmmaking--both silent and
sound--are given much attention, as are the later years
when the visitors to San Simeon included many film personalities. There is also an account of the making of
CITIZEN KANE, the contribution of Herman Mankiewicz, and
the resultant furor that the film caused in the Hearst menage. World War II prevented the film from having great
impact in 1941 and its subsequent emergence as a classic
in 1950 had little effect on Davies and Hearst.

Three picture sections illustrate various periods of
Davies' life clearly and objectively. This is a fine biographical portrait of an underrated film actress who was the
victim of an untruth promoted by a classic film. Highly
recommended for all collections.

2182.   Bette Davis, by Jerry Vermilye.   159 p.   (paper-
         back) illus. New York: Pyramid, 1973.
A volume in a new series, "The Pyramid Illustrated
History of the Movies," the standard structure of which includes an introductory overview of the life-career of the subject, followed by the films, conveniently divided into appropriate periods. In this case, we have The Early Years,
The First Triumphs, The Battle with Warners, The Vintage
Years, Years of Decline, The See-Saw Years, and The
Final Fright Films. Closing sections include a filmography,
bibliography, and an index, all of which add to the reference
value of the book.

This is another fine book in what promises to be
an outstanding series. All elements are of high quality:
reproduction of the many photographs is good, the text is
literate, spare, and critical, and there is enough unfamiliar
material to intrigue most readers--for example, several
illustrations are of Davis in scenes that the public never
saw. Along with the Dody biography (868), this is a basic
book on a legendary film actress; it belongs in all collections.

2183.   A DAY AT THE RACES. A script of the 1937 film,
         by Robert Pirosh, George Seaton and George Oppen-
         heimer (director: Sam Wood). 256 p. (paperback)
         illus. New York: Viking Press, 1972.
         Contains cast and production credits.

2184.   Deeper Into Movies, by Pauline Kael. 458 p. Bos-
         ton: Little Brown, 1973.
         What more can be said about Ms. Kael? She writes
film literature that can be read and re-read with profit and
enjoyment by many audiences. In this latest collection of
her reviews from The New Yorker, from September 1969 to
March 1972, she starts with BUTCH CASSIDY, considers
150 other films, and ends with WHAT'S UP, DOC? The
book is indexed. Highly recommended for inclusion in all
collections.

2185.   THE DEFIANT ONES. A script of the 1958 film,
         by Nathan E. Douglas and Harold D. Jacob Smith
         (director: Stanley Kramer). 548 p. (paperback)
         New York: Appleton-Century-Crofts, 1971.
         Contained in Film Scripts Two (2268).

2186.   The Detective in Film, by William K. Everson.
         247 p. illus. Secaucus, N.J.: Citadel, 1972.
         The idea of a photo-text survey of the detective in
films is provocative, but the resultant book is rather unsat-
isfying, especially from an author who is usually so reliable
in blending scholarship and entertainment. Perhaps the investigation uncovered much less quality material than other
genre studies.
         Tribute is paid to the "Master," Sherlock Holmes,
in the opening chapter, which is followed by an examination
of the silent screen detective. An insertion of three clas-
sics--THE KENNEL MURDER CASE, GREEN FOR DANGER,
and THE MALTESE FALCON--between silent films and talkies
seems awkward. Bulldog Drummond, Charlie Chan, Mr.
Moto, Philo Vance, Nick Charles, The Falcon and The Lone
Wolf are among the familiar names treated here in varying
detail. FBI agents, G-men, T-men, secret agents, district
attorneys, inspectors, sheriffs, investigators are all mentioned as examples of the detective genre. European sleuths,
with a separate section devoted to British detectives, are
noted, as are the detective characters of some of Hitchcock's
films. After a short chapter on comedy and camp, the
private eye--from Marlowe to Klute--is recognized. A full
index completes the book.

Picture quality is adequate but there has been a change in the paper used by Citadel for this series. Instead of the former semi-gloss type, a kind of dull-matte paper now appears and the effect on the visuals is to diminish their sharpness. Compare this volume to The Films of Clark Gable (505), for example, and the difference is apparent.

Everson's research, experience, and verbal ability are still apparent, but he seems to have had difficulty in placing the material into an appropriate framework or format. The disparate, unconnected chapters lack unity. Acceptable but not essential for all collections.

2187.   Development of the Film, by Alan Casty.   425 p.
         (paperback) illus. New York: Harcourt, Brace,
         Jovanovich, 1973.
         Casty uses a tri-part structure to present his critical history of the development of film as an art. The first portion covers silent films, with emphasis on Griffith, the Russians and the Germans, and notes the approach toward realism as evidenced in von Stroheim's work. The second section describes the two decades following the introduction of sound films, with social concerns and the establishment of realism as the dominant themes. In the final section Casty considers the new consolidations and directions seen in the films of the Italian neo-realists, the French New Wave, and the individual master directors--Bergman, Fellini, Antonioni, etc.
         The discussion is by no means limited to the three major themes. The author provides a review of many other films and genres. Emphasis throughout is on directors, and, in his attempt to cover as much as possible, the author sometimes mentions several films in one sentence. Those unfamiliar with the films will not find this especially informative. The many visuals are adequately reproduced. A lengthy index completes the book.
         This is an excellent text for college courses and is equally effective as a book for individual reading or reference. Highly recommended for all collections.

2188.   Dialogue on Film Series, by American Film Institute
         Staff. (paperback) illus. Washington, D.C.: American Film Institute, 1970-73.
         The dialogue series started with three small paperback books: Federico Fellini (2231); Rouben Mamoulian, Style is the Man (2515); and Frank Capra: One Man-One Film (2099). A format change followed and the next group

was issued as books to be placed in a three-ring binder. They included: Charlton Heston, Jack Nicholson (2375), Robert Aldrich (2012), Milos Forman, Ingrid Thulin (2299), John Cassavetes, Peter Falk (2105), Alfred Hitchcock (2382), Paul Williams (2889), Cable Television (2094). The most recent change is the reappearance of these publications as separate units resembling a periodical. Referred to as Volume 2, they include: University Advisory Committee Seminar (2844), David Wolper (2894), Stan Brakhage and Ed Emshwiller (2082), Richard Attenborough (2035), Liv Ullman (2837), and Television Seminar-NBC (2787).

2189. Dianying: Electric Shadows, by Jay Leyda. 515 p. illus. Cambridge, Mass.: MIT Press, 1972.
The title of this scholarly volume comes from the Chinese term for film and its literal translation--Dian (Electric) and Ying (Shadows). Further description of the book is given in the subtitle, "An Account of Films and the Film Audience in China." It is much more, of course, since it also treats the history, the production, the industry, and the personnel involved in Chinese filmmaking. Many films are described and examined as reflectors of Chinese thought and political philosophy. Leyda worked in China from 1959 to 1964 and a portion of this book derives from his first-hand observations. Another major source is a two-volume work, History of the Development of Chinese Cinema, by Cheng Chi-Hua, but there are also many others given. In fact, the section on sources which follows the text is a bibliography of impressive proportions.
The single section of visuals is bland and somewhat disappointing, while the scattered line drawings, cartoons, and symbols throughout the text do not compensate for the lack of adequate visual sampling of films.
The unusual reference value of the book is evidenced not only by the text but by the appendix, which includes the above section on sources, in addition to a selected list of important Chinese films from 1897-1966 and a fine collection of mini-biographies of Chinese film artisans. There is a lengthy index. The book will be a delight to the historians, scholars and researchers who use college libraries and large specialized collections. Leyda has treated an unknown area of world film history with diligence, wit, first-hand observation and reportage, and intelligence. The subject matter is too specialized and remote for the general reader, who may balk at 500 pages of unfamiliar names and films. However, even for smaller libraries that wish to include a book which will be a standard for many years to come, this one can be heartily endorsed and recommended.

2190   Dictionary of Film Makers, by Georges Sadoul.
        288 p. (paperback) Berkeley, Calif.: University
        of California Press, 1972.
        Translated, edited, and updated by Peter Morris,
this reference work is quite special. "Film Makers" in the
title refers to those persons "who have contributed something to the artistic industry of the cinema." Sadoul's original 1,000 entries have been increased and expanded about
15 percent by Morris.
        Bibliographic information, a filmography with dates,
and some critical comments make up most entries which
are arranged alphabetically. Directors, editors, writers,
animators, composers, art directors and cameramen from
more than 25 countries are represented. The emphasis is
on international cinema rather than on any one particular
country. As with any such compilation of artists, there are
probably some omissions, but with the added new material
it is hard to find them. Probably one of the most useful
and valuable reference books to appear in the English language in years. An essential for all film collections.

2191.   Dictionary of Films, by George Sadoul and Peter
        Morris. 432 p. Berkeley: University of California
        Press, 1972.
        In this dictionary there are 1,200 films, of which
the author claims to have seen 95 per cent. He suggests
that any inaccuracies in the listings are due to adaptations,
wording, or memory--either his or the reader's. Peter
Morris, the translator, has provided an introduction to this
English language edition explaining some of the changes he
made.
        Each entry has title, country, date, cast and produc-
tion credits, running time, and color or black and white.
A short synopsis, some background information, and critical
evaluation follow in most cases. An incomplete but quite
valuable reference work, most appropriate for all collections.

2192.   A Dictionary of Literary, Dramatic and Cinematic
        Terms, by Sylvan Barnet, Morton Berman and
        William Burto. 124 p. (paperback) Boston: Little,
        Brown, 1971.
        Based on an examination of this reference book,
cinematic terms can apparently be covered by explanations
of nine nouns: Cuts, Director, Documentary, Dubbing,
Film, New Wave, Sequence, Shot, and Soft Focus. All other
cinema terms are related to these nine--e.g., "auteur theory ... see director." The nine terms do not receive any

82

lengthy consideration. The inclusion of cinematic in the title
will mislead many readers. Such a small sampling does
not represent film terminology and even the terms selected
seem arbitrary; why, for example, use "soft focus" over
"deep focus" or "wide angle"? While this volume may be
helpful in the study of literature and drama, it offers little
to the student of cinema. Not recommended for film collections. Glossaries found in the back of many film books do
a far better job.

2193.   Dictionary of 1,000 Best Films, by R. A. E. Pickard.
        496 p. illus. New York: Association Press, 1971.
        One thousand sound and silent films representing the
best in world cinema from 1903 to 1970 are presented alphabetically. Each entry has the country of origin, the year, a
short plot synopsis, studio and production credits, and a few
cast names. Supportive information is sometimes also offered.

        The author's subjective selection includes such films
as APACHE, CAGED, FATHER'S LITTLE DIVIDEND, PLAT-
INUM BLONDE, and TAKE ME OUT TO THE BALL GAME.
Omitted, among others, are Kurosawa's IKIRU and YOJIMBO,
the emphasis falling on the American film. The treatment
of short films is superficial--THE RED BALLOON and TIME
OUT OF WAR are here but AN OCCURRENCE AT OWL
CREEK BRIDGE and NIGHT AND FOG are missing.

        Useful as a quick reference tool but whether it of-
fers much more than some far less expensive guides is for
the prospective purchaser to decide. Recommended, with
the above stated reservation, for all collections.

2194.   Directing Motion Pictures, edited by Terence St.
        John Marner. 158 p. (paperback) illus. New
        York: Barnes, 1972.
        This book, "compiled and edited" by Marner, uses
material "collected" from John Schlesinger, Jim Clark,
Charles Crichton, Sid Cole, Wolf Rilla, Jerzy Skolimowski,
Tony Richardson, and Joseph Losey, but the original sources
are not identified; whether they are from previously published
articles or from direct interviews is not divulged. The
author supplies the connective narrative and the supplementary diagrams and illustrations.

        The subject of directing is surveyed by attention to
role, preparation, script, shot selection, visual continuity,
composition, viewpoint, movement, acting, rehearsals, and
improvisation. On each of the above areas there are comments from each participant. This scheme works surprisingly well, probably because of the editor's expertise in selection,

arrangement and bridging. Visuals are plentiful and adequately reproduced. Two short script extracts appear in the appendix, and the book is indexed.

The diversity of opinion offered, the overall coverage of a difficult topic, and the common-sense selection of readable quotations all blend to make this a very entertaining, instructive and useful book. It belongs in most collections. Recommended.

2195.   Directors Guild of America Directory of Members.
369 p. (paperback) illus. Hollywood, Cal.: Directors Guild of America, 1971.

The fifth annual edition of a reference book that has value both within the film industry and in many libraries. It records in an alphabetical roster the largest membership in Guild history, along with a greater listing of credits and other information than ever before. Individual entries vary considerably in length. Some simply give the director's name, his home city and his ranking--assistant, associate or (full) director. Others give an extended list of credits along with agency and home addresses. Many of the credits refer to television programs. The total membership is divided into geographical groupings, with New York City, Hollywood, Chicago, Boston, Cleveland, Detroit and Florida represented. The latter five cities have small representation. Awards made by the Guild are noted, along with an index of agents, attorneys and business managers.

The book is a worthy addition to any reference collection, and future editions, which will probably increase the information given with each entry, may make it much more widely known than it is now. Currently it is distributed to libraries and universities around the world.

2196.   Directory of Film Libraries in North America,
edited by Joan E. Clark. 87 p. (paperback) New York: Film Library Information Council, 1971.

A listing of more than 1,800 film libraries in North America, this somewhat specialized reference work is of great value to film distributors and salesmen.

2197.   Directory of Non-Royalty Films for Television,
edited by T. M. Williams. 108 p. (paperback) Ames, Iowa: Iowa State, 1954.

Since this volume is almost twenty years old, it is of limited value today. However, its format and structure can serve as a model for similar books. A general introduction describes the organization of the material and discusses TV clearance problems. The latter topic consists of rights such as ownership, musical composition, musical performance, privacy, and other considerations. The films in the book are each given a clearance rating, on a scale of Class I (All risks in showing assumed by the producer) to Class V (All showings are made at the TV station's risk).

Films listed are largely the "free" films listed in other publications such as The Educator's Guide to Free Films (347). As noted in that annotation, the showing of commercially sponsored films without a preview is a risk. While many are entertaining, educational and technically excellent, others are simply one long hard-sell commercial. There is an alphabetical title listing, a subject listing, and a short listing of "Series" films. Information on obtaining government films is noted, along with the distribution sources.

This is more a model of the kind of reference material that will be needed in the era of Cable TV in libraries rather than a source of current useable information. See also 2828.

2198.   A Directory of 16mm Film Collections in Colleges
         and Universities in the United States, by Allan
         Mirwis. 74 p. (paperback) Bloomington, Ind.:
         Indiana University Press, 1972.
         This listing of colleges and universities which maintain film collections, using questionnaire responses from the institutions, gives the following data arranged by states: 1) Institution name, 2) address, 3) name, title of person in charge, 4) telephone number, 5) free loan policy, 6) rental policy, 7) number of titles, prints 8) catalog frequency, availability, 9) other comments. A time-saving section preceding the main body of the book lists all institutions which have out-of-state rental policies.

For anyone who uses film, this is a most helpful aid. It is arranged for easy use and will suggest possible sources of films that may not be noted elsewhere. On that basis it would seem to be essential for all colleges and secondary school libraries. Other libraries will also find it a valid addition.

2199.   Discovering the Movies, by Cecile Starr. 144 p.
         illus. New York: Van Nostrand, 1972.
         Imagine, if you can, a film study book that combines history, aesthetics, reference, criticism, and biography in 144 pages. Ms. Starr has designed such a text for a youth audience, and with considerable success. Beginning with pre-screen history, she quickly advances to Meliés, Porter, Griffith, and Chaplin. Flaherty, Grierson, and McLaren occupy the second section of the book. A few available

films supporting the text in each chapter are described and
evaluated. Distributor-rental-sale information is given in
the appendices along with some bibliography suggestions.
One of the outstanding appendices is entitled "Film Study in
the Classroom." A compilation of helpful suggestions on
using/studying films in a classroom situation, these few pages
seem to contain the distillation of the author's many years'
experience of teaching film. Picture work throughout is superior and a short but adequate index is provided.
    For the audience for which it is intended, this vol-
ume is a must. It cannot fail to excite, involve, and in-
spire any youngster toward further investigation of film.
More mature readers can cover the familiar ground quickly
but will find sufficient new material here to warrant attention.
Recommended enthusiastically for all collections.

2200.   A Discovery of Cinema, by Thorold Dickinson.
         164 p. (paperback) illus. New York: Oxford Uni-
         versity Press, 1971.
            Dickinson provides a very structured overview of
film, combining history, aesthetics, and criticism. Adapting
George Huaco's model from The Sociology of Film Art (1255),
Dickinson delineates four factors which determine the history
of film: Climate (political, economic, etc.), Technology,
Creativity, and Audience. Using these factors, he examines
three periods of cinema: The Silent Era (1895-1927), The
Early Sound Era (1927-1947), and The Modern Sound Era.
In his discussion, he gives attention to classic films, notable
directors (mostly European), film technology, and the film
industry. At times, he belabors a point--e.g., monochro-
matic film--but his encyclopedic knowledge and skill in
structuring his information more than compensate.
            The stills are well-reproduced and add considerably
to the book's effectiveness. A bibliography, an index and
several appendices complete the volume. This is an outstanding short volume that will appeal to a wide audience. Dickinson's approach is scholarly but it is that of an experienced,
secure teacher who guides his reader rather than overwhelms
him. Highly recommended for all collections.

2201.   THE DISPOSSESSED. An unfilmed screenplay, by
         Errol John. 194 p. London: Faber and Faber,
         1967.
            Found in FORCE MAJEURE; THE DISPOSSESSED;
HASTA LUEGO (2295).

2202.   DOCTOR DOLITTLE, by Harold Stern. 48 p. (paperback) illus. New York: National Publishers, 1967.

The first portion of this souvenir book contains the plot description, many fine stills, and the songs. Two articles, "Out of Dreams Comes Reality" and "Of Time and the Animals," provide background information about the film. Perhaps the outstanding feature included is the designer's sketchbook. The usual credits and individual biographies are also given. A most impressive example of what a souvenir book should be.

2203. DOCTOR ZHIVAGO. 32 p. (paperback) illus. 1965.

The spotlight is given to author Boris Pasternak, director David Lean, and screenplay writer Robert Bolt in this souvenir book. Major cast members are given a single page, including a still from the film. Producer Carlo Ponti is profiled and other production credits are noted. Many of the photographs are quite fuzzy, and the entire book is unimpressive.

2204. Documentary Explorations, by G. Roy Levin. 420 p. (paperback) illus. Garden City, N.Y.: Doubleday, 1972.

A brief outline of the history of documentary film introduces this collection of interviews. The history considers the documentaries of various countries in separate short statements. Following this serviceable section are the author's interviews with Basil Wright, Lindsay Anderson, Richard Cawston, Tony Garnett and Kenneth Loach from Britain; Georges Franju and Jean Rouch from France, and Henri Storck from Belgium. The United States is represented by Willard Van Dyke, Richard Leacock, D. A. Pennebaker, Albert Maysles, David Maysles, Arthur Barron, Frederick Wiseman, Ed Pincus, Michael Shamberg, and David Cort. A short biographical sketch is provided for each.

Although all of the interviews express ideas, opinions, attitudes or prejudices about making documentary films, the maximum effect of each statement will depend upon the reader's knowledge of the films. Filmographies are provided at the conclusion of each interview. A collection of stills, a short bibliography, and a useful index complete the book.

The author's qualifications for this work are evidenced by the filmmakers selected, the questions asked, and the final choice and arrangement of material. This fine book on documentary filmmaking will add dimension to any collection. Highly recommended.

2205.   (Bob Dylan) DON'T LOOK BACK. A script of the
         1967 film, by D. A. Pennebaker (director: D. A.
         Pennebaker). 159 p. (paperback) illus. New
         York: Ballantine Books, 1968.
         This transcript of the cinema-verité film concentrates
on the dialogue rather than the visuals. Since there was no
prepared script, what is recorded here is simply what is said
in the final print of the film.

2206.   DOUBLE FEATURE: Movies and Politics, by Mi-
         chael Goodwin and Greil Marcus. 128 p. illus.
         New York: Outerbridge and Lazard, Inc., 1972.
         The two major elements of this film program are
an extended interview with Jean-Luc Godard and Jean-Pierre
Gorin and the script of a-movie-to-be-read entitled "This Is
It: The Marin Shoot Out." An introduction of sorts, "The
Garbage Truck of the Proletariat," is the cartoon that precedes the two main features.
         Subtitled "Movies and Politics," the book addresses
itself to the assumptions and priorities of seeing and making
films. Early Godard films were made with the idea that the
film itself was more important than its effect on audiences.
This priority was reversed in later films, when Godard
joined with other French militants known as the Dziga Vertov
Group. Jean-Pierre Gorin was a member of that group
when the interview was given in New York City, 1970.
         Like most double bills, the main feature is padded
out by a lower-rung effort, the script. The provocative
topic of politics and film is handled in a gimmicky, ineffec-
tive format and is only intermittently satisfying. A few photographs are of no great assistance but the filmography of
Godard and the Dziga Vertov Group is a plus. Acceptable
for college and larger collections.

2207.   Carl Dreyer, edited by Soren Dyssegaard. 50 p.
         (paperback) illus. Copenhagen: Danish Ministry of
         Foreign Affairs, 1969.
         Much of the same material that appears in JESUS
(2446) is contained in this paperback distributed by the Danish
Ministry of Foreign Affairs. The Dreyer biography by Ib
Monty; the article, "Working with Dreyer," by Preben Thomsen; and five scenes from JESUS, the last Dreyer script,
are given, as is the tribute by Jean Renoir. The illustrations in this volume are beautifully reproduced and do not
appear in JESUS. This is splendid film material that belongs
in any collection. Libraries are advised to request a copy
as soon as possible.

2208.   DUCK SOUP. A script of the 1933 film, by Bert
         Kalmar and Harry Ruby (director: Leo McCarey).
         183 p. (paperback) illus. New York: Simon and
         Schuster, 1972.
         Found in MONKEY BUSINESS (2542).

2209.   The Early Development of the Motion Picture,
         1887-1909, by Joseph H. North.   313 p.   New York:
         Arno Press, 1973.
         One of six doctoral dissertations on film topics, re-
produced by Arno exactly as submitted to the degree granting
school.   The purpose of this study is to identify the accomplishments of film pioneers and indicate the relationship of
their work to that of Griffith and those after.   The period
covered is 1887-1909, the scene mostly Europe and America.
Some background is given about the inventors, the first ex-
hibitions, the early road showings, and the problems faced
by the exhibitors.   The films of the period are reviewed,
with several "longer" ones discussed in depth.   Films made
by scientists, business firms, The War Office, The Salvation Army and amateurs are noted.   Lawsuits, and the
change from episode films to narrative films are explained.
Motion picture exchanges, the screen theatre, mass production of films and a chapter on Griffith complete the work.
A bibliography supports the study.

2210.   Early Screenplays, by Federico Fellini and others.
         198 p. (paperback) illus. New York: Grossman,
         1971.
         Contains the scripts of: VARIETY LIGHTS, 1950
(2848) and THE WHITE SHEIK, 1952 (2883).

2210a.   EARTH. A script of the 1930 film, by Alexander
         Dovzhenko (director: Alexander Dovzhenko). 102 p.
         (paperback) illus. New York: Simon & Schuster,
         1973.
         Found in Two Russian Screen Classics (2833).

2211.   Viking Eggeling, 1880-1925, Artist and Filmmaker:
         Life and Work, by Louise O'Konor.   300 p.   illus.
         Stockholm: Almqvist and Wiksell, 1971.
         Eggeling is usually cited as the maker of DIAGONAL
SYMPHONY, a 7-minute abstract experimental film made in
1921.   O'Konor gives a biographical essay, a collection of
Eggeling's writings, some descriptions of his artistic works,
and a lengthy outline of DIAGONAL SYMPHONY. Some of
the text is concerned with the relationship between Hans

Richter and Eggeling and involves feuds, forgeries, and friendships. A specialized work suitable for very large film collections.

2212.   800 Films for Film Study, edited by D. John Turner. 112 p. Ottawa: Canadian Film Institute, 1970.
A catalogue of films available in Canada that are recommended for film study.

2213.   EL CID, by Harold Lamb. 26 p. illus. 1961.
The opening section of this souvenir book is devoted to supplying the history and background for the film. The two stars, Charlton Heston and Sophia Loren, are given individual attention and the major sequences of the production are described. They include: The Tournament at Calahorra, The Coronation at Burgos, and The Siege and Battle of Valencia. Other cast and production credits are given and the entire book is characterized by some interesting and nicely reproduced photographs.

2214.   The Electric Humanities, by Don Allen. 276 p. (paperback) illus. Dayton, Ohio: Pflaum, 1971.
McLuhan's influence is evident throughout this volume--spiritually in the text and physically in the non-linear lay-out. For most of the book, the author's words appear on the right-hand page while the opposite contains visuals, cartoons, quotes, and quips. These elements are intermingled to provide suggestions and encouragement for teaching mass media and popular culture, which the author terms "the Electric Humanities." He describes the "Electric Environment" as consisting in part of the Drugstore Library (popular literature), the Picture Show (popular theatre-movies-TV), and the AM/FM - LP (popular music). For each medium he suggests items for teaching.
The book will reinforce, support, and assist the instructer interested in these areas, but as a recruiting device to gather the older or squarer teacher into the electronic fold, it will probably discourage as much as attract. As a plea for changing curriculum, methodology, content, and teacher attitude, the book is provocative. It certainly belongs in all school libraries.

2215.   EL TOPO: A Book of the Film. A script of the 1970 film, by Alexandro Jodorowsky (director: Alexandro Jodorowsky). 172 p. (paperback) illus. New York: Douglas Book Corp., 1971.
Contains the script and an extended interview/conversation with Jodorowsky in which he talks about the making

and the meaning of his film, among other things. Both
film and conversation are designed to denigrate, attack, and
upset traditional values. Jodorowsky's unique style depends
rather heavily on surprise-shock.

2216.   Encountering Directors, by Charles Thomas Samuels.
         255 p. illus. New York: Putnam, 1972.
         This collection of interviews is unusual in several
respects.   All interviews were conducted by Samuels within
a three-year period, 1969-1972.   To prepare himself, the
author acquainted himself with all the films and with many
of the published interviews of each director.   Thus his
questioning represents a well-prepared, knowledgeable,
structured inquiry.   Perhaps the only quality missing is a
little lightness or humor, but since he was conducting many
of these sessions through language translators, that lack is
understandable.   But the book is a bit heavy at times, and
if the reader is not totally familiar with the films of a specific director, much of the interview's meaning may be lost.
Directors questioned include Michelangelo Antonioni, Francois Truffaut, Robert Bresson, René Clair, Ermanno Olmi,
Federico Fellini, Vittorio De Sica, Carol Reed, Ingmar
Bergman, Jean Renoir and Alfred Hitchcock.
         Each interview is preceded by a description of the
emotional and physical surroundings in which it was given.
A filmography is placed at the head of each unit.   Illustrations abound but there is no identification for many of them
and the reader (other than the film buff) can only guess as
to the identity of the persons shown and to which films they
refer.
         The book has an extended index which will be of
considerable reference value.   Produced in an oversized
coffee-table size, the book has attractive inside cover portraits of the subjects and the author.   Since the interviews
are comprehensive and well-planned, the directors are the
current legends, and the production is outstanding, the book
is a must for all collections.   Highly recommended.

2217.   Enter: The Comics, by Rudolphe Topffer; edited
         by E. Wiese. 80 p. illus. Lincoln, Nebr.: Uni-
         versity of Nebraska Press, 1965.
         Rudolphe Topffer (1799-1846), a lecturer on clas-
sical rhetoric at the Academy of Geneva, liked to draw
faces.   He noted that two faces could converse, and if the
conversation were preceded and followed by other drawings,
a story could be told by pictures.   Thus in the mid-1800s,
he created a base for the eventual development of both comics and the cinema.

This volume contains two different examples of his work. The first, a long piece called "Essay on Physiognomy," written in 1845, is an attempt to find a language for facial expressions. Many line drawings accompany the text which considers faces of all shapes, sizes, and with varying features. His faces are satirical and exaggerated.

The second offering is an early picture story, "The True Story of Monsieur Crepin," told in comic strip fashion, circa 1837.

The editor has not only translated and edited the original works but has written a fine introduction and supplied many explanatory notes and references to supplement the two major pieces. Pre-screen history is a specialized subject of limited appeal, but it is gratifying to discover a scholarly research work in this area that is readable, entertaining and informative. It represents a fine contribution to a neglected area of film history, and warrants consideration for inclusion in any collection.

2218. The Environment Film Review, by Alice S. Kurtz and Kevin J. Kelley. 155 p. (paperback) New York: Environment Information Center, 1972.

This annual guide to 627 films on environment appeared first in 1972, and one hopes for its continued publication. It begins with a list of film distributors and then proceeds to its two major divisions. The first review section is the longer and more interesting. Under each of 21 major environmental categories (air pollution, land use and misuse, wild life, etc.), appropriate films are arranged alphabetically. Reviews provide most or all of the following: critical rating, length, color or black and white, purchase/rental price, release date, sponsor, producer, distributor, director, writer, narrator and possible audiences, with some cross referencing to other reviews.

The second section contains an alphabetical index, a key word list, a subject index, an industry index, a sponsor index, and a list of acronyms for agencies, terms, and materials.

The reviews are originals, not excerpted quotes, and offer both descriptive and critical annotations. The length is usually several hundred words and one can only admire the thoroughness of the reviewers. The several reference elements offered here blend well to make an easy-to-use, valuable aid that belongs in most collections. Other organizations having specific subject interests would do well to use this book as a model. The resulting filmographies would fill an existing need for improved selection tools for the purchase or rental of films. Highly recommended.

2219.   THE ETERNAL RETURN. A script of the 1943
        film, by Jean Cocteau (director: Jean Delannoy).
        250 p. (paperback) illus. New York: Grossman,
        1972.
        Found in Jean Cocteau: Three Screenplays (2157).
Contains cast credits. Known as L'ETERNEL RETOUR in
France.

2220.   Every Other Inch a Lady, by Beatrice Lillie, John
        Philip and James Brough.   360 p. illus. Garden
        City, N.Y.: Doubleday, 1972.
        There is little mention of her films in this disap-
pointing autobiography of Beatrice Lillie. Although she
mentions EXIT SMILING and DR. RHYTHM briefly, she
neglects ARE YOU THERE?, ON APPROVAL, AROUND THE
WORLD IN 80 DAYS, and THOROUGHLY MODERN MILLIE.
Nor does the book make up in biographical excellence what
it lacks in coverage of her career. No valid picture of a
woman or a personality emerges and a series of thinly con-
nected stories and anecdotes is offered as a life story.
Further evidence of the lack of concern in creating the book
is its lack of an index. Over a period of years Miss Lillie
was reported from time to time as accepting royalty advances from her publishers, but not writing much. Two
co-authors and a dull book are further evidence of her dis-
interest. Not recommended.

2221.   Exam Questions and Answers on Sound Motion Pic-
        ture Projection, by James R. Cameron. (paper-
        back) illus. Coral Gables, Fl.: Cameron Pub.
        Co.
        Contains examples of questions asked by various
examining boards for a projectionist's operating license,
and answers to them. National Learning Publishers in New
York City distribute two volumes in a Civil Service Exam
Passbook Series: Motion Picture Operator and Film Editor,
both written by Jack Rudman.

2222.   EXODUS, by Tom Ryan. 64 p. (paperback) illus.
        New York: Random House, 1960.
        The subtitle of this souvenir book is "A Report
by Tom Ryan" and it gives the first portion a distinctive
newspaper format. Each page has a typical headline such
as "Exodus Location Search to Begin," or "Preminger Finds
His Karen." Cast and production credits form the center-
piece of the book and precede a photo preview of the film
itself. An admirable attempt to do something different; it
succeeds rather well.

2223.   Experimental Cinema: A Fifty-Year Evolution, by
         David Curtis. 168 p. illus. New York: Universe
         Books, 1971.
         "Film," as David Curtis shows, "can be painted,
scratched, slowed down, reversed, rephotographed, projected
onto one or a dozen screens, onto domes or people, shot
through distorting lenses and prisms, or directed by com-
puters.   Virtually anything and everything is possible."
         Using an historical structure, Curtis begins his
survey with the European avant-garde films of the twenties.
Some attention is given to the American scene between the
two world wars.   The American experimental cinema that
followed World War II receives the major spotlight, although
other world filmmakers are recognized.   The work of many
talented but unknown artists engaged in making experimental
films is described and evaluated.   A fine middle section of
illustrations gives some indication of the range and diversity
of the films.   A good bibliography is included and the book
is indexed.
         Most books which attempt a survey of this sort are
afflicted with minor errors and omissions and this one is
no exception.   However, the text is readable and enjoyable,
and quite free from rambling philosophical discourses on
implication, meaning, etc.   Some interpretation is offered
but it is concise, unpretentious, and never pedantic.   The
author's no-nonsense approach commands respect.   As a
statement of the fifty-year evolution of experimental cinema,
using the work of hundreds of filmmakers as data or support,
this book is most impressive.   Highly recommended for all
collections.

2224.   THE EXTERMINATING ANGEL.   A script of the
         1962 film, by Luis Buñuel and Luis Alcoriza (direc-
         tor: Luis Buñuel).   299 p. (paperback) illus.
         New York: Simon and Schuster, 1972.
         Contains: "Surrealism in THE EXTERMINATING
ANGEL" by Ado Kyrou, cast and credits.   Found in THE
EXTERMINATING ANGEL, NAZARIN, LOS OLVIDADOS
(2225).

2225.   THE EXTERMINATING ANGEL, NAZARIN, LOS
         OLVIDADOS, by Luis Buñuel.   299 p. (paperback)
         illus.   New York: Simon and Schuster, 1972.
         Contains scripts, articles, cast and production cred-
its for: THE EXTERMINATING ANGEL, 1962 (2224); NAZA-
RIN, 1959 (2588); and LOS OLVIDADOS, 1950 (2496).   See
individual entries for article titles.

2226.   [No entry]

2227.   Faces, Forms, Films: The Artistry of Lon Chaney,
         by Robert G. Anderson. 216 p. illus. New York:
         Barnes, 1971.
            Since there is very little about Lon Chaney available
in books, any new volume should be happily anticipated.
While there are reservations about the totality of this effort,
it is rewarding in many ways.
            First, it is profusely illustrated with examples of
Chaney's many film roles and his various makeups in them.
It also has a detailed filmography and indexes to both text
and illustrations.
            A biographical sketch of sorts begins the volume,
but it can scarcely be called a biography. The author's approach throughout is uniformly positive and noncritical. The
life story is related in factual terms and there is little attempt to explain the "person" of Chaney. The films and
film roles receive the greatest attention. At times the text
seems extremely repetitious, with explanations of the same
characters and the same films given in several different sections of the book. The frequent comments about the perfec-
tion of Chaney's makeup raise questions about the author's
bias. As an attempt to describe the work of Lon Chaney,
though, it is interesting and enjoyable. Recommended for
all libraries.

2228.   THE FALL OF THE ROMAN EMPIRE, by Will Durant.
         36 p. (paperback) illus. New York: National Pub-
         lishers, 1964.
            Will Durant provides the prologue to this souvenir
book. Each of the major cast members, producer Samuel
Bronston and director Anthony Mann are spotlighted. One
special section focuses on the Roman Forum, its ruins today
and how it was recreated for the film. Another is immodest-
ly titled, "Profile of an Epic." Other cast and production
credits are given. Like the film, this book is rather dull
and uninspired.

2229.   FANTASTIC VOYAGE. 18 p. (paperback) illus.
         Hollywood: 20th Century Fox, 1966.
            A souvenir book which should be much better than it
is when one considers the possibilities offered by the film it
describes. After the story outline there are accounts of the
preparation made for the filming and an article about "The
Incredible World of Inner Space." Some of the pages are arranged in a fold-out format which offers no great advantage
to the reader, merely awkwardness in handling. Color

photographs are carelessly reproduced. Cast and production credits are noted. The neglect that characterized the handling of the film is repeated here.

1130.　　FAR FROM THE MADDING CROWD, by Ray Freiman. 32 p. (paperback) illus. New York: National Publishers, 1967.

Bergen Evans provides the introductory essay, entitled "About Far From the Madding Crowd," in this souvenir book. A map of Essex during Thomas Hardy's time is reproduced. The remainder of the book is devoted to cast and film shots, many of which show director John Schlesinger in action. Cast and production credits are given.

2231.　　Federico Fellini, edited by James R. Silke. 15 p. (paperback) Washington, D.C.: The American Film Institute, 1970.

In January 1970, Federico Fellini, his wife, actress Giulietta Masina, actor Anthony Quinn, and director Sam Fuller held a discussion at the AFI Center in Beverly Hills. This short book is a transcription of the discussion which centered about Fellini and FELLINI SATYRICON. A bibliography, a filmography, and an index to the topics discussed are included. Acceptable for all collections and recommended for the larger ones.

2232.　　FIDDLER ON THE ROOF. 32 p. (paperback) illus. Englewood Cliffs, N.J.: Charnell Theatrical Enterprises, 1971.

The major portion of this souvenir book is devoted to a telling of the story by the use of narrative and stills taken from the film. One small portion details how the film was made, with appropriate attention given to director Norman Jewison and star Topol. Small capsule biographies of other cast members and some production credits are given.

2233.　　W. C. Fields: By Himself, by W. C. Fields and Ronald J. Fields. 510 p. illus. Englewood Cliffs, N.J.: Prentice-Hall, 1973.

There is a wealth of original material in this collection of letters, notes, scripts, and articles by W. C. Fields. A subtitle calls it "His Intended Autobiography" but this is wishful thinking on the part of Fields' grandson, Ronald, who cataloged, annotated, and provided linking commentary for the papers. Some sections are detailed and rather complete --such as the early pre-Ziegfeld years when Fields was developing his artistry as a vaudeville juggler. But the twenties and the thirties are only covered superficially. Some detail returns with the forties, and this suggests that the material available was in direct proportion to Fields' contact with his family.

The letters indicate that Field's generosity was greater than legend has it, and that his wife, Hattie, was a rather unloving and demanding woman. The relationship between Fields and his only son is distant, with some anemic effort at reconciliation during the early forties. This late tenuous reunion between father and son appears to be have been effected by Claude, Jr.'s acceptance of father's celebrity and by his wife, Ruth, who ingratiated herself with the comedian. Carlotta Monti, Field's mistress, who wrote W. C. Fields and Me (411), is given a nasty brushoff in two letters from Fields. The last was written from the sanitarium in which he died on December 7, 1946.

In spite of what seems like biased selection designed to suggest a family relationship that never was, the volume offers many evidences of Fields' personality, intelligence, wit, and hang-ups.

The illustrations vary in their effectiveness, the early vaudeville poses having an excellence that far surpasses the uninspired group from the sound film era. Many of Fields' drawings of himself are reproduced.

This collection of Fields materials is certain to interest and please many readers and fans. But the book promises more than it ultimately delivers and is weakened both by the absence of a strong linking commentary and by a suggested family image that reads as fabrication. Recommended for inclusion in all collections.

2234.   55 DAYS AT PEKING.   20 p.   (paperback) illus.
         New York: Program Publishing Co., 1963.
             A historical essay entitled "China, During the Siege at Peking" opens this souvenir book. The re-creation of Peking in Madrid, where this film was made, is described next. Stars Charlton Heston, Ava Gardner, and David Niven are given individual pages, as is producer Samuel Bronston. The final section is devoted to "The Men Who Made 55 Days at Peking."

2235.   Film and Literature: Contrasts in Media, edited by
         Fred H. Marcus.   283 p.   (paperback) Scranton,
         Pa.: Chandler, 1971.
             After an opening section on the art of the film, this anthology addresses itself to the differences and similarities between films and their literary sources. A few of the examples used are from novels (Catch 22, Hud, Lord of the Flies, The Grapes of Wrath, Tom Jones, Oliver Twist,

Midnight Cowboy), plays (Romeo and Juliet, Pygmalion) and the short story ("An Occurrence at Owl Creek Bridge"). Lists of films, distributors, and some films made from notable novels, stories, and plays appear as appendixes.

No argument can be made about the selection of the authors or of their specific articles. They are of varied opinions, and are representative of different time periods in film history. The emphasis on the novel as a film source is heavy, while the short story and play are given much less attention. This may be statistically valid but it unbalances the discussion. Illustrations are acceptable but only seven films are represented. The volume is a good compilation that should satisfy the reader interested in the relationship of literature and film. Acceptable for all collections.

2236. Film and Television Makeup, by Herman Buchman. 223 p. illus. New York: Watson Guptill, 1973.

Although intended for a specialized audience, this volume on makeup techniques is so clear and comprehensive that it will fascinate many a reader. By the use of many illustrations and a modest text, the author outlines procedures for all types of makeup. Beginning with a description of tools and materials, he indicates basic techniques for black and white film and for color film. There are chapters on Aging, The Bald Cap, Latex Rubber Face Pieces, Wigs, and Beards. One section is devoted to ways of obtaining special effects--blood, bruises, scars, tattoos, burns, etc. How to provide makeup for the black performer is also indicated.

Most of the book is devoted to film makeup; only one short chapter on television requirements is provided. The final rewarding section, a gallery of great makeup achievements, features Olivier, Guinness, Muni, Chaney, Laughton, Karloff, Barrymore and others. Very few females appear except under a subheading entitled "Their Individual Looks Became Their Trademark," which may be a bit of a cop-out by the author. Where, for example, is Crawford in A WOMAN'S FACE, Dietrich in WITNESS FOR THE PROSECUTION, etc.?

A list of suppliers and a general index conclude the book. Picture quality is uniformly excellent with both color photos and black and white illustrations reproduced with a care essential for this type of book. Anyone concerned with film makeup will find this book to be an essential. Libraries in colleges with courses on filmmaking and film study will find it a valid and necessary addition.

2237.   Film & TV Festival World-Wide Directory, edited
         by Shirley Zwerdling. 174 p. New York: Back
         Stage Publications, 1970.
      This compilation of information about film (and TV)
festivals is divided into three large classifications: U.S.A.
Festivals, International Festivals, and Amateur Film Festivals, world-wide. Other features include a list of awards,
a monthly calendar and a cross-index of categories. A final
index emphasizes countries, with a listing of all festivals
held within their borders.
      While some of the data seem repetitious, anyone
seeking information on festivals will find this a useful reference aid. With a reservation noted concerning the temporary status of some of the festivals, the book should serve
as a valuable guide. Essential for all schools and colleges
that teach filmmaking and quite valuable for other reference
collections.

2238.   Film and TV Graphics, edited by Walter Herdeg and
         written by John Halas. 119 p. illus. Zurich:
         The Graphis Press, 1967.
      This interesting book, presented in three languages--
English, German and French--examines the graphics found
in recent films of all types: the entertainment film, the
sponsored film, the commercial, and the experimental film.
The text begins with the visual revolution and ends with a
prediction about film and TV graphics in the future. Illustrations and text are outstanding. Although its topic is
specialized, it will offer the general reader who can get
beyond the title several hours of unusual reading and entertainment. For larger collections.

2239.   Film as Film, by V. F. Perkins. 198 p. (paperback)
         Baltimore, Md.: Penguin Books, 1972.
      As indicated in his subtitle, "Understanding and
Judging Movies," Perkins attempts to define what makes a
good movie and to establish criteria for evaluating films.
The films used for examples are popular ones rather than
art films or critics' choices. An overview of critical theories from Vachel Lindsay in 1922 (75) through Arnheim,
Balazs, Kracauer, Rotha, Manvell and others follows. He
concludes that their theories emphasized creation rather than
perception. For a better definition of film, it is necessary
to concentrate on the screen. He considers, in turn, the
photograph, technology, technique, form, discipline, world
image, participation, direction and authorship. His final
definition of fiction film is "A synthetic process whose conventions allow the creation of forms in which thought and

feeling are continually related to our common experience in the world."

What Perkins is proposing is a spectator-based aesthetic rather than one determined by imposed conventions and non-applicable criteria. "A theory of film is a theory of film criticism--not of film making." This volume can be read for the author's provocative and well-argued statement or for a review of some aesthetic theories advanced during the past 60 years. Recommended for all collections serving mature audiences.

2240.   Film as Film: Critical Responses to Film Art, by Joy Gould Boyum and Adrienne Scott. 397 p. (paperback) illus. Boston: Allyn and Bacon, 1971.

This exploration of the criteria for modern film criticism uses more than 100 examples of film criticism as they apply to 25 films. A short introductory portion entitled "Theory" talks of film as art, some inherent personal problems in the critical act, and other problems of criticism which stem from the nature of film itself. The major portion, logically called "Practice," gives several critical evaluations or reviews for each film. The number of reviews or criticisms varies: for example, 8-1/2 has three while BLOW-UP has eight.

A listing of ten books the authors recommend as being helpful in a study of film is offered. Included are Arnheim (440), Bluestone (1056), Eisenstein (462), Huss-Silverstein (457), Kracauer (1347), Lindgren (73), Manvell (422), Montagu (537), Pudovkin (531) and Stephenson-Debrix (212)--a rather heavy serving of film aesthetics.

The book can be used as a text, as a reference for the 25 classic films, or simply for reading pleasure. It brings together some provocative arguments on film criticism, but the meat of the book is the collection of reviews. Acceptable for all collections.

2241.   The Film Buff's Bible of Motion Pictures (1915-1972), edited by D. Richard Baer. Hollywood, Cal.: Hollywood Film Archive, 1972.

A rehash of film information taken from diverse sources including Maltin's TV Movies (1384) and Steven Scheuer's Movies on TV (992). Academy Awards and nominations, alternate film titles, and a general listing of more than 13,000 titles are included.

2242.   Film Course Study Guides, by Margot Kernan. (paperback) illus. New York: Grove Press

Films, 1973.

Three course outlines are available in this series: 1) The Politics of Revolution, 2) Racism, 3) Radical Voices. Each includes a short introduction and a series of suggested films for the course. The film is outlined, some information offered about its director, and the credits are listed. Naturally, many of the films are distributed by Grove Press. Additional features appear in the individual volumes. In Politics, for example, there is a chronology of how film began; in Racism there is a chronology on civil rights and the law. All three have suggested reading lists.

The outlines provide good starting points for building film courses, but it would be naive to think that they are sufficient by themselves. Much more film material is available on these subjects than is indicated here, and a more balanced program would probably result from its inclusion. Acceptable for college and university libraries.

2243.   The Film Criticism of Otis Ferguson, edited by
         Robert Wilson. 475 p. Philadelphia: Temple University Press, 1971.

A forgotten film critic for The New Republic, Otis Ferguson wrote during the years from 1934 to 1942. He was killed in World War II at the age of 36. A few essays accompany the hundreds of film reviews which are said to represent about 80 per cent of all his writing.

The reviews and articles are enjoyable, informative, perceptive, and timeless--an indication of a critic writing not only for his time but well ahead of it. A name index and a title index complete the book. As excellent reading, as a sample of exemplary film criticism and as a reference work, this book is simply outstanding. It belongs in all collections.

2244.   Film Daily Yearbooks, 1918-1922. illus. New
         York: Arno, 1973.

These are the first volumes of Film Daily Yearbook, known then as Wid's Year Book. This series includes: Volume I, 1918; Volume II, 1919-1920; Volume III, 1920-1921; Volume IV, 1921-1922. The first two are a larger page size than the latter pair. Interesting for historians and researchers, but libraries should note the availability of the Film Daily Yearbooks from 1918 to 1969 on microfilm (See next entry).

2245.   Film Daily Yearbooks, 1918-1969. illus. New
         York: Arno, 1972.

These volumes have been available previously as a

set (449) or individually. Now they have been published on
18 reels of microfilm, 35mm format, at about 25 percent
of the cost of the printed volumes. The amount and extent
of information in these volumes is enormous and encompasses
all aspects of the film industry. Highly recommended for all
collections which have the necessary hardware.

2246.   Film Editing Handbook: Technique of 16mm Film
          Cutting, by Hugh B. Churchill. 198 p. (paperback)
          illus. Belmont, Cal.: Wadsworth Publishing, 1972.
          This handbook was designed as a guide for students
who are relatively inexperienced in film editing. It does
not treat creative "editing" but addresses itself exclusively
to "physical" editing. Based on the author's teaching experiences, the material is divided into two major sections:
"Picture Cutting" and "Sound Cutting." In the opening silent
film portion, the basic cutting techniques are introduced,
and ultimately serve as a preparation for cutting the sound
track. Each of the techniques is given separate attention
with a purpose stated, followed by a step-by-step explanation. Drawings, charts, sample forms, and tables appear
as supplementary material throughout the book.
          The appendices, especially valuable, contain more
sample forms and charts, a survey of editing equipment, a
list of editing tools, and some manufacturer-supplier-dealer
information. A short bibliography lists only four books devoted totally to film editing. Other references contain only
individual chapters on either creative or physical editing.
A detailed glossary and an index complete the book.
          The book was designed to be read once and then
used simultaneously with the physical act of editing, as a
sort of lab manual or guide. Its effectiveness in actual use
is not evaluated here. It does appear to have the potential
for making a difficult complex technical task much easier
for the novice. Recommended for inclusion in college libraries.

2247.   Film: Encounter, by Hector Currie and Donald
          Staples. 272 p. (paperback) illus. Dayton, Ohio:
          Pflaum, 1973.
          This collection of 248 full-page stills from classic
films is divided into five parts, all of which have as a connecting theme, "Encounter." The Immediate Encounter,
which opens the book, treats gesture and space among other
philosophical concepts of film. On each page a still is offered with a quotation beneath it--the combination designed
to prod and provoke reader thought rather than to explain.

The Decisive Encounter, the Thematic, the Formal, and the Essential follow in the same pattern.

The book can be used on several levels. Simply as a collection of stills, it is quite beautiful. On another level, as an exercise in film aesthetics and theory, it takes on added value and fascination. In advanced classes, the book should generate unlimited discussion. The visual richness of the volume suggests many other uses--e.g., dismantling the book and using the visuals as illustrations of themes used in films, or as illustrations of filmmaking techniques. It will be a great aid to the teacher-librarian with imagination. The stills will suggest films for initial viewing or re-showing. Even the credits for the quotations provides a bibliography of sorts.

In summary, this is a volume which will appeal to many different audiences. It is enthusiastically recommended for all collections as one of the finest film books to appear thus far in the seventies.

2248.   Film Evaluation Guide: Supplement Two, edited
         by Esme J. Dick. 131 p. New York: Educational
         Film Library Association, 1972.
         The first Film Evaluation Guide (456) covered the
period 1946-1965, while Supplement One dealt with 1965-67. This current compilation is made from the film evaluation cards issued between September 1967 and August 1971. The films are arranged alphabetically by title and give a critical comment and a rating along with the usual data. Especially helpful is the subject index which directs the user to films which deal with a specific area--Asia, botany, city planning, sports, women, etc. An essential for all libraries.

2249.   Film Fantasy Scrapbook, by Ray Harry Hausen.
         118 p. illus. New York: Barnes, 1972.
         Author Harry Hausen began his film career with
George Pal and Willis O'Brien. Since then he has served as associate producer, special visual effects creator, or animator on many films. In this volume he is concerned with his specialty, the three-dimensional animated film. Using stills, sketches and diagrams from his personal collection, he has attempted to describe such special effects as front projection, traveling matte, sodium backing process, perspective photography, and the Dynamation Process.

The author considers individual films chronologically from KING KONG (1933) to THE VALLEY OF GWANGI (1969). For each he gives some short production background and then explains in detail some of the major challenges in visualizing the script. The sketches and stills are selected to correlate with specific sections of the text. An added bonus is the inclusion of advertisements for several of the later films.

There can be no quarrel with the author's credentials, the appeal of his topic, or the large number of effective visuals. However, there seems to be an editor-publisher willingness to settle for something less than excellence. Where, for example is a filmography for Harry Hausen, O'Brien, or of those films which belong to this genre? The year of release for each film in the text? Trying to find the year for THE VALLEY OF GWANGI can be a research challenge. An index to the specific techniques, names, titles, etc. in the text? Certainly this book has reference value. Production control on certain reproductions? (Pages 33, 41, 63, etc., are badly reproduced). If film frames must be used, why not with the care noted elsewhere in the book? The use of greyish-colored pages throughout gives a drab appearance to the book. Production control on the book's binding? After approximately three weeks, the covers on one edition began to buckle noticeably. The editor expertise in selecting an appropriate title? This one does not indicate the richness of information within the book.

As implied above, the total effectiveness of this book is diminished by the absence of several simple components. The strengths of the book are enough, however, to make it acceptable for all collections.

2250.   The Film Finds Its Tongue, by Fitzhugh Green. 316 p. illus. New York: Benjamin Blom, 1971 (1929).

This has the usual faults of such a specialized reprint: an exhorbitant price, poorly reproduced photographs, and no introduction or preface to the edition. The emphasis in the rather patronizing text is on Warner Brothers and will remind readers of a literary style long in disuse. Because of a slight historical interest, large special collections may consider this one, but most libraries should avoid it.

2252.   Film Guide to ... (A Series), edited by Harry Geduld and Ronald Gottesman. (paperback) Bloomington, Ind.: Indiana University Press, 1973.

This series of film guides appears most promising in its initial releases. Included are the following titles which are treated individually elsewhere in this book: THE GENERAL (2313); THE GRAPES OF WRATH (2336); LA

PASSION DE JEANNE D'ARC (2636); PSYCHO (2663); 2001:
A SPACE ODYSSEY (2835).

The format for each is similar and includes the
following elements: film credits, plot outline, a director
profile, some production history, a long analysis, and a
summary critique. Sections concluding the books are filmographies (usually simple title listings with director and
studio notes), bibliographies (sometimes nicely annotated),
rental sources, and notes to the text.

The series is designed to introduce the viewer to
the film, give background information for its viewing, examine its techniques and message, and encourage discussion and further study. The series should be greeted with
enthusiasm by teachers, students, and individual readers.

2253.   The Film Idea, by Stanley J. Solomon.   403 p.
         (paperback) illus. New York: Harcourt, Brace,
         Jovanovich, 1972.

A textbook on the narrative film, composed of three
major sections. The first examines the elements of the
film medium--time, space, motion, shots, editing, dimension, color, the craftsman and the artist. Part two is concerned with the historical development of the narrative
film, from Melies and Porter to Bergman. Theory and
aesthetics are the concern of the last part in which there is
further exploration of shots, movement, editing, verbal-
visual interactions and structure. The appendix contains
a glossary, a filmography of selected directors and a bibliography. Illustrations are plentiful and their reproduction
is uniformly excellent. A few pages of color illustrations
have received the same care and are quite attractive. The
quality and arrangement of the content is impressive, as
is the production care. As a textbook for college courses
in film study, the book is outstanding. All libraries will
find it a most worthy addition to film collections. Highly
recommended.

2254.   The Film in Education, by Andrew Buchanan.
         256 p. illus. London: Phoenix House, 1951.

A definition of the educational film begins this survey of the film in education, which deals with its history in
England and its development in specific academic fields.
Planning, production, and distribution are considered, with
much attention paid to two British national organizations:
1) The National Committee for Visual Aids; and 2) The
Educational Foundation for Visual Aids.

Presentation, with its elements of introduction,

projection, and discussion, is treated; a symposium of
teachers offer opinions and the author analyzes their conclusions; and the final topic is the effect of entertainment
films on children. A closing summary statement is made
by the author.

The author attempts too much, but this older volume
includes sufficient useful information, valuable comment and
good suggestions to warrant attention. The book is indexed
and has a bibliography that is of historical interest. Acceptable for all school and college libraries.

2255.   Filming THE CANDIDATE, by Bruce Bahrenburg.
         254 p. (paperback) illus. New York: Warner Pa-
         perback Library, 1972.
         THE CANDIDATE was a film about a young California
lawyer who runs for the U.S. Senate. In this behind-the-
scenes account of the making of that film, Bruce Bahrenburg
gives a detailed view of cast behavior, production activities,
economics, compromises and other aspects of filmmaking.
The material is arranged in chronological fashion with individual chapters emphasizing the star, the director, supporting actors, and some of the production personnel. A series
of candid photos in the center section supplement the narrative nicely.

The author's approach is interesting, honest, and
sympathetic to the filmmaking process. His coverage is
quite complete and the reader will have a good comprehension of both process and people. For example, he writes of
Natalie Wood who played a cameo role in the film: "As
unobtrusively as she had appeared on the set, Natalie was
gone, back to Los Angeles and her child. She brought to
the set of THE CANDIDATE the presence of a movie star.
She was one of the last, and there would always be those
eyes pleading for affection. "

Entertaining, informative and well-written, this book
is one of the better accounts of the creation of a specific
film. It is recommended for all collections.

2256.   Filming Works Like This, by Jeanne Bendick and
         Robert Bendick. 95 p. illus. New York: McGraw
         Hill, 1970.
         An earlier book by the Bendicks, Making the Movies
(887), was a pioneer in the field of film books for young
readers, and its excellence is continued here. Using a combination of supportive text, line drawings and sketches, the
authors consider all facets of student filmmaking. Design
of the volume is so attractive that even the most reluctant
student will be encouraged to try.

There is little need to analyze content; it is all
here--cameras, lenses, film, lights, sound, scripts, budgets,
schedules, editing, titles, animation, processing, projectors
and sources. These and many other topics are presented
in a usable and concise arrangement. The suitability and
appeal of the visuals is undeniable; even a short index is
provided. For the young person who may not or cannot respond to the professional books usually provided, this one
will be attractive. The temptation to overpraise occurs when
books such as this are published; it is so completely right in
all its qualities--its knowledge of subject, treatment, and intended audience. It belongs in every school library.

2257.   The Film Maker and His World: A Young Person's
        Guide, by R. J. Minney. 160 p. London: Victor
        Gollancz, Ltd., 1964.
        Aimed at a young audience, this volume surveys the
usual topics in filmmaking. Starting with a short account of
early films, the text concentrates on the roles of various
participants in the filmmaking process--the producer, director, actor, art director, etc. Other topics such as casting,
trick photography, film schools, and art vs. industry are
discussed. Somewhat dated and rather uninspired to start
with, this volume has been surpassed by many recent ones
on the same topic.

2258.   Filmmaking for Children, by Arden Rynew. 144 p.
        (paperback) illus. Dayton, Ohio: Pflaum, 1971.
        One of the most frequently voiced needs has been
an adequate book on filmmaking for elementary school students. Rynew's book may satisfy that need, although most
of the book is for teachers. Only the last section, the handbook, is suggested as a student text. The book is divided
into four large divisions: I, Background; II, The Implementation of a Filmmaking Program; III, Additional Filmmaking
Information; IV, Motion Picture Production Handbook (the
student text). The accompanying text is informative, somewhat technical, and practical when appropriate. Rynew is a
practicing art teacher in an elementary school and much of
what he suggests seems based on his own experience. All
the sections are valuable, but the "Handbook" portion will
probably get the greatest teacher use.
        It may be indelicate to indict an art teacher for his
illustrations, but they are quite unimpressive. The drawings
seem amateurish. Line drawings are cluttered with too much
information, and the full-page blowups of 8mm film are murky
and hard to interpret. However, there is enough valuable

information, suggestion, and direction in the text to justify recommending this volume for all school libraries.

2259.   Film Making in Creative Teaching, by Keith Kennedy. 128 p.   illus.   New York: Watson-Guptill, 1972.
This British book was designed for use by teachers of junior high students.   Its primary concern is communication, with film regarded as one method of communication. Suggested ways of using film in the learning process are supplemented by explanations of the equipment needed and an emphasis on the use of imagination and creativity.   The hardware includes not only motion picture cameras, but still cameras, polaroids, tape recorders, and loop projectors. The latter portions of the book suggest projects such as camera adventures, photopoems, photo hunts, collages, montages and improvisations.   A list of suppliers, a bibliography, and an index complete the book.
The admirable intentions of this volume are larger than the achievements.   Some of this may be due to its British origin, for there are wide differences in the respective curricula of England and America, and in the structure for teaching and methodologies.   Some of the suggestions seem awkward to implement, others seem dated.   Whenever a book employs illustrations of technology, the risk of their being quickly out-of-date is great.   Some of the illustrations are of older machines (page 43) and are of brands more familiar to European purchasers (Philips, Rank Aldis, Eumig Mark, etc.)   Certain references are outdated--for example, Limbacher's Guide to 8mm and 16mm Films is now published by Bowker and has a new title.
These reservations are minor when one considers the total effort.   The rationale for the book's dominant theme--using film to communicate--is presented with intelligence and argument based upon teaching experience.   This volume is appropriate for the professional collection of most 7-12 schools, although some of its content is pertinent for a wider audience.   Some adjustment and compromise will be required before full communication can take place.

2260.   Filmographic Dictionary of World Literature, Volume I: A to K, by Johan Daisne.   681 p.   illus. New York: Humanities Press, 1972.
That the judgment of a book by its cover and appearance is inadvisable is demonstrated by this attractive looking volume.   The cover, printed in four languages, catches the eye and the explanation of the contents in the introduction is impressive.   Paper used is of very high quality

and it all looks very promising.

Written in English, German, Dutch, and French, the book has three major parts. First, there is a list of certain selected authors, arranged alphabetically with a filmography supplied for each. Volume I begins with French writer Charles Abadie and ends with American Peter B. Kyne. The Kyne entry lists "Cappy Ricks," "Cappy Ricks Returns," and "Three Godfathers" as the source literature for several films which are noted beneath the appropriate book title. Any differences between film title and book title are indicated along with the country and year of production, and the name of the director. A few cast players are noted, sometimes with the name of the character they portray in the film.

The second section is a gallery of stills which covers approximately 340 pages and is an almost complete waste of space in a reference book. Pictures are poorly selected, badly reproduced, and presented unattractively. Some take up less than half a page, leaving large empty areas of white space. The illustrations are also arranged by literary author name.

The final section is a combined alphabetical index of all the films and literary sources noted in section I. The reader is referred to the author name rather than to a specific page.

If the book is to have any reference value, it must be in the content of its first section which runs about 240 pages. Reservations about these pages appear quickly:

.... authors have been chosen in a selective fashion. Missing are Cervantes, Clark, Kazantzakis, Heller, etc.

.... listings beneath each author are partial--under Raymond Chandler only THE BIG SLEEP is noted.

.... no distinction is made between literary source genre--novel, short story, play, musical comedy, tv script, etc.

.... some annotations seem incomplete, erroneous, or misleading--under Noel Coward we find him credited with STAR. Most sources indicate that he contributed some uncredited dialogue for the Coward character but the film was based on a screenplay derived from the two Lawrence biographies and other sources. Then, too, BRIEF ENCOUNTER is taken from the short play, "Still Life," a part of the Coward "Tonight at 8:30" series. Here it is indicated as the original title of a literary work.

.... there are omissions within filmographies--Dashiel
Hammett's The Maltese Falcon was also made
under the title of SATAN MET A LADY in 1936.
The author notes only the 1931 and the 1941 versions.
.... certain credits are distorted. Here Kathryn
Forbes is given credit for I REMEMBER MAMA,
said to be taken from her novel, Mama's Bank
Account. Most sources indicated the film was
based primarily on John Van Druten's play taken
from the novel.

The above reservations and comments are based on
only a partial and cursory examination. When the author
states he has worked with "scientific accuracy" and that the
material is "the work of a lifetime," the reader/user may
feel a bit intimidated. Another statement, "We want this
book to illustrate how the whole of literature forms the basis
of the seventh art," is simply irritating in its bias and partial ignorance.

The high price, the low level of a concentrated content and the vulnerability of some entries make this a most
questionable purchase for any library. Consider instead
Dimmitt's A Title Guide to the Talkies and Enser's Filmed
Books and Plays.

2261.   Film: Readings in the Mass Media, by Allen
Kirschner and Linda Kirschner. 315 p. (paperback) New York: Odyssey Press, 1971.

Perhaps the rationale for this anthology is explicit
in its title, but one wishes the introduction offered some
further elucidation. We are given instead a capsule history
of film in four parts: One Minute Please (1896-1912), You
Are Living the Story (1912-1927), You Ain't Heard Nothin'
Yet (1927-1950), and Movies Are Better than Ever (1950 on).

The body of the book consists of three major divi-
sions with appropriate reprintings under each. Section I,
"Form and Technique," features personalities such as Mc-
Luhan, Agee, Griffith, Hitchcock, Antonioni and Mekas.
Persons familiar with film literature anthologies can probably
guess the titles of the articles. Section Two is entitled
"Audience and Effect," the majority of authors here being
critics--Schickel, Kerr, Kauffmann, Knight, Crist, etc.
Critics are also heavily represented in the last section,
titled "Critics and Criticism." Kael, Adler, Tyler, Alpert,
Crowther, Morgenstern and others appear. A further section reproduces statements on "The Future of the Film" by
members of the National Society of Film Critics. A selected
bibliography completes the volume.

As a text for a film or communications course, the
book may offer a service to the student by bringing together
a collection of well-known articles, but since many of the
articles appear elsewhere in film collections, the volume
may be redundant or extravagant for most libraries. Its
rather high price and the absence of a unifying statement
by the authors are other negative factors.

2262.   Film: Real to Reel, by David Coynik.   274 p.
        (paperback) illus. Dayton, Ohio: Pflaum, 1972.
        The author denies this is a textbook, preferring to
call it a companion to film study. And he is quite right,
for the style, approach and tone all suggest informality and
exchange of ideas rather than pure exposition.
        Film aesthetics is the first major topic considered.
Starting with a discussion of the shot, Coynik proceeds to
editing, rhythm, sound, motion, light, and color. Film
forms and genres appear next and they include feature films,
documentaries, animation films, and experimental or "now"
films, as the author calls them. A final chapter suggests
that the reader make his own film and offers encouragement
and advice.
        The numerous visuals used are well-reproduced and
supplement the text in excellent fashion. Some small reservation may be expressed at the absence of color illustrations in the section which deals with color. Some of the
captions on the photographs seem a bit calculated--a shot
of Orson Welles splattered with mud has a sentence under-
neath telling of his difficulties with the studios. Many of
the stills and the examples cited in the text are taken from
the classic films that usually appear in film study courses.
        As a book for individual or group reading, this
volume is excellent. The examples used are clearly explained, no attempt is made at verbal acrobatics, and the
experience of reading it is both comfortable and rewarding.
It can be used with equal effectiveness by young adults or
more mature readers. It certainly belongs in every school
and college library. Highly recommended.

2263.   Film Research, compiled by Peter J. Bukalski.
        215 p. Boston, Mass.: G. K. Hall, 1972.
        The title of this book may be somewhat misleading,
for the topic is not film research but suggested aids for
doing film research. It is largely a bibliography of film
books. An introductory essay provides a general overview
of film study and film literature. Fifty books are listed in
the next section, "Essential Works," with a brief annotation
for each title. Short chapters listing film rental and film

sales agencies are followed by a listing of periodicals. The bibliography, the major portion of the text, divides film books into the usual categories: 1) Film History, Theory, Criticism, and Introductory Works; 2) Film Production and Technology; 3) Film Genre; 4) Sociology and Economics of Film; 5) National Cinemas; 6) Film Scripts; 7) Particular Films; 8) Personalities, Biographies, Filmographies; 9) Film Education; 10) Film Related Works; 11) Careers in Film; 12) Bibliographies, Guides and Indexes; 13) Selected Works in Foreign Languages. Book titles listed under these categories are not annotated; only author, title, publisher and date are given.

Since the material used in this volume so closely parallels that of Cinema Booklist and this supplement, the following comments may not be impartial or objective.

A listing of book titles without evaluation or even description is of limited value. The Larry Edmund's Book Catalog gives many more titles and annotations than Bukalski does here and at far lower cost.

The fifty annotations that are given vary in quality: e.g., on MacGowan's Behind the Screen--"....it is best in its accounts of technological developments of film but less than inadequate in its discussion of many historical films." Why include it as an essential work? Why not include Jacobs' The Rise of the American Film instead? This latter book is recognized by most film scholars as one of the classics in film literature. Incidentally, Jacobs wrote this book; he did not edit it, as indicated in Bukalski's non-annotated bibliography.

The arrangement of the books is questionable. To place introductory books in one listing along with history, theory, and criticism may not offer the best service to the researcher. For example, into what categories do the following fall: Contemporary Film, Movie Reader, Black Magic, Image Maker, or The New Spirit in the Cinema? The absence of an annotation for this last title can be misleading, since it is a reprint of a 1930 book. The arrangement assumes that the searcher will know the author's specialty. No index is given to overcome these important limitations for reference use.

The script section lists books which are not scripts; they merely contain visuals from the films--e.g., "Yellow Submarine" or "Zuckerkandl" or "Young Aphrodites."

There are other disturbing features--omissions, incorrect placement, and poor arrangement--that diminish the value of this volume to a considerable degree. It cannot be recommended, other than as a checklist.

2264.   Film Review Index, edited by Wesley A. Doak and
         William J. Speed.   Pasadena, Cal.:   Audio-Visual
         Associates, 1972.
         This annual index to film reviews offers a unique
service.   Available in several formats, including loose-leaf
and microfilm, the index is published in quarterly cumulative
installments with volume four being the compilation for the
entire year.   More than 90 publications are indexed and they
are listed at the front with complete data on publication
schedule, address, subscription price, etc.   The films are
first arranged alphabetically by title, with a separate line
for each review.   Since several film formats are included,
differentiation is made by symbols: M for 16mm films, FF
for feature film, F for filmstrip, E for 8mm, L for film
loop, C for cartridge, S for slide, T for transparency, K
for kit, VT for video tapes.   The type of entry--review, annotation or mention--is noted, and the source volume, issue
date, page and reviewer's name are listed.   The format
makes it relatively easy to trace a review.
         The films are then rearranged under subject head-
ings in a separate guide following the alphabetical listing.
A list of distributor names and addresses completes the
book.   An abbreviation list for the periodicals is given but
there is none for the distributors.   Appreciation must be expressed for the intent of this service.   To bring some order
to the chaotic world of film evaluation, selection, purchase
and rental is an accomplishment indeed.   Highly recommended
for consideration by all libraries.

2265.   Films and Broadcasts Demeaning Ethnic, Racial or
         Religious Groups, by Subcommittee on Communica-
         tions and Power.   97, 67 p.   (paperback)   Washing-
         ton, D.C.:   U.S. Gov't. Printing Office, 1970, 1971.
         The reports of two hearings by the Subcommittee on
Communication and Power of the Committee on Interstate and
Foreign Commerce of the House of Representatives, the first
on September 21, 1970, the second April 27-28, 1971.   The
rationale for the hearings was more than 70 similar resolu-
tions which suggested that "Congress finds ethnic, racial or
religious defamation or ridicule existing in motion pictures
... and that the producers ... should develop and adhere to
a code of ethics that would rule such material out-of-bounds."
The testimony of various witnesses, along with letters, exhibits, and appendices, all speak to the perpetuation of ster-
eotypes by the media.   The victim most often cited is the
Mexican-American, although other nationalities are represented.

Noted here as a source of information about film, censorship, pressure groups, governmental regulation of media and other aspects of film history. Government documents can provide a rich source of such information.

2266   Film Scripts--a series. New York: Simon & Schuster; London: Lorrimer, 1968-1973.
        Since 1968 Simon and Schuster has published a series of scripts in two categories: Modern Film Scripts and Classic Film Scripts. The dividing date between the two categories seems to be World War II. The scripts seem to appear first under the Lorrimer banner in London. The time-lag in publication sometimes is a matter of more than a year, and it is not unusual for a title to appear in London long before it is seen here. Occasionally the title is changed. The following is a list of the scripts that Simon and Schuster has published or announced thus far:

Modern Film Scripts
ALPHAVILLE (Godard) - 25
ASHES AND DIAMONDS (Wajda) - 2034
BELLE DE JOUR (Buñuel) - 2056
THE BICYCLE THIEF (De Sica) - 130
A BLOND IN LOVE (Forman) - 2498
BLOW UP (Antonioni) - 2072
CLAIRE'S KNEE (Rohmer) - 2146
CLOSELY WATCHED TRAINS (Menzel) - 2150
LA COLLECTIONEUSE (Rohmer) - 2157a
THE FIREMAN'S BALL (Forman) - 2290
GENERATION (Wajda) - 2315
IF (Anderson) - 743
IKURU (Kurosawa) - 744
JULES AND JIM (Truffaut) - 808
KANAL (Wajda) - 2453
LOVES OF A BLOND (Forman) - 2498
A MAN AND A WOMAN (Lelouche) - 890
MY NIGHT AT MAUD'S (Rohmer) - 2581
OEDIPUS REX (Pasolini) - 2613
LE PETIT SOLDAT (Godard) - 1092
PIERROT LE FOU (Godard) - 1111
THE SEVEN SAMURAI (Kurosawa) - 1221
THE SEVENTH SEAL (Bergman) - 567, 1224
THE THIRD MAN (Reed) - 1352
THE TRIAL (Welles) - 1374
TRISTANA (Buñuel) - 2822
WILD STRAWBERRIES (Bergman) - 567, 1466

Classic Film Scripts
L'AGE D'OR (Buñuel) - 14

THE BLUE ANGEL (von Sternberg) - 140
THE CABINET OF DR. CALIGARI (Wiene) - 522
UN CHIEN ANDALOU (Buñuel) - 198
CHILDREN OF PARADISE (Carné) - 202
DUCK SOUP (McCarey) - 2208
EARTH (Dovzhenko) - 2210a
ENTR'ACTE (Clair) - 368
GRAND ILLUSION (Renoir) - 621
GREED (von Stroheim) - 2167, 2346
IVAN THE TERRIBLE (Eisenstein) - 791, 792
LE JOUR SE LEVE (Carné) - 805
M (Lang) - 874
METROPOLIS (Lang) - 2533
MONKEY BUSINESS (McLeod) - 2542
MOROCCO (von Sternberg) - 2548
MOTHER (Pudovkin) - 2550
NEVER GIVE A SUCKER AN EVEN BREAK (Cline) - 2591
A NOUS LA LIBERTE (Clair) - 1054
PANDORA'S BOX (Pabst) - 2633
POTEMKIN (Eisenstein) - 355, 1121
RULES OF THE GAME (Renoir) - 1178, 1939
SHANGHAI EXPRESS (von Sternberg) - 2730
STAGECOACH (Ford) - 2754
TILLIE AND GUS (Martin) - 2810

2267.   Film Scripts One, edited by George P. Garrett,
         O.B. Hardison, Jr. and Jane R. Gelfman.   544 p.
         (paperback) New York: Appleton-Century-Crofts,
         1971.
            Contains: Introduction; HENRY V, 1944 (2372); THE
BIG SLEEP, 1946 (2066); A STREETCAR NAMED DESIRE,
1951 (2762).   Appendix: Initial and closing pages of final
shooting schedule of THE BEST MAN, 1963; Glossary; Bibliography.

2268.   Film Scripts Two, edited by George P. Garrett,
         O.B. Hardison, Jr. and Jane R. Gelfman.   548 p.
         (paperback) New York: Appleton-Century-Crofts,
         1971.
            Contains: Introduction (Same as Volume I); HIGH
NOON, 1952 (2376); TWELVE ANGRY MEN, 1957 (2829);
THE DEFIANT ONES, 1958 (2185).   Appendix: Initial and
closing pages of final shooting schedule of THE BEST MAN,
1963; Glossary; Bibliography.   Appendix is the same as in
Volume I.

2269.   Film Scripts Three, edited by George P. Garrett,

O. B. Hardison, Jr. and Jane R. Gelfman. 618 p. (paperback) New York: Appleton-Century-Crofts, 1972.

Contains: Introduction (Same as Volume I); THE APARTMENT, 1960 (2028); THE MISFITS, 1961 (2538); CHARADE, 1963 (2114). Appendix: Initial and closing pages of final shooting schedule of THE BEST MAN, 1963; Glossary (changed somewhat from Volumes I, II); Bibliography (updated since Volumes I, II).

2270.   Film Scripts Four, edited by George P. Garrett, O.B. Hardison, Jr. and Jane R. Gelfman. 500 p. (paperback) New York: Appleton-Century-Crofts, 1972.

Contains: Introduction (Same as Volume I); A HARD DAY'S NIGHT, 1964 (2363); THE BEST MAN, 1964 (2060); DARLING, 1965 (2179). Appendix: Initial and closing pages of final shooting schedule of THE BEST MAN; Glossary (changed somewhat from Volumes I, II); Bibliography (updated since Volumes I, II).

2271.   Film 70-71, edited by David Denby. 319 p. (paperback) New York: Simon and Schuster, 1971.

The fourth yearly anthology by the National Society of Film Critics. The editor this time is David Denby, film critic for The Atlantic, and the usual representation can be noted--Kael, Simon, Knight, Alpert, Gilliatt, Schickel, Sarris, Kauffmann, Morgenstern, etc. There are 22 members in the group. An account of the voting for the 1970 awards, some short critic identifications and an index complete the book. Another fine collection of film criticism, this volume is highly recommended for all collections.

2272.   Films for Universities, by British Universities Film Council. 292 p. (paperback) London: British Universities Film Council, 1968.

This is a list of films found to be useful in some aspect of university work. Since the origin of the book is British, the films and the distributors are out of England rather than America. It is noted here since some of the films are world wide and others may be obtained if they are special enough and have no counterpart elsewhere. The entries are arranged under the Universal Decimal Classification system.

2273.   Films For Young Adults, by New York Library Association. 54 p. (paperback) New York: Educational Film Library Association, 1970.

There is much to recommend in this brief list of
annotated short films. Descriptions of certain films are concise and accurate. There is a bibliography, a subject index,
a list of filmmakers and a list of distributors. Most of this
information is useful and pertinent.

Some reservations must be noted. Admittedly this
is a selected list, but certain films are short-changed by being included within the description of another film. For
EYE OF THE BEHOLDER the reader is referred to THE
SWORD where the annotation reads: "With EYE OF THE BE-
HOLDER (Stuart Reynolds) and 12-12-42 (Xanadu), it evokes
an extraordinary comment on perception and sensitivity."
Good programming perhaps, but poor annotation for a film
in the list. The user would have to use another source for
full information.

Another selected list of feature films for young
adults is given that should send the knowledgeable librarian
scurrying to Media and Methods for suggestions. Finally,
certain of the distributors seem to be rather high in their
film prices. Ninety dollars for THE GREAT TRAIN ROB-
BERY seems exhorbitant today. Acceptable for all collections
with limitations as noted above.

2274.   Films in Depth, by Paul A. Schreivogel. (paper-
          back) illus. Dayton, Ohio: Pflaum, 1970.

This unusual package of film study materials contains 13 booklets. The first is an introduction and overview
of the series; each of the others addresses itself to a specific short film. Titles of the films are: FLAVIO (2293),
THE LANGUAGE OF FACES (2467), THE LITTLE ISLAND
(2491), NIGHT AND FOG (2602), NO REASON TO STAY
(2608), AN OCCURRENCE AT OWL CREEK BRIDGE (2611),
ORANGE AND BLUE (2623), OVERTURE--OVERTURE/
NYITANY (2630), A STAIN ON HIS CONSCIENCE (2755), SUN-
DAY LARK (2767), TIMEPIECE (2811), TOYS (2817). For
information on each film, see individual entries as noted.

Each study guide offers an analysis of the film and
attempts to relate it to some aspect of film technique or appreciation. The latter part of each guide suggests questions,
offers background, script excerpts and other materials designed to stimulate thought and discussion. The guides are
available separately. This elaboration of what Kuhns (1345b)
and others have done is an improvement over such sturdy,
proven material since each title provides more background
and greater depth to the analyses of the films. Essential
for schools and colleges, and public libraries would do well
to use it at their showings, too.

2275. Films in Review, 1950-1953, edited by Henry Hart.
illus. New York: Arno, 1973.
Announced for publication are the first four years
of Films in Review, a publication of the National Board of
Review. Begun in 1950, the periodical is concerned primarily with film history, aesthetics and criticism, although it
deals with all aspects of the motion picture. The first series will consist of four volumes, one for each year from
1950 through 1953.

2276. Films Kids Like, by Susan Rice. 128 p. (paperback) illus. Chicago: American Library Association, 1973.
Ms. Rice's book is an annotated listing of 229 short
films that were tested by the Center for Understanding Media
with children from ages three to twelve. Readiness and
follow-up activities were included in making the determination
of each film's effectiveness. Several grants aided the investigation.
The results are presented in a most attractive and
usable form. An introductory essay discusses The Children's
Film Theater and offers some practical advice on showing
films for children in libraries, schools, and elsewhere.
The main body of the work consists of the film listings,
which include: the film title; an annotation which tends to
be mostly descriptive, with some helpful hints on use; running time, color or black and white, animation or live action, narration or no narration, the distributor, and the
country of origin. Missing is the release date of the films.
A key to the distributors concludes the book. Visuals used
throughout are either stills from the films or candid shots
of the youngsters enjoying the films. They are reproduced
nicely and add variety to the listing. The book will be of
great assistance to all professionals dealing with young children. As an aid for selection, evaluation, or use, it is
essential for all public libraries and elementary schools.

2277. Film Sneaks Annual, 1972. Ann Arbor, Mich.:
Pierian Press, 1972.
Announced as a guide to 4,500 non-theatrical films
which cumulates ratings of these films by librarians from
40 major libraries over the last seven years. The sample
page shows title, distributor, and a rating scale of six
values: excellent, very good, good, average, fair, and
poor. The film ANYONE FOR DIVING? had the score,
VG--2; G--1; A--2, which would seem to indicate that five
reviewers thought the film to be somewhere between average
and very good.

2278.   A Film Society Handbook, edited by R. C. Vannoey.
         56 p. (paperback) illus. London: Society for
         Education in Film and Television, 1966.
         One section of this handbook offers practical advice
on organizing a film society for young people, the other relates some actual experiences, problems, successes, and
failures that established societies have had. The British
ads and letters to the editor are amusing and helpful. An
acceptable addition to all film collections.

2279.   Film Society Programmes, 1925-1939, by London
         Film Society. 456 p. illus. New York: Arno,
         1972.
         These are the programs for 108 showings organized
by the London Film Society during the years 1925 to 1939.
Approximately 900 films were shown and notes about them
appeared in the programs. Directors, players, production
facts, casts, credits and other data are given. The programs
indicate certain movements and trends in the history of motion pictures. Of interest primarily to researchers and historians, this volume is most suitable to larger film collections.

2280.   The Films of ... (A series). illus. New York:
         Citadel Press, 1963-73.
         A series of oversized volumes, most of which are
devoted to individual film personalities, with a few about
character-types in films--The Rebel, The Detective, The
Bad Guys, etc.--or about a genre, such as The Musical.
The personality format is fairly standard, consisting of an
introductory essay section, the films arranged in chronological order, and a short account of other show business appearances, if pertinent. The section devoted to the films is
the major emphasis and follows a predictable structure:
stills, cast and production credits, a plot outline, review
excerpts, and occasionally some background information. Although similar in structure, the books vary greatly in quality.
         When the volumes first appeared in the early sixties
the words "The Films of" were given equal prominence with
the subject. In preparing Cinema Booklist they were placed
alphabetically using those first three words. Recent volumes
in the series minimize "The Films of" and maximize the
subject name. However, rather than depart from the procedure established earlier, the books will continue to be
treated as "The Films of ..." with the hope that this entry
and the subject index will facilitate any necessary searching.
         Titles in the series include:

All Talking! All Singing! All Dancing! (20)
The Bad Guys (91)
Bogey (146)
The Detective in Films (2186)
The Films of Ingrid Bergman (494)
The Films of Marlon Brando (2282)
The Films of James Cagney (2283)
The Films of Charlie Chaplin (497)
The Films of Gary Cooper (498)
The Films of Joan Crawford (499)
The Films of Bette Davis (500)
The Films of Cecil B. DeMille (501)
The Films of Marlene Dietrich (502)
The Films of Kirk Douglas (2284)
The Films of W. C. Fields (503)
The Films of Errol Flynn (504)
The Films of Clark Gable (505)
The Films of Greta Garbo (506)
The Films of Jean Harlow (509)
The Films of Katharine Hepburn (510)
The Films of Laurel and Hardy (513)
The Films of Carole Lombard (2286)
The Films of Frederic March (514, 2287)
The Films of Marilyn Monroe (515)
The Films of Paul Newman (516)
The Films of Frank Sinatra (2288)
The Films of Spencer Tracy (521)
The Films of John Wayne (524)
The Fondas (55)
Judy (807)
A Pictorial History of the Western Film (1105)
Rebels: The Rebel Hero in Films (1153)
Tarzan of the Movies (1318)

The titles in this series are shuffled around quite a bit between subsidiary companies, book clubs and paperback reprints. Names such as Bonanza Books, Cadillac Publishing, Lyle Stuart, Movie Book Club, and others are associated at times with Citadel Books. The editions put out by the several companies vary greatly in the quality of paper used, photo reproduction and binding.

2281. The Films of Ingmar Bergman, by Jorn Donner.
276 p. (paperback) illus. New York: Dover, 1972.

This is the same book as The Personal Vision of Ingmar Bergman, published in 1964 by Indiana University Press (1090). For this edition some new illustrations have been provided and the entire production is more impressive than the original.

2282. The Films of Marlon Brando, by Tony Thomas.
illus. Secaucus, N.J.: Citadel Press, 1973.

A most satisfying account of Marlon Brando, told through his films. While much of the personal life story is omitted, the professional life is covered completely. Starting with a biographical essay that emphasizes the pre-Hollywood life and career, the book departs from the usual Citadel format in the main film section. A descriptive evaluation of each film is given instead of the standard synopsis plus critical excerpts. Cast and production credits are listed as always. LAST TANGO IN PARIS is the final film discussed. Pauline Kael contributes a foreword and there is an afterword about Brando's refusal of the Oscar.

The substitution of critical narrative for factual rehash is commendable. However, in the rush to cash in on the Brando revival, the editors were most lax in proofreading; spelling, grammatical, and name errors abound and certain sentences lack meaning because of word omissions. Picture quality is acceptable in the film section but poor in the biographical portion. There is no index.

Tony Thomas has written a fine, biased, evaluation of the film work of Brando. It is a better total book than any of the biographies and can be recommended for all collections.

2283. The Films of James Cagney, by Homer Dickens.
249 p. illus. Secaucus, N.J.: Citadel, 1972.

Since this volume was obtained through the Movie Book Club at a reduced price, it may be a special cheaper edition. This information is given because the immediate observation is that the paper is a less expensive kind and the reproduction quality of the photographs extremely variable. Because James Cagney is such an ideal subject and because Homer Dickens is one of the more dependable authors in the Citadel series--Dietrich (502), Cooper (498), and Hepburn (510)--the negative production factors are most unfortunate.

A short essay, "The Anti-Hero," is followed by a gallery of Cagney portraits. The long filmography has stills, credits, synopsis, critical excerpts, and notes. It is in this last section that Dickens demonstrates his knowledge and understanding of the subject's career. A theatre chronicle of the plays that Cagney did before Hollywood (1920-1930) closes the book, which is not indexed. Acceptable for all

collections, but Cagney has been shortchanged by Citadel
(or Cadillac, as printed on the binding).

2284.   The Films of Kirk Douglas, by Tony Thomas.   256 p.
          illus. Secaucus, N.J.: Citadel, 1972.
          A better book than most of the newer titles in this
series. Starting with a biography, it is primarily a record
of the 54 films that Douglas had made up to the book's publication. It contains casts, credits, and synopses as well
as the author's own evaluations. Other data are also noted.
Photographs in this book are adequately reproduced and some
come from Douglas' private collection. Acceptable for all
collections.

2285.   The Films of Alice Faye, by W. Franklyn Moshier.
          182 p. (paperback) illus. San Francisco (312
          Teresita Blvd.): Moshier, 1971.
          This personally produced tribute contains a biograph-
ical essay, complete credits, and notes on each of Alice
Faye's films. Most impressive is the disclosure of the
songs and scenes which were omitted from the final versions
of the films.
          The book is available only from the author, who is
probably more of an authority on Alice Faye than she is her-
self--which may suggest a combined effort toward an autobiography. Acceptable for all collections.

2286.   The Films of Carole Lombard, by Frederick W.
          Ott.   192 p.   illus. Secaucus, N.J.: Citadel,
          1972.
          The usual format of this series is applied to Carole
Lombard. Picture quality is good. Acceptable for all collections.

2287.   The Films of Frederic March, by Lawrence J.
          Quirk.   255 p. illus. New York: Citadel, 1971.
          The format is consistent with previous publications
in the Citadel Series. A long biographical essay is followed
by a chronological recall of March's films. Starting with
THE DUMMY (1929) and finishing with TICK... TICK... TICK
(1970), each film has a player listing, production credits,
a descriptive narrative that includes both supportive information and plot description, and finally some review excerpts.
This data surrounds the many illustrations which are the
strength and richness of the book. A final section gives a
chronological listing of the 18 Broadway plays in which March
appeared from 1920 to 1961.

March's career has covered the entire Hollywood era of sound films and his performances have been consistently excellent. This tribute to him is not only justified but the execution and quality of the work is most appropriate for the subject and his career. This is one of the better Citadel volumes and is recommended for all collections.

2288.   The Films of Frank Sinatra, by Gene Ringgold and Clifford McCarty. 249 p. illus. New York: Citadel, 1971.
       The opening biographical sketch is factual rather than analytical and is followed by the films--from LAS VEGAS NIGHTS (1941) to DIRTY DINGUS MAGEE (1969). The text states that many of the films are poor but appropriately commercial in nature. Examination verifies this statement-- especially with such examples as THE KISSING BANDIT, DOUBLE DYNAMITE, 4 FOR TEXAS, and the above DIRTY DINGUS MAGEE. The authors are careful to include some kind words about each in their selection of review excerpts.
       The photographic reproduction and the selection of illustrations are remarkably fine. One exception is THE LIST OF ADRIAN MESSENGER where Sinatra is not shown in his gypsy stable-boy makeup. There is an index and some miscellaneous short film appearances are noted at the end. The photographs and the reference data are the important contribution here. Other than the opening essay, there is no critical contribution from the authors, merely a task of assembling material. Acceptable for all collections.

2289.   FINIAN'S RAINBOW, by Burt Sloane. 48 p. (paper- back) illus. New York: National Publishers, 1968.
       Two background articles introduce this souvenir book: "The Fanciful Joy of Finian's World: How It All Came to Be," and "Touching Finian's Magic to the Screen." Small illustrations from the film are used rather ineffective- ly throughout. Single pages are given to Fred Astaire, Petula Clark and Tommy Steele, with similar attention to producer Joseph Landon and director Francis Ford Coppola. Flat and unsatisfying--just like the film.

2290.   THE FIREMAN'S BALL. A script of the 1967 film, by Milos Forman, Jaroslav Papousek and Ivan Passer (director: Milos Forman). (paperback) illus. London: Lorrimer, 1972.
       Found in Milos Forman (2298). Announced by Simon and Schuster.

2291.   Five Screenplays, by Harold Pinter. 367 p. Lon-
         don: Methuen & Co. Ltd., 1971.
         Contains scripts of: THE SERVANT (1963), THE
PUMPKIN EATER (1964), THE QUILLER MEMORANDUM
(1966), ACCIDENT (1967), THE GO-BETWEEN (1971). Only
casts and director are given.

2292.   A Flask of Fields, edited by Richard J. Anobile.
         272 p. illus. New York: Norton (Darien House),
         1972.
         The format of this volume is the same as that of
Anobile's Why A Duck? (2887) and Who's On First? (2885).
Frames from 10 films made for Paramount and Universal
are used along with script dialogue to provide the "verbal
and visual gems of W. C. Fields." An introduction by
Judith Crist sets the stage for the print recreation of some
of Fields' better film moments. The illustrations are acceptable and help to recapture some of the special quality of
Fields' humor. The book should be quite popular in all collections. Not essential but a pleasant entertainment.

2293.   FLAVIO, by Paul A. Schreivogel. 20 p. (paper-
         back) illus. Dayton, Ohio: Pflaum, 1970.
         A study guide for the 1964 film directed by Gordon
Parks.   Found in Films in Depth (2274) and also available
separately.

2294.   Focus on ... (a series), edited by Ronald Gottes-
         man and Harry Geduld. (paperback) illus. Engle-
         wood Cliffs, N.J.: Prentice Hall, 1972-1973.
         This fine series of books concentrates predominately
on individual films, directors and genres. Usually there
are an introduction, essays, reviews, script excerpts, illus-
trations, a filmography and a bibliography--but individual
books may vary somewhat. When used in connection with
film showings or film study, they can serve as enrichment,
reference, and recreational reading. The titles include:
   Focus on THE BIRTH OF A NATION (2070)
   Focus on BLOW-UP (2073)
   Focus on BONNIE AND CLYDE (2079)
   Focus on Chaplin (2113)
   Focus on CITIZEN KANE (548)
   Focus on Godard (2322)
   Focus on D. W. Griffith (2349)
   Focus on Howard Hawks (2367)
   Focus on Hitchcock (2383)
   Focus on The Horror Film (2398)

Focus on RASHOMON (2674)
Focus on The Science Fiction Film (2707)
Focus on THE SEVENTH SEAL (2722)
Focus on Shakespearean Films (2727)
Focus on SHOOT THE PIANO PLAYER (2733)

2295.   FORCE MAJEURE. An unfilmed script, by Errol
         John. 194 p. London: Faber and Faber, 1967.
         Found in FORCE MAJEURE; THE DISPOSSESSED;
HASTA LUEGO (2296)

2296.   FORCE MAJEURE; THE DISPOSSESSED; HASTA
         LUEGO, by Errol John. 145 p. London: Faber
         and Faber, 1967.

2297.   John Ford and Andrew V. McLaglen, by Michael
         Burrows. 32 p. (paperback) illus. Primestyle
         Ltd: (21 Highfield Ave., St. Austell, Cornwall,
         England), 1970.
         This second "Formative Film" booklet uses quota-
tions from interviews, letters and reviews, straight narrative, critical and analytical interpretation, and photographs
in describing John Ford and his disciple, Andrew McLaglen.
The text is potpourri of material used to create overall impressions of the two subjects. Some of it is chatty, informal and unfocused. A structured formal approach may have
served better. A filmography and several full page illustrations conclude the booklet. Picture reproduction is only
average. This volume is inexpensive, unassuming and pleasant but adds little to the material already available on Ford.
The section on McLaglen may justify its inclusion in certain
collections.

2298.   Milos Forman, by Milos Forman, etc. (paperback)
         illus. London: Lorrimer, 1972.
         Contains script, cast and production credits for:
THE FIREMAN'S BALL, 1967 (2290); A BLOND IN LOVE
(LOVES OF A BLOND), 1965 (2498). Announced for publica-
tion by Simon and Schuster.

2299.   Milos Forman, Ingrid Thulin, edited by Bruce
         Henstell. 27 p. (paperback) Washington, D.C.:
         American Film Institute, 1972.
         The seminar session recorded here took place with
Forman at the AFI Center in Beverly Hills. The occasion
was the release of TAKING OFF. Lynn Carlin, Ultra Violet,
and John Klein were also present at this interview conducted
by Frank Daniel. The Thulin interview coincided with the

125

release of THE DAMNED and the interest of the participants
is evident from the transcription. She also discusses acting
for Pasolini, Fellini, Bergman and Visconti. A filmography
is given for both but only the Forman piece has a bibliography. Acceptable for all collections.

2300.　　Forming and Running a Film Society, edited by Jon
　　　　　Evans and Margaret Hancock. 24 p. (paperback)
　　　　　London: British Film Institute, 1961.
　　　　This small book, a joint venture of the British Film
Institute and the Federation of Film Societies, treats the past
history of film societies, their aims, how to form one, budg-
eting, rules and regulations. Advice is given on launching
a society, planning programs, booking, operation, insurance,
royalties, etc. Final sections discuss the work of the two
sponsoring organizations. Here is sound practical advice
that has been hard to come by in the U.S. until recently. A
worthwhile addition to any film collection.

2301.　　Forty Years in Hollywood, by Roman Freulich and
　　　　　Joan Abramson. 201 p. illus. New York: Barnes,
　　　　　1971.
　　　　The title suggests biography but the data furnished
about the author-photographer of this book is so brief as to
be almost unnoticeable. He worked first at Universal and
later at Republic, where he was head of the photographic de-
partment. The book is primarily a collection of photographs.
Two sections of illustrations of Universal films and stars are
offered, and a third one is of Republic films and stars. A
final section is a mixture of United Artists and independent
productions, a few afterthoughts, some second chancers, and
a number of fillers. Introducing each of the four pictorial
sections is a collection of hoary stories, tired anecdotes,
and some rather flat narratives about unrelated subjects. An
index is provided.
　　　　The pity is that the book constantly indicates how
good it might have been. Nearly all the visuals are very
clearly reproduced and many are examples of memorable
photography. Others, such as the early Universal groups,
have a nostalgic interest. Occasionally the text goes beyond
blandness to discuss the directorial methods of Welles, Whale,
Ford, etc. But ultimately the book is defeated by poor organization, faulty selection of text and visuals, and inadequate
development of what was used. Freulich received four Academy Awards but specific mention of these honors is almost
impossible to find in this book.
　　　　Because the photographic work is of high quality and

is so well reproduced, the book is acceptable for any collection. Perhaps the author's long experience with Universal and Republic has conditioned him to a world of "B" efforts --good visuals but no story.

2302.   The Four Seasons of Success, by Budd Schulberg. 203 p. New York: Doubleday, 1972.
Schulberg relates the experiences of six famous writers who journeyed to Hollywood to improve their fortunes: Scott Fitzgerald, Dorothy Parker, William Saroyan, Nathanael West, Thomas Heggen and John Steinbeck. Since he knew all the subjects, Schulberg's story is personal, intimate and goes beyond the usual factual accounts. This is an unusually rewarding book that tells what happens to writers when critics, institutions and audiences cool in admiration for them. Recommended for inclusion in all collections.

2303.   The Fox Girls, by James Robert Parish. 722 p. illus. New Rochelle, N. Y.: Arlington House, 1971.
This detailed look at "15 Beautiful Vixens and One Adorable Cub" gives a possible clue to the master plan of author Parish. "The Paramount Pretties" followed this volume and used an identical format. Are we to expect "The MGM Ladies" and "The Warner's Liberated Women" as upcoming volumes? Let us hope so, for there are some nice things about this book. It provides a light, entertaining and up-to-date look at the careers of some screen ladies and legends.
     Each subject in this collective biography is given a chapter-essay, with the emphasis placed on career and films rather than on personal life. A gallery of photographs, mainly stills from films, accompanies each narrative portrait. Concluding each section is a filmography listing major cast and production credits for each of the star's films.
     The fifteen ladies are: Theda Bara, Anne Baxter, Jeanne Crain, Linda Darnell, Alice Faye, Janet Gaynor, Betty Grable, June Haver, Sonja Henie, Carmen Miranda, Marilyn Monroe, Sheree North, Gene Tierney, Raquel Welch, and Loretta Young. The "cub" is Shirley Temple. The biographies are descriptive rather than critical, and the reader will have the "public image" reinforced rather than gain any privileged insight into a human personality.
     One major reservation concerns picture quality, which is only average. A questionable decision to use more photographs but to reduce their size results in a disservice to the illustrations. Their impact is diminished considerably. The book will probably have a wide and deserved success,

127

however. Its likely popularity and its reference value make it an appropriate candidate for inclusion in all collections.

2304.   The Frankenscience Monster, by Forrest J Acker-
           man. 191 p. (paperback) illus. New York: Ace
           Publishing Co., 1969.
           The author of this unusual book is known for his
creation of "Film Monster" magazines and many other activities which derive from his interest in horror and fantasy
films.   In this volume he has assembled a tribute to Boris
Karloff which consists of articles, interviews, biographies,
and appreciations.   Most of the items are quite enjoyable and
a few have a value beyond casual reading.   For example, a
tribute to Jack Pierce, the makeup artist who created the
Frankenstein monster, would have pleased Karloff, who acknowledged his debt to Pierce many times.   Several long articles on Karloff, two filmographies--one alphabetical, the
second chronological--and a reading version of Frankenstein
based on the film are all quality elements in this rewarding
book.   Almost as good are a long picture section and listings
of his television and stage appearances.   With this volume
and the newer one by Denis Gifford (2644) readers will have
access to a richness of materials on Karloff.   This excellent
volume belongs in all collections.

2305.   The Frankenstein Legend, by Donald Frank Glut.
           398 p.   illus.   Metuchen, N.J.: Scarecrow Press,
           1973.
           The complete story of Frankenstein's monster--in
legend, literature, theatre, motion pictures, radio, television, comic books, toys, and other forms.   The illustrated
volume's subtitle is "A Tribute to Mary Shelley and Boris
Karloff."
           The major portion of the book is concerned with
films, dividing them roughly into the silent films, the Karloff-
Universal films, and the Hammer films of the sixties.   Much
of the information is quite detailed and deals with all aspects
of the films--stars, scores, stories, etc.   Picture quality
is acceptable, and the book is indexed.
           The book is unique, specialized, and impressive in
the range of its coverage.   Libraries may consider two cop-
ies--one for circulation, the other for reference.   If only
one is possible, it should be placed in circulation for the
enjoyment of the many devotees of horror films and books.

2306.   FREEDOM TO LOVE.   A script of the 1970 film,
           by Phyllis and Eberhard Kronhausen (director:

Phyllis and Eberhard Kronhausen). 191 p. (paperback) illus. New York: Grove, 1970.
    Contains cast and credits. Also has interviews with
Hugh Hefner, Kenneth Tynan, Michael McClure (author of the
play, Beard), a Danish porno shop owner, "swingers," and
Daughters of Bilitis.

2307.   From Fiction to Film: ... (A Series), by Gerald
        R. Barrett and Thomas L. Erskine. (paperback)
        illus. Encino, Calif.: Dickenson Publishing Co.,
        1972.
    This series is concerned with the teaching of short
stories, films, and the art of adaptation. For each, Barrett
provides the same introduction, which considers the problems
of changing material from one medium to another. The original short story is reprinted with selected critical essays
appended. The film section contains the script with correlated visuals. Selected critical essays are also given for
the film, as are some suggestions for student papers on both
the short story and the film.
    The first two releases, treated individually elsewhere
in this book, are: An Occurrence at Owl Creek Bridge
(2612) and Silent Snow, Secret Snow (2736). Announced as
the third title in the series is D. H. Lawrence's The Rock-
ing Horse Winner. Increasing interest in literary adaptations
and the quality of the first two releases more than justify
this series.

2308.   Samuel Fuller, by Nicholas Garnham. 176 p. (pa-
        perback) illus. New York: Viking, 1972.
    The premise that Welles, Mankiewicz and Fuller are
the clearest American examples of auteur theory begins this
examination of Samuel Fuller's work. The approach to the
films is as a total body of work rather than as individual
statements. A broad overview describes the influences,
settings, camera techniques, editing, and themes found in
the films and provides the base for what follows. In suc-
ceeding chapters, the continual appearance of large themes
such as the individual, love, society, national identity, energy and, finally, madness is noted.
    A concluding section suggests the influence that
Fuller has had on Godard. The filmography which closes
the book is detailed and helpful in recalling the films, most
of which were low-budget B films. The cult which has
grown about Fuller and his work should find strong support
in this well-written and different examination. The arguments are logical and objective in spite of the author's

obvious admiration for his subject. Picture quality is only
fair and no index is provided. Recommended for larger collections.

2309.   FUNNY GIRL, by Jack Brodsky. 48 p. (paperback)
         illus. New York: National Publishers, 1968.
         Stars Barbra Streisand and Omar Sharif, and director
William Wyler are introduced in the opening sections of this
souvenir book. "Behind the Cameras of FUNNY GIRL" includes
producer Ray Stark, dance director Herb Ross, and scriptwriter Isobel Lennart. "Presenting Miss Fanny Brice" pays
tribute to the original subject, while "Words and Music" discusses the musical portions of the film. Supporting players
Walter Pidgeon, Kay Medford, and Anne Francis are each
given one biographical page, along with listings of the cast
and production credits.

2310.   Clark Gable, by Rene Jordan. 159 p. (paperback)
         illus. New York: Pyramid, 1973.
         As one of the initial releases in a series called,
"The Pyramid Illustrated History of the Movies," this volume
is consistent in quality with the others. A good opening section distills much of the copious material previously published
on Gable into a succinct, perceptive overview of the man, the
actor, and the legend. The title, "The Right Time for the
Right Face," is a sample of the author's ability to be economical and still totally informative.
         The films are placed in chronological divisions: the
First Dozen, the First Oscar, the Star Years, and the Final
Post-War Years. A bibliography, filmography and index conclude the book. The many illustrations are quite acceptable
and complement the objective text nicely. Trying to define
Gable's appeal is an impossible task, but the author makes
a creditable, intelligent attempt. This is as good a book on
Gable as any that have appeared thus far. It is recommended
for inclusion in all collections.

2311.   The Gangster Film, 1930-1940, by Stephen Louis
         Karpf. 299 p. illus. New York: Arno, 1973.
         This is one of six doctoral dissertations on film
topics which are reproduced exactly as submitted to the degree-granting school. An introduction which explains the
study is followed by an analysis of some archetypical films--
LITTLE CAESAR, THE PUBLIC ENEMY, SCARFACE and
THE PETRIFIED FOREST. The decay of the gangster film,
and how and why it occurred, is explored by the examples
of Robinson, Muni, Cagney and Bogart. A concluding section tries to isolate the positive contributions made by the

genre to later films. Some other pertinent films are examined by script excerpts, synopses, cast and production credits. A bibliography completes the study. Acceptable for large academic libraries.

2312.   Garbo, by Ture Sjolander. 139 p. illus. New
        York: Harper and Row, 1971.
        This attempt at Garbo's biography is told largely via oversized photographs, a brief text, and supporting evidence such as a horoscope, handwriting analysis, and caricatures. Photographs used in the major portion of the book are family snaps, publicity pictures, candids, and newspaper shots. The film stills are located on the last four pages. Thus we have many portraits of Garbo off-screen which can be interpreted to a large extent by the viewer. The text supplied by the author supplements but never dictates interpretation of the Garbo charisma or mystery. Quality of photo reproduction is unusually good with a few exceptions. Several double-page illustrations place the subject near the centerfold thus limiting their effectiveness. The nature of the volume does not suggest an index.
        This is a specialized, high-priced volume that will enrapture a small audience, generally please a larger audience, and probably mystify the youth audience. Selection by libraries should be on a most considered basis. The amount of knowledge this book adds to the Garbo legend is debatable and it is a rather costly entertainment.

2313.   THE GENERAL, by E. Rubinstein. 83 p. (paper-
        back) Bloomington, Ind.: Indiana University Press,
        1973.
        This filmguide gives equal attention to THE GENERAL and its creator, Buster Keaton. After a few pages of credits and plot outline, the author summarizes the Keaton career, with emphasis on the production of THE GENERAL. In the next section, an in-depth analysis of the film is offered. Not only are the film's scenes described in detail but much description and evaluation of Keaton's technique is included. The summary critique is largely the author's rather than other critics'. A partial filmography, a bibliography with some annotations, rental and purchase sources and some notes to the text complete the book.
        The biographical sections are somewhat familiar, probably because of the earlier biographies and books, but the analysis section is new and provocative. Visual comedy cannot be described in print; thus, the author's aim here is not to make you laugh but to facilitate your understanding

and appreciation of Keaton's artistry. In this endeavor, he succeeds. Since the film is easily available for detailed study, this volume can enrich that study experience to a great degree. Especially valuable for schools, the book is a fine addition to any collection. Recommended.

2314.   General Bibliography of Motion Pictures, edited by
         Carl Vincent, Riccardo Redi and Franco Venturini.
         252 p. New York: Arno, 1972.
         This bibliography is presented in three languages--
Italian, French and English--and includes both books and selected articles from periodicals. The classifications used
are: General Works; History; Aesthetics, Criticism; Techniques; Social, Moral Problems; Legal, Economic; Cinema
and Science; 16mm and Amateur Films; Documentation, Anthologies; Subject, Screenplays; Unclassified Books. The titles
are arranged by author, and the annotations vary considerably. In some entries a complete table of contents is given,
in others only a few words.
         Use of this reference is not easy and some of the
materials listed are too obscure for anyone except the most
dedicated researcher. Acceptable for large collections.

2315.   A GENERATION. A script of the 1955 film, by
         Bodham Czeszko (director: Andrzej Wajda). 239 p.
         (paperback) illus. New York: Simon & Schuster,
         1972.
         Found in The Wajda Trilogy (2861).

2316.   Gentlemen to the Rescue: The Heroes of the Silent
         Screen, by Kalton C. Lahue. 244 p. illus. New
         York: Barnes, 1972.
         Another in the series of books ground out by the
same author and publisher. Someone, somewhere, must be
buying them, but this one is as bad as the others. Purportedly a collective biography of silent screen male stars, it
has the predictable format. Two or three pages of narrative
for each, followed by four or five pages of stills. A lifetime compressed into a few pages usually deteriorates into a
series of factual sentences, and the bland recitals here are
no exception. In most cases the picture quality is poor, with
dark hues predominating to such an extent that the visual
becomes murky and indistinct. A few stills are reproduced
adequately.
         Perhaps the greatest service this book can offer is
the biography that is scarce or unavailable. To aid the
searcher the list of players treated includes: King Baggot,
John Barrymore, Richard Barthelmess, Carlyle Blackwell,

Francis X. Bushman, Lon Chaney, Ronald Colman, Maurice
Costello, Richard Dix, Douglas Fairbanks, William Farnum,
John Gilbert, Sessue Hayakawa, Johnny Hines, Jack Holt,
Houdini, Rod LaRocque, Elmo Lincoln, Tommy Meighan,
Tony Moreno, Ramon Novarro, Herbert Rawlinson, Charles
Ray, Wallace Reid, Will Rogers, Milton Sills, Rudolph Va-
lentino, Henry B. Walthall, Bryant Washburn, Ben Wilson.
This book should be considered only when other sources are
not available. It is not recommended for most collections.

2317. The German Cinema, by Roger Manvell and Heinrich
 Fraenkel. 159 p. illus. New York: Praeger,
 1971.
 Until the appearance of this volume, the books by
Eisner (659), Hull (470), Krakauer (577) and Wollenberg
(417) were the principal sources of information on the German film. Each deals with only a portion of German film
history, but Manvell and Fraenkel have attempted to survey
the entire history in this fine overview. They divide the
history into eight eras: Pioneer Films, The Twenties, Sound
Films Before Hitler, Early Nazi Films, Later Nazi Films,
Aftermath Films, Decline in the 50's, and the New German
Cinema of the 60's. The text is supported by many notes
and sources: it departs somewhat from Kracauer and is in
greater agreement with Eisner on the Expressionist films
and Hull on the Nazi films. It stands alone on the German
films made after World War II.
 A bibliography, an index of names and a separate
one for selected films end the book. Many illustrations are
used and they are mostly effective. Since this volume is
unique in its coverage of an important national cinema, and
because it is uniformly excellent in text, photographs, production, and supporting material, it should be included in
all film collections.

2318. The Ghouls, edited by Peter Haining. 383 p. illus.
 Stein & Day, 1971.
 This volume was included in Cinema Booklist (601)
but appeared too late for any annotation. It is an unusual
anthology of 18 short stories which were the source material
for a like number of horror films. Included are the original
stories which inspired THE PHANTOM OF THE OPERA,
FREAKS, THE MOST DANGEROUS GAME, DRACULA'S
DAUGHTER, THE BEAST WITH 5 FINGERS, THE FLY, and
other films. Abbreviated cast and production credits are
given for each film in the appendix. Vincent Price introduces the book and Christopher Lee contributes an afterword.

With only a limited value for film collections, the book is
noted here to clarify its earlier listing.

2319. John Gielgud, by Ronald Hayman. 276 p. illus.
New York: Random House, 1972.
Although this sterile biography is largely a recital
of theatrical triumphs and disasters, a few films are men-
tioned in passing: SECRET AGENT, THE PRIME MINISTER,
JULIUS CAESAR, THE LOVED ONE, and THE CHARGE OF
THE LIGHT BRIGADE--each acknowledged with a paragraph
or two.

2320. GIGI. 13 p. (paperback) illus. New York: Al
Greenstone Co., 1957.
This small souvenir book does not reflect the quality
of the film it attempts to describe. Most of the illustrations
are selected poorly and printed in either black and white or
with a color tint. The story is related, with the songs noted
at the point in the narrative in which they are sung or performed. One section indicates that Paris is really the star
of the film. Producer Arthur Freed, director Vincente
Minnelli, and designer Cecil Beaton along with Alan Jay
Lerner and Frederic Loewe are the creative people profiled.

2321. THE GO-BETWEEN. A script of the 1971 film, by
Harold Pinter (director: Joseph Losey). 367 p.
London: Methuen & Co. Ltd., 1971.
Found in Five Screenplays by Harold Pinter (2291).

2322. Focus on Godard, edited by Royal S. Brown. 190 p.
(paperback) illus. Englewood Cliffs, N.J.: Prentice-Hall, 1972.
A series of interviews with Godard, accompanied by
one with a continuity girl and another with the Dziga-Vertov
Group are followed by reviews, essays, and commentaries.
Of all the New Wave directors, probably Godard has received
the most attention, both in-print and out. This collection of
articles is sufficiently wide so that the reader will receive
a sound introduction to this important New Wave director,
his films and the controversy they have caused.
An unusually detailed filmography, a bibliography,
and an index support the articles. The few illustrations used
in the centerfold are well-selected and reproduced. As an
introductory study of Godard and his films, this volume is
quite good. The collection of interviews alone is a unique
feature; when added to the other elements, it contributes
much to the picture of Godard. Recommended for all collections.

2323.   Godard on Godard, by Jean-Luc Godard.   292 p.
         (paperback) illus.   New York: Viking, 1972.
         Tom Milne has translated and edited this collection
of selected writings by Jean-Luc Godard.   The early pieces
are film criticism; the later essays and interviews deal with
Godard's experiences as a filmmaker.   The period from
1950 to 1967, which includes his participation in La Gazette
du Cinema and Cahiers du Cinema, is covered.   Milne offers
comment on each of the Godard articles in a lengthy section
following the main text.   There is an index of names and
a separate index of films.   Richard Roud, the author of
Godard (606), provides an introduction.
         A good number of visuals add dimension to the ar-
ticles, though reproduction of them is only average.   In some
ways this collection of writing resembles his films and will
affect readers as the films affect viewers.   Godard fans will
find it rich, others will wonder what all the shouting has
been about.   Recommended for all collections.

2324.   THE GODFATHER.   24 p.   (paperback) illus.   New
         York: Souvenir Book Publishers, 1972.
         This souvenir book is almost too concise in dealing
with its important subject.   Opening pages describing the
making of the film are followed by short biographies of the
cast members.   Production credits complete the book.   Perhaps the several extended accounts written about making the
film intimidated the creators of this book.

2325.   THE GODFATHER Journal, by Ira Zuckerman.
         143 p.   (paperback) New York: Manor Books,
         1972.
         Ira Zuckerman was given a grant from the Amer-
ican Film Institute which enabled him to serve as an assis-
tant to director Francis Ford Coppola during the filming of
THE GODFATHER in New York City.   From the journal he
kept during the 70 days he created this informative paperback.   The reader is treated to a partial look at the problems, procedures, and pleasures of making a high budget
film.   The views of the participants are clearer and in
greater depth than in some total biographies.   Brando, Coppola, Albert Ruddy, Robert Evans, and others are seen in
a working situation rather than posing for a verbal portrait.
         Only the journal is offered; there are no illustrations.
The quality of the observations--factual, objective, avoiding
sensation--and the author's experience and intelligence in
selecting those matters which describe the totality of filmmaking are the book's strong points.   This modest effort is

135

an unexpectedly good look at filmmaking and is a most valid
addition to all film collections.

2326. THE GODFATHER Papers and Other Confessions,
by Mario Puzo. 252 p. New York: G. P. Putnam's, 1972.
THE GODFATHER Papers is a misnomer for this
book since only one short article, "The Making of THE GOD-
FATHER," is about the film. The bulk of the book is "other
confessions"--a compilation of reviews, interviews, stories,
articles, etc., written by Puzo in pre-GODFATHER days.
The one article is acceptable but the rest of the book is
dross for a film collection. It may be wiser to wait until
a reprint of THE GODFATHER article appears in a film
anthology. See entry 2325 for an account of the making of
THE GODFATHER.

2327. God in Hollywood, by Alyce Canfield. 160 p. (paperback) New York: Wisdom House, 1961.
This paperback inspirational sermon uses screen
personalities as persuasion. Jane Russell is the first subject
and her story is followed by descriptions of the various
church groups in Hollywood, the stars who turn to Judaism,
off-beat religions, June Haver, Hollywood failures, and finally, Pat Boone. Throughout, an attempt is made to link
career and personal misfortunes to a lack of faith in religion. Examples of success are cited for those who are open-
ly religious. It is ironic that many of the positive examples
cited by the author have turned into negative failures since
this book appeared. Ms. Canfield is on shaky ground in her
attempt to prove a relationship between success, happiness
and religion. Acceptable only for large collections, as an
unusual book which may interest researchers.

2328. The Golden Days at San Simeon, by Ken Murray.
163 p. illus. Garden City, N.Y.: Doubleday,
1971.
This book contains a collection of photographs of
many Hollywood personalities enjoying the hospitality of
William Randolph Hearst and Marion Davies at San Simeon
and at his beach house in Santa Monica. It tells of the con-
struction of San Simeon, and a good part of the book provides a tour of it as it appears today. There is some discussion of Hearst's involvement with films.
The book may be of interest for several reasons:
Davies, Hearst as film producer, CITIZEN KANE analogies,
or simply because of some of the persons in the photographs.

As in most of Ken Murray's efforts, the subjects are far
more interesting than the treatment provided. Murray appears to be a writer-producer-actor-speaker who succeeds
not on his ability but through his acquaintance with the important people of Hollywood. Ronald Reagan has written the
foreword to this particular volume. Acceptable for all collections.

2329.   GOLDFINGER. 16 p. (paperback) illus. New
         York: Program Publishing Co., 1965.
            A fan magazine approach is used in this brief sou-
venir book. Close-up pictures of star Sean Connery and
supporting players Gert Frobe, Honor Blackman, Shirley
Eaton, and Harold Sakata accompany the usual studio-created
biographies. One interesting page is devoted to the devices
used in the picture but it is not enough to redeem the rest
of this book.

2330.   GONE WITH THE WIND, by Bob Thomas. 32 p.
         illus. New York: National Publishers, 1967.
            This is not the original 6-page program book from
1939 but the souvenir book printed for the 1967 revival. In
addition to "The Story of GONE WITH THE WIND," it contains
full page portraits of Clark Gable, Vivien Leigh, Leslie
Howard, and Olivia deHavilland. Other impressive visuals
include the burning of Atlanta and the railway station hospital
scene. The original world premiere in Atlanta is recalled
and cast and production credits are given.

2331.   Good-Bye, Baby, and Amen, by David Bailey and
         Peter Evans. 239 p. illus. New York: Coward-
         McCann, 1969.
            Subtitled "A Saraband For the Sixties," this over-
sized picture book has as its subjects many persons concerned
with film. Actors, actresses, directors, writers and producers populate its pages. Some of the subjects receive a double treatment--usually a full page photo and a full page of
text; others are represented only via visuals. While the text
is entertaining, it is the visuals that give the book its great
appeal. It is a book that will also tempt rip-off artists.
Highly recommended for all collections that serve a mature
audience. The nudity may limit its use in schools.

2332.   GOODBYE, MR. CHIPS. 20 p. (paperback) illus.
         New York: National Publishers, 1969.
            A photo-postcard-album format is used in this short
souvenir book but as a compensation there is a large poster

inside. In addition to the cast and the production credits, there is a section devoted to the making of the 1969 film.

2333.   Good Night Sweet Prince: The Life and Times of
         John Barrymore, by Gene Fowler.   477 p.   illus.
         New York: Viking Press, 1944.
         The fact that John Barrymore appeared in more than 70 motion pictures may not be apparent to the casual reader of this excellent biography. Some attention is given to this facet of Barrymore's career but most of the films are not even mentioned. Barrymore will certainly be remembered more for his performances in BILL OF DIVORCEMENT, ROMEO AND JULIET, TOPAZ, GRAND HOTEL and other films than by his stage performances, including Hamlet. The biography is candid, honest, affectionate. A beautiful tribute to a man who was an actor in every sense of the word.

2334.   GRAND PRIX, by Gordon Arnell.   32 p.   (paperback)
         illus. New York: National Publishers, 1966.
         A most interesting approach to a souvenir book: many of the pages have a montage of shots from the film bordered by a descriptive narrative. Some short actor biographies are followed by the professional racers who appeared in the film. Ten of the most famous racing tracks in the world are noted as are the world champion drivers from 1950 to 1966. Even a vocabulary of circuit sayings is offered. Cast and production credits complete this fascinating and specialized program book. A noteworthy attempt to do something different.

2335.   Cary Grant, by Albert Govoni.   233 p.   illus.
         Chicago: Henry Regnery Co., 1971.
         Author Govoni has not succeeded in capturing the life, personality, and charisma of his subject. The phrase, "unauthorized biography," here means nearly complete reliance upon newspapers and periodicials for content. The attempts of the author to pad the book by providing either period description (The Early Depression), or critical evaluation (INDISCREET) are ineffective and embarrassing. Inaccuracies and errors occur (GRAND HOTEL was not the Academy Award film when Hepburn and Laughton received their first awards). There is no mention of relationships between Grant and his directors--Hitchcock, Donen, Capra, Hawks, Stevens, Cukor, McCarey, Kanin, etc.--an imposing roster if there ever was one.
         No attempt is made to present a portrait of the human being, the author being content to offer an introductory apology followed by a recitation of chronological facts. There-

fore, the text is unbalanced, with the earlier years getting
minor attention and the later years--Grant-with-Betsy Drake
and Grant-with-Dyan Cannon--getting excessive coverage.
The photograph selection is also lopsided. INDISCREET gets
6 stills, WALK, DON'T RUN, CHARADE, and FATHER
GOOSE each receive 5 stills, MR. LUCKY and OPERATION
PETTICOAT get 2 apiece and there is one each for TO
CATCH A THIEF, DREAM WIFE, THAT TOUCH OF MINK,
and NORTH BY NORTHWEST. There is nothing from Grant's
first decade of filmmaking and a total of 62 films are not
represented by stills. An unsatisfactory attempt is made to
overcome the film omissions by including a critical filmography. The book is not indexed, probably because the text
does not offer sufficient material. This disappointing volume
is not recommended.

2336. THE GRAPES OF WRATH, by Warren French.
       87 p. (paperback) Bloomington, Ind.: Indiana Uni-
       versity Press, 1973.
       Appreciation must be expressed to Warren French
for his approach to this volume, one of the initial Filmguides.
Although he covers some familiar ground--Bluestone's (1056),
and Asheim's pioneer works on novels into film--he does it
with the eye of the Seventies critic. Dividing the film into
15 sequences and 50 scenes, he establishes a structure which
serves him (and the reader) well. The outline and the analysis make use of these divisions, as does the film-novel
comparison given in the appendix.
       Other elements are not neglected--the credits, a
short Ford biography and appreciation, the production history
and a summary critique are given. The Ford filmography is
a listing of titles along with studio origin. Much more valuable is an annotated bibliography describing materials about
Ford and THE GRAPES OF WRATH. The design of this
volume and the noteworthy selection of material makes it a
most valuable addition to any film collection. Schools which
use THE GRAPES OF WRATH should welcome it with much
enthusiasm. Highly recommended.

2337. The Great Comedians Talk About Comedy, by Larry
       Wilde. 382 p. illus. New York: Citadel, 1968.
       This collection of interviews has a certain impor-
tance for film collections since many of the subjects have
made films. However, comedy is defined throughout in a
very broad sense, covering much more than film comedy.
Those interviewed are Woody Allen, Milton Berle, Shelley
Berman, Jack Benny, Joey Bishop, George Burns, Johnny

Carson, Maurice Chevalier, Phyllis Diller, Jimmy Durante, Dick Gregory, Bob Hope, George Jessel, Jerry Lewis, Danny Thomas, Larry Wilde, and Ed Wynn. All comedy resists analysis and that is evident in the interviews. But the book will interest readers and the Jerry Lewis interview is reason enough to consider the volume. Acceptable for all collections.

2338. The Great Dane and The Great Northern Film Company, by Bebe Bergsten. 116 p. illus. Los Angeles, Calif: Locare Research Group, 1973.

The Dane referred to in the title is Ole Olsen, a pioneer who began making films in 1906. In middle age, after careers as a carnival barker and peep show owner, he arrived in Copenhagen and opened a motion picture theatre. To obtain product, he produced his own films, via the Nordisk Film Company. More than 100 films were produced in 1906. He continued to expand his activities to the point where he had branches in Berlin, London, Vienna, Genoa and New York City. In 1912 and 1913 the company made films of two or three reels, thus preparing the way for the feature film. Sixteen Nordisk films are described in the latter section of the book by cast and production data, a synopsis, some frame reproductions and a beautifully reproduced publicity still. The book is indexed.

Some unfamiliar subjects are described with respect, scholarship and intelligence. The research necessary to produce the quality seen here is obvious. In addition, production values--the binding, print, layout, and photo reproduction--are superior. The book is highly recommended for all large collections. Although its specialized topic may limit general reader interest, it is also a good addition to smaller collections.

2339. THE GREATEST STORY EVER TOLD. 34 p. illus. New York: Ivy Hill Lithograph, 1965.

Oversized stills from the film are used to illustrate an essay on religion and film in this unusual souvenir book. The latter section is devoted to portraits of the various characters in the film, nearly all of whom are portrayed by noted actors. The same concept which was distracting in the film is again at work here--a guessing game as to which actor is playing what role. The book clarifies it all on the last pages by indicating all cast credits along with other technical and production credits. The producer-director is identified only in the subtitle, "A Film by George Stevens."

2340.   Great Monsters of the Movies, by Edward Edelson.
        101 p.   illus.   Garden City, N.Y.:   Doubleday,
        1973.
            This is written for a juvenile audience.   Edelson
divides his book into sections such as legends, pioneers,
frightening men, big beasts, and a miscellany of monsters.
Melíes, Chaney, Karloff, Lugosi and Chaney, Jr. receive
individual attention.   The illustrations are passable at best,
and the approach, content, format, and design are overly
familiar.   With the experience most kids have had with horror films on TV, they could probably come up with a better
book than this.   Manchel's volume (1338) is still the one to
choose for children's collections.

2341.   The Great Movie Serials, by Jim Harmon and
        Donald F. Glut.   384 p.   illus.   New York: Dou-
        bleday and Co., 1972.
            In an introductory note, the authors state that the
one essential element of the film serial was action.   This
may be the reason for the lack of excitement in this book:
action is hard to describe, tedious to read in words and
needs to be visualized.   The first illustrations follow page
171 and use only eight pages; another eight page section appears after page 194.   The visuals are mostly half-page
and the selection is poor.   Thus an essential element of a
book such as this is damagingly weak.
            The well-researched text divides the serials (mostly
sound) into types or categories: The Girls, Science Fiction,
The Westerns, The Boys, Real Life Heroes, The Jungle,
Aviator, Detectives, Super-Heroes, etc.   This latter group
includes Superman and Captain Marvel, while The Girls considers Pearl White, The Jungle Queens, The Tiger Woman,
The Female Zorro, Linda Stirling, Phyliss Coates, and
others.   In addition to much factual information about production, special effects, and casts, there are plot outlines,
script excerpts, and evaluative comments.   A general index
completes the book.
            Unless one is an afficionado of the serial, the book
will have a limited appeal.   A far more effective treatment
of the subject is available in books such as To Be Continued
(2812) and Days of Thrills and Adventure (282).   One positive quality about the book is its potential for reference,
via the copious text and detailed index.   Acceptable for collections which need a supplement to other volumes or a reference to this film genre.

2342.   The Great Movie Series, edited by James Robert
        Parish.   333 p.   illus.   New York: Barnes, 1971.

This impressive oversized volume reviews 25 of the sound motion picture series made by Hollywood from 1930 to 1968. One non-Hollywood series, the James Bond films, completes the group. Each series has an introductory essay --more descriptive than critical--followed by selected stills and a filmography of the entire series. A seemingly complete cast listing, along with studio, date, running time, director, author, screen play, art direction, music direction, camera, and editing credits are noted in most instances.

The series considered include: ANDY HARDY, BLONDIE, BOMBA, BOSTON BLACKIE, BOWERY BOYS, CHARLIE CHAN, CRIME DOCTOR, DR. CHRISTIAN, DR. KILDARE, ELLERY QUEEN, THE FALCON, FRANCIS--THE TALKING MULE, HOPALONG CASSIDY, JAMES BOND, JUNGLE JIM, THE LONE WOLF, MA AND PA KETTLE, MAISIE, MATT HELM, MR. MOTO, PHILO VANCE, THE SAINT, SHERLOCK HOLMES, TARZAN, THE THIN MAN.

Since this is a rather ambitious reference attempt, one is tempted to forgive errors in spelling, e.g., Adele Jerkins for Adele Jergens; confusion in story plots, e.g., Smersh or Spectre in the Bond outlines, and other small slips. Although, with an editorship consisting of one chief, one associate and three contributors, perhaps a higher degree of accuracy might be expected. The numerous stills are nicely reproduced and the total text is more than acceptable. As either a reference book or an entertainment, the volume qualifies for inclusion in all collections.

2343.   The Great Movie Shorts, by Leonard Maltin.   236 p.
        illus.   New York: Crown, 1972.
        Anyone who regards this volume as "a coffee table book" does it and its potential audience a great disservice; it is much more than the usual book in that genre. Providing a broad survey of the one- and two-reel short films (taken mostly from the 30's and 40's), the author has researched his work with such diligence that he establishes a standard that will be difficult for most writers to meet. Some indication of his potential for writing this book can be noted by examining his earlier book, Movie Comedy Teams (966), which treated some of the same material.

Starting with the studios, he progresses quickly to the film series where he gives extended attention to Our Gang, Laurel and Hardy, Charley Chase, Harry Langdon, W. C. Fields, Thelma Todd, Zasu Pitts, Patsy Kelly, Andy Clyde, Edgar Kennedy, Leon Errol, The Three Stooges, Pete Smith, Buster Keaton, Robert Benchley and Joe McDoakes. The short films of other comedians are also described.

Filmographies listing cast, director, date, studio, and a short synopsis follow each performer's section. The work is not limited to comedy shorts. Series such as "Crime Does Not Pay," "Screen Snapshots," "John Nesbitt's Passing Parade," and newsreels, travelogues, musicals, documentaries and sport shorts are also included. Cartoons and World War II shorts are not considered. More than 200 rather special illustrations supplement the text. Reproduction quality is above average and the selection is unique, nostalgic, and frequently exciting. An extended index further enhances the book's reference value.

The book will appeal to a wide range of audiences--scholars, buffs, historians, nostalgia lovers, the curious, and the library browsers--and all will be well rewarded by Maltin's affection for his topic, his impressive research, and the total production of what can only be called a fine contribution to cinema literature. Highly recommended for inclusion in all collections.

2344.   The Great Movie Stars, by David Shipman.   568 p.
         illus.   New York: St. Martin's Press, 1972.
         Written as the follow-up or sequel to his earlier book (631), this volume surpasses that effort. Subtitled "The International Years," the book covers film performers active in the period following World War II to the present. More than 220 mini-biographies are offered and some tell more about the subject than full-length life stories elsewhere. Shipman not only offers the factual information, but is critical about the films, gossipy about the private lives and temperaments, and extremely biased in his treatment of a few favorites. (For a typical example of Shipman at his best, try "Susan Hayward.")

Reading this book recalls the pleasurable experience of discovering the Blum pictorial books: it is addictive, charmingly prejudiced, enormously entertaining; its picture selection criteria are similar to Blum's, and it is a book that can be re-read and re-used many times. The many illustrations have been reproduced with care, a brief bibliography is given, and there is a listing of film title changes.

With a book of this size and scope, some errors and omissions are a certainty--e.g., isn't the still on page 214 from DEADLINE AT DAWN rather than from THE HAIRY APE? Is Goldie Hawn with her one Academy Award (included) more a star than Jack Hawkins (excluded)? This last situation is even more puzzling in view of Shipman's rather British viewpoint. Perhaps his introductory explanation on criteria for selection explains it, but it still seems quite subjective.

These are strictly minor matters, for this book is a most welcome arrival. It is an ideal reference and a rich entertainment. Highly recommended for all collections.

2345.   THE GREAT RACE.   33 p.   (paperback)   illus. Hollywood: Warner Brothers, 1965.
Some familiar faces appear in this attractive souvenir book. After the plot is related in great detail, there are individual sections devoted to Jack L. Warner, the producer, and to Blake Edwards, the director. Each of the three stars gets a double page consisting of a center narrative and a perimeter of photographs. Although some attempt at quality can be detected, many of the photographs are only average in color fidelity and focus. An amusing section on the devices that were used in the film and the supporting cast and production credits complete the book.

2346.   GREED. A script of the 1924 film, by Erich von Stroheim (director: Erich von Stroheim).   352 p. (paperback) illus. New York: Simon and Schuster, 1972.
Found in GREED (2347).

2347.   GREED, by Erich von Stroheim.   352 p.   (paperback) illus. New York: Simon and Schuster, 1972.
In addition to reprinting von Stroheim's original 10-hour shooting script, a comparison is made between the release version of the film and the original script. Scenes contained in the original script but missing from the film are bracketed. Entire sequences which were deleted are indicated by footnotes.
Supporting articles include the following: "Dreams of Realism" by Erich von Stroheim; "Introducing GREED" by Joel W. Finler; "Stroheim's GREED" by Herman G. Weinberg; "My Experience With Stroheim During the Making of GREED" by Jean Hersholt; "Shooting GREED" by William Daniels; "The Making of GREED" by Erich von Stroheim; two contemporary reviews of GREED (1924, 1925), and cast credits. Libraries are directed to this excellent book which is much less expensive than the Weinberg reconstruction of GREED for Arno Press. It belongs in all film collections.

2348.   Graham Greene on Film, by Graham Greene.   284 p. illus. New York: Simon and Schuster, 1972.
This volume of collected film criticism from the years 1935-1939 has several virtues and one severe fault. Any collection of reviews of classic, forgotten, neglected

and unknown films from the Golden Thirties has a lot going
for it initially. Add many nicely reproduced stills from the
films discussed and you've strengthened the brew. If the
subjects include many unknown British features and a few
documentaries along with a sprinkling of other European films,
the appeal is further increased. If all of the above is placed
in an attractively produced book, a success seems assured.
However...

Styles in film criticism change and Greene as film
critic is much different from Greene as story teller, novelist
or screenplay writer. A definite aesthetic seems lacking and
his reliance on emotional reaction to personality rather than
evaluation of an individual performance is indicative of a kind
of intellectual fan dance. He is never at a loss in sounding
informed, witty, and sophisticated but the passage of some
30 years shows the evaluations to be incorrect more often
than not--e.g., WUTHERING HEIGHTS ("The whole picture
is keepsake stuff"), LITTLE TOUGH GUY ("One of the best
melodramas in recent years"), SARATOGA ("One of Miss
Harlow's better films"), FOLLOW THE FLEET (Miss Harriet
Hilliard ... is infinitely to be preferred to Miss Irene Dunne")
and so on. The comments read today as if they were written by a cynical scholar with an entertaining literary style
but with only a meagre background in films, their history
and evolution.

As an exercise in recreating a by-gone period of
film history, and as a reminder of a large sampling of the
films of that period, the book is pure pleasure, but it cannot be considered as serious film criticism. As nostalgia,
it is recommended for all larger collections.

2349.   Focus on D. W. Griffith, edited by Harry Geduld.
         182 p. (paperback) illus. Englewood Cliffs, N.J.:
         Prentice-Hall, 1971.
         A major portion of this book is devoted to the writ-
ings of D. W. Griffith. Essays on his films and his artistry
provide the remainder. A filmography, bibliography, an index, and a few stills complete the book.
         Geduld has performed a service for the reader in
gathering the original Griffith pieces. Together with the
biographical articles that introduce the book, and the critical
essay that completes it, they contribute much to solving the
enigma that was Griffith. Perhaps the weakest portion is the
collection of visuals. They are all familiar, the reproduction is only fair, and they are too few in number to add any
great dimension to the portrait. Contributing authors, other
than Griffith, include Lillian Gish, Linda Arvidson, A. Nich-

olas Vardac, Lewis Jacobs, Jay Leyda, and Erich von Stroheim. The bibliography is lengthy and annotated.

With all the recent print attention directed toward
Griffith, it is rewarding to discover a fine volume such as
this in the group. Whether for film study, research, general reading, or simple entertainment, this book can be
highly recommended for inclusion in all collections.

2350. D. W. Griffith: His Life and His Work, by Robert
M. Henderson. 326 p. illus. New York: Oxford
University Press, 1972.

Before the appearance of this volume, the Focus book
(2349), and the one edited by James Hart (2519), the major
work on Griffith was a special edition of Film Culture in
1965 compiled by Seymour Stern. Other available materials
were either poor--Croy (1277), or partial--Barry (634),
Gish (990), Griffith (1454), O'Dell (635), and Henderson
(636).

Although this fussy account is heavily detailed and
documented, it does present most of what is publicly known
about Griffith. At this point it would be foolish to charge
that "the real Griffith does not emerge...." Because of his
guarded private life and the delayed recognition accorded
him, that portrait will probably never be drawn. Why argue
over his possible Jewish ancestry, the old-age decline into
lechery, his secret mistress, etc? These matters do not
help explain his importance to film history and art.

Henderson has gone through mountains of information, sifted it, and offered what must be the definitive biography of Griffith. If it has traces of a scholar showing off
by reciting bits of remote and non-essential trivia, this de-
tracts little from the total achievement.

The visuals, reproduced nicely, are a joy, but they
would have been more helpful to the text if they had been
scattered rather than lumped together. An appendix lists
all the Griffith films with cast and credits for the features.
Notes and an index complete the book. This volume attempts
the impossible and almost succeeds. Highly recommended
for all collections.

2351. D. W. Griffith's THE BATTLE AT ELDERBUSH
GULCH, by Kemp R. Niver. 65 p. illus. Los
Angeles, Calif.: Locare Research Group, 1972.

Kemp R. Niver is a dedicated historian-researcher.
Here, he offers a reconstruction of the film, using many of
its frames and titles, and surrounds this with original Biograph materials. Using sources such as The Bioscope, The
Moving Picture World, trade magazine summaries, and The

Biograph, he recreates some of the introduction to the industry that the film received. He notes the many errors
made by other authors concerning this film--Mrs. D. W.
Griffith, Billy Bitzer, Kevin Brownlow, and Robert Hender-
son--and offers his recreation of it to set the record straight.
    The illustrations are largely reproductions of frames
taken directly from the paper prints on deposit with The Library of Congress. An index completes the volume. The
scholarship evidenced here is gratifying; like Niver's previous
works, this one is a contribution to film history. Especially
recommended for large collections, but smaller libraries
might also consider it.

2352.   Groucho, Chico, Harpo and Sometimes Zeppo, by
         Joe Adamson. 512 p. illus. New York: Simon &
         Schuster, 1973.
    Although a late entry in the Marx Brothers-in-print-
sweepstakes, this is one of the better ones. Blending history, biography, criticism, analysis, and dialogue excerpts,
the author indicates the factors involved in the rise and fall
of the Marx teams. A biography and some illustrations support the text. The popularity of this book with audiences is
assured. Recommended for all collections.

2353.   Guide Book to Film, by Ronald Gottesman and Harry
         M. Geduld. 220 p. (paperback) New York: Holt,
         Rinehart, Winston, 1972.
    Called an eleven-in-one reference, this book con-
tains: 1) An annotated list of books and periodicals, 2) Theses and dissertations about film, 3) Museums and Archives,
4) Film schools, 5) Equipment and supplies, 6) Distributors,
7) Book-stores, publishers, etc., 8) Film organizations and
services, 9) Festivals and contests, 10) Awards, 11) Terminology.
    Like any other volume which attempts such broad
reference coverage in so relatively few pages, this one has
serious drawbacks. Much of the material appears to be a
condensation or extract from more detailed sources such as
Festivals (2237); Awards (35); Film Organizations (364), etc.
The annotations in the book section range from a single
phrase to a few sentences. To some readers the most interesting section will be the theses and dissertations (taken
from Journal of the University Film Association by Raymond
Fielding). The volume may have some value for a smaller
library with limited funds, but in most cases reference collections should opt for the primary sources.

2354.   Guide to College Courses in Film and Television,
         edited by Michele Herling. 309 p. (paperback)
         Washington, D.C.: Acropolis Books, 1973.
         The annual survey of film study in colleges conducted
by the American Film Institute. Some 613 colleges are listed,
of which 194 offer degrees in film/television. Some general-
izations based on the data are made following forewords by
Arthur Knight (film) and George C. Stoney (television). Several listings of the schools are offered--by state, by degrees
offered, by major areas of concentration, and by alphabetical
arrangement. This is a valuable reference book for school
libraries as well as for colleges and universities. The attempt by AFI to keep it current and to improve each edition
is most commendable.

2355.   Guide to the Ford Film Collection, by National Ar-
         chives and Records Service. 118 p. (paperback)
         illus. Washington, D.C.: General Services Admin-
         istration, 1970.
         The film records described in this guide are the
more than one million feet of motion pictures contained in
the Ford Historical Film Collection.

2356.   THE GUNS OF NAVARONE. 20 p. (paperback)
         illus. New York: Program Publishing Co., 1961.
         This souvenir book is below average in appearance
and content. By the use of much portrait art work, the
stars and cast of the film are shown. Production and technical credits are also listed, and a map is reproduced on
the back cover. Everyone concerned deserves better treatment.

2357.   HALF A SIXPENCE. 32 p. (paperback) illus.
         New York: National Publishers, 1968.
         The story of the film is told with a minimum of
narrative and a maximum of illustrations in this souvenir
book. In addition to a page devoted to H. G. Wells, the
author of the original work on which the film was based,
there are several pages devoted to the cast and production
crew. Here is one case where the book is probably better
than the final film.

2358.   THE HALLELUJAH TRAIL. 20 p. (paperback)
         illus. New York: Alsid Distributors, 1965.
         This oversized souvenir book reflects the concept
employed in making the film--everything much larger than
life and told with a tongue-in-cheek style. Some cartoon

art is intermixed with the illustrations from the film and the portraits of the cast. Both production and cast credits are noted. The book, like the film, should be clever and wittier than it is.

2359.   Handbook of Film Production, by John Quick and Tom La Bau. 304 p. illus. New York: Macmillan, 1972.
        The title of this valuable resource has been well selected. Covering the many phases of filmmaking with thoroughness, the authors make extensive use of illustrations, charts, and diagrams to supplement a well-written text. Though the book is technical at times, it will probably be comprehensible to most readers. Outstanding among the 26 chapters are unique ones on screen history, the definition of a film, direction, special effects, editing and storage-care of films. The remaining sections are almost as impressive, and it is difficult to find a weak portion of the text.
        In keeping with the consistent quality of the book, the authors include a bibliography listing most of the film production volumes of recent years. A list of equipment suppliers and dealers and a lengthy index complete the book. Because of the excellence of all aspects of this book--coverage, style, production values--it can be enthusiastically recommended without reservation for all collections. It is one of the best books on filmmaking to be published in the last decade.

2360.   HAND IN HAND, by Diana Morgan, etc. 57 p. illus. Surrey: The World's Work, 1963.
        This children's book is based upon the 1961 film. Since the book consists almost entirely of stills from the films, linked by the barest of narrative, it is noted here as a film book rather than a novel. Credits are complex, reading as follows: HAND IN HAND, a screen play by Diana Morgan, based on an adaptation by Leopold Atlas of a story by Sidney Harmon. The film is shown frequently on television and this pictorial-print version of the material should delight youngsters.

2361.   THE HAPPIEST MILLIONAIRE. 32 p. (paperback) illus. New York: National Publishers, 1967.
        This souvenir book begins with "The Story Behind the Story"--that of Anthony J. Drexel Biddle. It continues with pages devoted to the cast, which includes Fred McMurray, Tommy Steele, Greer Garson, Geraldine Page, Gladys Cooper and even George, the alligator. Some attention is

paid to the design of the sets and costumes, and supporting cast and production credits are noted.

2362. A HARD DAY'S NIGHT. 12 p. (paperback) illus. New York: Program Publishing Co., 1964.
This poorly produced souvenir book features only a dozen pages and has practically no color photography. The black and white illustrations are from the film and of The Beatles in off-screen activities. Some small attention is paid to the songs featured in the film and to the supporting cast and production crew. An easy day's labor to earn a fast dollar.

2363. A HARD DAY'S NIGHT. A script of the 1964 film, by Alun Owen (director: Richard Lester). 500 p. (paperback) New York: Appleton-Century-Crofts, 1972.
Found in Film Scripts Four (2270).

2364. HASTA LUEGO. An unfilmed script, by Errol John. 194 p. London: Faber and Faber, 1967.
Found in FORCE MAJEURE; THE DISPOSSESSED; HASTA LUEGO (2296).

2365. HATARI! 42 p. illus. Japan: Arthur L. Wilde Co., 1962.
This souvenir book is excellent on all counts--color, content, photography, and format are uniformly impressive. Opening with an article by the Chief Game Warden of Tanganyika, Major Bruce Kinloch, the book contains a plot summary, production stories and articles, biographies of director Howard Hawks, stars John Wayne and Hardy Kruger, and others. Other supplemental features include "Delinquents of the Animal World" and "Catcher in the Veldt." In addition to stills from the film, there are candids, and some original art work including a large double page map of Tanganyika. Composer Henry Mancini also is alloted one complete page of biographical data. An outstanding example of what a souvenir book should be.

2366. HAWAII. 32 p. illus. New York: National Publishers, 1966.
With a few fuzzy exceptions, the illustrations in this souvenir book are so impressive that the reader will wonder why the final film was so dull and unmoving. Using scenery, portraits, film stills, and even tintypes, the story and the background of the film are related. Stars, supporting

cast, director George Roy Hill, producer Walter Mirisch, composer Elmer Bernstein, and costume designer Dorothy Jenkins are all given special attention. Based upon the evidence here, one suspects there may have been too much material for one film.

2367.   Focus on Howard Hawks, edited by Joseph McBride. 178 p. (paperback) illus. Englewood Cliffs, N.J.: Prentice-Hall, 1972.

Two short articles are followed by an audience interview of Hawks which took place in Chicago, 1970. The essays which are the bulk of the text are fewer than usual with this series, but in greater depth. One by Andrew Sarris, for example, takes 30 pages. Mostly, the essays explore Hawks' methods, themes, films, and his place among major American directors. A few of his films receive individual notice: RIO BRAVO, MAN'S FAVORITE SPORT, EL DORADO and RIO LOBO. The filmography offers a short plot outline in addition to the usual information, while the bibliography refers mostly to French publications. An index and a few stills complete the book.

Hawks is probably one of the least known American directors. His work has been shown continuously for almost 50 years and shows no sign of subsiding on the TV screen. This book remedies some of the neglect, as did an earlier one by Robin Wood (661). Recommended for all libraries.

2368.   Hedda and Louella, by George Eels. 360 p. illus. New York: G. P. Putnams, 1972.

Dual biography is a rarity and George Eels, who impressed so with his work on Cole Porter (2481), succeeds once more with this volume. Tracing the careers of each of his subjects in alternate chapters, he manages to capture not only their disparities and similarities but also the absurdity of the society in which they lived and worked.

Both women have written several books, including autobiographies, so the basic information about their careers is known. The challenge to Eels was not only to purify their accounts but to interpret and assess their importance to Hollywood and filmmaking. He does this with clarity and ease, yet remains objective and readable. Illustrations, grouped together in the center of the book, are quite good; in fact, more would be welcome. An index is also provided. While not essential, this volume will be popular with mature readers, and is recommended for all collections.

2369.   HELEN OF TROY. 12 p. (paperback) illus. Hollywood: Warner Brothers, 1956.

The production of this short souvenir book is unusual and rather attractive. The text is centered on the pages, with a border of illustrations. The pictures are tinted in a pleasing monochrome. Some description of "The World's Largest Prop" is given and the two stars--Rossana Podesta (Helen) and Jack Sernas (Paris)--are profiled. Supporting cast members and production personnel are noted. Brigitte Bardot played a minor role as one of Helen's hand maidens.

2370.   HELLO DOLLY, by Jack Hirschberg. 48 p. (paperback) illus. New York: 20th Century Fox Film Corp., 1969.
Photographs are outstanding in this souvenir book and include not only the stars, Barbra Streisand and Walter Matthau, but director Gene Kelly and other production personnel. The songs used in the film are given special attention and there are listings of the supporting cast and backstage technicians.

2371.   HELP. 28 p. illus. New York: Random House, 1965.
This souvenir book is an improvement over the one issued for the first Beatles film. Containing both color and black and white photographs, the format is similar: the story, the songs and lyrics, and some behind-the-scenes candid shots. The hardcover production supplied by publisher seemingly makes the difference.

2372.   HENRY V. A script of the 1944 film, by Laurence Olivier and Reginald Beck (director: Laurence Olivier). 544 p. (paperback) New York: Appleton Century-Crofts, 1971.
Included in Film Scripts One (2267).

2373.   Katharine Hepburn, by Alvin H. Marill. 160 p. (paperback) illus. New York: Pyramid, 1973.
Since there are only about three previous books on Hepburn, this volume in "The Pyramid Illustrated History of the Movies" series is most welcome. Although some of the illustrations are not reproduced as well as those in other series volumes, remaining aspects are of equal quality.
Probably because of the non-existence of a full-length biography, no opening overview of the star's personal-professional life is given here. Instead the book is divided into four major divisions: The Stage Years, The RKO Years The MGM Years, and The Independent Years--into which the biographical elements and the films are interwoven. Throug out her long career, Hepburn has returned often to the stage.

and her appearances in that medium are noted also. A filmography, a bibliography, a list of radio appearances, and an index complete the book.

As indicated, the book's strength is its review of the Hepburn films and the notation of her appearances on stage and radio. The missing ingredient is the personal-biographical one. The quality, content, and reference material in this volume warrant its inclusion in all collections. A recommended book.

2374. Heroes, Heavies and Sagebrush: A Pictorial History of the "B" Western Player, by Arthur F. McClure and Ken D. Jones. 350 p. illus. New York: Barnes, 1972.

Here is a more ambitious and more successful book than the other volumes in what is apparently a series. An earlier effort by McClure (1420) treated the minor film players whose faces were familiar although their names were not. In this volume it is the player in the "B" western film who is considered. Subjects range from "Superstars" John Wayne, Tom Mix, Buck Jones, and Gene Autry to such unknowns as Syd Saylor, Nacho Galindo, and Iron Eyes Cody. The oversized book is divided into five sections: 1) Heroes, 2) Sidekicks, 3) Heavies, 4) Indians, and 5) Assorted Players. A short biographical sketch is given for each subject, with one or two stills which identify him facially. Films mentioned in the biography are selected and are limited to westerns. Obviously, certain faces and names keep reappearing throughout the various sections and in the many illustrations.

The reference value of the book could have been increased greatly by a single-page alphabetical listing of all the subjects. Under the present format, a reader might have to check five sections to locate the desired biography. Fortunately the notoriously bad picture reproduction that characterizes many Barnes volumes is not present in this one. Nearly all the pictures are well printed and they include many full page portraits. This volume represents a step forward for publisher and author. Most qualities are improved but there is still a way to go. First, the material should be designed with more than the casual browser in mind. The biographies could be extended by using consistent abbreviations for statistical data. However, it is a good addition to most collections.

2375. Charlton Heston, Jack Nicholson, edited by Bruce Henstell. 31 p. (paperback) Washington, D.C.: The American Film Institute, 1972.

These two individual pieces are part of the Dialogue On Film Series (2188). Heston talks about the directors he has worked for--Orson Welles, William Wyler, Sam Peckinpah, and Franklin Schaffner. Nicholson offers similar comments as he tells of his work with Roger Corman. The book concludes with selected bibliographies on both men. Acceptable for all collections.

2376. HIGH NOON. A script of the 1952 film, by Carl Foreman (director: Fred Zinnemann). 548 p. (paperback) New York: Appleton-Century-Crofts, 1971. Contained in Film Scripts Two (2268).

2377. HIGH NOON. A script of the 1952 film, by Carl Foreman (director: Fred Zinnemann). 394 p. (paperback) illus. New York: Globe Book Co., 1972. Included in Three Major Screenplays (2805). The script is preceded by: 1) "About the Author," 2) "About the Screenplay," and followed by: 1) "What the Critics Said," 2) "To Enrich Your Reading."

2378. High Speed Photography, by Raymond F. Saxe. illus. New York: Amphoto, 1966.
A section of this book deals with high-speed cine cameras. Other topics include streak and framing cameras, short exposure picture-taking devices, flash X-rays, and other electronic techniques.

2379. A Historical Study of the Academy of Motion Picture Arts and Sciences (1927-1947), by Pierre Norman Sands. 262 p. New York: Arno, 1973.
This is one of six doctoral dissertations on film topics reproduced by Arno exactly as they were submitted to the degree-granting school. This study is a historical investigation of the Academy of Motion Picture Arts and Sciences and its contribution to education and the Industry during the years, 1927-1947. The historical portion covers the founding period, the first banquet, constitution, by-laws, boards, facilities, publications, membership, officers, awards, etc.
The Academy's contributions to education are more provocative and include: institutions, the commercial community, and the military--all covered in a rather short section. Its service to the film industry itself is much larger.
A summary and conclusions are presented. A bibliography and some appendixes support the rather weak argument. The study seems to lack objectivity and was based on

what the Academy said or wrote rather than an evaluation by disinterested parties. Acceptable for large academic collections.

2380.   The History of the British Film, 1918-1929, by Rachel Low. 544 p. illus. London: George Allen & Unwin, 1971.

This, the fourth volume in Ms. Low's monumental survey of British film history, covers the period of the twenties. Topics considered include the emergence of film as an art form, the formation of the British Board of Censors, foreign competition, and the Quota Act of 1927-28. Names of films, directors, actors, and producers are scattered throughout the book, as are quotes and interviews with pioneers of the period.

Perhaps the most impressive feature is the list of feature films of the Twenties. Using more than a third of the book, the author gives an alphabetical arrangement with title, producer, length, trade showing date, director, cast, screenwriter, art director, film editor, and other data indicated. A bibliography, a long index and many well-reproduced illustrations add to the overall impressiveness of this work.

For a sample or model of research scholarship, it would be difficult to top Ms. Low's work with the history of the British film (675). This volume is essential for all large film collections. The fact that it is quite specialized and treats only one decade may limit it for smaller libraries but it should be considered whenever and wherever possible.

2381.   The History of World Cinema, by David Robinson. 440 p. illus. New York: Stein & Day, 1973.

Using a similar structure to that of Thorold Dickinson (2200), who acknowledged George Huaco (1255), Robinson states that those films which appear on the screen during a specific time and at a particular place are determined by four factors: an Esthetic, a Technology, an Economy and an Audience.

With that approach in mind he examines world cinema from the pre-screen era to the seventies. His divisions of this continuum are named with imagination: Heritage (pre-1895), Discovery (1895-1908), Metamorphosis (1908-18), Apogee (1918-27), Revolution (1927-30), On the Eve (1930-39), Realities (1939-46), Survival (1946-56), Revival (1956-72) and Legacy. A most pleasing and comprehensive outline told in a few words and dates. The text is both factual and

critical and covers many facets of film's history. The one
area that seems minimized is the American film. For ex-
ample, the 1946-56 period gives one short paragraph to the
American musical and two sentences to the Western. The
author neglects A STAR IS BORN, AN AMERICAN IN PARIS,
SINGIN' IN THE RAIN, FUNNY FACE, THE BANDWAGON,
SHANE, etc. He makes an error in this same section when
he says Ford's THE SUN SHINES BRIGHT contributes to the
western legend, naming it along with MY DARLING CLEM-
ENTINE, WAGON MASTER, and SHE WORE A YELLOW
RIBBON. It was a rework of the Judge Priest stories by
Irvin S. Cobb in which Will Rogers had starred back in 1934.
In any event, the coverage is world-wide and arguments over
emphasis and selection are subjective. Robinson's attempt
to describe the whole of film history is admirable if not always successful.

A final short article on animated film is followed by
selected or complete filmographies for many of the directors
named in the text. A rather cramped bibliography and three
separate indexes (General, Films, Names) complete the book.
There are more than 100 photographs, most of which are
nicely reproduced. They appear throughout the book rather
than in one or two concentrated sections.

Since this is the first "longer" general history of
world cinema in about 30 years--if one omits Dickinson
(2200), Mast (1233) and Casty (2187)--it is welcome in spite
of its omissions, emphases, and mistakes. It attempts an
almost impossible task and succeeds much of the time. Highly recommended for inclusion in all collections.

2382.   Alfred Hitchcock, edited by Bruce Henstell.   27 p.
        (paperback) Washington, D.C.: American Film In-
        stitute, 1972.
        In February 1970 Hitchcock visited the AFI Center
in Beverly Hills after completing a publicity tour for his
film, TOPAZ. In typical fashion, Hitchcock departed from
any pre-arranged structure and allowed the questions to range
over many diverse aspects of filmmaking. A bibliography
and a filmography are included. Acceptable for all collections.

2383.   Focus on Hitchcock, edited by Albert J. LaValley.
        186 p.   (paperback) illus. Englewood Cliffs, N.J.:
        Prentice-Hall, 1972.
        How much more there is to say about Hitchcock is
debatable, but this fine collection does gather together some
opinions about him that have been offered in the past. It

begins with two interviews and two articles by Hitchcock
himself. The next section contains evaluations of Hitchcock
and his films by Lindsay Anderson, André Bazin, Robin
Wood, Andrew Sarris, and Raymond Durgnat. The remaining articles address themselves to specific films: NOTORI-
OUS, STRANGERS ON A TRAIN, THE WRONG MAN, PSY-
CHO, and the television series.

An unusual and surprisingly good analysis of the
plane-cornfield sequence from NORTH BY NORTHWEST appears next. Utilizing some 30 pages, the sequence is analyzed shot-by-shot, using story boards to suggest the frame
composition. A filmography, a bibliography, an index and
a few stills complete the book. As a survey of Hitchcock's
work and his contribution to film, this volume would be
hard to beat. It is excellent in all ways and that shot-by-
shot analysis is worth the price alone. This is another
superior title in the "focus on" series and is highly recommended for all collections.

2384.   Hollywood at Sunset, by Charles Higham.   181 p.
          illus. New York: Saturday Review Press, 1972.
          The reference in Higham's title is to the period
from 1946 to 1971, a sunset lasting a quarter century and
not altogether invisible even now. In 1946 the highest yearly attendance at films in the United States was recorded.
Immediately thereafter a series of events occurred which
contributed to the demise of a business system that had been
enormously successful for nearly three decades. A temporary loss of the European market, government actions which
ended block booking and theatre ownership by distributors/
producers, and the investigations of Communism in Hollywood Studios by the House Un-American Activities Committee are cited as destructive factors appearing in the late
forties. Television and post-war leisure habit changes were
felt in the early fifties. Experiments in wide screen, 3-D,
or Cinerama processes did not bring the lost audiences back.
Blockbuster films such as CLEOPATRA and MUTINY ON
THE BOUNTY debilitated the studios even more, making
them easy acquisitions for agencies, conglomerates and other
Wall Street tenacles. The auctions at the MGM and Fox
Studios close the book on a sad and melancholy note.
          Short biographical sketches of the men behind the
scenes--studio heads, 3-D inventors, agency presidents,
etc.--are placed in the appropriate chronology of the story
and these brief portraits give the book its strength.
Higham is not nearly so effective when he evaluates films
since he offers only subjective opinion without corroborating

argument: "Jerry Lewis' THE NUTTY PROFESSOR--an inspired comedy that was a witty exception to such inane films as BREAKFAST AT TIFFANYS."

A short center pictorial section shows a few of the major characters discussed in the text. Why the book is without a table of contents and an index is a mystery. Segments of Higham's material are certainly most pertinent to students and scholars and their retrieval from the book in its present form is quite difficult. There is much to appreciate here but one wishes there had been a firmer editorial hand; the book could have and should have been better. With the above reservations, the book is acceptable for all libraries.

2385.　Hollywood in the Fifties, by Gordon Gow. 208 p. (paperback) illus. New York: Barnes, 1971.
The changes that took place in Hollywood during the 1950s are noted in this volume, which is one of a series. Because of the competition from home television, Hollywood tried new methods to bolster the sagging box office receipts. 3-D, Cinemascope, overseas locations, super-spectacles and independent productions were all elements of change in this period. Gow examines films, film sources, social comment in films, the free screen film types such as the individual or the misfit, acting styles, show business films and comedies. The survey manages to mention many of the films made within the decade. An index is provided and the book is illustrated with an average collection of stills, most of which tend to be quite small in reproduction size. Gow's narrative account of this period of change is informed, entertaining, and rather subjective at times. As a critical historian, he mentions films he did not like while others did, e.g., VERTIGO; and films he thinks were underrated by other critics, e.g., RED GARTERS.
The book is fairly typical of the others in the series (690, 691, 692, 2386), though each differs in some respects, as each has a different authorship. When the books are used together, a valuable historical record of the Hollywood film results. (An interesting oversized volume could be made by combining all five.) As part of this series, this is a highly recommended volume. As a single book, it is also a good addition to any collection.

2386.　Hollywood in the Sixties, by John Baxter. 172 p. illus. New York: Barnes, 1972.
This volume covers some of the same ground as Higham's Hollywood At Sunset (2384) but the emphasis is

quite different. Baxter explores films rather than individuals and studios. The first two chapters outline the decline of the studios and the disappointing efforts of some of the outstanding directors of earlier years--Zinnemann, Kramer, Preminger, Kazan, Rossen, Minnelli, etc. Contrasted with these are newer directors such as Mike Nichols, Sidney Lumet, Frank Perry and Arthur Penn. Remaining chapters are devoted to film genres--the musical, the mystery, the western, the sex comedy, etc. A lengthy index is provided, and the illustrations are mostly above average.

The book's weakness is the interjection of personal bias as accepted truth. Baxter is most vulnerable when he states: 1) Rosalind Russell gave a performance of wit and animation in GYPSY. (Most critics thought she watered down so much of the character of Rose that the motivation for the story was lost. The rest of Baxter's comments about GYPSY are equally unfounded. It was a poor movie based upon a great musical.) 2) Debbie Reynolds gave a "spirited performance" in THE UNSINKABLE MOLLY BROWN. (Her distasteful shrieking put the entire film out of perspective.) 3) The score to SWEET CHARITY is called "routine." (Yet he singles out three songs for individual positive comment in the paragraph that follows) 4) Of all Billy Wilder's parodies, KISS ME STUPID is both the funniest and most accurate. (Most critics thought otherwise.)

Since most of the volume consists of film criticism, there has to be reservation about such solo opinions, lacking any stated corroboration or evidence. Presented as film history, the book is suspect. As a personal overview of the films of the sixties, it will please and entertain the noncritical reader. Because of its broad coverage and the fine index, it also has some reference value. Acceptable for most libraries.

2387.   Hollywood Leg Man, by Jaik Rosenstein. 212 p.
         Los Angeles, Calif.: Madison Press, 1950.
         A collection of short pieces about Hollywood by a man who was a press agent and a legman for Hedda Hopper. His responsibility in this latter job was to hunt up or check out items for Hopper's column. The proximity to Hopper had its effect, for the text reads like old-fashioned Hollywood gossip. Many blind items are used and the whole book promises to divulge much but delivers little. Of very limited interest today and suitable only for very large collections.

2388.   The Hollywood Musical, by John Russell Taylor and
         Arthur Jackson. 278 p. illus. New York: Mc-
         Graw-Hill, 1971.

Five related essays consider various aspects of the musical film in this handsome book's opening pages. Among the topics are the translation of stage musicals into film, the composers, the performers, the directors, and an evaluation of the genre. Linking these chapters is a sort of critical history. The two main sections follow, the first being a selected filmography listing 1,443 pictures with the usual data--title, year, running time, cast credits, and production credits. The bonus here is the inclusion of the songs from each, with a key to the actor(s) who performed them. The filmography is flawed by inconsistency in selection. For example: THE COUNTRY GIRL is included but GOOD NEWS is not; A DAY AT THE RACES is in but A NIGHT AT THE OPERA is not; ONE NIGHT OF LOVE is in but THE GREAT CARUSO is not; THE GLENN MILLER STORY is in but THE BENNY GOODMAN STORY is not.

The second section is an index of names, which gives some bits of biographical data and a listing of credits --but only in relation to musical films. Those films listed in the filmography appear here in bold print. Again, some inconsistency occurs. IN OLD CHICAGO (Ameche), LITTLE BOY LOST (Crosby), LOVE AFFAIR (Dunne), JUKE GIRL (Sheridan) may have a song hidden somewhere but are not musicals in any way. There are alphabetical indexes for the songs and for the film titles at the book's end. Many fine illustrations appear and several in color are most pleasing.

In spite of the inconsistency and the assignment of some titles, the book has a fine reference potential. It seems limited to that use since the opening essays are not strong enough to attract reader interest and the indexes and filmography are not reading material except for the dedicated musical buff. Recommended for inclusion as a reference in all collections.

2389.   Hollywood Now, by William Fadiman.   174 p.   New
        York: Liveright, 1972.
The author has had an impressive career in films, having been a producer, a vice president, and an executive literary advisor in Hollywood. He is certainly qualified to write this volume, a view of Hollywood today, which contains elements of filmmaking, industry organization, history, and sociology. It is an honest, absorbing and useful book. Key topics considered by Fadiman are the industry, the agent, the director, the star, the writer, the producer, and the future. The book is not illustrated but it has a short bibliography and an index.

The text is informed, witty, sometimes cynical, practical, and, most of all, respectful. It avoids that com-

mon practice of today, taking pop-shots at the remains of
Hollywood. Fadiman reminds us of what failed in the past
but also of what is still valuable or functional today. In general, his attitude is cautiously pessimistic; he sees subsidiza-
tion and a change in film content as two possible remedies
for Hollywood's ills. A concise, intelligent view of Hollywood, past and present, this volume is recommended for all
collections.

2390.   Hollywood Panorama, by Bob Harmon. 95 p. (pa-
         perback) illus. New York: Dutton, 1971.
         This delightful book consists of 30 full-color panels
of caricatures of movie stars--past and present--all drawn
by Bob Harmon. Some are costumed for their most famous
roles: Garbo as CAMILLE, Leslie Caron as GIGI, W. C.
Fields as Mr. Micawber, etc. Others are portrayed in various activities: swimming, tennis, socializing, etc. Identification is the game and most buffs will find it easy, for
Harmon has been highly successful in capturing the uniqueness
of his many, many subjects. The nonbuff will find it more
challenging but will be helped by the reverse side of each
plate, on which there appears an identification diagram, the
names, and the film role, if applicable.
         The use of this volume in libraries is limited only
by the creative imagination of those in charge. With care
against mutilation, it can circulate with much user popularity
and appreciation. The publisher suggests a mural made by
combining all 30 plates. Projection via the opaque projector
is possible; contests could be held prior to film showings;
and simply as pictorial aids for display, the plates are fine.
This book should be ordered in duplicate so that its full potential for pleasure is realized. Different and highly recommended.

2391.   The Hollywood Professionals, by Kingsley Canham.
         (paperback) illus. New York: Barnes, 1973.
         Announced as the first book in a series, this one
discusses the film careers of three Hollywood directors who
have been somewhat neglected by today's critics: Michael
Curtiz, Raoul Walsh, and Henry Hathaway. The promise of
a full filmography for Curtiz alone justifies the book.

2392.   The Hollywood Screen-Writers, edited by Richard
         Corliss. 328 p. (paperback) New York: Avon,
         1972.
         This original paperback anthology focuses attention
on a neglected and misunderstood area in filmmaking: the

161

creation of a script. By a judicious choice of articles and interviews about screenwriters, the editor has managed an eloquent arrangement for the re-evaluation of their role. A loose chronological arrangement of the material presents Anita Loos as an early representative of the craft. The Golden Years feature Jules Furthman, Ben Hecht, Preston Sturges, Dudley Nichols and Howard Koch. During the House Un-American Committee Hearings and the McCarthy Era, the intent of the screenwriter was questioned by the Government. Ring Lardner, Jr., Bordon Chase, Dalton Trumbo, and James Poe were names familiar during this period. Writer rebirth is indicated by Eleanor Perry, Penelope Gilliatt, Jules Feiffer and others. A symposium section which records the responses of 12 noted writers to the same questionnaire precedes the final section, fifty filmographies of perhaps the best known screenwriters in the American cinema. Each article or interview has a filmography appended.

The book, which derives much of its material from the periodical, Film Comment, is promised as the first of a series, which is good news. The description of the screenwriting craft along with individual portraits of noted writers makes informative, vital, and enjoyable reading. The editor can be criticized on one major count. The reference value is less than adequate. The provision of a simple index of writer names would have helped immeasurably. With so many filmographies in the book, it could have approximated a poor-man's version of Who Wrote the Movie and What Else Did He Write? (1462). The table of contents is of some assistance, but two poor reference situations exist: first, with the writers who are "buried" within a general article--Paul Mazursky, Larry Tucker, David Newman, Robert Benton, etc.--and secondly with the 50 names included in the final filmography. A single-page index to the names would have made the book much more useful. Even with this large reservation, the quality of the book is such that it is recommended enthusiastically for all collections.

2393.   Hollywood: The Golden Era, by Jack Spears. 440 p. illus. New York: Barnes, 1971.
The title of this fine volume may be misleading to some readers. A collection of 12 articles which originally appeared in Films in Review has been updated and revised with impressive results. Chapters are devoted to surveys of films dealing with World War I, comic strips, baseball, doctors, and the Indian. Other chapters deal with the work of Max Linder, Norma Talmadge, Colleen Moore, Marshall Neilan and Robert Florey. Other sections deal with Mary Pickford's directors and Chaplin's collaborators.

The book has separate indexes for films and subjects and offers filmographies for Talmadge, Florey, Neilan and Moore. Illustrations are fascinating in content but small in size and only fairly reproduced. The care with which the author has selected his subjects and the thoroughness of his work are evident throughout. Here is a fine example of scholarly writing/research made into fascinating reading by the ability of the author. Highly recommended for all collections.

2394.   Hollywood Voices, edited by Andrew Sarris.   180 p.
         illus.   New York: Bobbs-Merrill, 1971.
         This volume is a bit of a puzzle.   Directors Cukor, Preminger, Huston, Losey, Welles, Ray, Polonsky, Mamoulian and Sturges are represented by interviews taken from the total of 40 that appeared in Sarris' Interviews With Film Directors (770).   The only discernible changes here seem to occur in the filmographies, and they are minimal indeed. A few acceptable illustrations accompany the text here which are not found in the paperback version of the longer work. Although the format and production quality on this "spin-off" are quite high, so is the price.   Nowhere except in the book's title is there any mention that this is about 20 per cent of the content of the earlier book, and it suggests the possibility of that total content appearing now in five volumes at nearly five times the original price.   There is no quarrel with the excellence of the material (see 770), but prospective purchasers should be completely aware of what they are buying.

2395.   Hollywood When Silents Were Golden, by Evelyn F.
         Scott.   223 p.   illus.   New York: McGraw-Hill,
         1972.
         The author's mother, Bellah Dix Flebbe, came for a short visit with the DeMille family in Hollywood and remained 50 years.   As description of life in Hollywood from 1916 to about 1930, the book is an affectionate tribute. Names and nostalgia for the period abound.   The view is antiseptic and will scandalize or offend no one.   A picture section is disappointing in both selection and size.   The volume seems like an afterthought attempt to capitalize on the current popularity of Hollywood nostalgia.   Acceptable but not at all essential for library collections.

2396.   The Home Movie Scenario Book, by Morrie Ryskind,
         C. F. Stevens and James Englander.   174 p.   New
         York: Richard Manson, 1927.
         This historical curio consists mostly of 20 scenarios

163

designed for the amateur to film. Titles will give the reader a clue to the content and quality: "The Golf Widow," "The Way of a Transgressor," "What to Do With Chaperones," "A Modern John Alden," etc. The second section deals with the elements of amateur filmmaking, starting with the establishment of the home movie company--a director, cameraman, technical helpers, players, etc. Directing, acting, sets, lighting, makeup and editing are treated next. A glossary of terms completes the book. Commercial sound films appeared almost simultaneously with this book. No mention is made of sound, however. The book is an attractive piece of memorabilia that may have historical interest but is of little practical value today. Noted for the record.

2397.   Horror and Science Fiction Films: A Checklist, by Donald C. Willis. 612 p. Metuchen, N.J.: Scarecrow, 1972.
As the title indicates, this reference book is a listing of 4,400 titles in the film genres of horror and science fiction. For each entry, the following information is given: title, country of origin, studio, production credits, cast credits, synopsis and comment. Some of the data indicated above were not available on early silent films. Four addenda complete the book: "Titles Announced for 1971-72," "Shorts, Animated, Puppet Films," "Out List," and "References."
Some attempt is made to define the criteria for the placement of a film in the main listing or the out list, but decisions seem more subjective than objective. Annotations are short, prejudiced, elementary, and even poor at times, appearing as if they are condensations of the outlines appearing in TV movies or other film listings. For example: JUST IMAGINE is described as a "S-F musical set in New York in 1980." The annotation on DOCTOR X reads: "Synthetic flesh! silly; once in a while silly enough to be some fun; at any rate better than Curtiz's other early thirties horror hit, MYSTERY OF THE WAX MUSEUM." On DR. JEKYLL AND MR. HYDE (1932): "This may or may not be the best version of the tired old story (which wasn't much to begin with) but good it isn't. There are some impressive touches, mainly in the treatment of Hyde, but Hopkins is dull, and there are the usual obligatory time-filling scenes with Jekyll. Better than Mamoulian's early 'Classics'." These words seem self-contradictory and unfair to the films.
Perhaps the most important service provided is the almost all-inclusive main listing. Nearly any horror film or science fiction film that one can recall is listed. The coverage is impressive. As a specialized reference tool, the book is fine and most suitable for large libraries and col-

lections. As a recreation or pleasure book, it would have been much better if the annotations had reflected general critical consensus rather than the author's personal bias.

2398.   Focus on The Horror Film, by Roy Huss and T. J. Ross. 186 p. (paperback) illus. Englewood Cliffs, N.J.: Prentice-Hall, 1972.
   The three dozen articles in this compilation are ar-ranged in four groups: The Horror Domain, Gothic Horror, Monster Terror, and Psychological Thriller.   Under this last category, for example, there are essays on Val Lewton, THE BIRDS, ROSEMARY'S BABY, REPULSION and TAR-GETS. In addition there are a chronology, a filmography, a bibliography, an index, and a few stills. Excerpts from the scripts of a 1910 version of FRANKENSTEIN and from THE BRIDE OF FRANKENSTEIN (1935) appear in two of the articles.
   There is enough here to satisfy most horror film buffs.   While one might question the absence of certain films --THE HAUNTING and THE INNOCENTS--the presence in the text of so many classic films of this genre more than compensates.   This volume is a natural audience pleaser and can be recommended for all collections. It is ideal sup-port material for courses in film study, which usually in-clude one or more sessions on horror films.

2399.   Hot Line! The Letters I Get and Write, by Burt Reynolds. 128 p. (paperback) illus. New York: Signet Books, 1972.
   "When you're hot, you're hot"--thus, this snicker-ing, leering appeal to prurient curiosity is a product of the Reynolds' centerfold celebrity.   The visuals and the text in this example of publishing garbage are dirty, simple-minded, and ultimately insulting.   Noted here as an example of the length to which limited performers will go to promote them-selves. Devices such as hair pieces, retouching, and pad-ding are obvious in the visuals and the letters seem to be the product of an overstimulated but underexercised ghost-editor.

2400.   Hound and Horn: Essays on Cinema. New York: Arno, 1972.
   The Hound and Horn was a little magazine which appeared in the late twenties and the early thirties.   Devoted to all the arts, it was one of the first to carry critical re-views and essays on film.   This compilation includes the following:
   "Eisenstein's New York" by Jere Abbott

"In Memory of Harry Alan Potamkin, 1900-1933, Anonymous

"Nationalism in German Films" by Alfred H. Barr, Jr.

"Spoilation of QUE VIVA MEXICO" by Kirk Bond

"The Art of Kipps" by Grant Code

"The Dynamic Square" by Sergei Eisenstein

"Periodical Reviews: Movie Magazines" by Henry-Russell Hitchcock Jr.

"James Cagney and the American Hero" by Lincoln Kirstein

"Eisenstein and the Theory of Cinema," by Harry Alan Potamkin

"A Proposal for a School of the Motion Picture," by Harry Alan Potamkin

"Pabst and the Social Film," by Harry Alan Potamkin

"Pudovkin and the Revolutionary Film," by Harry Alan Potamkin

"Animated Cartoons" by Kenneth White

"F. W. Murnau" by Kenneth White

"Garbo and Dietrich" by Kenneth White

"The Style of Ernst Lubitsch" by Kenneth White

"Movie Chronicle" by Kenneth White

Acceptable for large film collections.

2401.   Howard, The Amazing Mr. Hughes, by Noah
         Dietrich and Bob Thomas.   303 p.   (paperback)
         illus.   Greenwich, Conn.:   Fawcett Publications,
         1972.

For 32 years, Noah Dietrich was a close associate of Howard Hughes, acting as business associate and confidante. Bob Thomas is the experienced biographer of Irving Thalberg, Walt Disney, Harry Cohn, David Selznick, and others. This combination of experiences applied to a subject like Howard Hughes seems sure-fire. For the most part it does work well in this volume.

The familiar Hollywood stories--Jean Harlow, Billie Dove, HELL'S ANGELS, COCK OF THE AIR, Multicolor, RKO, Jane Russell, Jean Peters--all receive attention. The personal side of Hughes is emphasized throughout, getting as detailed at times as a discussion of his chronic constipation. While the writing style is a bit naive and amateurish--unlike Thomas' King Cohn--it is bearable, and the content and the visuals compensate for the lack in literary quality. The book is not indexed. This is the best biography of Hughes currently in print. Acceptable for those libraries which serve mature readers.

2402. How Films Are Made, by Stanley Reed and John
Huntley. 90 p. Illus. London: The Educational
Supply Assoc. Ltd., 1955.
An older volume designed for educational use, this
book covers the making of a film from script to screen.
The contribution made by each artisan is explained, sometimes by the use of invented dialogue. Some of the illustrations are excellent in content but poor in reproduction. The
book is indexed. Since much of the material is either out-
of-date or seems to "talk down" to the reader, the book is
only of minor historical interest for libraries.

2403. HOW THE WEST WAS WON. 36 p. illus. New
York: Random House, 1963.
Since there were so many stars and co-stars in this
Cinerama-MGM production, each receives only a small portrait and a paragraph of biography. The central section contains a collection of photographs from the film, arranged to
approximate the continuity of the film. Directors Henry Hathaway, John Ford, and George Marshall, along with other production personnel, are given special attention, and there is
a rather good diagram of the Cinerama process included.
The care that the publisher takes in producing these program
books is again evident.

2404. How to Break Into the Movies, by Albert Zugsmith.
173 p. (paperback) New York: Macfadden, 1963.
Remember Phillipa Fallon? She had roles in Producer Zugsmith's GIRL IN THE KREMLIN, HIGH SCHOOL
CONFIDENTIAL, and PRIVATE LIVES OF ADAM AND EVE.
With his success in guiding Miss Fallon in films as an im-
petus, Zugsmith offers his rules for film fame, punctuated
by tidbits of information--e.g., Doris Day sang with a band,
John Wayne was a stuntman, etc. The text is always predictable. There are also chapters on writing, producing,
direction and other behind-the-camera careers. Zugsmith's
films and the book are consistent: the films are obvious,
cheap, intellectually insulting, and promise more than they
deliver. So does the book. The strongest portion is the appendix, which offers job descriptions along with some union-
guild names and addresses. The remaining information is
obsolete today. Noted for the record.

2405. How to Make Exciting Home Movies and Stop Boring
Your Friends and Relatives, by Dodi Schultz and Ed
Schultz. 152 p. illus. Garden City, N.Y.: Dou-
bleday, 1973.

167

This volume has an imaginative title but a rather predictable and pedestrian text. The usual topics are covered, with a disappointing difference: instead of having visuals appear throughout the book, they are grouped into two sections. There are 35 color visuals and 38 black and white --which sounds bountiful--but many of these are grouped two to a page. The book is unrelieved text for the most part, and a better presentation of the identical material can be obtained at a much lower price at most photography stores.

2406.   How to Make Films at School, by J. D. Beal.
         147 p. illus. London: Focal Press, 1968.
         The first section of this book makes a strong argument for filmmaking in school, and notes some educational trends and aims in support. The central portion of the book is a broad general discussion of the techniques, processes, and problems of filmmaking. Final pages make a plea for school cooperation in filmmaking and offer some suggestions toward achieving such cooperation. A good glossary and an appendix complete the book.
         This volume is unusual in its attempt to relate and correlate filmmaking with the schools. It is of British origin and some of the academic approach may differ from that of other countries but there is enough valid information and suggestion here to warrant inclusion in any school collection.

2407.   How to Make Movie Magic, by Julien Caunter. 348 p.
         illus. Philadelphia: Chilton Book Co., 1971.
         Originally published in two volumes titled How to Do the Simpler Tricks and How to Do Tricks, this book is a revised and combined edition. The book is addressed to the amateur filmmaker and offers suggestions on camera magic via exposure, focus, lens, speeds, distortions, reflection, filters, and chemicals. Fades, wipes, dissolves, the special effects box, reverse action, stop-motion, superimposition, ghosts, masks and post-filming treatments are described in the second half. An indexed glossary completes the book. Visuals and diagrams throughout are quite helpful.
         Here is a small book that can be used by the nonprofessional filmmaker or by the reader interested in knowing how some film effects are obtained. Recommended for all collections, with a special recommendation to those that support filmmaking courses in schools and libraries.

2408.   How to Organize and Run a Film Society, by Janet
         Weiner. 210 p. (paperback) illus. New York:
         Collier Books, 1973.

This valuable book has some outstanding features and a few unnecessary ones. Stronger sections appear at the beginning where organization, selection of films, and publicity are treated. Whether listing 900 films and indicating the distributors for them is necessary is debatable, especially when it takes up half of the book. The inclusion of some film bookstores is also an isolated resource; certainly the prices for posters and stills from these sources are rather prohibitive, and most film books today can be found in libraries, discount stores or on paperback racks. The discussion on programming is quite good, as is the chapter on publicity which contains some practical suggestions. There are diagrams, drawings, and some poster reproductions. The book is indexed. A surface coverage of what usually turns out to be a complex operation, but a starting point, nevertheless. Acceptable for all collections.

2409.   How to Use a Motion Picture, by William H. Hartley. 8 p. (paperback) Washington, D.C.: National Council for the Social Studies, 1965.

This pamphlet is included here as an example of the kind of information on films and film use that is available from many national associations. In a very few pages, this publication gives a rationale for film use, suggestions on use, an overview of what is available in classroom, government, theatrical, and commercial films, and several pages on the steps necessary for effective use of the film. A selected bibliography is offered, too. Excellent material is available in this format but it takes some digging to discover titles and organizations.

2410.   How to Write and Sell Film Stories, by Frances Marion. 365 p. New York: Covici-Friede, 1937.

This older volume on screenplay writing is by a well-known author who recently wrote her autobiography (2614). The first section deals with characters, plot, motivation, theme, dialogue, emotions, etc.; the second section presents the script of THE ADVENTURES OF MARCO POLO.

2411.   How to Write for Moving Pictures, by Marguerite Bertsch. 275 p. illus. New York: George H. Doran, 1917.

Author Bertsch subtitles her book "A Manual of Instruction and Information" and bases her offering on her experience as director and editor for the Vitagraph Company and the Famous Players Film Company. Written in 1917, the book's seven major divisions are: Writing, Production, Hackneyed Themes, Themes Based on Conflict, Themes Based on Social Conflict, Divided Interest and Censorship. Since this was the era of BIRTH OF A NATION and INTOLERANCE, it is a bit surprising to find chapters on the dissolve, double exposure, the cut-back, and the close-up. There are 14 illustrations to help explain the text. This book for historians and researchers is noted here for the record.

2412. HUSBANDS. 30 p. (paperback) illus. 1970.
This is not the typical souvenir book but an attempt to present mostly oversized visuals of shots from the film. There is little text aside from the usual cast and production credits. All the performers are pictured and identified. A beautiful presentation and production.

2413. THE HUSTLER. A script of the 1961 film, by Robert Rossen (director: Robert Rossen). 274 p. (paperback) illus. New York: Doubleday, 1972. Found in: Three Screenplays (2806).

2414. I Am Gazing into My 8-Ball, by Earl Wilson. 182 p. Garden City, N.Y.: Doubleday, 1945.
A World War II book that offered escapism via gossip column nonsense and press agentry. Names like Lana Turner, Carol Landis, Ann Sheridan, Howard Dietz, Tallulah Bankhead (on LIFEBOAT), Jimmy Durante, Garbo, Nunnally Johnson, Betty Hutton, Gregory Ratoff, Dorothy Lamour, Charles Boyer, Veronica Lake, Katharine Hepburn, and Rags Ragland are featured in the short anecdotes and paragraphs that make up the book. The book has some value as an indication of the public's interest three decades ago. It hasn't changed much since then. Noted for the record.

2415. ICE STATION ZEBRA, by John Tobias. 32 p. (paperback) illus. New York: National Publishers, 1968.
The format of this souvenir book makes it a bit more difficult to follow since the content is spread over two pages at times and is visualized with rather small photographs. Included are a diagram of a nuclear submarine, some explanation of the special effects used in the film, and the usual cast, director, and producer credits. The photographs tend to resemble those found in National Geographic rather than stills from a film.

2416. The Image Maker, edited by Ron Henderson. 96 p. (paperback) illus. Richmond, Va.: John Knox Press, 1971.

170

Six interviews with directors--Miklos Jansco, Abraham Polonsky, Jaromil Jires, Jean Renoir, Ingmar Bergman, and Peter Fonda--make up the first part of this book. An introduction is provided to each interview except Fonda's. The second section is a collection of six essays on various topics. According to Henderson, their commonality is that they all point to film as image maker. Perhaps. Some rather good visuals are included.

The interviews are the major attraction here and one suspects the essays were fillers. Were they written for this book? No sources are given for the essays, but Schillaci's "Film As Environment" appeared earlier in Films Deliver (487). Acceptable for all collections.

2417. The Image Makers: 60 Years of Hollywood Glamour, by Paul Trent and Richard Lawton. 327 p. illus. New York: McGraw-Hill, 1972.

This book is aptly subtitled because everything about it indicates glamour: visuals, layout, dust jacket, type style, paper quality, etc. are all apart from the ordinary. An introductory essay discusses those stars who had a public image, usually created and prized above all else by the studio master minds. Some were able to change this image, others could not--e.g., Mary Pickford, Garbo. The studio photographers are named and an informal history of the film star photo is delineated.

The substance of the book is the pictures, which are of two major types--the gallery portrait and the candid. Concentration is on the former; only a very few candids are included. Presented in a chronological fashion by decades, the visuals are consistently breathtaking. When the charisma of these unique people was exposed by the photographer, you have the almost perfect blending of subject and artist. Selection is wide, with Barbara Stanwyck, Bette Davis and Marlene Dietrich, with six pictures each, among those most represented. A few of the later photographs are in full color. In the book's closing pages the subjects are indexed by year, photographer, film studio, film title, and page reference.

This is a visual experience and feast that will please many readers and lookers. Care will have to be taken against vandalism, for many of the portraits will suggest permanent possession. No matter how the book is handled in libraries, it is an exciting addition to any collection. With few words and much beauty, it indicates that quality of the Hollywood movie star that is sadly missing in today's acting professionals.

2418.   Image Maker: Will Rogers and the American Dream,
         by William Brown. 304 p. illus. Columbia, Mo.:
         University of Missouri Press, 1970.
         Brown attempts to explain and analyze Will Rogers as
a national idol with four faces: the American Adam, the
American Democrat, the Self-Made Man, and the American
Prometheus. The book concentrates on the public image rather than the private man. It emphasizes the comments and
writings of Rogers but ignores Rogers as a screen performer
both in silents and in the sound eras. Even as supporting material to a study of Rogers, the book is limited. The approach is worshipful and prejudiced, extolling Rogers' virtues
and minimizing his faults or omissions. Not recommended
for film collections.

2419.   THE IMMORTAL ONE. A script of the 1963 film,
         by Alain Robbe-Grillet (director: Alain Robbe-
         Grillet). 173 p. illus. London: Calder and Boyars,
         1971.
         Includes preliminary notes; cast and production cred-
its; a shot-by-shot description of the film which the author
calls "a Cine-Novel."

2420.   An Impersonation of Angels: a Biography of Jean
         Cocteau, by Frederick Brown. 438 p. illus. New
         York: Viking, 1968.
         Another fine biography of Jean Cocteau which gives
brief accounts of the films and their making. The book is
absorbing and compassionate, yet objective. Film stills are
not used in the illustrations; these are mostly informal poses
of Cocteau and his friends. The book has a detailed index,
a bibliography of French and English books, and many explanatory notes. Acceptable for all collections which serve
mature readers.

2421.   Independent Filmmaking, by Lenny Lipton. 432 p.
         (paperback) illus. San Francisco: Straight Arrow
         Books, 1972.
         Subtitled "A Complete Guide to 8mm, Super 8, Single
8 and 16mm Moviemaking," this is an encyclopedia for the
non-professional filmmaker. Each of its ten chapters is
crammed with information, opinion, charts, diagrams, tables
and visuals. Chapter titles encompass the totality of independent film making--the format, the film, the camera, the
lens, shooting, splicing and editing, sound and magnetic recording, preparing the sound track, the laboratory's role,
and a final mixed bag of topics.

In addition to the detailed text, the visuals, which are chosen wisely and reproduced beautifully, add to the clarity of the book. Understanding the technical portions should be no great problem for most readers, since Lipton uses an easy informal personal style. An index enhances the reference value of the book and a second index of the illustrations should satisfy the curious. Stan Brakhage supplies a well-written, witty introduction. This is one of the best books on independent filmmaking to appear in some time. It can be used effectively by junior high students and anyone older who needs a comprehensive guide to filmmaking. Highly recommended for all collections.

2422.   Index to Film Culture: No. 1 to No. 46. (paper-
        back) New York: Film Culture, 1968.
        This is not an index in the usual reference sense.
It is simply a listing of the tables of contents of the periodical, Film Culture, from volume 1 to volume 46. This short
work should be of some assistance but one wishes that a more
usable index had been produced.

2423.   Index to Films in Review: 1950-1959, by Marion
        Fawcett. 105 p. New York: National Board of
        Review of Motion Pict., 1961.
        This valuable index to an important film periodical
first lists all of the article titles from 1950 to 1959 alphabetically, then by subject, using headings such as Arts,
Biography, Interviews, Aesthetics, Film Music, etc. Other
sections are devoted to book reviews, film titles, illustrations, author names, directors, actors, actresses, etc. The
index is quite easy to use and the cross listings will be of
great assistance to the searcher who has meager information
to begin with.

2424.   Index to Films in Review, 1960-1964, by Marion
        Fawcett. 196 p. New York: National Board of Re-
        view, 1966.
        This second index to Films in Review covering the
years 1960 to 1964, differs from the earlier index; a straight
alphabetical arrangement is used here rather than the earlier
section/division format. The claim that this is more effi-
cient is debatable, but the ultimate value of this research tool
is not. A valuable reference work for most libraries.

2425.   Index to Films in Review, 1965-1969, by Sandra
        Lester. 234 p. New York: National Board of Re-
        view, 1973.

2426.   Index to the New York Times Film Reviews.   1142 p.
          illus.   New York: Arno, 1970.
          This valuable reference source has other uses than
as a guide to the five volumes in the original set (1040).   For
those libraries which have the Times on microfilm, or for
the small library that simply wants the name index with the
accompanying film titles, the citations to the Times reviews,
the title index, the corporate index, the awards section, or
the picture collection of 2,000 performers, this single volume
may suffice.

2427.   Industrial Motion Pictures, by Eastman Kodak.   76 p.
          (paperback) illus.   Rochester, N.Y.:   Eastman
          Kodak.
          The concern here is with the service film rather than
the promotional one.   Its aim is to show how good service
films can be produced simply and inexpensively.

2428.   IN OLD CHICAGO.   A script of the 1938 film, by
          Lamar Trotti and Sonya Levien (director: Henry
          King).   263 p.   illus.   Beverly Hills: Twentieth
          Century Fox Film Corp., 1937.

2429.   In Search of Dracula, by Raymond McNally and Radu
          Florescu.   225 p.   illus.   Greenwich, Conn.:   New
          York Graphic Society, 1972.
          In this overview of all the aspects of the Dracula
legend, one chapter is devoted to "Bram Stoker and the Vam-
pire in Fiction and Film."   More important, perhaps, is the
filmography given at the book's conclusion which lists silent
and sound films from 1896 to 1971 that dealt with vampires.
Melies' THE HAUNTED CASTLE begins the list and THE
RETURN OF COUNT YORGA is the last film noted.   Noted
here for the record.

2430.   Inside Linda Lovelace, by Linda Lovelace.   184 p.
          (paperback) illus.   New York: Pinnacle Books,
          1973.
          For the few who may not have heard or seen Linda
Lovelace in recent months, she is the star of DEEP THROAT.
In a book that is supposedly an autobiography, the author tells
of her early life, the making of the film, and then offers
some sexual advice.   A group of pictures of the author from
the age of one to the present make up a centerfold gallery.
No one else intrudes on these photographs, which are of the
early Playboy variety.   The text, however, is something else
and deserves an X rating--only for adults over 21.   Ms.

Lovelace not only believes in sexual freedom but also in sexual excess.

There is some information about the making of the film but it is surrounded by sexual escapades and other fantasies. Most readers will be turned off after a few pages by the uninspired pornography and the author's apparently insatiable appetite for sexual adventure. Not for libraries but noted here for the record. Tina Russell, another porno film actress, covers the same ground and the same people in her book, Porno Star (2654).

2431. International Directory of 16mm Film Collectors, edited by Evan Forman. 69 p. (paperback) Mobile, Alabama (P.O. Box 969): E. Forman, 1973.

Mr. Evan publishes this directory from time to time. His information is obtained by requesting any collector who wishes to be listed to send him the particulars--name, address, types of films desired, gauge, etc. The listing is without cost but the catalog has a printed price of $15. In this recent issue, there are 5000 names arranged by state. Unfortunately, they are not arranged in any fashion under each state. Some entries do list the special interests of the collector, but most are simply names and addresses. A very specialized reference that is suitable only for large collections and for individual collectors.

2432. The International Encyclopedia of Film, edited by Dr. Roger Manvell. 574 p. illus. New York: Crown, 1972.

This reference concentrates on the world history of film as an art and as an industry. It avoids film technology and all other complex facets of film production. Between general terms (animation, censorship, documentary, screen writing) and the national cinemas of countries (Canada, India, Japan, Spain, etc.) are placed individual biographies (Brook, Louise; Lupino, Ida; Hunter, Ross; etc.) and definitions (bridge, dubbing, pre-release, etc.) In addition, there is 1) a chronological outline of film history with the major events of each year indicated; 2) a lengthy bibliography; 3) an index of principal title changes; 4) an index of films; and 5) an index of names.

Both color and black and white illustrations are used with considerable success. They support the text immeasurably and are reproduced with a clarity that is unusual today. The efforts of everyone concerned here should be applauded. It is an ideal reference book that belongs in every library.

2433.   IN THE MESH (L'ENGRENAGE). An unfilmed script,
         by Jean-Paul Sartre. 128 p. London: Andrew
         Dakers Limited, 1954.

2434.   An Introduction to Cinematography, by John Mercer.
         200 p. illus. Champaign, Ill.: Stipes, 1968.
         A much admired text on the basics of cinematography.
Emphasizes the practical rather than the theoretical, with
much attention to costs. However, the big studio influence
pervades.

2435.   Introduction to Film and TV Law, by Johnny Minus
         and William Storm Hale. illus. Hollywood, Cal.:
         Seven Arts Press, 1972.
         Announced as an introductory volume on film and
television law, the book will deal with such topics as contracts, copyright, right of privacy, taxation, F.C.C., libel,
guilds, unions, forms, obscenity, etc. The authors were
responsible for The Movie Industry Book (967).

2436.   ISADORA. 48 p. (paperback) illus. New York:
         Universal Picture Corp. , 1968.
         The story of Isadora Duncan is told in this souvenir
book both by narrative and photographs. There is also a
section on the making of the film. Individual attention is accorded stars Vanessa Redgrave, James Fox, and Jason Ro-
bards. Production, direction, and supporting cast credits
are also given.

2437.   IS PARIS BURNING?, by Nathan Weiss. 32 p.
         (paperback) illus. New York, 1966.
         This souvenir book is sprinkled liberally with quota-
tions from persons who played major roles in the liberation
of Paris from the Nazis. Historic background is provided
and there is some discussion of the making of the film. The
many stars are noted along with the production people and
supporting cast. The book is almost as confusing as the film.

2438.   The Italian Cinema, by Pierre Leprohon. 256 p.
         illus. New York: Praeger, 1972.
         An enormous amount of detailed information appears
in this most welcome critical history of the Italian film,
which is divided into seven periods: The Early Years (1895-
1908), The Golden Age (1909-1916), The Period of Decline
(1917-1929), The Cinema Under Fascism (1930-1943), The
Period of Neo-Realism (1943-1950), The Difficult Decade
(1951-1959), and New and Young Cinema (1960-1969). Each

is surveyed in depth and data on names, dates, locations, etc. are given along with critical comment, historical analyses, and trend identifications. The author uses a serious, rather determined approach that is compatible with the scholarly tone of the work. His evaluations of the classic Italian films are enlightening, balanced, and most valid. The frequent provision of background information about the making of the films is laudable.

Picture quality is acceptable, as are the notes, references, bibliography and the index. An added feature to be appreciated is a biographical dictionary of 150 people who have contributed to the shaping of the Italian cinema. This extended section (25 pages) is a reference work in itself. The quality of the content, its arrangement for reference use, and the production values all qualify this book for inclusion in all collections. It is a study that enriches film literature. Highly recommended.

2439. ITS A MAD, MAD, MAD, MAD WORLD. 36 p.
       (paperback) illus. New York: Mar-King Publishing Co., 1963.
       An account of the making of this challenging film opens this souvenir book. Its conception and the problem of using so many comedians to full advantage are discussed. Other interesting features of the book include a centerfold cartoon of all the performers, a two-page montage, and individual biographies of the stars, each written by one of the other performers in the film. Supporting players, director and producer are noted. A most satisfying program book.

2440. It's Only a Movie, by Clark McKowen, William Sparke and Mel Byars. 188 p. illus. Englewood Cliffs, N.J.: Prentice-Hall, 1972.
       Using quotations, visuals, interviews, quizzes, words, titles, advice, criticism, and many other print devices, the authors have put together a labyrinth on films and filmmaking. All of these items are put into Madison Avenue ad montages by Mel Byars. The appeal of this type of volume is dissipated quickly by the continual cuteness and the exhausting fragmentation of material. If experienced in small doses, like a book of crossword puzzles, it may be more rewarding. The list of literary and photo-art permissions runs two tightly-spaced, small-print pages, and indicates the number of participants in this McLuhan stew. The college student with some film background may be enthusiastic about the book, as will the film buff, but the general reader may well wonder what it is. Acceptable for academic collections.

2441.   It Was Fun While It Lasted, by Arthur H. Lewis.
320 p. illus. New York: Trident Press, 1973.
This lament for "the Hollywood that was" consists
mostly of observations and comments by the author supplemented by interviews with Mae West, Glenn Ford, Zsa Zsa
Gabor, Ida Lupino, Joan Blondell, Barbara Stanwyck, Betty
Blythe, Lewis Milestone, Dore Schary and John Wayne. No
connecting theme other than the general topic exists, and the
pieces bear little relationship to each other. However, they
are entertaining and they generate a range of emotions, from
sadness to hilarity. The book has been carelessly prepared
and errors--factual, grammatical, and spelling--abound. Not
essential, but acceptable for all collections.

2442.   I Was Born Greek, by Melina Mercouri. 253 p.
illus. Garden City, N.Y.: Doubleday, 1971.
Much of this autobiography is political but some attention is given to Mercouri's film work. Starting with her
film with Michael Cacoyannis, STELLA, she tells about her
initial meeting with Jules Dassin, their first film, HE WHO
MUST DIE, and making THE LAW, PHAEDRA, NEVER ON
SUNDAY, TOPKAPI and other films. A short collection of
photographs appears in the mid-section. The book is not indexed.
An attempt has been made by the author to duplicate
in words the Mercouri personality, which depends upon so
many diverse physical, emotional and mental elements. The
result is only partially successful. She is at her best when
she is the light comedienne, at her tedious worst when she
is the militant authoress. The autobiography has sufficient
pleasurable moments to make it acceptable for all collections.

2443.   James Bond in the Cinema, by John Brosnan. 176 p.
illus. New York: Barnes, 1972.
With the exception of the Bond fanatics, most readers
will find this book to be too much of a good thing. Beginning
with an appreciation, the book covers the seven James Bond
films with individual chapters devoted to each. Using the
film or film script as the structure, the author describes the
action, quotes a bit of dialogue and adds production information, novel-film comparisons, etc. The films are: DR. NO
(1962), FROM RUSSIA WITH LOVE (1963), GOLDFINGER
(1964), THUNDERBALL (1965), YOU ONLY LIVE TWICE
(1967), ON HER MAJESTY'S SECRET SERVICE (1969), DIA-
MONDS ARE FOREVER (1971).
The book is adequately illustrated and there are full
credit listings for the films in the appendix. One other appendix considers the offshoots of the Bond series--Matt Helm,

Derek Flint, Modesty Blaise, etc. For the devotees and
aficionados of Bond, the book will be a delight; others will
find it of moderate interest at best. For this reader, the
James Bond section found in series collections (2342, 2702)
would probably serve better. Acceptable for larger collections. Smaller collections should invest their money in one
of the above-mentioned series books.

2444. Japanese Cinema: Film Style and National Character,
by Donald Richie. 261 p. (paperback) illus. Garden City, N.Y.: Doubleday, 1971.
An updating of Richie's early works (796, 797), emphasizing themes, directors, and films of Japan. The volume
is illustrated, indexed, and contains a list of Japanese films
available in the United States. Recommended for all collections.

2445. Jazz in the Movies, by David Meeker. (paperback)
illus. London: British Film Institute, 1972.
Announced as an index to the work of jazz musicians
in the film.

2446. JESUS. An unfilmed script, by Carl Theodore
Dreyer (director: Carl Theodore Dreyer). 312 p.
illus. New York: Dial Press, 1972.
There is much more in this volume than the script
of Dreyer's planned film on the life of Jesus. Three essays
by Dreyer about the film and why he wanted to make it,
along with tributes to Dreyer from Renoir, Fellini, and
Truffaut, are included. An essay entitled "Working with
Dreyer" by Preben Thomsen and a short review of his career by Ib Monty also supplement the main text--the script
of JESUS, which is quite detailed, with many explanatory
paragraphs describing the shots and scenes. A fine collection of illustrations of stills from Dreyer's films introduces
the book in appropriate fashion.
The quality of this volume is high in all respects--
content, selection, arrangement and production. While a
script that was never filmed may have a limited appeal, the
remaining materials serve a double purpose: they enhance
the reading of JESUS and give background for the appreciation of Dreyer's other film classics. This is a beautifully
produced book that is recommended for all collections.

2447. Jolson, by Michael Freedland. 256 p. illus. New
York: Stein and Day, 1972.
This affectionate retelling of Jolson's life offers much
new information, with attention focused primarily on the per-

forming aspects: minstrels, theatre, recording, films, radio
and entertaining G.I.s. Apparently Jolson was an egomaniac
who only came completely alive when appearing before an
audience. Much of the book describes these performances.
His career in films never equalled his stage triumphs in the
World War I period. The only exception is the most famous
Jolson film, THE JOLSON STORY--an irony because he is
portrayed by another actor, Larry Parks. According to the
author, Jolson does play himself in one blackface number,
"Swanee," in that film.

The attention to his film appearances from an abor-
tive attempt with D. W. Griffith to RHAPSODY IN BLUE in
1943 is gratifying. The two biographical films, THE JOL-
SON STORY and JOLSON SINGS AGAIN get major attention,
but adequate mention is made of the others. There are some
things, however, that diminish the book's total effectiveness.
Time periods are treated casually by Freedland--e.g., did
Ruby Keeler sign for 42ND STREET in 1929? The portrait
of Ruby Keeler is altogether rather phantom-like and unsatisfactory. This is unfortunate since the Keeler-Jolson relationship is so important to the story. Perhaps the book is
at its best when persons who knew Jolson reminisce via anecdotes and professional put-downs. George Jessel's statement, "He was a no-good son of a bitch but he was the
greatest entertainer I've ever seen," tells the reader a great
deal in a few words. The author, for all his prose, fails
to provide such succinct clarity in his portrait.

Other weaknesses are the absence of 1) a filmography, 2) a discography, 3) a bibliography, and 4) a list
of theatrical appearances. Some photographs are included
but they seem carelessly chosen and they are poorly reproduced. The book is indexed. Jolson is a blend of strong
and weak (or absent) components that will bring mixed reactions from readers. With more attention to the research
and listing of specific performances, better illustrations, and
a more extensive use of the resource people, the book could
have been excellent. Because of its intelligent treatment of
the Jolson films, it can certainly be recommended for film
collections.

2448.   A Journal of the Plague Years, by Stefan Kanfer.
         306 p. illus. New York: Atheneum, 1973.
         Another book about those years from 1947 to 1962
when the HUAC, the blacklist, Red Channels, and J. Parnell
Thomas were familiar and frightening names to many persons
in show business. Kanfer takes to task all those who capit-
ulated in one form or another to the pressure; he is unfor-
giving of Elia Kazan and Larry Parks for having "sung" to

the HUAC, of talent agencies for having used the blacklist, and of film studios for their purges.

Although Robert Vaughn's book (2622) is superior in all respects, this volume indicates enough passionate anger on the part of the author to make the reader forgive some rather poor writing and organization. The conclusion of both books is similar: tracking down and punishing persons whose political views differ from those in power is not a new governmental activity. The warning is implicit throughout: to guard against a repetition of these events today. Acceptable for all collections.

2449. The Journal of The Society for Education in Film and Television, Autumn 1972, edited by Sam Rohdie. 136 p. (paperback) London: The Society for Education in Film and Television, 1972.

Although this is a journal available by subscription, its appearance is similar to many paperback books, and it is sold in individual issues in bookstores. For those reasons it is noted here. The Autumn 1972 issue is an anthology containing articles on John Ford's YOUNG MR. LINCOLN, Hitchcock's British films, cinema verité in America, and an interview with Ivor Montagu. The material is specialized and best suited for large collections.

2450. JUDGMENT AT NUREMBERG, by Mike Kaplan. 32 p. (paperback) illus. New York: Souvenir Program Co., 1961.

Black and white photography is used exclusively in this souvenir book, probably because of the nature of the film rather than for economic measures. The portraits of Tracy, Lancaster, Widmark, Dietrich, Schell, Garland and Clift are quite impressive. Writer Abby Mann and director-producer Stanley Kramer are also given attention. The story of the film is told largely by visuals and the supporting cast and production credits are given.

2451. JUDGMENT AT NUREMBERG. A script of the 1961 film, by Abby Mann (director: Stanley Kramer). 182 p. illus. London: Cassell, 1961. Contains cast and production credits.

2452. JULIUS CAESAR. 24 p. (paperback) illus. New York: Al Greenstone Co., 1953.

After the players, director, and producer are introduced in this souvenir book, the task of filming Shakespeare's play is discussed. Many stills from the picture and quotations from the play are used throughout. For the uninitiated, a synopsis is also provided.

2453.   KANAL. A script of the 1957 film, by Jerzy Stefan
         Stawinski (director: Andrzej Wajda). 239 p. (pa-
         perback) illus. New York: Simon & Schuster,
         1972.
         Found in The Wajda Trilogy (2861).

2454.   Karloff, by Peter Underwood. 238 p. illus. New
         York: Drake Publishers, 1972.
         It is difficult to believe that a man who created so
much excitement for so many audiences in several media
should be the victim of such a dull, uninspired biography.
The reason may be that only a few major sources--two previously published interviews and one actual meeting with
Karloff--are relied upon heavily. Other snippets of interviews, newspaper and magazine comments are used so frequently as to create an impression of padding. Another indication of stretching is the inclusion of several pages devoted
exclusively to Lon Chaney. The narrative section of the book,
then, is a recital of factual information dressed up to resemble a biography written with the complete cooperation of
the subject.
         The other sections of the book are more valuable
since they are straightforward reference--a bibliography, a
discography, and an annotated filmography. A detailed index
and a gallery of photographs are also assets. In summary,
the book is a mixed bag of the good, bad and indifferent. It
may do as a temporary source, enriched by its reference sections, but readers are advised to look at Gifford (2455) and
Ackerman (2304).

2455.   Karloff, The Man, The Monster, The Movies, by
         Denis Gifford. 352 p. (paperback) illus. New
         York: Curtis Books, 1973.
         Everything you've ever wanted to know about Boris
Karloff is probably contained in this volume. Starting with
a factual biography that is liberally sprinkled with quotes
from previously published articles and interviews, the book's
major section examines the Karloff films. He started his
screen career as an extra in Fairbank's HIS MAJESTY THE
AMERICAN in 1919 and was still active in HOUSE OF EVIL,
a film made for a Mexican company in 1968. For most of
the films, extended cast and production credits are given,
along with a detailed synopsis and some critical comment.
Occasionally an excerpt from a review is included. Closing
pages list his recordings, his writings, and a list of unfilmed productions that were announced as "vehicles" for

182

him. A small pictorial section suggests that, from the large number of films made by Karloff, a very fine pictorial account could be created. One did appear in the sixties but it was only 64 pages in length (810). The task of indexing this volume would have been enormous but it would have added greatly to the reference value.

There is little comparison between this excellent book, which appears in a modest production, and the more elaborate Underwood biography (2454). This one wins on nearly all criteria except size, visuals, and paper quality. Highly recommended for all collections.

2456.   Gene Kelly, by Michael Burrows. (paperback) illus. Cornwall, England: Primestyle, 1971.
Pictures, films, discussion about Kelly in the usual Burrows-Primestyle fashion. Acceptable for all collections.

2457.   KHARTOUM. 32 p. (paperback) illus. New York: Alsid Distributors, 1966.
Many of the pictures in this unusual souvenir book extend over two pages, across the width of the book. A comparison is made between the typical studio portrait and the actor made up for his role in this film. Attention is also given to research, costume design, action sequences, and the encampments used in the film. The usual cast and technical credits are noted. The book is as pleasantly surprising as was the film.

2458.   KING OF KINGS. 32 p. illus. 1961.
The usual format is followed in this souvenir book. Beginning with a prologue, the book offers the cast and the production in words and photographs. Closing sections are devoted to remaining cast and production credits. It should be emphasized that this is the book for the 1961 production which starred Jeffrey Hunter. A souvenir book was also produced for the 1927 silent version which starred H. B. Warner.

King Vidor on Filmmaking see Vidor.

2459.   KNIGHTS OF THE ROUND TABLE. 14 p. (paperback) illus. New York: Al Greenstone Co., 1954.
This modest souvenir book opens with the legend and the story followed by the cast and production credits. The photographs are rather unattractive; a color process was used that results in exaggerated hues rather than soft natural colors. Some attention is given to Cinemascope and how it differs from the normal ratio.

2460. KRAKATOA EAST OF JAVA. 32 p. (paperback)
       illus. 1969.
       A souvenir book which contains many shots from the
film, a synopsis, cast and production credits, and one section on the new single-projector Cinerama process. The use
of one projector rather than three narrows the field of vision
from 146 degrees to 120 degrees. This change hastened the
demise of the Cinerama process.

2461. Stanley Kubrick Directs, by Alexander Walker.
       272 p. (paperback) New York: Harcourt, Brace
       Jovanovich, 1971.
       This excellent account of the work and persona of
Kubrick appears at a time when the director's reputation is
quite high. From his first films, FEAR AND DESIRE and
KILLER'S KISS, to his later works, 2001: A SPACE ODYS-
SEY and A CLOCKWORK ORANGE, he has never failed to
bring artistry, excitement, and controversy to the film medium. His total filmography is rather short; it includes, in
addition to the above, PATHS OF GLORY, SPARTACUS,
LOLITA, DR. STRANGELOVE, and two early documentary
short films.
       The first portion of this book gives a narrative ac-
count of his career and films. Style and content are discussed next and the major portion of the book is devoted to
detailed analyses of three films: PATHS OF GLORY, DR.
STRANGELOVE and 2001: A SPACE ODYSSEY. It should
be noted that only a few descriptive pages are devoted to
A CLOCKWORK ORANGE since it was in production when
this book was being prepared. The text is impressive and
treats Kubrick and his films with affection and respect. The
photographs range from average to excellent, although many
of them are too small to be effective. An excellent addition
to all collections; likely to be very popular with young people.

       Stanley Kubrick's A CLOCKWORK ORANGE see 2149.

2462. [No entry]

2463. [No entry]

2464. LA DOLCE VITA, by Mario deVecchi. 24 p. (paper-
       back) illus. New York: National Publishers, 1961.
       A synopsis of the film is given in both text and
stills in this souvenir book. The cast is listed in the centerfold, in the chronological sequence in which they appear.
Technical credits are also given. Fellini and the major cast

names are given some special attention and there is an article entitled, "The Sweet Life's Hard Knocks" by Mario de Vecchi.

2465.   Lana: The Public and Private Lives of Miss Turner, by Joe Morella and Edward Z. Epstein. 297 p. illus. New York: Citadel Press, 1971.
       Based for the most part on public documents, previously published news releases, and private interviews, this unauthorized biography is an exercise for imaginative minds. Much of what is said is familiar but the chronological arrangement of the material and the carefully phrased innuendo suggest much more than is stated. As a result, a rather unhappy and at times lurid biography unfolds. The story of Lana Turner is told in terms of her films, her affairs, seven marriages, one sensational courtroom trial, a successful screen comeback, and a recent theatrical tour in "Forty Carats."
       The care that was necessary to avoid legal action is reflected continually by the text. The illustrations seem chosen with greater freedom. A center picture section covers almost all the personalities who played a role in Miss Turner's professional/private life. Index and filmography are omitted, probably because they would be of slight interest to the audience for whom this book was designed.
       The book has value only in its depiction of the minimal difference between Miss Turner's screen life and her personal life. Although it is not a vital addition to any film collection, the volume should enjoy great popularity with the non-discriminating general reader.

2466.   Landing Rightside Up in TV and Film, by G. William Jones. 128 p. (paperback) illus. Nashville: Abingdon Press, 1973.
       G. William Jones has given us another valuable little book in this attempt to offer some new advice on the problems of communicating with young people via television and films. Using a semi-serious programmed approach, the book consists of double-paged units, each having a cartoon on the left page and approximately one-half page of narrative on the right. The reader supposedly can read only those units which are pertinent to his need, but the book is so knowledgeable and entertaining that most users will probably read it all. Since Mr. Jones is not one to labor his points, the book is also concise, yet it does cover the major problems that film-users encounter. For example:
       What do you say before a film showing?

How do you capture the greatest benefit of a film or program in a follow-up discussion?
How do you find appropriate material?

The cartoon style may not please all readers--a tendency to overdraw seems evident. A simpler, uncluttered format would have been more in keeping with the text. A good bibliography is given. For anyone communicating with audiences of any age via films or television, the book is a most helpful aid. Recommended for all collections.

2467.   THE LANGUAGE OF FACES, by Paul A. Schreivogel. 20 p. (paperback) illus. Dayton, Ohio: Pflaum, 1970.
A study guide for the 1961 film directed by John Korty. Found in Films in Depth (2274) and also available separately.

2468.   Mario Lanza, by Matt Bernard. 224 p. (paperback) New York: Macfadden-Bartell, 1971.
This sensationalized biography emphasizes the excesses of Mario Lanza rather than his accomplishments. As a result, a most unflattering portrait of a gifted artist is presented. Many reconstructed conversations and some rather personal information cause the reader to wonder what Bernard's sources were. The book is nevertheless a fascinating curiosity, since it is the only one currently available on Lanza, who was always bigger than life, on screen and off.
There is no supporting material here--only the text. Because of its sexual content, the book is acceptable only for those collections serving a mature audience. A good biography of Lanza has yet to appear. This melange of gossip, innuendo, and sensationalism is a disservice to his memory. But if made available, it will undoubtedly be read.

2469.   Mario Lanza, Max Steiner, by Michael Burrows. (paperback) illus. Cornwall, England: Primestyle, 1971.
Another dual presentation--this time Mario Lanza and Max Steiner. Typical Burrows-Primestyle approach with illustrations, filmographies, comments, quotations, etc. Acceptable for all collections.

2470.   Las Vegas is My Beat, by Ralph Pearl. 251 p. illus. Secaucus, N.J.: Lyle Stuart, 1973.
A history of Las Vegas from the forties to the present, along with short vignettes of the artists who have appeared there. Since many film personalities have appeared

on the stages of Las Vegas, their respective fates there
make interesting reading. Tony Curtis, Susan Hayward,
Mario Lanza, Elvis Presley, Judy Garland, Jayne Mansfield,
Marlene Dietrich and others are discussed. The author is
a Las Vegas columnist and his writing style, his concept of
humor, and his sense of proportion are all deficient. Only
his subjects matter, and he succeeds in making them seem
deficient, too. The book is noted for the record.

2471.   Charles Laughton and Frederic March, by Michael
         Burrows. (paperback) illus. Cornwall, England:
         Primestyle, 1970.
         Another dual presentation with many photographs,
quotes, comments, filmography, etc. Acceptable for all collections.

2472.   LAWRENCE OF ARABIA, by John R. Woolfenden.
         32 p. (paperback) illus. New York: Richard
         Davis & Co., 1962.
         One of the better examples of a souvenir book. An
excellent section entitled "The Legend of Lawrence" is followed by some fold-out visuals and historical maps. Cast
and production names are treated in some detail, and there
is a Lawrence chronology plus a bibliography.

2473.   Leading Film Discussions, by Madeline S. Fried-
         lander. 42 p. (paperback) New York: League of
         Women Voters, 1972.
         This valuable little book is divided into four main
sections: Planning a Program, Conducting a Discussion,
Training Leaders via Workshops, and Making Arrangements
for the Program. The final section is devoted to films and
film sources. Each section is a small treasure by itself.
Together they form a vital reference for anyone who uses
film with an audience. Most of the suggestions and advice
are first rate, practical, and pertinent. The list of recommended films reflects the interests of the League and deals
mostly with environment, government, urban problems, racial problems and the United Nations. A bibliography and
a directory of film sources conclude the volume.
         The material offered here is unique and should sug-
gest to both the beginner and the experienced professional
many new ways in which a film-discussion program can be
improved. An essential book for all libraries; a copy should
also be placed in the professional's collection.

2474.   Val Lewton: The Reality of Terror, by Joel E.

187

Siegel. 176 p. (paperback) illus. New York: Viking, 1973.

This long awaited book on the films that Val Lewton produced during the forties is completely satisfying; in most ways it is equal to the quality of the previous volumes in the fine Cinema One series. An account of Lewton's life and work opens the book. Included here are references to older interviews, letters, reminiscences of people who worked with Lewton, and background information about making the films. The films themselves occupy the second portion of the book. Cast and production credits are given, with a short plot synopsis and some production data. A critical essay follows in which the author evaluates in depth the strengths and weaknesses of each film.

Lewton's films number only 14 and some of the later ones were quite undistinguished, but the popularity, the frequency on TV, and the critical rediscovery of I WALKED WITH A ZOMBIE, THE SEVENTH VICTIM, ISLE OF THE DEAD, THE BODY SNATCHERS and others more than justify this book's attention. Siegel has written with enthusiasm, respect, and a scholar's eye. Along with the comprehensive coverage of a relatively short career, he has included bits of information which fascinate and surprise--e.g., was Hitchcock's shower scene in PSYCHO really lifted or suggested by Lewton's THE SEVENTH VICTIM?

The illustrations are disappointing, not so much in their selection as in their reproduction. Many are given only a third of a page and in some there is too much contrast, the black being far too dark. The book is not indexed but there is a list of Lewton's credits to 1937, compiled by himself. By his sympathetic understanding of his subject, Siegel has provided a tribute to Lewton unlike any received in his lifetime. A fine book that can be recommended for all collections.

2475.   The Library of Communication Techniques (A series). illus. New York: Hastings House, 1973.

This excellent series is published by Hastings House in cooperation with Focal Press of London. The titles provide a complete basic library in the techniques of filmmaking. Each volume is handsomely produced with many illustrations, diagrams, charts and other visuals. While the texts tend to range from basic introduction to more complex technical matters, they are usually comprehensible to most readers. The books are constantly revised and updated to keep pace with technological change and innovations in practice. The titles include:

The Technique of Documentary Film Production (1323)
The Technique of Editing 16mm Films (1324)
The Technique of Film Animation (1326)
The Technique of Film Cutting Room (1330)
The Technique of Film Editing (1327)
The Technique of Film and Television Makeup (1325)
The Technique of Film Music (1328)
The Technique of Lighting for Television and Motion Pictures (2783)
The Technique of Motion Picture Camera (1331)
The Technique of Sound Studio (1332)
The Technique of Special Effects Cinematography (1329)

2476.   Life and Death in Hollywood. (paperback) illus.
         Cincinnati, Ohio: Zebra Picture Books, 1950.
         This small photograph collection covers familiar
ground, mostly the Hollywood scandals, but with visuals rather than text. Divided into chapters, the predictable subjects
appear in chronological order: D. W. Griffith, Mack Sennett,
Mary Pickford, Fatty Arbuckle, Wally Reid, William Desmond Taylor, Chaplin, Valentino, Garbo, Clara Bow, Harlow,
and Hayworth. Noted here as one of the early picture books
--a preview of the genre that was to appear in the sixties
via Citadel, Crown and other publishers.

2477.   The Life and Legend of Tom Mix, by Paul E. Mix.
         206 p. illus. New York: Barnes, 1972.
         The author, who is not directly related to Tom Mix,
has done an enormous amount of investigation in preparing
this biography. Unfortunately, its base of research-data
shows continually through the narrative which, instead of inviting reader involvement, becomes largely a recital of facts,
quotes, and historical references. Its intention and its thoroughness must be admired, but it is not much fun to read.
         The pedantic-statistical text might have been more
palatable if greater care had been taken with the numerous
illustrations. The selection shows depth (the home of the
employer of Tom's father), originality (the highway marker
denoting Mix's fatal accident) and variety (stills, frames,
posters, ads and candids), but all of these qualities are defeated by murky production, over-exposure and fuzzy printing.
Granted that some of the original material has deteriorated,
it should be possible to obtain better quality control over the
illustrations.
         The impressive research carries over to the appendix which lists the museums, libraries, and companies that
provided materials on Mix. A good filmography is given

and some microfilm records are described but their location
is not noted. Had the author been able to apply some critical, analytical and narrative style to his talent for research,
this would be a far more entertaining book. Devotees of
western films will probably find the book quite satisfying and
it does provide much reference material on Mix. On this
latter basis, it is acceptable for inclusion in all film collections.

2478.   THE LIFE AND TIMES OF JUDGE ROY BEAN. A
         script of the 1972 film, by John Milius. (director:
         John Huston). 180 p. (paperback) illus. New
         York: Bantam, 1973.
         Contains cast and production credits.

2479.   The Life of Robert Taylor, by Jane Ellen Wayne.
         349 p. (paperback) illus. New York: Warner
         Books, 1973.
         Biographies of screen personalities range widely in
quality and it is unusual for one as good as this to be published as an original paperback. It exhibits some interesting
features, including the author's access to many letters written by Taylor and the cooperation of many persons close to
him. While outside sources and references are few, the
privileged inside information seems plentiful.
         The portrait that emerges is not one of charisma or
strength. Taylor was a beautiful male who lacked aggressive-
ness. For much of his life he was a puppet dominated by
his mother, by his wife (Barbara Stanwyck), and by Louis B.
Mayer. His ever-present concern about his masculine image
would obviously make an interesting psychoanalytical study.
Even toward his life's end, he seemed content to relinquish
his role as master in favor of fussiness, penny-pinching and
image-worry. The portrait of Stanwyck presented here is
fascinating: constantly sedated, hard, foul-mouthed, and
money-hungry--another meaty role, but this time self-created.
         A few pictures show Taylor with his more famous
leading ladies. There is no index but a rather good filmography completes the volume. Only infrequently does the book
lapse into questionable taste, and that mostly when sex is the
topic. The recreated dialogue may bother some purists, too,
but, all in all, this is a better-than-average biography. The
book can be highly recommended for public libraries and is
a good addition to all film collections.

2480.   A Life on Film, by Mary Astor. 245 p. (paper-
         back) illus. New York: Dell, 1972.

The genre of film biography goes forward a few steps with this fascinating, absorbing life story. Miss Astor's first volume, Mary Astor, My Story (79), emphasized her personal life, with little attention given to her many films. The situation is reversed here and the bulk of this volume tells about the films, her co-workers, and the industry. The privileges, responsibilities and the disadvantages of being the "total professional" are fully delineated. In her writing, as on the screen, Miss Astor has the ability of the true artist --that of being able to command the sympathy and respect of an audience without apparently trying for it. In turn, she can be intellectual, witty, compassionate, and even bitchy, but she always appears totally honest. At the book's conclusion, she emerges with stature, not only as a consistently fine actress but as a strong human being.

The photographs in the paperback edition are only fair. The book does contain a filmography, listing rather complete credits for 109 feature films in which she appeared. There is also an index which is quite helpful. It is a pleasure to give high recommendation to a film star autobiography. This one is in the same thoroughbred class as Bette Davis' The Lonely Life and can be placed without hesitation in any film collection. Miss Astor obviously deserves one more award.

2481.   The Life That Late He Led, by George Eels. 447 p. (paperback) illus. New York: Berkley Publishing, 1967.

Most people associate Cole Porter with the Broadway theatre, and rightfully so. What they may not be aware of is his long and prolific musical contribution to motion pictures. Not only were many of his stage musicals translated into film, but he wrote several memorable original scores for films. His filmography is fascinating: 1929, BATTLE OF PARIS; 1930, 50 MILLION FRENCHMEN; 1934, WAKE UP AND DREAM and THE GAY DIVORCE; 1935, ADIOS, ARGENTINA; 1936, BORN TO DANCE and ANYTHING GOES; 1937, ROS-ALIE; 1938, BREAK THE NEWS; 1939, THE SUN NEVER SETS; 1940, BROADWAY MELODY OF 1940; 1941, YOU'LL NEVER GET RICH; 1942, SOMETHING TO SHOUT ABOUT and PANAMA HATTIE; 1943, DUBARRY WAS A LADY and LET'S FACE IT; 1944, HOLLYWOOD CANTEEN and MISSIS-SIPPI BLUE; 1945, NIGHT AND DAY; 1946, THE PIRATE; 1949, ADAM'S RIB; 1953, KISS ME KATE; 1956, HIGH SO-CIETY; 1957, SILK STOCKINGS and LES GIRLS; and 1960, CAN-CAN.

The volume also contains a 1936 diary of his days in Hollywood, preparing his first full score for the film

BORN TO DANCE. Names of film celebrities proliferate in this detailed and factual book. Porter's wit, talent, courage, and sophistication are made known in an affectionate but objective text by Eels. For those who were adults during Porter's reign as one of America's top composers, the book is a total pleasure.

The book is indexed, contains a few illustrations and a chronological listing of all Porter's musical activities. Although only partially concerned with film composing, this volume can be recommended for all collections.

2482.   Light of a Star, by Gwen Robyns. 256 p. illus.
         New York: Barnes, 1970.
         The American edition of the Vivien Leigh biography that appeared in England two years earlier. It is surprisingly good and many of the usual criticisms of star biography cannot be applied here. A rather clear portrait of the complex person that Vivien Leigh was does emerge by the book's end. According to the author, Miss Leigh was a total professional and a perfectionist, always working to improve her performances--with only one notable exception, her role as wife to Laurence Olivier. She seems to have taken that part for granted and the discovery of the marriage's failure was a principal cause of her early death. The text notes her positive qualities such as thoughtfulness, humility, and emotional control, and balances them against her over-ambition, vanity, and a candor that could be mistaken for bitchery.

Some attention given to her major films--GONE WITH THE WIND, A STREETCAR NAMED DESIRE, THE ROMAN SPRING OF MRS. STONE and SHIP OF FOOLS. The important film neglected is CAESAR AND CLEOPATRA; other than noting friction between Gabriel Pascal and Leigh, not much is said about her fine performance. Ironically, all her theatrical appearances, including out of town failures, are described in detail. The author handles discreetly and sensitively the nervous breakdowns, sicknesses, emotional relationships, and other happenings in the star's personal life. There are some illustrations, but they fail completely to capture the physical beauty of this fine actress. The book is indexed but a listing of the plays and films, which would seem essential, is not given.

The total portrait given here is affectionate yet objective, probably because much of the author's material came from persons who knew Vivien Leigh. The book is a deserved tribute to a fine actress and a complex human being. Recommended for those collections serving a mature audience.

2483.   Light Up Your Torches and Pull Up Your Tights, by
         Tay Garnett. 416 p. illus. New Rochelle, N.Y.:
         Arlington House, 1973.
         Tay Garnett had a variety of careers before he be-
came a writer for Mack Sennett in the twenties. Since that
time he has been writing and directing films and in recent
years has been most active in television. The richness of
his experience should have resulted in a far better autobiography than this. But his films leave one with the feeling
that they could have been much better in most instances if
Garnett had greater control and discipline, and the book
reads the same way: narrative and interest are sacrificed
in favor of a gag, a wisecrack, or an unimportant anecdote.
         Often he refuses to state the reasons why a film did
not succeed, sometimes using courtesy as his out: "As a
kindness to many people, I shall forgo a recital of most of
the tragedies of that misbegotten film." Most of the personalities who populate his little stories are presented in sugar-
coated prose: "gallant Gable ... utterly lovely Martha Scott
... serious-minded Robert Taylor ... multi-talented Gene
Kelly ... wise Walter Pidgeon ... etc." A fear of becoming
too serious seems to hover over the narrative which loses
reader involvement by using many unrelated shots rather than
settling for a well-defined scene.
         Illustrations are quite small and mounted several to
a page. This is acceptable for portraits but the reader will
have to squint to see some of the actors mentioned in the
captions. An index, a filmography and a listing of TV and
radio credits are added values. Acceptable for all collections.

2484.   LILIES OF THE FIELD. A script of the 1963 film,
         by James Poe (director: Ralph Nelson). 394 p.
         (paperback) illus. New York: Globe Book Co.,
         1972.
         Included in Three Major Screenplays (2805). The
script is preceded by: 1) "About the Author," 2) "About
the Screenplay"; and is followed by: 1) "What the Critics
Said," and 2) "To Enrich Your Reading."

2485.   LILITH. A script of the 1963 film, by Robert Ros-
         sen (director: Robert Rossen). 274 p. (paperback)
         illus. New York: Doubleday, 1972.
         Found in Three Screenplays (2806).

2486.   Vachel Lindsay: The Poet as Film Theorist, by
         Glenn Joseph Wolfe. 191 p. New York: Arno,
         1973.

One of six doctoral dissertations on film topics which are reproduced exactly by Arno as submitted to the degree-granting institutions. Probably the first American to advance a theory of film was the poet-writer, Vachel Lindsay (75). This study concentrates on Lindsay's film writings and looks at the factors which influenced him: his interest in many arts--sculpture, painting, architecture, etc.--and his concern with religion, politics, society, and his fellow man, all of which had an effect on his interpretation of film as art.

The first section deals with his social views, ideas on art, and his religious beliefs. Social problems and how film could help in solving them is considered next. Other sections indicate the relationships between Lindsay's social beliefs and his theories on the arts, including film. A final section compares Lindsay's theories and those of his contemporaries. A bibliography is included. Acceptable for large academic collections.

2487. THE LION IN WINTER. 32 p. (paperback) illus. New York: Ronark Program Co., 1968.
A map of the domains which provide the motivation for the story is given at the beginning of this souvenir book. Some historical background precedes a discussion of the making of the film. Tribute is paid to the cast and production personnel in the final sections of this impressive book. Production values here are much above the average.

2488. THE LION IN WINTER. A script of the 1968 film, by James Goldman (director: Anthony Harvey). 139 p. (paperback) illus. New York: Dell Publishing Co., 1968.

2489. The Lions of LIVING FREE, by Jack Couffer. 96 p. illus. New York: E. P. Dutton, 1972.
Jack Couffer's career as a naturalist photographer, which began with Walt Disney, was described in his book, Song of Wild Laughter (1256). Recently, Couffer directed two films for other studios--RING OF BRIGHT WATER and LIVING FREE. It is the making of the latter film that is related in this book. Attention is given to the actors--Susan Hampshire and Nigel Davenport--the lions, the territory of East Africa and its people. The film was an unsuccessful attempt to duplicate the success of the original, BORN FREE. Just as audiences felt that one film about a mature woman's "attraction" to lions was quite enough, the reader will find most of this account familiar and predictible. The book On Playing With Lions (1066), which accompanied the original film, covered some of the same material presented here.

There are some illustrations which are consistent with the total effort--flat, unimaginative, and repetitive. No index is provided. Chalk this book up as a sequel which depended upon another sequel. A case of too much inbreeding resulting in an anemic offspring. Young readers may have some interest in this book but it is not generally recommended.

2490. The Literature of Cinema (Arno Press Cinema Program--A Series). General Editors: George Amberg and Martin S. Dworkin. New York: Arno Press, 1972.

This ambitious and commendable publishing series has made another 36 books on film available. The first grouping in 1970 included 48 titles (858). Prices range from $7 to $65 for individual books. With these books, libraries should exercise care and selection since the volumes in this series vary in audience appeal.

Titles in the second series selected by George Amberg include:

Friese-Greene: Close-Up of an Inventor (576)
Theory of the Film (1348)
Let's Go to the Movies (843)
Brigitte Bardot and the Lolita Syndrome (93)
Art and Design in the British Film (64)
Report on Blacklisting, Part I (1165)
Que Viva Mexico (1143)
Dynamics of the Film (331)
The Odyssey of a Film-Maker (1059)
Charlie Chaplin (190)
Hollywood on Trial (697)
Hollywood Scapegoat (701)
The Film Answers Back (438)
Anatomy of the Film (41)
The Use of the Film (1405)

Three original compilation volumes complete the Amberg selections:

The Art of the Cinema (2033)
Origins of the American Film (340, 103, 816)
Hound and Horn (2400)

The complete GREED of Erich von Stroheim (2167) is a separate Arno publication edited by Herman Weinberg, that can be considered as part of the series.

Martin S. Dworkin selected 17 titles for this series which include:

Around Cinemas, 2 Volumes (62)
Cinematographic Annual, 2 Volumes (2135)

Scrutiny of Cinema (1205)
British Film Music (161)
The Motion-Picture Cameraman (2552)
Movement (2560)
Sociology of Film (1254)
Film and Theatre (433)
20 Years of British Film, 1925-1945 (1388)
Soviet Cinema (1261)
Scandinavian Film (1189)
The Italian Cinema (783)
French Film (575)
50 Years of German Film (417)

2491.   THE LITTLE ISLAND, by Paul A. Schreivogel.
         20 p. (paperback) illus. Dayton, Ohio: Pflaum,
         1970.
         A study guide for the 1958 film directed by Richard
Williams. Found in Films in Depth (2274) and also available
separately.

2492.   LITTLE MURDERS. A script of the 1968 film, by
         Jules Feiffer (director: Alan Arkin). 144 p. (pa-
         perback) illus. New York: Paperback Library,
         1968.

2493.   LIVING FREE, by Leonard Reeves. 14 p. (paper-
         back) illus. London: Sackville Smeets, 1972.
         The film that this souvenir book honors, a spin-off
of BORN FREE, did not fare nearly as well as its predeces-
sor. The few pages are devoted to articles with such titles
as: "The Men Who Took Lions to Kenya," "The Film That
Couldn't Be Made," "Facts About Lions," etc. Carl Foreman, the producer, is the only human to receive individual
attention.

2494.   THE LONGEST DAY, by Fred Hift. 40 p. (paper-
         back) illus. New York: Program Publishing Com-
         pany, 1962.
         The profile of producer Darryl F. Zanuck which
opens this souvenir book is followed by a section entitled
"Making THE LONGEST DAY Come True--Again." Many of
the visuals are candid shots taken during the making of the
film. There are also shots from the film, maps, line drawings, and small photographs of the cast members. The official cast credits are divided into four sections: Who's Who
in the American Cast, the British Cast, the French Cast,
and the German Cast.

2495.   LORD JIM.   28 p.   (paperback)   illus.   New York:
         Mar-King Publishing, 1964.
         Perhaps the outstanding feature of this souvenir book
is the use of large stills from the film.   Richard Brooks, the
writer-director of the film, gets attention, as do the major
cast members.   One page is given to Joseph Conrad, author
of the book upon which the film is based.   Other cast and
production credits are noted.

2496.   LOS OLVIDADOS.   A script of the 1950 film, by
         Luis Buñuel, Luis Alcoriza and Oscar Dancigers
         (director: Luis Buñuel).   299 p.   (paperback)   illus.
         New York: Simon and Schuster, 1972.
         Contains: "Cruelty and Love in LOS OLVIDADOS"
by Andre Bazin; credits and cast.   Found in: THE EXTER-
MINATING ANGEL, NAZARIN, LOS OLVIDADOS (2225).

2497.   LOVE AT TWENTY.   A script of the 1962 film, by
         Francois Truffaut (director: Francois Truffaut).
         320 p.   illus.   New York: Simon and Schuster, 1971.
         Contained in The Adventures of Antoine Doinel (2006).
LOVE AT TWENTY was an international sketch film with por-
tions directed by Marcel Ophuls, Renzo Rossellini, Andrzej
Wajda, Shintaro Ishihara, and Truffaut.   The script referred
to here is for the Truffaut episode entitled ANTOINE AND
COLETTE.

2498.   LOVES OF A BLOND.   A script of the 1965 film,
         by Milos Forman, Jaroslav Papousek and Ivan Pas-
         ser (director: Milos Forman).   (paperback)   illus.
         London: Lorrimer, 1972.
         Found in Milos Forman (2298).   Announced for pub-
lication by Simon and Schuster.

2499.   LOVE STORY, by Marvin Saunders.   28 p.   (paper-
         back)   illus.   New York: National Publishers Inc.,
         1970.
         Consisting mostly of stills from the film, this sou-
venir book is rather unimpressive.   Brief biographies of Ali
McGraw, Ryan O'Neal, Ray Milland, John Marley, producer
Howard G. Minsky, director Arthur Hiller and author Erich
Segal are given.   Perhaps the most interesting feature is an
advertisement from the publishers for 32 other titles in the
souvenir book series that they publish.   This is the first
such instance noted.

2500.   The LOVE STORY Story, by Nicholas Meyer.   224 p.
         (paperback)   illus.   New York: Avon, 1971.

197

Meyer was the unit publicist on LOVE STORY, which meant that all material about the making of the film had to go through his hands. Much of it is repeated here. In an introduction, he promises to be honest rather than protective. To a degree he succeeds, but nearly all the participants emerge as rather saintly figures and one assumes that, if honest, he also does not tell all. The account is nevertheless quite detailed, although much of it is trivial. It does give the reader a final impression of having "been with" the film from beginning to end.

There are portraits of Ali McGraw, Ryan O'Neal, Arthur Hiller, Howard Minsky, Erich Segal and others. The similarity of LOVE STORY to CAMILLE is noted also. The book is nicely illustrated but there is no index. This is an interesting account of present-day filmmaking that is sure to please those readers who know LOVE STORY as a film, a book, or both. Recommended for all collections.

2501.   Low Budget Features, by William O. Brown. 240 p. (paperback) illus. Hollywood, Cal. (1054 N. Cahuenga): W. O. Brown, 1971.

This volume is available only from its author at the address given above. Most of the elements involved in making low-budget films are discussed: finance, budget, schedules, etc. Charts and forms are pictured, and other data is presented. The approach is a no-nonsense straightforward one that emphasizes spareness and efficiency, which are essential to anyone interested in low-budget features.

2502.   Lucy: The Bitter Sweet Life of Lucille Ball, by Joe Morella and Edward Z. Epstein. 281 p. illus. Secaucus, N.J.: Lyle Stuart, 1973.

Lucille Ball has been a performer for more than 40 years. This unauthorized biography describes both her personal and professional life, with the emphasis on the years following the early fifties. It was then, with the enormous success of "I Love Lucy," that she was able to synthesize all her previous experiences as a chorus girl, extra, dramatic actress, comedienne, singer, dancer and general all-around performer. The book skips over the early film years and concentrates on the relationships with Desi Arnaz, their children, Luci and Desi, Jr., and finally her second marriage to Gary Morton. Some attention is given the accusation that she had "Communist Ties" during the witch-hunt years of Joe McCarthy.

Two sections of photographs are average in quality, but there is no index or filmography. Acceptable until a fully documented biography appears.

2503.   MACKENNA'S GOLD. 32 p.   (paperback) illus.
1969.
Gold is the major motivation in the film upon which
this souvenir book is based.   Beginning with a map, the
book relates gold with the land, the people, and their quest
for same.   The usual cast and production credits are given.

2504.   Macmillan Audio-Brandon Films, edited by Michael
Kerbel and Robert Edelstein.   630 p.   Mount Vernon,
N.Y.:   Macmillan Audio-Brandon, 1973.
This beautiful catalog, subtitled "16mm Collection of
International Cinema, 1974-75," belongs in every film collec-
tion.   Resembling a Sears Roebuck Catalog in size and shape,
the book is divided into three major sections: Feature Films,
Experimental Films and Short Films.   The sound feature,
the silent feature and the silent short categories are sub-
divided by country of origin.   Experimental films are placed
into the classic period, American, foreign, and miscellaneous.
The sound short films are arranged according to subject area
(art, music, etc.), with special listings accorded Robert
Benchley, W. C. Fields, Laurel and Hardy, and Mack Sennett.
The sound feature films are the major product, and
the greatest attention is given to them, with representation
of some 30 countries in 448 pages.   Additional features include an index of selected directors with a filmography beneath each, and an alphabetical title list.   The majority of
films are treated individually with many occupying a complete
page.   For example, the entry for GIANT gives the year of
release, running time, color, rental schedule, and rather
complete cast and production credits.   A short plot outline
is followed by background information, interpretation, and a
listing of awards or recognition the film received.   A few
critical excerpts, some of which are a paragraph or more,
are also given.   Four stills from the picture are placed
around the side and bottom of the page.
The book is a browser's delight, but its reference
value cannot be overemphasized.   Information on many of the
foreign films is not easy to retrieve elsewhere, but locating
it here is a simple operation.   How easy is it, for example,
to find information on a film called A WORKER'S DIARY?
It happens to be one of the six films described quite satisfactorily on pages 206-207 in a section entitled "Films From
Finland."
Obviously the purpose of the catalog is to promote,
encourage and facilitate the rental of films.   The by-product
of good will engendered by making such a fine book available
can only be an eventual source of satisfaction (and profit)

to Macmillan Audio-Brandon. Simply stated, this book belongs in every film collection. It is a blend of commerce, publishing, and film art that is highly recommended.

2505. Steve McQueen: Star on Wheels, by William Nolan. 143 p. (paperback) New York: Berkley (Medallion Books), 1972.
Equal time is given to McQueen's racing and professional experiences. The biographical portion is largely factual, with a sprinkling of statements from McQueen obtained during several interviews done originally for a racing magazine. This appears to be a spinoff of that material supplemented with additional information obtained from McQueen's friends and professional associates.
The films are mentioned ever so quickly, with only BULLITT and LE MANS getting extended coverage. No critical judgments are made about the films and the book closes with what already seems an ironic tribute to the lasting McQueen marriage to Neile Adams. There are no illustrations, filmography or index.
If the reader skips over the racing portions, he will have the equivalent of a magazine article on McQueen's life and career. While this biographical content is similar in style to that found in some higher priced volumes, it is too abbreviated to serve as anything but a temporary source. Until a fuller treatment of McQueen is written, this book is acceptable.

2506. The Magic Factory: How MGM Made AN AMERICAN IN PARIS, by Donald Knox. 217 p. illus. New York: Praeger, 1973.
Called an oral history by the author, this volume is really a group of interviews, broken apart and re-set as a mosaic on a specific example of filmmaking. In addition, the working of a major studio during the declining years of Hollywood is exemplified. The quotes are from a wide variety of personalities--director, stars, prop men, and other studio workers, including an office boy. The statements were made in 1970, some two decades after the film's release. Supporting this unusual text, there are illustrations, sketches, diagrams, script excerpts, budget forms, and advertising posters. All of these are clearly reproduced, although the color of the film is missing. Musical numbers are noted in the appendix, along with the staff list and the cast. Andrew Sarris has written a foreword and there is a preface by the author.
With this provocative manner of recreating a specific experience and a general era, the author has acted unobtru-

sively; but one senses that the interviews, their rearrangement, and the background research were not small challenges. This is a fine reading experience that can be recommended for all collections. Using it before a viewing of the film would seem to be a prime example of what film study is all about.

2507. MAIDSTONE, A Mystery. A script of the 1968 film, by Norman Mailer (director: Norman Mailer). 191 p. (paperback) illus. New York: Signet, 1971.
Includes: "A Combined Account of the Filming of MAIDSTONE," by Sally Beauman, J. Anthony Lukas and James Toback; "A Course in Filmmaking," by Norman Mailer; "A Numbered Listing of the Shots/Cuts in the Dream Sequence"; foreword, notes, cast, production credits by Norman Mailer.

2508. MAJOR BARBARA. A script of the 1941 film, by Bernard Shaw (director: Gabriel Pascal). 160 p. (paperback) illus. Baltimore: Penguin Books, 1951.

2509. Make Your Own Professional Movies, by Nancy Goodwin and James N. Manilla. 209 p. New York: Macmillan, 1971.
This book on filmmaking describes the act rather than giving "how-to" instruction. Relying completely on words to express the art of filmmaking is a courageous act but in this case not an especially successful or rewarding one. Most of the book is pure exposition--first a glossary, then the role of the crew, sample scripts to shoot, movie festivals and contests to enter, etc.
Emphasis on the different topics is puzzling. The instruction on editing and splicing is given in a total of six pages. The suggested scripts use more than 113 pages. Although there is a "helpful hints" approach to the material that some readers may appreciate, most will be disappointed by the imbalance in the text. The word "professional" in the title is certainly a misnomer. With no index and no illustrations to support the questionable text, the book cannot be recommended for any perceivable situation. The quality of other available volumes--Bobker (2511), for example--is much superior to that of this book.

2510. Making Films Work For Your Community, by The Committee on Community Use of Film. 71 p. (paperback) illus. New York: Educational Film Library Association, 1946.

This short anthology treats topics such as community film problems, managing a film forum, film aesthetics, film sources and the use of equipment. Later sections are devoted to film programs in small communities, public libraries, museums, churches, and young people's groups. Much of the material is still valid and, of course, the general topic is more important than ever. However, the anthology approach to this vital community service is too fragmented to be effective or useful. An up-dating by a single author might provide the unifying quality that this volume lacks.

2511.   Making Movies: From Script to Screen, by Lee R. Bobker with Louise Marinis. 304 p. (paperback) illus. New York: Harcourt, Brace, Jovanovich, 1973.

As the title indicates, this volume attempts to explain the filmmaking process from script to screen. Attention is paid to both the technical and creative aspects: scripts, budgets and schedules are considered first, with cinematography, sound recording, and editing following as the major emphases of the book. Some shorter final sections deal with film distribution and careers. Suggested reading and viewing lists follow many of the sections.

The description above cannot convey in any way the quality, depth and inclusiveness of the book. Readers familiar with Bobker's Elements of Film (358) will have some idea of what to expect but even they will be surprised at the excellence here. The structure is linear--pre-film, filming, and post-filming--and logical. The content is comprehensive, not-overly technical, and supported by a very fine collection of visuals. All are beautifully reproduced, with several in full color, and in addition, there are charts, diagrams and contractual forms.

The book may be used by many audiences--filmmakers, students, general readers, etc. Since it is indexed, it can answer many questions about filmmaking that arise in classrooms and libraries. This is the best book on filmmaking to appear in the 70s thus far. It is enthusiastically recommended for all collections. Teachers of filmmaking should consider it as a text for their courses.

2512.   The Making of ONE DAY IN THE LIFE OF IVAN DENISOVICH, by Alexander Solzhenitsyn and Ronald Harwood. 271 p. (paperback) illus. New York: Ballantine, 1971.

This volume contains: 1) An introduction by Ronald Harwood which tells how the film was made; 2) The original story by Alexander Solzhenitsyn, translated by Gillon Aitken;

3) The screenplay by Ronald Harwood; 4) Cast and production credits.

2513.   Making Wildlife Movies: A Beginner's Guide, by
         Christopher Parsons. 224 p. illus. Harrisburg,
         Pa.: Stackpole, 1971.
         Expert advice from an experienced professional who
enjoys his work and is able to communicate his enthusiasm
to his audience. Acceptable for all collections.

2514.   Making Your Own Movies, by Harry Helfman. 95 p.
         illus. New York: Morrow, 1970.

2515.   Rouben Mamoulian: Style is the Man, edited by
         James R. Silke. 35 p. (paperback) illus. Wash-
         ington, D.C.: The American Film Institute, 1971.
         A transcription of an interview with Mamoulian held
in April 1970 at the AFI Center in Beverly Hills. Includes
a bibliography, a filmography, and a listing of the stage productions that Mamoulian was involved with. The book has an
index-guide to the topics discussed during the interview and
a few illustrations. Acceptable for all collections and recommended for the larger ones.

2516.   A MAN FOR ALL SEASONS. 31 p. (paperback)
         illus. Englewood Cliffs, N.J.: Ronark Program
         Co., 1966.
         This souvenir book is made up mostly of stills from
the film. Some attention is given to the cast members and
production personnel, but director Fred Zinnemann and play-
wright Robert Bolt--who was responsible for the script taken
from his original play--are the special subjects of this interesting volume.

2517.   MAN OF LA MANCHA. 30 p. (paperback) illus.
         Englewood Cliffs, N.J.: Charnell Theatrical Ent.,
         1972.
         Dale Wasserman, the author of the original play,
contributes an opening article entitled "A Long Time in La
Mancha." The remainder of this souvenir book is devoted
to telling the story with illustrations and narrative. Photographic quality is extremely variable. Individual pages are
given to Peter O'Toole, Sophia Loren, James Coco, and
director Arthur Hiller. Other cast and production credits
are listed.

2518.   Jayne Mansfield, by May Mann. 277 p. illus. New
         York: Drake Pub., 1973.

A biography that emphasizes the sensational rather than the professional, this book by a Hollywood columnist who was a friend of Ms. Mansfield is never dull--just badly written. When you consider that the subject was a Philadelphia Main Liner with an I.Q. of 163, a Hollywood sex symbol, and a sympathetic, warm female who had continual trouble with men, it's hard to be uninteresting. The author tells of Mansfield's struggle to achieve stardom, her marriages, and the sad events that led up to the final tragic automobile accident.

The weakness of this book lies not with the subject but with the author. She never seems to present a heroine the audience can admire. Instead, she settles for mysticism, spiritualism, and the influence of the devil, and indicates that Jayne Mansfield came back from beyond to tell her to write this book. Some private photographs are among the 60 illustrations. Not a very good biography, this volume will still be popular with the general audience. Acceptable for all collections.

2519. The Man Who Invented Hollywood, edited and annotated by James Hart. 170 p. illus. Louisville, Ky.: Touchstone Publish. Co., 1972.

The major portion of this book is an autobiography of D. W. Griffith, written in a predictable romantic, southern-Victorian style. Supporting the autobiography are an introduction by Frank Capra, some interview notes taken by Hart, many illustrations, and some concluding information. The latter is necessary since the autobiography was unfinished. With the interest in and constant reevaluation of Griffith's work, a book such as this becomes important source material. If the reader is willing to penetrate the old fashioned prose, there is much rewarding information and observation.

Picture quality is quite good for the most part and James Hart's attempts to add more pertinent information to the Griffith life story must be appreciated. There is a Griffith chronology but no index. Recommended for all collections.

2520. Marilyn: A Biography, by Norman Mailer. 270 p. illus. New York: Grosset and Dunlap, 1973.

One of the big events in publishing circles in 1973 was the first printing of 400,000 copies of this Marilyn Monroe biography. The original intent was to have Norman Mailer write a preface of 10,000 words to a coffee table book of Monroe photographs. It didn't quite work out that way; he wrote some 90,000 words and the photographs now supplement his biographical essay.

Mailer's writing has been called "novelistic biography," "a meditation," "inaccurate," "careless," and "plagiarism." The last charge stems from Mailer's reliance on two earlier Monroe biographies by Maurice Zolotow (931) and Fred Lawrence Guiles (1047). Not noted by the critics was the duplication of much material that appeared in a 1968 paperback by James A. Hudson (2583).

Monroe's lust for fame and her self-destruction wish seem familiar to Mailer. He wrote this material in 60 days, inventing scenes, checking only 14 persons who knew Monroe (he didn't), and ultimately denying the book was a biography (why, then, the final title?). What is offered is Mailer's stylistically brilliant interpretation of two major biographical sources on Monroe, accompanied by his personal speculations about her sex life, her death, and her real self. Style notwithstanding, the book is unfair to everyone except Mailer who seems to believe he can write it all ways--part novel, part biography, part interpretation, and part conjecture. He can't.

The photographs are varied, fascinating and ultimately relate a better biography than Mailer does. The book is an assured success because of the controversy, publicity, subject matter, author personality and other factors that have surrounded its publication. It will be popular in all collections and it is an acceptable although disappointing addition.

2521.   Marinetti, edited by R. W. Flint. 363 p. New
         York: Farrar, Straus & Giroux, 1972.
         A compilation from the writings of Filippo Tommaso
Marinetti (1876-1944), one of the major personalities in the
Italian avant-garde movement during the early years of this
century. His predictions about the cinema, much ahead of
their time, were quite accurate. Acceptable for all collections.

2522.   MAROONED, by Harold Stern. 24 p. (paperback)
         illus. New York: National Publishers, 1969.
         A space glossary and a section entitled "Tomorrow
Is Now" are the unusual features of this souvenir book. The
visuals concentrate on the space flight and space activities.
Gregory Peck gets the most attention as star, and producer
Mike Frankovich and director John Sturges are also spotlighted. Other cast members and production personnel are
noted.

2523.   Marquee Ministry, by Robert G. Konzelman. 123 p.
         illus. New York: Harper and Row, 1972.

Does the idea of transforming your local theatre into a community forum seem radical? Can there be cooperation between the film industry, the local theatre manager, and the members of the community? Konzelman, a Director of Educational Research for the American Lutheran Church, believes in both ideas and discusses the power of the church in determining future films. He opts for cooperation, understanding, and interaction between the church and the film industry rather than censure, threats, and control. A dialogical film study which considers motion pictures as a communication both to and from our culture is recommended. Some evaluation criteria for the selection of those films which might be used in such a study are suggested. Final chapters offer advice on leading discussions, the role of the church pastor, organizing film festivals, and other matters which might help to bring about the effective use of secular films. A short bibliography is appended.

In theory, the ideas proposed certainly are stimulating and workable; in practice, some of them may be defeated by economic, political, or self-serving motivations. Many people consider the motion picture theatre as a doomed or dying institution. (Statistical and observational evidence supports this view.) Reasons for this belief are many but foremost is the reluctance of people to leave the house. The attraction outside must be strong, indeed. In other words, people should do the things suggested by Konzelman but will they?

In any event, the comments, advice, and suggestions for using films have much general application and will interest those who teach film. Recommended for those audiences which are willing to take the time to select the sections applicable to their individual situations.

2524.   MARY POPPINS. 16 p. (paperback) illus. New York: National Publishers, 1964.
In a straightforward fashion this souvenir book treats author, cast, music, animation and production of the film. Stars Julie Andrews and Dick Van Dyke are singled out for special treatment.

2525.   Mass Media in a Free Society, edited by Warren K. Agee. 96 p. (paperback) Lawrence, Kansas: The University Press of Kansas, 1969.
This book consists of six presentations which were originally made at the William Allen White Centennial Seminar at the University of Kansas in 1968. The general theme was the challenges to be met today and in the future by news-

papers, TV, motion pictures and magazines. Bosley Crowther gave the presentation on films, entitled "Magic, Myth and Monotony: A Measure of the Role of Movies in a Free State."

What was acceptable writing on film in the thirties and forties now seems naive, up-tight, and senile. Crowther should have quit when he was ahead. Acceptable for the rest of the book--especially Stan Freberg on TV--but the film article is a disservice.

2526.   The Matinee Idols, by David Carroll.   159 p.   illus.
         New York: Arbor House, 1972.
         Divided into two portions, The Theatre and The
Film, this collective biography of male performers who appealed primarily to the female audience is a fascinating sample of memorabilia. Each biography is accompanied by several varied illustrations--portraits, stills, candids, sketches, etc.--and sometimes reprints of articles by the subject. Film stars include Francis X. Bushman, Lou Tellegen, Douglas Fairbanks, William S. Hart, Tom Mix, Wallace Reid, Rudolph Valentino, Ramon Novarro, John Gilbert, and John Barrymore; some others--Antonio Moreno, Ricardo Cortez, Jack Holt, Charles Ray, Richard Barthelmess--are pictured but not discussed in the text. Picture quality is acceptable and the book is indexed.
         Interesting but hardly essential material, this volume will have a curiosity appeal for the general reader. The material presented lacks depth and other books like Blum's (1103) supply more and better visuals.

2527.   MAYA.   14 p.   (paperback) illus.   1966.
         The souvenir book of MAYA is like the film--small, unassuming, and pleasant. Stars Clint Walker and young Jay North are given some attention but the backgrounds shot in India and the elephants steal it all.

2528.   [No entry.]

2529.   The Media Works, by Joan Valdes and Jeanne Crow.
         282 p. (paperback) illus. Dayton, Ohio: Pflaum, 1973.
         Although concerned with the broad field of media
and mass communication, there is sufficient attention given to motion pictures in this volume to warrant its inclusion here. An up-to-the-minute textbook designed for young adults, this outstanding compilation of narrative, suggestions, questions, problems, bibliographies, filmographies and visuals should find rapid acceptance in schools. It would be unfortunate if its readership was limited to the student, for there is much to stimulate, provoke and even excite all

207

readers.   There are three major sections: I, The Workings;
II, The Mass Message; III, The Personal Message.   In addition to films, other mass media examined are television, advertising, magazines, comics, radio and newspapers.

Format, presentation, organization, style and content are top grade, as are the production values.   Illustrations, drawings, and cartoons are abundant and appropriate.
There is much creativity, intelligence, and obvious effort apparent in this quality text, which may initiate much needed
courses in mass media in our schools.   It is enthusiastically
recommended for inclusion in school libraries; other libraries will also find it to be a valuable acquisition.

2530.   Meeting Mrs. Jenkins, by Richard Burton.   24 p.
         illus.   New York: William Morrow & Co., 1966.
         Originally written for Vogue, the Burton text has
been embellished here by some color portraits of Elizabeth
Taylor.   Three scenes--a home in Bel Air, a restaurant
five years later, and Paris--provide the physical settings
for this portrait of Taylor.   The book is trivial, but Burton
writes well and the visuals are beautiful.   Noted here for
the record.

2531.   Melville on Melville, edited by Rui Nogueira.   176 p.
         illus.   New York: Viking Press, 1971.
         Jean-Pierre Melville, a French filmmaker, is un-
known to most Americans; his eleven feature films have had
few showings in this country.   An individualist who usually
writes his own scripts and has assumed many other roles
in filmmaking, he prefers the thriller genre.   He frequently
voices his admiration for American films and directors of
the thirties, and their influence can be detected in his films,
most of which were made in the sixties.

This volume is structured like Truffaut's Hitchcock--
a series of questions proposed to Melville which cause him
to review his films in chronological order.   While the quality
and value of Melville's responses is unquestionably high, the
reader who has not seen his films is at a disadvantage.   The
familiarity factor was certainly important in the success of
Truffaut's book.

Illustrations are adequate and there is a detailed
filmography.   Since Melville is an important French filmmaker of the sixties, this specialized volume may serve to acquaint readers with his work.   Acceptable for large collections.

2532.   Memo from David O. Selznick, edited by Rudy
         Behlmer.   518 p.   illus.   Viking Press, 1972.

A different approach to film literature is used in this collection of memoranda written by David O. Selznick over the period 1926 to 1962. Selected from a reservoir of two-thousand file boxes, the memos have been edited and arranged to give the book a narrative framework. Major attention, as might be expected, is given to the memos issued during the GONE WITH THE WIND era (1936-1941). REBECCA (1938-1941) is also singled out for an extended chapter. Since Selznick worked at Paramount, RKO, and Metro before forming his own company in 1935, the memos of those early years indicate his influence and effect on the careers of many famous actors--Hepburn, Astaire, Crawford, etc. The decline which coincided with his almost total devotion to the career of Jennifer Jones is indicated in the latter sections. One senses that the author is not sympathetic to the actress. Although she was a major focus of Selznick's activities from 1942 to 1963, the memos indicate that any achievement by Jones was due largely to Selznick's perseverance and backstage savvy. It should also be noted that Val Lewton (THE CAT PEOPLE, THE BODY SNATCHER, ISLE OF THE DEAD, etc.) served as story editor to Selznick in the thirties.

Introducing each section is a montage of Selznick's statements, and these give a certain coherence to the material that follows. The appendix contains an edited Selznick lecture on the producer's function and the making of feature films. Another section called "Cast of Characters" identifies many of the names mentioned in the memos. An index is included, as are several groupings of illustrations. Photographic reproduction and selection are uniformly excellent.

This is a rich book about a larger-than-life personality, written in his own words. Not a biography, the volume will probably give the reader a more valid portrait of the real Selznick than any of the other biographical materials. Certain memos reveal him as uncertain, insecure, and annoying--a man who interfered, nagged and needled when he should have been occupied by other matters. They show his errors in judgment were as numerous as his correct decisions. Reading the memos concurrently with the Thomas biography (1215) is a most rewarding excursion. The work of a dedicated editor is obvious throughout and his shaping of the voluminous material into this fascinating collection is impressive. Highly recommended for all collections.

2533.　METROPOLIS. A script of the 1927 film, by Thea Von Harbou (director: Fritz Lang). (paperback) illus. London: Lorrimer, 1972.
　　　　Announced for publication in the U.S. by Simon and Schuster.

2534.   MGM Library of Film Scripts.   (paperback)   illus.
New York: Viking Press, 1972.
This attractive series supplies the original script
with notations indicating how the script was changed into the
final film.   Illustrations are plentiful, clearly reproduced
and well selected.   Occasionally there are introductory pieces
by persons concerned with making the film.   Casts and production credits are noted.   The first six titles include:
    NINOTCHKA (2606)
    NORTH BY NORTHWEST (2609)
    ADAM'S RIB (2005)
    A NIGHT AT THE OPERA (2603)
    A DAY AT THE RACES (2183)
    SINGING IN THE RAIN (2738).

2535.   The MGM Years, by Lawrence B. Thomas.   138 p.
illus.   New Rochelle, N.Y.:   Arlington House, 1972.
This oversized book deals primarily with 40 MGM
musicals which are each given several pages of stills, cast
and production credits, plot outlines, etc.   In addition to the
selected musicals, more than 160 others are mentioned.
Sections on dubbing, soundtrack recording, songs from non-
musical films, awards, and rental films are also given.
Several indexes, a bibliography and a discography complete
the volume.   This is specialized material that is given affectionate treatment.   The selection of visuals is rather
good, although many of them require color for full appreciation.   Acceptable for all collections.

2536.   Miller's High Life, by Ann Miller with Norma Lee
Browning.   283 p.   illus.   Garden City, N.Y.:
Doubleday, 1972.
The durable Ann Miller tells about her life as a tap
dancer, from the age of five to her most recent TV success
dancing on the giant soup can for a commercial.   It's fan
magazine material blown up to book size with little apparent
help by Ms. Browning.   Acceptable for all collections.

2537.   MINNIE AND MOSKOWITZ.   A script of the 1972
film, by John Cassavetes (director: John Cassavetes).   116 p.   illus.   Los Angeles: Black Spar-
row Press, 1973.
Includes an introduction by the writer/director.
Also included are production and cast credits.

2538.   THE MISFITS.   A script of the 1961 film, by Arthur
Miller (director: John Huston).   618 p.   (paperback)

New York: Appleton-Century-Crofts, 1972.
Found in Film Scripts Three (2269).

2539. THE MISFITS. A script of the 1961 film, by Arthur
Miller (director: John Huston). 132 p. illus.
New York: Viking Press, 1961.

2540. Miss Tallulah Bankhead, by Lee Israel. 384 p.
illus. New York: G. P. Putnams, 1972.
This fascinating biography contains short accounts
of the few films that Bankhead made. Emphasis is on LIFE-
BOAT, A ROYAL SCANDAL, DIE DIE MY DARLING and
THE DEVIL AND THE DEEP. Although she was not primarily a film actress, the legacy of LIFEBOAT offers sufficient proof of Bankhead's artistry.

2541. The Robert Mitchum Story, by Mike Tomkies. 271 p.
illus. Chicago, Ill.: Regnery, 1972.
The sub-title for this one originally was "It Sure
Beats Working," and it gives a clue to the tone of the book.
Mitchum always had a colorful and smart way with words
and Tomkies uses that talent to give an enlightening portrait
of a unique man.

2542. MONKEY BUSINESS. A script of the 1931 film, by
S. J. Perelman, Will B. Johnstone and Arthur
Sheekman (director: Norman McLeod). 183 p.
(paperback) illus. New York: Simon and Schuster,
1972.
Contains: MONKEY BUSINESS, 1931; DUCK SOUP,
1933; Casts and credits.

2543. Monsters from the Movies, by Thomas G. Aylesworth. 160 p. illus. Philadelphia, Pa.: J. B.
Lippincott, 1972.
This book for children is part of a series called
"The Weird and Horrible Library." Two other subjects,
mummies and poltergeists, will give some idea of the range
of the series. The first chapter combines film showings
with a recap of Melies' career. The remaining chapters
categorize the monsters into man-made, self-made, human
fiends, the living dead, and creatures from another world.
An appendix of some selected horror films and an index
complete the book.

2544. The Moon's a Balloon, by David Niven. 380 p.
illus. New York: G. P. Putnams, 1972.

This has been one of the most popular film autobiographies ever published, and the reason may be Niven's refusal to be terribly serious about it all. The light touch is applied constantly, whether to career, love, or philosophy of life. Only in a few spots is the book sombre or sad--and one senses that these were traumatic moments in Niven's life.

In the second half of the book Niven gets around to his career as an actor. His near appearance with Mae West in GOING TO TOWN, and his screen test for Edmund Goulding were among his first experiences in Hollywood. The signing with Goldwyn, the acceptance by the Hollywood "British Colony," the small parts which led up to "Edgar" in WUTHERING HEIGHTS and other major roles are described. World War II, the accidental death of his first wife, career renewal, and his second marriage complete the story. Several illustrations from Niven's own private collection are used and these are snapshots rather than studio stills. The book is indexed.

There is a slight overbalance in space given to the early years and a shortchanging of the film years, but that is Niven's prerogative. His view of himself is charming, witty, and quite objective. Recommended for all collections, but with a warning for schools--Niven is casual about his sexual experiences and short of naming names, tells all.

2545. The Morals of the Movie, by Ellis Paxson Oberholtzer. 251 p. New York: Jerome S. Ozer, 1971 (1922).

This book by a member of the Pennsylvania State Board of Censors appeared first in 1922 under the banner of the Penn Publishing Company of Philadelphia. It is currently reprinted by Ozer as part of the "Moving Pictures--Their Impact on Society" series. It purports to be a record of the author's experiences during a six-year period of operating the Censor's office. His philosophy is expressed by "Not many of us wish to violate correct standards of deportment in other departments of life. But we are not unmindful of our duty to our fellows, and we make rules to hinder and prevent that little part of the population which now or at some future time, shall stand ready to do damage to society. The laws which we would enact are not for those who direct their courses rightly: they are meant for and will only touch and restrict those who on some account are minded to act in another sense."

Examined are sex films, melodramas, serials, and comedies; and child audiences, censor boards, the industry, and politics. In the appendix there are several examples of censorship laws from locations such as Chicago, Portland,

Oregon, Missouri, Massachusetts, and Quebec. The author does not quite follow his original premise--that of a record of experiences. What he offers is a rather long inspirational essay and justification for his activity. Of interest mostly to historians, this volume should be considered only for large collections.

2546.   More About ALL ABOUT EVE, by Joseph L. Mankiewicz and Gary Carey. 357 p. New York: Random House, 1972.
        A lengthy interview-article called "A Colloquy" introduces this volume. In it Mankiewicz speaks of the creation of the film with emphasis on the script and the characterization. Carey's role is to add pertinent background and detail. The script of the film follows. (It was printed separately in 1951.)

2547.   The Morning After, by Wilfred Sheed. 304 p. New York: Farrar, Straus and Giroux, 1971.
        Wilfred Sheed is a versatile writer who is equally at ease in judging books, films, theatre, sports or politics. A sampling of his critical essays is offered in this book. The film section has an even dozen reviews written originally for Esquire; they deal mostly with the foreign or the specialized film: THE HIPPIE REVOLT, GREETINGS, etc. Sheed's style is a mixture of intelligence, wit, and sophistication. The sampling here is too small to discern any unique aesthetic other than his apparent preference for the imported or important film. His subjects are chosen according to his own taste rather than as a sampling of what's available. Sheed is a critic whose film reviews make rewarding reading. This sampling suggests the publication of a book devoted solely to his essays and reviews about films.

2548.   MOROCCO. A script of the 1930 film, by Jules Furthman and Benno Vigny (director: Josef Von Sternberg). (paperback) illus. New York: Simon and Schuster, 1972.
        Found in 2549.

2549.   MOROCCO, SHANGHAI EXPRESS, by Josef von Sternberg. (paperback) illus. New York: Simon and Schuster, 1973.
        Contains scripts for: MOROCCO, 1930 (2548); SHANGHAI EXPRESS, 1932 (2730).

2550.   MOTHER. A script of the 1925 film, by V. I. Pudovkin and N. Zarkhi (director: V. I. Pudovkin).

102 p. (paperback) illus. New York: Simon & Schuster, 1973.
Found in Two Russian Screen Classics (2833).

2551. Motion Picture and Television Film Image Control and Processing Techniques, by D. J. Corbett. 231 p. illus. New York: Amphoto, 1968.
This volume provides detailed coverage of motion picture laboratory work. It covers the elements of film processing and some theoretical aspects of photometry. For the professional engineer, cameraman, or technician.

2552. The Motion-Picture Cameraman, by Edwin George Lutz. 248 p. illus. New York: Arno, 1972 (1927).
Originally published by Scribner in 1927, this book describes the cinematographic techniques of that period. There are chapters on cameras, lenses, locations, trick photography, development of film and other topics. Many illustrations and diagrams help to explain the text. Of interest to historians, researchers and scholars. Acceptable for large academic collections.

2552a. Motion Picture Directors, by Mel Schuster. 418 p. Metuchen, N.J.: Scarecrow Press, 1973.
The very prolific Mr. Schuster has done it again. After providing an essential reference book, Motion Picture Performers (946a), he has repeated the format, this time with directors. The result is a bibliography of articles on directors which have appeared in 340 periodicals from 1900 to 1972. More than 2,300 directors, filmmakers, and animators are listed.
Directors are arranged alphabetically by surname, making the volume very easy to use. Articles are listed under each chronologically. For example, the first entry for Cecil B. DeMille is from Photoplay, June 1915 while the last is from the May 1970 issue of After Dark. A total of 110 articles are listed in all. While DeMille is admittedly a unique entry, many others have equally exhaustive periodical coverage, e.g., Disney, Chaplin, Godard, Hitchcock, Welles, etc. The introduction contains a valid explanation of the criteria for selecting the directors for inclusion. Directors for whom no articles were found are listed. The 340 periodicals which were researched are named in the appendix.
The effort required to compile this thorough reference is obvious throughout. The book is essential for all

those libraries which support film study courses and is highly recommended for all others.

2553.   The Motion Picture in the Soviet Union 1918-1952:
        A Sociological Analysis, by John David Rimberg.
        238 p.   New York: Arno, 1973.
        This one of six doctoral dissertations of film topics
reproduced by Arno exactly as they were submitted to the
degree-granting school.   The thesis of this study is that the
content and volume of film production in the Soviet Union
are determined by compromise between three groups--govern-
ment officials (propaganda), creative artists (works of art),
and audiences (entertainment).
        After a review of previous research studies of Soviet
Union, the content desired by each group and their power potential are examined.   Using the three areas of content,
films from various periods of Soviet film history are examined.   A summary seems to confirm Rimberg's main thesis.   A bibliography and an appendix complete the work.
Acceptable for large academic collections.

2554.   Motion Picture Photography, by Carl Louis Gregory.
        435 p.   illus.   New York: Falk Publishing, 1927.
        This is now a historical curiosity rather than the
how-to-do-it volume it was back in 1927.   Several things
make it unusual.   Through its text and the photographs of
filmmaking in the twenties, the reader can gain insight into
the technology of the period.   Certain chapters are especially interesting--animated cartoons, airplane photography,
trick work, double exposure, submarine photography, etc.
There is even a chapter on The History of Cinematography.
Only for very large collections but noted here for the record.

2555.   Motion Picture Projection, by James R. Cameron.
        1010 p.   illus.   Coral Gables, Fla.:   Cameron Pub-
        lishing.
        This is the 14th edition of this standard book de-
signed for operators of projection and sound systems.   Includes data on Cinemascope, Vistavision, Todd AO, Cinerama, Superscope, Perspecta Sound, etc.

2556.   Motion Pictures: A Catalog of Books, Periodicals,
        Screen Plays and Production Stills.   1169 p.   Boston,
        Mass.:   G. K. Hall, 1973.
        Announced as a guide to the collection at the Theatre
Arts Library, University of California at Los Angeles.   It
is divided into three sections:

I. Books and Periodicals: includes the research collection of books on all aspects of film and the film industry, personal papers of film personalities (Stanley Kramer, Jack Benny, Charles Laughton, King Vidor, etc.), clippings, records, screenplays from Republic Studios.

II. Production Stills: includes 87,000 stills from American and foreign films as far back as 1905. Jessen Collection, Richard Dix Collection, and the Columbia Pictures Stills Collection are represented.

III. Screenplays: includes more than 3,000 unpublished American, British, and foreign scripts.

This valuable reference tool will appear in two volumes, and should be a welcome addition to all large film collections.

2557. Motion Pictures: A Study in Social Legislation, by Donald Ramsey Young. 109 p. New York: Ozer, 1971 (1922).

A reprint of the 1922 edition, now part of the series, "Moving Pictures: Their Impact on Society," this volume is an examination of the problem of moral standards in motion pictures. The author is a reformer who argues for state censorship as the only way of controlling film content to make it acceptable to local audiences. Any film which does not "uplift" an audience should be either censored or eliminated, according to Young. If the reader can overcome annoyance at the narrow viewpoint presented, the book may have some historical value. Acceptable for large collections.

2558. Motion Pictures 1960-1969: Catalog of Copyright Entries Cumulative Series. [Identified from the records of the U.S. Copyright Office.] 744 p. (paperback) Washington, D.C.: Government Printing Office, 1971.

This is the latest volume in the series (948, 949, 950, 951) and the format employed for this volume is less informative than the ones used previously. Producer, director, and certain writing credits are omitted. Remains a necessary reference work for all collections.

2559. Motion Picture, TV and Theatre Directory, by John B. Low. 148 p. (paperback) illus. Tarrytown, N.Y.: Motion Picture Enterprises Public, 1972.

This guide to commercial services and products appears semi-annually in the Spring and the Fall. While it contains large amounts of commercial advertising, it also gives information that may not be easily available through other sources. It resembles Audio Visual Market Place (81) somewhat, but each has unique offerings. A very long index lists well over 100 services or products for the AV field-- including basics such as motion picture labs by state, film treatment, film schools, etc., and such rarities as animals for rent (trained), helicopters, underwater filming, etc. The directory posts a price of $2.50 but is sent free once your name is on the mailing list. A good reference item for all film collections. Recommended.

2560.   Movement, by Etienne Jules Marey. 323 p. illus.
         New York: Arno, 1972 (1895).
         Marey was a French scientist who was interested in the analysis of motion back in the mid-1880's. He was the first to "shoot" motion pictures with a single camera. This book, originally published in 1895, summarizes his work and thought on the subject. It has chapters on measuring time and space by photography, chronophotography, and loco-motion--of man, of quadrupeds, in water and in air. A chapter on comparative locomotion also appears. Many photographs and charts help the text. Historically important and acceptable for all collections.

2561.   The Movie Business: American Film Industry Prac-
         tice, edited by A. William Bluem and Jason E.
         Squire. 368 p. New York: Hastings House, 1972.
         This anthology addresses itself to film considered as "a vast economic enterprise." The feature motion picture made for theatrical release is the ultimate concern of all the articles. There are sections on developing the story and screenplay, finance and budget, company management, production, distribution, and exhibition. Two concluding sections discuss the audience and the new technology.
         The several articles that appear in each section have either been written specifically for this volume or adapted from previously published works. Author names are interesting and impressive: Charlton Heston, Russ Meyer, Stanley Kramer, Stirling Silliphant, Walter Reade, Jr., etc. The appendix contains excerpts from contracts of the major creative guilds (writers, directors, actors) and the craft unions (stage employees, moving picture operators). An index is also provided.
         The intention of the authors is to fill the gap that exists in most college filmmaking curricula, and their selection and arrangement of material is commendable. As a text the book is a good addition to the literature and certainly belongs in university and college collections. For general collections the book is a bit too specialized and will have limited appeal. At this point, however, it is almost the

217

only recent volume that looks at the total industry (circa 1972) in a competent, professional manner and that may qualify it for inclusion in all collections.

2562. Movie Journal: The Rise of the American Cinema, 1959-1971, by Jonas Mekas. 434 p. New York: The Macmillan Co., 1972.

When Mekas began writing his weekly columns for The Village Voice, he considered both the commercial film and the experimental film. Since his passion was for the latter film form, he relinquished the commercial film assignments to Andrew Sarris and concentrated on the New American Cinema. This anthology consists of about one-third of the Voice columns from the period 1959-1971.

Mekas is a beautiful self-creation. An individual who writes in a conversational style flavored with charm, anger, pity and rage, he is opinionated and defensive at times, open-minded and receptive at others. He is never dull. Readers unfamiliar with the American Experimental film may find some of the topics remote and of little interest, but anyone who has followed the growth and development of this film movement will be fascinated.

A fine collection of film writing that will have much appeal for a special audience. The index is a decided asset to the book. Recommended for most collections.

2563. Movie Making in 18 Lessons, by George Cushman. 128 p. (paperback) illus. New York: Amphoto, 1971.

Each of these 18 lessons is composed of several paragraphs which follow the opening explanatory statement. The paragraphs, which are alphabetically numbered, present a single concept, idea, or technique that can be understood when taken out of context. The format resembles an outline that has been filled in. For example, the outline for Lesson 3 might be:

Taking Scenes

Introduction
A - Hand vs. Tripod
B - Length of Scene
C - Panning
D - Shots vs. Long Takes
E - Long Shot
F - Medium Shot
G - Close-Up

When it is expanded to a narrative form in the book, it takes
almost five pages. Lesson titles are standard--Lenses, Titles, Lighting, Editing, Sound, etc. The illustrations, charts,
and diagrams are most helpful. This is a sort of pro-
grammed approach that simplifies the process of filmmaking.
It is readable, helpful, and informative. Recommended for
inclusion in all collections.

2564. Movie People, edited by Fred Baker and Rose Firestone. 193 p. illus. New York: Douglas Book
Corp., 1972.
Each chapter in this volume represents one step in
the total process of making a feature film. The pre-produc-
tion section deals with the producer (Roger Lewis) and the
distributor (David Picker). Production chores are divided
between the director (Sidney Lumet, Frances Ford Coppola),
the screen writer (Terry Southern, James Salter), the actor
(Rod Steiger), the editor (Aram Avakian) and the composer
(Quincy Jones). After the film is released, the exhibitor
(Walter Reade, Jr.) and the critic (Andrew Sarris) begin
their work.
Inspired by a series of lectures, the individual presentations were edited, updated and augmented by adding
some missing elements. For each of the contributors there
is an introductory page which contains a small picture, some
biographical data and a filmography. The articles are uniformly interesting but because of the disparate experiences,
the book does not have the unity it might have had if all had
been working together on the same film. Taken as an anthology rather than a unified work, the book is more than
satisfying. Recommended for all collections.

2565. The Movie Rating Game, by Stephen Farber. 128 p.
Washington, D.C.: Public Affairs Press, 1972.
An examination and critique of the movie rating system that came into being after the abolishment of the Code.
A brief opening traces the history from censorship to code
to the current rating or classification system. The thin line
between a GP and an R rating is discussed. Other aspects
of the system are evaluated and the total result is quite negative. Some appendices are included. Most persons concerned
with film are aware of the message of this book, but for the
uninformed it may be useful. Acceptable for large collections.

2566.   Movie Reader, edited by Ian Cameron.   120 p.
illus.   New York: Praeger, 1972.
The first item of interest in this book appears opposite the title page: a summary chart by the editorial
board of Movie evaluating directors.   Since all the articles
in this reader are from the magazine, the chart gives some
indication of the content to follow.
The principles of the "auteur" theory are evident
in the selection and content of the articles.   Alfred Hitchcock and Howard Hawks (chart rating: great) are recognized
by several articles, as are Otto Preminger, Nicholas Ray,
Joseph Losey (brilliant).   Appreciated but rated lower are
Michael Powell (competent or ambitious), Frank Tashlin
(very talented).   Two directors--von Sternberg and Chabrol--
do not appear on the chart but are given article treatment.
Reviews and discussions of some specific films close the
book.
The periodical Movie was initiated to offer some
balance to the one-side bias of the French Cahiers School of
Film Criticism.   Its aim was the critical recognition of underrated American and British directors and their films.
The above rationale explains most satisfactorily this book
and its organization and content.   Since writers such as Ian
Cameron, Paul Mayersberg, Robin Wood, and Raymond
Durgnant are each represented by several pieces, the high
quality of the writing will be obvious to anyone familiar with
cinema literature.   Picture quality varies from excellent to
some poorly reproduced illustrations that are far too dark
and murky.   Although the emphasis is on directors who are
already well represented in print analyses, the freshness of
approach here is sufficient to invite reader attention.   Recommended for those collections which serve a more mature
audience.   College libraries will find this a most valid and
popular addition.

2567.   Movies and How They Are Made, by Frank Manchel.
71 p.   illus.   Englewood Cliffs, N.J.:   Prentice-
Hall, 1968.
This delightful book is designed for students in
grades three to seven but many readers beyond those grades
will enjoy it.   Using a blend of line drawings and an intelligent text which is never condescending, Manchel manages
to inform, teach, and entertain.   Such terms as "Mass Entertainment," "Treatment," "Associate Producer," "Unit
Manager," and so on are defined and explained with economy
and clarity.   The book treats all of the elements of filmmak-
ing--budgets, scripts, schedules, shooting, locations, music

and preview. A glossary and an index complete the volume. The line drawings by Kelly Mark throughout are most appropriate for the intended audience, relying on subtlety rather than exaggeration. Highly recommended for intermediate and junior high grades, and others may want to consider it, too.

2568. Movies and Morals, by Anthony Schillaci. 181 p. (paperback) Notre Dame, Ind.: Fides, 1970.
The main thesis of this small but vital book is "that motion pictures, rather than being an object of fear and suspicion as far as morals are concerned, are in fact a vital source of emotional maturity and moral sensitivity." Using topics such as a new kind of cinema, art and morality, film as modern man's morality play, religion and film, and cultural exorcism, the author argues for a knowledgeable use of films rather than their dismissal as entertainment or depravity. The author's style is persuasive, personal, and dedicated. His belief in his cause is evident but the pitfall of sermonizing has been avoided.
The appendices are commendable, too. There are a paperback bibliography, some examples of workshops on the use of film, a few sample film series, a filmography for religious topics, moral problems, and the human condition. A final section lists the major distributors of films. Although the book has a religious origin, there is so much of value and quality here that the book has pertinence for anyone who uses films. Many other readers will enjoy its arguments, too. It is highly recommended for all libraries.

2569. The Movies: A Picture Quiz Book, by Stanley Applebaum and Hayward Cirker. 244 p. (paperback) illus. New York: Dover Publications, 1972.
Here is a sleeper of a film book. Intended for a specialized audience, it has value and pleasure for a much larger group. The reader who ignores the quiz format and simply browses through the admirable collection of stills will be exposed to a short, selected pictorial chronology of outstanding films from the period of 1900 to 1960. The quality of picture reproduction here puts many higher priced volumes to shame. Selection is thorough and covers all genres and major personalities. In addition, the book has two indexes, one for performers and one for film titles.
The quiz format may result in greater sales but it is an added attraction, not the main feature. Questions are posed in a serious but provocative paragraph or so. Answers are found in an informative listing near the book's closing pages. In libraries, the book is adaptable to a variety of uses and purposes, and will bring pleasure to many

readers. The low price and high quality will probably encourage others to buy a copy for personal use or as a gift.
Highly recommended.

2570.   Movies in America, by William Kuhns. 248 p. (pa-
         perback) illus. Dayton, Ohio: Pflaum, 1972.
         One of the first books used widely as a text in film
study courses was Kuhns' Exploring the Film. Since the
qualities that distinguished that earlier volume are present
to a greater degree in this volume, an even wider success
is indicated. The title refers to movies in America, not the
American Movie. The emphasis, however, is almost exclusively on American films, directors, columnists, and performers. A historical account provides the general framework but there are entertaining digressions and time-period
juxtapositions of material. Kuhns' intention is to present an
account of the film in America by tracing its development
from a novelty to an art form and by examining the relationship between certain short periods of post-1900 American
history and the films that appeared within them. He is
mostly successful in this endeavor.
         The creativity evident throughout this volume makes
it unique among film books. Production quality is outstanding, with hundreds of unusual stills carefully arranged and
reproduced. The book is a visual feast, a stimulating arrangement of what could easily be too-familiar material,
and it has an intelligent text to cement the elements of the
book. Because of the large number of pages, the oblong
book format may be awkward to handle. There is a short
bibliography and an index. Highly recommended for all librarians and for consideration by all teachers of film study
as a class text.

2571.   Movies Into Film, by John Simon. 448 p. New
         York: Dial Press, 1971.
         "Vicious, vicious, vicious" could easily be applied
to Simon. He spares no one and is especially hard on females. His comments on Streisand ("a repellent, egomani-
acal female impersonator"), Brenda Vaccaro ("a 'Dikey'
kewpie doll"), Sandy Dennis ("walking catarrh") and others
are devastating. His main obsession seems to be sex--with
an emphasis on homosexual-lesbian relationships, which are
plentiful in the films he reviews. These approaches to film
criticism--bitchiness and sex--are not likely to limit a critic's celebrity. Add constant appearances on TV talk shows,
on-going feuds with fellow critics, and some occasional fire-
works in the Sunday New York Times and you have a recipe
for certain success.

222

Simon has a background of knowledge and information about all the arts that serves him well in his film criticism. He can write in a style that informs, challenges, entertains, and shocks, but he is often guilty of monumental bad taste in speaking of other human beings.

The essays in this volume are mostly from The New Leader and take up where Private Screenings (1130) left off. They cover a period of about four years, from 1967 to 1970, and are arranged under subject headings rather than chronologically, i. e., Adaptations, The Youth Film, Young Directors, Musicals, etc. The introduction, which takes on both Pauline Kael and Andrew Sarris, should be required reading for anyone interested in film criticism. The book is indexed. John Simon is probably the most controversial critic writing today. He enjoys a love-hate relationship with his readers, his professional contemporaries, and his critics. Any book of his film criticism deserves a place in all collections. Highly recommended.

2572.   Movie Techniques for the Advanced Amateur, by George Regnier and Myron Matzkin. illus. New York: Amphoto, 1959.
The usual steps in filmmaking are described: shooting, scripting, lighting, direction, etc. Aimed at the more experienced or serious amateur.

2573.   Moving Pictures: Their Impact on Society (a series). Advisory editor: Garth S. Jowett. New York: Jerome S. Ozer, 1972.
The intent of this collection is to provide reprints, for scholars and students, of books long out of print and difficult to obtain in the used book market. The books examined in this reprint edition are bound in silver cloth and are facsimile reproductions of the original editions. Charts, illustrations, indexes, and bibliographies have been retained. Titles in the series are:

The Business Man in the Amusement World, by Robert Grau (2092)

Censored: The Private Life of the Movies, by Morris Ernst and Pare Lorentz (183)

Children and Movies, by Alice Miller Mitchell (2116)

Children in the Cinema, by Richard Ford (201)

The Community and the Motion Picture, by the Hays Office (2160)

Decency in Motion Pictures, by Martin Quigley (284)

Economic Control of the Motion Picture Industry, by Mae Dena Huettig (338)

The Hays Office, by Raymond Moley (662)
The Morals of the Movie, by Ellis P. Oberholtzer (2545)
The Motion Picture Industry, by Howard Thompson Lewis (945)
Motion Pictures: A Study in Social Legislation, by Donald Ramsey Young (2557)
The Movies on Trial, by William J. Perlman (991)
New Courts of Industry, by Louis Nizer (2594)
The Public and the Motion Picture Industry, by William Marston Seabury (2664)
The Public Relations of the Motion Picture Industry, by The Federal Council of Churches of Christ in America (2665)
(Selected Articles on) Censorship of the Theater and Moving Pictures, by Lamar Taney Beman (2110)
Sociology of Film, by Jakob Peter Mayer (1254)
The Story of Films, by Joseph Patrick Kennedy (1291)
What's Wrong With the Movies?, by Tamar Lane (2879)
World Wide Influences of the Cinema, by John Eugene Harley (1491).

2574.   The Moving Picture World. 10,158 p. illus. New York: Arno, 1972.
Announced as a reprint of the first five years of the magazine, The Moving Picture World. There will be 10 volumes in the series: 1907 - Volume I; 1908 - Volumes II, III; 1909 - Volumes IV, V; 1910 - Volumes VI, VII; 1911 - Volumes VIII, IX, X.

2575.   Multi-Media Reviews Index, edited by C. Edward Wall. Ann Arbor, Mich.: Pierian Press, 1970, 1971.
An index to reviews of films, filmstrips, non-classical records, tapes, slides, transparencies, and other media. In addition to being a guide to the reviews, MMRI offers information about the films: title, distributor, date of release, gauge, running time, silent or sound, color or black and white, etc. The tone of the reviews is indicated by a plus or minus sign.
Two volumes are available, 1970 and 1971, with the latter now indexing over 130 periodicals and containing nearly 20,000 citations. This is a most needed reference work. Essential for all school libraries and recommended for others.

2576.   Music for the Movies, by Tony Thomas. 270 p. illus. New York: Barnes, 1973.

224

A welcome survey of movie music. After a general introduction, the influence of European composers on film music is noted, along with the eventual emergence of the American composer. Mancini and others are given some special attention. An attempt is made to note recordings of film scores but as usual there is confusion between record labels and record numbers here and in Europe. Recommended for inclusion in all collections.

2577.   MUTINY ON THE BOUNTY, by Morgan Hudgins.
        36 p. illus. New York: Random House, 1962.
        This souvenir book of the 1962 film furnishes much background material. In addition to the inevitable credits for cast and production, this volume has features on the ship, its sail plan, and a portion of its log. Tahiti yields many fine illustrations and other features include a map of the Bounty's journey, some historical notes, and an account of what happened to both the mutineers and the faithful members of the crew. This is one of the more interesting and admirable books made to accompany a film.

2578.   Eadweard Muybridge: The Man Who Invented the
        Moving Picture, by Kevin MacDonnell. 158 p. illus.
        Boston: Little, Brown & Co., 1972.
        Although Eadweard Muybridge was born and died in England, he accomplished much of his important work during the many years he spent in America. He achieved fame as a photographer, inventor, writer, speaker, and even as a defendant in a murder trial. His great contributions were the changing of scientific understanding of animal and human locomotion and the invention of their pictorial representation.
        The biographical essay which opens this oversized volume concentrates on the professional accomplishments and only suggests bits of the personal life. (A full length biography by Robert Bartlett Haas is in preparation.) Following, there are samples of Muybridge's photographic work grouped under specific periods or topics: Alaska, Yosemite Valley, The Modoc War, Central America, Palo Alto, and Other Travels. The two last sections describe his work at Pennsylvania University and his invention of the Zoo-praxiscope. In the appendix there are extracts from his trial and two articles: the first on Muybridge's technique, the second on the author's search for the material presented in the book. A bibliography is included but there is no index.
        An exhibit of Muybridge's photographic work in New York City in 1973 was held in commemoration of Muybridge's collaboration in 1872 with Leland Stanford on horses in motion. That was the beginning of the studies that ultimately

225

led to the projected motion picture. Visuals selected for
this volume will give the reader a far greater understanding
and appreciation of Muybridge's contribution to the art of
motion pictures. They also stimulate the readers' desire
to know more about the man himself. The small evidence
presented here indicates that he was a unique personality and
a creative artist of considerable dimension. This volume
provides enlightenment about an era and a personality. The
nude studies may affect its placement in certain school libraries, but the book is highly recommended for all collections.

2579. MY FAIR LADY. 44 p. illus. New York: Warner
       Brothers, 1964.
       Using a chronological arrangement of the songs as
they appear in the film as the structure for the many visuals,
this attractive souvenir book also describes the making of the
film, its stars, and all the major names involved in the production. Included are director George Cukor, composer
Frederick Loewe, author-lyricist Alan Jay Lerner, designer
Cecil Beaton, musical supervisor Andre Previn, and producer Jack Warner. The author who started it all, George
Bernard Shaw, is acknowledged only briefly. Supporting
cast and other production credits are noted.

2580. My Ivory Cellar: The Story of Time Lapse Photog-
       raphy, by John Ott. 157 p. illus. Old Greenwich,
       Conn.: Devin.
       An account of the author's experiences with time
lapse photography. This is not a how-to-do-it book.

2581. MY NIGHT AT MAUD'S. A script of the 1970 film,
       by Eric Rohmer (director: Eric Rohmer). (paper-
       back) illus. London: Lorrimer, 1972.
       Found in Eric Rohmer (2694). Announced for pub-
lication in the U.S. by Simon and Schuster.

2582. Myself Among Others, by Ruth Gordon. 389 p.
       New York: Atheneum, 1971.
       This series of character observations of varying
lengths--one paragraph to a chapter--has a rambling, un-
structured quality. Opinions, reminiscences, and recreated
dialogues are given in a "Dear Diary" fashion. The book is
noted here since Miss Gordon's life has included many film
personalities and experiences. While some film personalities
are mentioned, the legitimate stage supplies the setting for
the largest number of anecdotes. Not pertinent for film
collections.

2583.   The Mysterious Death of Marilyn Monroe, by James
          A. Hudson. 112 p. (paperback) illus. New York:
          Volitant Publishing Co., 1968.
          This paperback quickie raises the following ques-
tions:
     What was Monroe's place in the "White House Set"?
     Who started the rumors about Monroe and Bobby Kennedy?
     Who talked to her on the last night of her life?
     Who was she telephoning as she died?
     How sure are authorities that Monroe was not murdered?
     Was vital evidence destroyed?
     Was Monroe a lesbian?
     Was Monroe a nymphomaniac?
          It answers none of them.   Noted here for the record.

2584.   My Way of Life, by Joan Crawford.   224 p.   illus.
          New York: Simon and Schuster, 1971.
          Although the book claims to be "autobiography and
more," it is mostly "more."   Ms. Crawford offers copious
advice on dress, figure, face, hair, and other personal
grooming matters.   In addition she gives hints on travel,
holding a job, keeping a man, entertaining, decoration, soli-
tude, competing in a man's world, and many other such topics.   These helpful hints for the incompetent have little place
in any film collection.

2585.   [No entry]

2586.   Naked Hollywood, by Weegee and Mel Harris.   illus.
          New York: Pellegrini & Cudahy, 1953.
          The pictures in this collection were taken by Arthur
Fellig (Weegee) during a four-year stay in Hollywood.   Text
and layout are by Mel Harris.   Both men attempted to "define" Hollywood but admit to failure in the foreword.   Nevertheless, the book does give a rather disillusioning portrait of
Hollywood at the start of its demise.   Its four acts are titled:
I.   Dream Factory; II. The People; III.   Private Lives;
IV.   Street Scene.   Noted here as one of the early picture
books about film topics.   It is out of print but it would not
be surprising to see Weegee photographs resurface.   Noted
for the record.

2587.   NANOOK OF THE NORTH, by Robert Kraus and
          Robert Flaherty.   32 p.   illus.   New York: Wind-
          mill Press, 1972.
          Using Flaherty's classic, the author has selected
pictures and captions to give young people an idea of Eskimo
life.

2588.   NAZARIN. A script of the 1959 film, by Luis
         Buñuel and Julio Alejandro (director: Luis Buñuel).
         299 p. (paperback) illus. New York: Simon and
         Schuster, 1972.
         Contains: "The Passion According to Buñuel" by
J. Francisco Aranda; cast and credits. Found in THE EX-
TERMINATING ANGEL, NAZARIN, LOS OLVIDADOS (2225).

2589.   Patricia Neal and Margaret Sullavan, by Michael
         Burrows. 42 p. (paperback) illus. London:
         Primestyle Ltd., 1971.
         The Burrows-Primestyle books resemble magazines
or periodicals devoted to a pair of subjects--in this case,
Patricia Neal and Margaret Sullavan. The treatment consists of biographical bits, quotes, comments by the subject,
and a critical appreciation. Stills from films and some
portrait shots are usually included. A simple listing of the
star's films closes the book. Acceptable for all collections.
         Other volumes in this series include:
    Mario Lanza and Max Steiner
    Charles Laughton and Frederic March
    John Ford and Andrew McLaglen
    The Films of John Steinbeck.

2590.   Need Johnny Read?, by Frederick Goldman and
         Linda R. Burnett. 238 p. (paperback) illus.
         Dayton, Ohio: Pflaum, 1971.
         The question proposed by the title of this book chal-
lenges the position of print literacy in the educational experience. The authors present abundant evidence to identify
their position in the first section. In the remaining portion
they offer positive suggestions for enriching humanities
courses, mostly by the use of films and by film study. Using six components of film--visuals, sound, editing, acting,
narrative, symbolism and metaphor--is recommended as a
base for film study. Other suggestions are intriguing--the
use of short films only, a plea for teachers rather than
pedantic scholars, etc.
         The book is a strong argument for introducing
courses in visual literacy into our schools. Reasons put
forth are not only emotionally persuasive but are supported
by citations, quotes, and references from authorative sources.
This book belongs in the collections of all school and college
libraries. It is highly recommended reading for all educators.

2591.   NEVER GIVE A SUCKER AN EVEN BREAK. A
         script of the 1941 film, by John T. Niville, Prescott

Chaplin and W. C. Fields (director: Edward Cline).
124 p. (paperback) illus. New York: Simon and
Schuster, 1973.

Contains: NEVER GIVE A SUCKER AN EVEN
BREAK (1941); TILLIE AND GUS (1933); an introduction by
Andrew Sinclair; casts and credits.

2592. The New Bohemia, by John Gruen. 180 p. illus.
New York: Shorecrest, 1966.

This volume deals with the avant-garde of today, including those working with film. Gruen feels that filmmakers
like Warhol or the Kuchar brothers will bring about an artistic renaissance by their irrationality. The volume also deals
with musicians, playwrights, actors, etc.

2593. New Cinema in Eastern Europe, by Alistair Whyte.
159 p. (paperback) illus. New York: Dutton,
1971.

For the purposes of this book, Eastern Europe consists of Poland, Hungary, Czechoslovakia, Yugoslavia, Bul-
garia, Albania, Romania and East Germany. As usual with
the Studio Vista series, the many visuals are superbly reproduced. Nearly every page contains a visual large enough
to reinforce the ideas of the accompanying text. Emphasis
is on the new directors appearing in these countries. The
recurrent theme in many of the films seems to be the role
of the individual in society. The book has a short bibliography and an index. Beautifully done and highly recommended for all collections.

2594. New Courts of Industry: Self Regulation Under the
Motion Picture Code, by Louis Nizer. 344 p. New
York: J. S. Ozer, 1971 (1935).

One of the series entitled, "Motion Pictures: Their
Impact on Society," this 1935 volume was originally published
by Longacre Press. It is a detailed analysis of the operation of the Hays Office and the administration of the Production Code. Problems, solutions, and the explanation of specific actions by the Office are discussed. The use of members of the industry to act as a court to settle disputes was
a valid method then and remains so today. This volume is
of historical interest and belongs in large collections only.

2595. [No entry]

2596. New Singer New Song, by David Winter. 160 p.
illus. Waco, Texas: Word Books, 1967.

The name Cliff Richards is relatively unknown in this country. In England, during the early sixties, he was a top recording personality who also made several successful films. American audiences saw him in only one or two; the others were never given any distribution here. The best known is EXPRESSO BONGO, in which he played the title role, a rock singer who achieves a sudden celebrity. Richards' life story does not present an especially flattering or inspiring example. He appears to be a determined, disciplined, ambitious, rather cold person who had more than a usual share of good luck. In the last chapter, Richards finds religious salvation via Billy Graham, the Christian Youth Crusade, and other Christian endeavors.

A filmography (six films) and a complete discography are included, as are several good illustrations. Whenever a book appears to have the sponsorship of a religious group, one suspects persuasion, propaganda and a hard sell for conversion--see Dale Evans (2176, 2895). While there are such elements in this book, they are minimal. The biography itself is unintentionally revealing, as much by its omissions as by its statements. Acceptable for larger collections.

2597. The New Swedish Cinema, by Nils Petter Sundgren. 57 p. (paperback) illus. Stockholm: The Swedish Institute, 1970.

Sundgren is a film critic and educator who addresses himself here to the rebirth of Swedish cinema in the Sixties. The topics discussed are the Swedish Film Institute, the new directors, and the veterans. Bo Wilderberg, Jan Troell, Jörn Donner, Vilgot Sjöman are among the former group, Ingmar Bergman, Alf Sjöberg and Arne Sucksdorff in the latter. The book is illustrated with pictures of most of the directors, and offers a short bibliography which separates its listings by language--English, French, Hungarian, Italian and Portuguese. A short surface assessment of Swedish cinema during the sixties, this book is an acceptable addition to all collections.

2598. The New York Times Directory of the Film, by Staff of the New York Times. 1,243 p. illus. New York: Arno, 1971.

An introduction by Arthur Knight begins this spin-off from the massive six-volume set, The New York Times Film Reviews, 1913-1968. The contents include: 2,000 small photos of actors and actresses; nearly 900 pages of credits (covers all 18,000 films of the large set); awards section, including Academy (from 1927), New York Film Critics (from 1935), and New York Times Ten Best (from 1924);

500 reviews, with selection based on awards listed above, arranged chronologically; a listing of 1,500 film companies and their product. Much of the material here is selected from the key or index volume to the large set. This does not in any way diminish its value or potential. The vast amount of film information in this single volume makes it a "must" for all school, academic and public libraries that do not have the larger set.

2599. The New York Times Film Reviews, 1969-1970. 333 p. illus. New York: The New York Times, 1971.
This is the seventh volume in the set of New York Times Film Reviews and it now extends the collection from 1913 to 1970. Some 809 films are considered with illustrations and an index of over 10,000 entries. The volume is available by itself or as part of the complete set, which was evaluated as essential for any large collection. Smaller libraries are referred to the two mini-versions of the large set (2598, 2600).

2600. The New York Times Film Reviews, 1913-1970: A One-Volume Selection, by George Amberg. 495 p. illus. New York: Quadrangle Books, 1971.
The blurb on the dust jacket says it right off: "For people who really deserve the enormous 7-volume set of the New York Times Film Reviews but just can't spare $425." Insert the words "and libraries" after "people" and it's even more valid.
George Amberg has done a brilliant job in his one-volume selection of 400 of the reviews. This testimonial is based upon the experience of using the volume for several years and not finding it lacking more than once or twice. Reviews of nearly all of the critical and popular classics of film seem to be here. In addition, there are six essays which divide the reviews into general eras, and an introduction, all by Amberg. A portrait section of the stars is unnecessary and the title index would be more functional if it were placed up front, rather than with those portraits. All of this is unimportant compared with the reference value of this book for the smaller public or school library, or even its appeal to the individual who wants a basic reference work on film. Essential for all film collections that do not own the seven-volume set.
NOTE: The annotation (1040) for the New York Times Films Reviews lists only six volumes covering 1913-1968. A further collection (2599) has since been published

for the 1969-1970 period and it is this volume that now makes up the seven-volume set mentioned above.

2601.   NICHOLAS AND ALEXANDRA.   28 p.   (paperback) illus.   Englewood Cliffs, N.J.:   Charnell Theatrical Enterpr., 1971.
The emphasis is on history in this oversized souvenir book which includes several double-paged illustrations. In addition to the interesting historical background material, a diagram showing the royal line of Russian Nobility is included.   Cast and production credits are noted.

2602.   NIGHT AND FOG, by Paul A. Schreivogel.   20 p. (paperback) illus.   Dayton, Ohio: Pflaum, 1970.
A study guide for the 1955 film directed by Alain Resnais.   Found in Films in Depth (2274) and also available separately.

2603.   A NIGHT AT THE OPERA.   A script of the 1935 film, by George S. Kaufman, Morrie Ryskind, James McGuiness (director: Sam Wood).   256 p. (paperback) illus.   New York: Viking, 1972.
Contains cast and production credits.

2604.   A NIGHT TO REMEMBER.   16 p.   (paperback) illus.   New York: Program Publishing Co., 1958.
There is very little narrative in this souvenir book but some of the other features are quite unusual: for example, a diagram of the damage done by the iceberg to the Titanic, shown in a cross-section view, and a reproduction of a newspaper report of the disaster.   Also included are the usual cast and production credits.

2605.   99+ Films on Drugs, edited by David O. Weber.   68 p.   (paperback) New York: Educational Film Library Association, 1970.
Here is a filmography which must be approached with caution and additional information.   Originally published by the University of California with a grant from the Maurice Falk Medical Fund, the book lists more than 99 films that deal with some aspect of drugs.   Each entry begins with the title, year of release, time, color or black and white, distributor and producer.   A lengthy descriptive annotation is followed by an evaluation.   There is a final rating (Poor, Fair, Average, Good, Very Good, Excellent) and a recommendation for appropriate audiences (primary, intermediate, junior high, high school, college, adult, professional).   For convenience there is a rating summary of all the films (only

two are rated as excellent), and a classified index which groups films into areas of interest such as community action, rehabilitation, research, history, etc. Some drug films not reviewed are named, along with some titles that are currently unavailable. A distributor directory completes the volume.

The caution indicated in the opening sentence is occasioned by a report by the National Coordinating Council on Drug Education, a consortium of 133 organizations. In a publication entitled Drug Abuse Films--An Evaluation Report, they state that the majority of drug abuse films available today are "unacceptable." Of the 220 films reviewed, only 35 (16%) were approved as "scientifically and conceptually acceptable." Thirty-one per cent were totally unacceptable and 53 per cent were considered "restricted" since they require special care in presentation. There are precautions urged in this volume but one wonders how many of the 99+ films fit into the categories of the NCCDE Report. The filmography is therefore a reference to be used with an awareness of its potential for good--or possible harm.

2606.   NINOTCHKA. A script of the 1939 film, by Charles Brackett, Billy Wilder and Walter Reisch (director: Ernst Lubitsch). 114 p. (paperback) illus. New York: Viking Press, 1972.
Contains cast credits and production credits.

2607.   Non-Fiction Film: A Critical History, by Richard Meran Barsam. 332 p. (paperback) illus. New York: Dutton, 1973.
This new critical history has much to recommend it. In considering the major periods and creators of documentary-factual films, it discusses the early films of Russia and America, the British school led by John Grierson, films surrounding the decade of World War II, the contribution of Robert Flaherty, the new documentaries of the 60s, and much more. The author describes a large number of films and provides political and sociological background to explain their origin and importance. The narrative is lively, respectful, and objective.

Supporting sections are equally fine. Illustrations abound and they are well selected and nicely placed throughout the book. Films discussed in detail are listed in the appendix along with distributor information. An awards section, a strong bibliography and a lengthy index complete the book. While non-fiction films have been neglected in the past, there is evidence of an awakening interest and enthusiasm for them today. This volume will reinforce, encourage

233

and expand that interest. It is highly recommended for all collections.

2608.   NO REASON TO STAY, by Paul A. Schreivogel.
         19 p. (paperback) illus. Dayton, Ohio: Pflaum,
         1970.
         A study guide for the 1966 film directed by Mort
Ransen. Found in Films in Depth (2274) and also available
separately.

2609.   NORTH BY NORTHWEST. A script of the 1959
         film, by Ernest Lehman (director: Alfred Hitch-
         cock). 148 p. (paperback) illus. New York:
         Viking, 1972.
         Contains cast and production credits.

2610.   NOT RECONCILED. A script of the 1965 film, by
         Jean-Marie Straub (director: Jean-Marie Straub).
         176 p. (paperback) illus. New York: Viking,
         1972.
         Found in Straub (2761).

2611.   AN OCCURRENCE AT OWL CREEK BRIDGE, by
         Paul A. Schreivogel. 28 p. (paperback) illus.
         Dayton, Ohio: Pflaum, 1970.

2612.   AN OCCURRENCE AT OWL CREEK BRIDGE, by
         Gerald R. Barrett and Thomas L. Erskine. 216 p.
         (paperback) illus. Encino, Cal.: Dickenson Pub-
         lishing Co., 1973.
         This second title of the "From Fiction to Film"
series is consistent in quality with the first (2736). An introduction is followed by the original short story, "An Occurrence at Owl Creek Bridge," by Ambrose Bierce. Six
short articles of criticism about the story conclude the fiction section. The section devoted to the film is unique. A
shot analysis approach to the scripts is employed. Explanations of shots, transitions, camera movement, camera angles and sound precede the presentation of two scripts derived from Bierce's original story. The first is THE
BRIDGE (or THE SPY), an 11-minute film directed in 1931
by King Vidor and notable for the use of Soviet editing techniques. More famous is Robert Enrico's short film, AN
OCCURRENCE AT OWL CREEK BRIDGE, which is presented
next. Five critical articles on the films complete the film
section. A list of questions leading to the writing of papers
completes the book.

The concept, design, and selection of materials in the book is laudable. In secondary schools and colleges, the potential for use is enormous. In addition, the book is most acceptable for general collections. For this audience the book is highly recommended.

2613.   OEDIPUS REX. A script of the 1970 film, by Pier Paolo Pasolini (director: Pier Paolo Pasolini). 150 p. (paperback) illus. New York: Simon and Schuster, 1971.
Contains: "Why That of Oedipus is a Story" by Pier Paolo Pasolini; cast and credits; "Cutting Continuity."

2614.   Off With Their Heads, by Frances Marion. 356 p. illus. New York: Macmillan, 1972.
Frances Marion enjoyed a career in Hollywood for more than 50 years, working as actress, writer, director and producer. Her greatest renown came as the author of screenplays for films such as THE WIND, ANNA CHRISTIE, DINNER AT EIGHT, and CAMILLE. The story she relates is only coincidentally autobiography--in fact, she tells little of her personal life, preferring to relate the story of Hollywood with an emphasis on the personalities. The pages are strewn with all the famous names but there is always a rationale for inclusion; the author is never guilty of name-dropping. Her style is that of a screenplay writer who likes "scenes" rather than gossipy sensationalism. Thus the effect on some readers may be one of historical distrust but the book is interesting in spite of a few slight inaccuracies. Because it lacks the "best-seller" elements of wit, exposé, cynicism, and bitchiness, it may not reach a wide audience, but it is a memoir that many would appreciate and enjoy.
Supporting the warm, engrossing narrative is a fine collection of photographs that are accurately reproduced. In addition there is a detailed index and a filmography which lists 137 entries from A GIRL OF YESTERDAY (1915) to THE CLOWN (1953). Similar in certain ways to Anita Loos' A Girl Like I (604), this volume covers a longer period of Hollywood history and offers a broader but gentler view. The book will need the librarian's recommendation since the title may not attract the readership that would appreciate author Marion's affectionate, lady-like, discreet style. Recommended for all collections.

2615.   THE OLD MAN AND THE SEA. 14 p. (paperback) illus. New York: Souvenir Program, Inc., 1958.
The focus is on people in this souvenir book. It

shows a few highlight scenes and then spotlights author Ernest Hemingway, star Spencer Tracy, producer Leland Hayward, director John Sturges, composer Dimitri Tiomkin, and cameraman James Wong Howe. Even Jack Warner gets into the act by furnishing an introduction to the book.

2616.   OLIVER, by Nathan Weiss.   48 p.   (paperback)
        illus.   New York: National Publishers, 1968.
        The attractive color photography in this souvenir
book is its outstanding feature.   Following an exposition of
the story and an account of the making of the film, the large
cast of featured players is given special attention.   Other
supporting cast members are noted, as are many of the behind-the-camera people including director Carol Reed and
dance director Oona White.

2617.   The Oliviers, by Felix Barker.   371 p.   illus.
        Philadelphia: J. B. Lippincott, 1953.
        This early partial biography of the famous acting
team takes the reader up to early 1953.   Viewed from the
seventies, the story is quite incomplete.   Vivien Leigh had
an active career up to the time of her death in 1967 and, at
this writing, Lord Olivier is still very busy professionally.
Ironically, the book ends with the leading characters happily
married.   The divorce of the Oliviers took place in 1960.
        The part of their lives that is related here is fully
detailed; this is an "authorized" biography.   During its writing the author had access to the subjects, their friends, letters, documents, and diaries.   The accent is on a recount-
ing of professional matters rather than personal relationships.
The filmmaking of both actors receives an adequate coverage.
Olivier's early disasters with Garbo, WUTHERING HEIGHTS,
HAMLET, and his other films are all described, as are
Leigh's GONE WITH THE WIND, CAESAR AND CLEOPATRA,
and A STREETCAR NAMED DESIRE.   The book is a prime
source of biographical information (see 2482) about two of
the most famous film actors of this century.   Many illustrations and a good index add to the book's reference value.
A chronology of their appearances in plays and films would
have helped considerably.   For larger collections the book
would seem to be an essential, in spite of its early cut-off.
For other collections it is a worthy addition.

2618.   On Cukor, by Gavin Lambert.   276 p.   illus.   New
        York: G. P. Putnams, 1972.
        When one examines the Cukor filmography, it ap-
pears that he has directed almost every other well known

film--and probably every major star except John Wayne. Since he is still active, he may get to Wayne yet.

This book is taken from Oral History Tapes sponsored by The American Film Institute and is a long edited interview with Cukor. An introduction, an index, and the filmography support the text which resembles the Truffaut-Hitchcock collaboration. In a loose chronological order, films or groups of films are used as chapter bases for discussion. A few general observations on persons, ideas, and techniques called "Interludes" punctuate the chapters. Lambert seems a superior interviewer for he does not display the awe and hero-worship that flawed the earlier model. He has obviously done his planning for this project extremely well, and his knowledge of the Cukor films is encyclopedic. Highly appreciative and respectful of Cukor's artistry, he does not hesitate, however, to express a difference of opinion. All this makes for fascinating reading.

A full portrait of the professional Cukor emerges, but the personal is never considered. His memory is not infallible--for example, he forgets Minnelli's THE CLOCK when he states that Garland had not played a serious role before A STAR IS BORN. He offers some obvious truths that have gone relatively unnoticed till now--e.g., the similarity between the Harlow-Beery pairing in DINNER AT EIGHT and the Holliday-Crawford duo in BORN YESTERDAY. In all of his responses Cukor seems honest, open, and relaxed, and most sensitive to the memory of the persons he has worked with. It is difficult to find any malice or bitterness, except toward those unnamed persons who cut several of his films into unrecognizable forms.

All of the illustrations--and there are many--are first rate in selection, correlation, content and reproduction. The book is an example of successful chemistry between interviewer and subject, recorded in a nicely produced book that warrants hard cover format. Highly recommended for all collections.

2619. ONE DAY IN THE LIFE OF IVAN DENISOVICH. A script of the 1970 film, by Ronald Harwood (director: Casper Wrede). 271 p. (paperback) illus. New York: Ballantine, 1971.
Found in The Making of ONE DAY IN THE LIFE OF IVAN DENISOVICH (2512).

2620. On Film, by Vernon Young. 428 p. Chicago: Quadrangle Books, 1972.
Vernon Young is an international film critic whose

work appears regularly in The Hudson Review. The author may be correct in his subtitle, "Unpopular Essays on a Popular Art," but only partially. Many of these witty and learned pieces will please enormously. A strong point of view coupled with the exposition of a knowing teacher characterize the writing. He is never afraid to champion a minority film cause or to search diligently to locate a forgotten film in order to reassure the correctness of his memory. The entertaining attacks he makes on other film critics, directors, etc. are never as devastating as he believes they are. Mr. Young is an eclectic writer whose statements indicate sensitivity, wit and experience.

The range of his topics is quite wide, taking in Nazi, Danish, Japanese, and Italian films; directors such as John Ford, Kurosawa, Eisenstein, Arne Sucksdorff; and re-evaluation of individual films such as THE THIRD MAN and THE LONG VOYAGE HOME. The reader who can come to these essays with a film aesthetic background, some open-mindedness, and initial patience will be rewarded immeasurably. The book is indexed. For any adult collection, the book is highly recommended. Younger readers may find it a bit too demanding.

2621.   The Only Good Indian, by Ralph and Natasha Friar. 332 p. illus. New York: Drama Book Specialists, 1972.
This unusual book explores the portrait of the Indian as reflected in both silent and sound films. Some attention is also paid to the image presented by literature. Final sections of the book include a listing of actors who frequently played Indians, and a long filmography that lists both sound and silent films. The films in this listing are arranged by subject category. There are some interesting visuals and the book is indexed. This is at present the definitive study of the Indian's portrayal in films. With the recent Brando action, perhaps more attention will be paid to the problem of the image of the American Indian. This volume should aid in any discussion which may ensue. Recommended for all film collections.

2622.   Only Victims, by Robert Vaughn. 355 p. New York: G. P. Putnams, 1972.
The original source for this book was Vaughn's doctoral dissertation, done at the University of Southern California. It quotes Dalton Trumbo's trenchant comment about there being no heroes, villains, saints or devils but only victims in that dark time of 1938 to 1958. This was the

period when investigations by the House Committee on Un-American Activities (HUAC) were prevalent. The study concerns itself with five different HUAC hearings: Martin Dies (1938), J. Parnell Thomas (1947), John Woods (1951-52), Harold Velde-Francis Walters (1953-55), and the Passport Hearings (1958). Vaughn tries to examine the effects of HUAC by considering three possibilities: Actual Effects (theatre closings, jobs lost, etc.), Probable Effects (moral, personal, and procedural), and Possible Effects (constructive, evolutionary, unapparent as yet). His conclusions are twofold: first, that the major goal of the Committee was punishment; and second, that the stifling of creative artists who lived in fear of the Committee is an incalculable loss. There are, of course, implications for us today and Vaughn notes these.

Senator George McGovern introduces the book; it has several appendices, a detailed bibliography and an index. While the book will appeal to a limited audience, its sound argument deserves a wider one. This book is one of the best of several recent ones on the hearings. All deserve the attention of anyone concerned with misuse of power, governmental or otherwise. Highly recommended for public and academic libraries.

2623. ORANGE AND BLUE, by Paul A. Schreivogel. 20 p. (paperback) illus. Dayton, Ohio: Pflaum, 1970.
A study guide for the 1962 film directed by Peter Chermayeff and Clare Chermayeff. Found in Films in Depth (2274) and also available separately.

2624. The Original Sin, by Anthony Quinn. 311 p. Boston: Little, Brown, 1972.
This is at best a partial autobiography, emphasizing the pre-screen years. Using psychiatric sessions and the literary metaphor of an 11-year-old boy to represent his immaturity, Quinn resorts to shock words and situations, frank descriptions of sexual encounters, and mental flagellation to interest the reader. It doesn't work too well.

The first third of the book tells of his parents and his life as a chicano in the slums of Los Angeles during the twenties. Later, encounters with Aimee Semple McPherson, Mae West, John Barrymore, Carole Lombard, Gary Cooper and Cecil B. DeMille are described. The book concludes with his discovery of his ability to love and the inevitable banishment of the "boy" Quinn. The two short sections that deal with his film career are fine. His experience as a beginning film actor in DeMille's THE PLAINSMAN is a fascinating reminiscence while the early contract negotiations

239

will give the reader some insight into the operations of film studios of the thirties. The writing style is compounded of egotism, confession, sex and search. There are no illustrations, nor is an index provided. It is simply not "that kind of a book."

Admirers of Quinn will appreciate the exposure of self and others. Those who are less enthusiastic about his abilities will be bored by the heavy priority given to personal problems over professional matters. Acceptable for all collections. High school libraries may be sensitive to the frankness and candid style.

2625.   Origins of the American Film, by Gordon Hendricks.
         592 p. illus. New York: Arno, 1972.
         Arno has performed a public service in gathering
three books by Gordon Hendricks and publishing them in one volume. A new introduction by Hendricks sets the stage for these remarkable researches. Titles are: The Edison Motion Picture Myth (340); Beginnings of the Biograph (103); The Kinetoscope (816).

2626.   The Origins of American Film Criticism, by Myron
         Osborn Lounsbury. 547 p. New York: Arno, 1973.
         This is one of six doctoral dissertations reproduced
by Arno exactly as they were submitted to the degree-granting school. Keeping in mind Ernest Callenbach's appraisal of American film literature as mostly a debate between form and content, an examination of the film literature preceding the second World War is attempted here. The purpose is to offer an account of the evolution and growth of serious film criticism from 1909 to 1939, and its effect on the development and improvement of film techniques. The Film Index (465) was used as a major source in this study, which spotlights Vachel Lindsay, Hugo Munsterberg, Gilbert Seldes, Victor Freeburg, and other early writers. Publication in 1939 of Lewis Jacobs' The Rise of the American Film provides the cut-off point of the study.

         A conclusion suggests the existence of six basic
types of critical opinion: Liberal Patrician, Modern Liberal, Social Radical, Popular Cultist, Aesthetic Idealist, and Modern Aesthete. The film critics of the pre-1939 period did not achieve a blend of form and content to any extent. A bibliography and an index complete the book. Acceptable for large academic collections.

2627.   ORPHEUS. A script of the 1950 film, by Jean
         Cocteau (director: Jean Cocteau). 250 p. (paper-
         back) illus. New York: Grossman, 1972.

Found in Jean Cocteau: Three Screenplays (2157).
Contains cast credits.

2628.	The Other Hollywood, by Edward Thorpe.	174 p.
London:	Michael Joseph, 1970.
Another nail in Hollywood's coffin! It purports to
examine Hollywood today, and some idea of the approach can
be seen by the chapter titles: Hideous Hollywood; Hi-Life
Hollywood; Has-Been Hollywood; Housewives' Hollywood; High
School Hollywood; Hustler's Hollywood; Homosexual's Hollywood; Hard Core Hollywood; Hybrid Hollywood; Hopeful Hollywood. The book is an example of sensationalized sociology.
Acceptable only for very large collections.

2629.	Our Will Rogers, by Homer Croy.	377 p.	New
York:	Duell Sloane Pearce, 1953.
Homer Croy was the author of They Had to See
Paris, a novel upon which Will Rogers' first sound film was
based. The men became friends in 1930, at the beginning
of Rogers' second career in films. This is evident in the
attention given by Croy to Rogers in the Hollywood of the
30's. The early chapter on the silent films is also well
written. In fact, the book is surprising when one recall's
Croy's disastrous biography of D. W. Griffith (1277). The
sources for the text are listed in a long appendix and the
book is indexed. Since there is more attention to the films
in this volume, it is the one that might be included in a collection to represent Rogers. Acceptable for all collections.

2630.	OVERTURE, OVERTURE/NYITANY, by Paul A.
Schreivogel.	20 p.	(paperback) illus.	Dayton,
Ohio:	Pflaum, 1970.
A study guide for the 1958 film, OVERTURE, and
the 1965 film, OVERTURE/NYITANY, directed by Janos
Vadasz. Found in Films in Depth (2274) and also available
separately.

2631.	THE OXBOW INCIDENT. A script of the 1943 film,
by Lamar Trotti (director:	William Wellman).
394 p.	(paperback) illus.	New York:	Globe Book
Co., 1972.
Included in Three Major Screenplays (2805). The
script is preceded by: 1) "About the Author," 2) "About
the Screenplay," and followed by: 1) "What the Critics
Said," and 2) "To Enrich Your Reading."

2632.	PAINT YOUR WAGON. 32 p.	(paperback)	illus.
New York:	National Publishers, 1969.

Peter Max's influence is apparent in the graphics work for this souvenir book. Cover designs and titling are unusual for the subject matter and probably reflect the lack of faith the producers had in their original material. All the songs used in the film are listed, along with other cast and production credits. Stars Lee Marvin, Clint Eastwood, and Jean Seberg share the spotlight with director Joshua Logan, composer Frederick Loewe, and author-lyricist Alan Jay Lerner.

2633.   PANDORA'S BOX. A script of the 1928 film, by G. W. Pabst (director: G. W. Pabst). 136 p. (paperback) illus. New York: Simon and Schuster, 1971.
Contains: "Pabst and Lulu" by Louise Brooks; "Pabst and the Miracle of Louise Brooks" by Lotte Eisner; cast and credits.

2634.   Milton's PARADISE LOST. A screenplay for the Cinema of the Mind, by John Collier. 144 p. (paperback) New York: Alfred Knopf, 1973.
John Collier has written "Paradise Lost" as a screenplay with interesting results. Called "a screenplay for the cinema of the mind," it offers teachers of English and creative writing an example of what might be done as a student exercise. An article, "The Apology," precedes the script. Acceptable for all collections.

2635.   The Paramount Pretties, by James Robert Parish. 587 p. illus. New Rochelle, N.Y.: Arlington House, 1972.
The ladies have an almost exclusive spotlight in this collective biography. The subjects have been selected from the Paramount Studio contract list but the text considers films made for other studios as well. In approximately chronological order, according to their tenure at Paramount, the "Pretties" are: Gloria Swanson, Clara Bow, Claudette Colbert, Carole Lombard, Marlene Dietrich, Miriam Hopkins, Sylvia Sidney, Mae West, Dorothy Lamour, Paulette Goddard, Veronica Lake, Diana Lynn, Betty Hutton, Joan Caulfield, Lizabeth Scott, and Shirley MacLaine.
A short biographical overview introduces the detailed account of each subject's professional life, and only minor attention is paid to the personal side. Each portrait closes with a filmography containing technical and cast credits and a picture collection of about two dozen stills, portraits, and candids squeezed into 5 or 6 pages. The appendix has brief biographical sketches of the producers who

furthered the careers of the main subjects: Jesse Lasky, Emanuel Cohen, William Le Baron, Ernst Lubitsch, B. P. Schulberg, Hal Wallis, and Adolph Zukor.

Most of the narrative is informational--a recital of facts, film plots, quotations, etc. When a negative criticism is offered, it is softened so that all the subjects emerge as rather nice ladies. That the author apparently loves 'em all is reflected in the star-worship approach used throughout. Male actors on the Paramount list do not fare nearly as well: "The rare exception of virile sexuality was Alan Ladd --the rest were as bland as could be: Fred MacMurray, Joel McCrea, Ray Milland, William Holden, Brian Donlevy, Sonny Tufts, and Robert Preston." Similar barbed comments appear about performances in films mostly forgotten.

Although there is much familiar material in the book (several of the ladies have individual biographies in print at this time), the reading is still entertaining, informative, and memory-prodding. Filmographies appear rather complete and are a fine supplement to the text. The pictures seem to be an afterthought and their small size and poor reproduction lessen their effectiveness. No index is provided and the only introduction is that which appears on the book's dust jacket. Although there are minor faults with this volume, the abundance of data presented in a readable, entertaining way should insure its appeal to a wide range of readers. Good for all collections.

2636.   LA PASSION de JEANNE d'ARC (PASSION OF JOAN OF ARC), by David Bordwell. 83 p. (paperback) Bloomington, Ind.: Indiana University Press, 1973.

This filmguide takes on a most demanding task: that of providing an analysis of a film that consists of many titles, a minimum of action, and a maximum of facial closeups. David Bordwell, a young author and obvious admirer of Carl Dreyer, is more than able to meet the challenge.

The book provides the usual credits, plot outlines, and production details. It is in the section on director Carl Dreyer and in the long analysis of the film that the quality is apparent. Both sections indicate a scholarship and drive not unlike the determination the author attributes to Dreyer. The summary critique is also a model for future authors in this series to emulate. A filmography-listing, a fine annotated bibliography, two rental sources and some notes to the text complete the book.

One minor reservation concerns the author's limited attention to the sound version of the film which is a desecration of Dreyer's original. The potential user of this film should be warned that the sound version is to be avoided if at all possible. Turning off the sound, as Bordwell suggests, is only a minimum help. The removal of titles in favor of narration and the third-rate dramatic readings alter the pace of the original film completely. The above notwithstanding, the book is admirable on all counts and is highly recommended for all collections.

2637.   The Path of Fame of the Czechoslovak Film, by Jaroslav Broz. 112 p. (paperback) illus. Prague: Ceskoslovensky Filmexport, 1967.
Produced in rather primitive fashion, this short paperback is a history of Czech film. While the many illustrations are uniformly excellent, the text is somewhat pedantic and plodding. The typewritten pages do not add to the book's values.

It is, however, indexed, and includes a listing of prize-winning films. Since so many of the films are obscure to American audiences, the book has most value to the researcher or the historian and belongs only in the larger collections.

2638.   Patterns of Realism, by Roy Armes. 226 p. illus. New York: Barnes, 1972.
This study of the Italian Neo-Realist cinema begins with a discussion of realism and an attempt to describe the roots and origins of this movement in the pre-World War II cinema and literature of Italy. Visconti's OSSESSIONE is the link between the past and the Neo-Realist years (1945 to 1953) of the Italian cinema. Roberto Rossellini, Luchino Visconti and Vittorio De Sica (with writer Cesare Zavattini) are given major attention, and the works of Aldo Vergano, Giuseppe De Santis, Alberto Lattuada, Pietro Germi, Luigi Zampa, Luciano Emmer and Renato Castellani are also noted. Films which are analyzed in depth include OSSESSIONE, ROME OPEN CITY, PAISAN, GERMANY YEAR ZERO, LA TERRA TREMA, SHOESHINE, BICYCLE THIEVES, UMBERTO D, and MIRACLE IN MILAN. A final evaluative section summarizes the Italian Neo-Realist movement and denotes its contribution to films and directors who followed.

A filmography arranged in chronological order is given of the films mentioned in the text, and there is a lengthy bibliography. The book is indexed and illustrated with many excellent photographs. This serious study is impressive for several reasons: the importance of the topic, the scholarly but unstuffy treatment, the excellence of the supporting illustrations and documentation, and the willingness of author Armes to take a frequently vulnerable position with confidence. Recommended for all collections and specifically for college and university libraries.

2639. PEPE, by Harold Wilson. 36 p. illus. New York: Columbia Pictures, Inc., 1960.
Supposedly written as a diary by Cantinflas, this souvenir book describes the making of the film in studio press-release fashion. The latter sections are devoted to full page biographies of the other two major stars, Dan Dailey and Shirley Jones, and director-producer George Sidney. Cameo stars are grouped in page quartets and major production personnel get individual attention. The complete cast and production credits are given on the inside back cover pages, along with a listing of the musical numbers used in the film.

2640. PERSONA. A script of the 1966 film, by Ingmar Bergman (director: Ingmar Bergman). 191 p. (paperback) illus. New York: Grossman, 1972. Found in Bergman: PERSONA and SHAME (2058).

2641. Perspectives on the Study of Film, edited by John Stuart Katz. 339 p. illus. Boston: Little, Brown & Co., 1971.
The aim of editor Katz in this anthology is to offer the educator some suggestions for approaching film or film study. Four major sections indicate the large areas of concern: 1. Film Study and Education; 2. The Film As Art and Humanities; 3. The Film As Communications, Environment, Politics; 4. Curriculum Design and Evaluation in Film Study. The range of authors represented is very wide and many impressive names are included: Huxley, McLuhan, Balazs, Sontag, Bluestone, Sarris, Kael, Mekas, etc.
This is not a textbook but a collection of writings designed to encourage a philosophy about film and film study. The articles are well-selected, a few illustrations are provided, and a bibliography completes the book. As with any compilation, certain of the articles are familiar, but the majority offer new insights and ideas that will stimulate anyone concerned with teaching film. A specialized book that will have a limited appeal to the general reader but which belongs in all school collections.

2642. PETER PAN. An unfilmed script, by James M. Barrie. 250 p. London: Peter Davis, 1954.
Found in Fifty Years of Peter Pan by Roger Lancelyn Green. This book contains information on the numerous productions of this play.

2643.   Photoplay Treasury, edited by Barbara Gelman.
373 p.   illus.   New York: Crown, 1972.
If a reader is told that an oversized coffee-table
book containing "nostalgic picture-and-word stories" from
Photoplay Magazine from the teen years through the forties
is due, he anticipates something quite special.   The anticipa-
tions are not fulfilled in this case; the book is a disappointment.

Very little quarrel can be made with the selection--
there was a sameness about the fan-magazine articles of the
period; only the names of the subjects were changed.   The
objection here is to the poor, indistinct, murky and sometimes nearly black reproduction of the illustrations.   Examples are abundant but pages 52, 60, 69, 75, 115, 116,
131, 214, 215, 227, 273, 327, 366, 367 are especially bad.
Where was production control on this vital element of the
book?   Today's reader will not have the patience to wade
through too many pages of studio press agentry verbiage;
visual nostalgia is the primary interest.   There are some
fine visuals in the book (pages 165, 308), which suggests
that the poor reproduction of many of the others was avoid-
able.   Stronger proof is available in a similar volume, The
Talkies (2776), which also used Photoplay articles but much
more satisfactorily.

There is so much potential enjoyment in this book
that it is disheartening to see it undermined by the careless
production.   Not recommended; instead, libraries are referred
to the above mentioned book by Richard Griffith, The Talkies
(2776).

2644.   A Pictorial History of Horror Movies, by Denis
Gifford.   216 p.   illus.   New York: Hamlyn, 1973.
Any book that extolls the fascination of the horror
movie can't be all bad; the trouble with this one is that it
could have been a lot better.   The author has a fine Dutton-
Vista book called Movie Monsters (971) to his credit.   Ex-
panding on that spare volume, he has produced an oversized
book which is very much like one of his topics, Jekyll and
Hyde.   It was written and printed in London, and some of
its attempts to appeal may be hard to comprehend here.
For example, the chapter headings and the text often strain
for humor where none is needed.   Do headings like "Dr.
Jekyll is Not Himself," "A Chip Off the Old Hump," and
"How Grand Was My Guignol" help?   Another reservation
concerns the identification of the stills.   In most cases all
stills on a two-page spread are identified in a paragraph
placed strategically on the page.   The reader will become

impatient rather quickly with uppers, lowers, lefts, rights, opposites, and bottoms.

The book does have some fine visuals. One of Claude Rains as the Phantom is almost worth the price alone, and there are many others of almost equal fascination. Reproduction ranges from good to excellent. An appendix contains a filmography for collecters, one bibliography for books and another for magazines, and a list of "H" certificate films ("H" meant "Horrific" in England, and no one under 16 was admitted to films marked as such). A rather complete index follows.

When the author is serious in his text, the material offered is very good. Visuals are mostly superior if the reader can bear the identification handicap mentioned above. To all these qualities, add an inexpensive price and the book can be recommended for all collections. It will certainly appeal to a large audience.

2645.   A Pictorial History of Westerns, by Michael Parkinson and Clyde Jeavons. 217 p. illus. New York: Hamlyn, 1973.

Similar to Gifford's A Pictorial History of Horror Movies (2644), this book has some of the same virtues and faults. The text is divided into sections on the films, the stars, the stalwarts, the directors and two sub-genres: the spaghetti westerns and the TV westerns.

Visuals again play a vital part and their quality ranges from exceptional to poor. The latter include poorly contrasted shots which obliterate faces while the former are some full-page portraits and several beautiful color stills. Fitting the scope of the western outdoor scene to a small illustration seems to be a problem. Many of the pictures are hard to interpret, with tiny figures seen against an enormous landscape. Identification is also a problem here, with one explanatory paragraph for all the visuals on one or a double page. The reader again encounters the upper, lower, right, left, top, bottom, opposite, across syndrome. A lengthy index completes the book. The text is above average, the visuals satisfactory for the most part, and the arrangement a valid one for such a survey. Acceptable for all collections.

2646.   Picture Pioneers, by G. J. Mellor. 96 p. (paperback) illus. Newcastle-upon-Tyne, England: Frank Graham, 1971.

Subtitled "The Story of the Northern Cinema, 1896-1971," this short book was prepared as a tribute to the 75th anniversary of the first film showing in England. Its aim is to acknowledge the role played by the North of England in the development of cinema. Since much of the information was provided by the pioneers of the title, the emphasis is on the early years. Hundreds of unfamiliar names stud this factual account, along with brief descriptions of the technology, the theatres, and the films of the time. The narrative works its way up to the introduction of sound films and concludes with a short chapter on the 1930-1971 period. An interesting finale is provided by the statements of more than 30 pioneers, who are each allotted a few paragraphs for a flashback.

Picture quality is only fair because of the age of the photographs used. An index of names and theatres is provided. The local accounts may be correct but the author's general knowledge of cinema history is suspect; for example, he overlooks DON JUAN completely in the account of sound films. This is very specialized history that belongs only in larger collections.

2647.   Playboy Interviews Peter Fonda and Joan Baez. 144 p. (paperback) illus. Chicago: Playboy Press, 1971.
The interview with Fonda gives his predictions about film, his attitudes toward life, and a filmography.

2648.   Playboy Sex in Cinema # 2, by Hollis Alpert and Arthur Knight. 144 p. (paperback) illus. Chicago: Playboy Press, 1972.
The usual three parts appear in this annual: the films of 1971, a photo section, and the stars of the films. Acceptable for collections serving mature audiences where it will be quite popular for any one of a number of reasons. The sections by Alpert and Knight are, of course, quite good, but one wonders how many of the borrowers will read them.

2649.   Politics and Film, by Leif Furhammar and Folke Isaksson. 257 p. illus. New York: Praeger, 1971.
The authors attempt to show the political content or purpose of some films made during or about the wars of the last 60 years. Attention is also given to some of the newer revolutionary films. After the historical framework has been established, certain individual films are described: TRIUMPH OF THE WILL, MRS. MINIVER, THE HITLER GANG, TORN CURTAIN, THE GREEN BERETS, CHE, etc. The concluding section summarizes the aesthetics of propaganda, the development of leader by film image (Churchill,

248

Kennedy, Hitler, etc.), the unification of a diverse population into a "We," and finally the image of the enemy. Some conclusions complete the text which is supplemented by an extensive bibliography, an index and many fine illustrations.

Although the text is lacking in definition and an overall structure, it is still an intelligent introduction to a neglected topic in film literature. Written with clarity, the book often indicates scholarship and background. For many it will be provocative and exciting; others will take issue with its lack of focus and viewpoint. Essential for all college collections and recommended for all others.

2650.   Popcorn and Parable: A New Look at the Movies, by Roger Kahle and Robert E. A. Lee. 128 p. illus. Minneapolis: Augsburg Publishing House, 1971.

As stated in the preface to this compact volume, its purpose is "to find in feature films a resource of our own faith and for our communication of religious truths to others." The authors urge the reader to study, to understand, and then to use films rather than think of them as a threat.

After an initial overview of the feature film of today, attention is given to topics such as film communication, fads, exploitation, sex, violence, etc. Many constructive suggestions are given in the closing sections which deal with film criticism and film festivals. A short bibliography and some explanatory notes are appended.

This is another volume in the growing list of books addressed to church workers. It is sound enough in its argument to merit consideration by many lay readers. Points are made with clarity and succinctness, the style is readable and the content is impressive. In summary, a fine small volume, suitable for all collections.

2651.   Pop Culture in America, edited by David Manning White. 279 p. (paperback) Chicago: Quadrangle Books, 1970.

An anthology designed to inform the reader about what's going on in radio, television, film, theatre, art, music, and books. Articles on film include the fine debate between Carl Foreman and Tyrone Guthrie on film vs. theatre (Foreman wins easily); "The Movies are Now High Art," by Richard Schickel; "Biggest Money-Making Movie of All Time--How Come?" by Joan Barthel; and "The Bard Competes with The Body" by C. A. LeJeune. The Foreman-Guthrie debate alone is worth the price of the book. Recommended for all film collections.

2652.   The Popular Arts: A Critical Reader, edited by
         Irving Deer and Harriet A. Deer. 356 p. (paper-
         back) New York: Charles Scribners Sons, 1967.
         A few of the more familiar articles on film appear
in this anthology: "The Gangster As Tragic Hero" by Robert
Warshow; "History on the Silver Screen" by Gilbert Highet;
"From the Film" by Albert Hunt; "The Witness Point" by
Vernon Young; and "Comedy's Greatest Era" by James Agee.
A group of study questions follows each article. These five
excellent articles listed are surrounded by several general
articles on popular art topics--Kitsch, Pornography, Aes-
thetics, etc.--and a few specific ones on Architecture, Jazz,
Literature, Television, Still Photography, the Western novel,
Science Fiction, Detective Story, American Musicals, Comic
Strips and Best Sellers; the appeal of the book is apparent.
For anyone looking for broad exploration and discussion of
the popular arts with an emphasis on films, this volume will
be quite satisfying. It is a good addition to all collections.
         Another book with the same major title exists, writ-
ten by Stuart Hall and Paddy Whannel (1118). It is a detailed
presentation of the popular arts as the authors perceive them
rather than an anthology. The approach is an integrated one
with film examples and references used throughout the text.
The effort, scholarship, and originality found here makes for
the difference between a good book (the Deer's volume) and
an excellent one (the Hall-Whannel volume).

2653.   PORGY AND BESS, by Ray Freiman. 36 p. illus.
         New York: Random House, 1959.
         This souvenir book published by Random House is a
model for other publishers to emulate: photography, arrangement, art work, and content are all outstanding. Beginning
with a tribute to producer Sam Goldwyn, who gets more acknowledgment than anyone else, the book uses stills from the
film to outline the story. A biography of George Gershwin
is followed by Deems Taylor's account of the creation of the
opera, "Porgy and Bess." Leo Lerman provides additional
information on changing DuBose Heyward's story from a book
into a play and then into the Gershwin opera. Major cast
members are given short biographical sketches; the production personnel fare somewhat better. Closing pages list the
songs and complete cast and production credits.

2654.   Porno Star, by Tina Russell. 224 p. (paperback)
         New York: Lancer Books, 1973.
         The author has appeared in more than 75 full-length
pornography films and is obviously well-qualified to discuss
the porno film business. Real names have been changed in

the text and, since there are no pictures in the book, the
question of authenticity arises. If porno filmmaking is really as the author describes it here, that any film ever gets
made is amazing. The performers never seem to tire of
sexual activity with other actors, crew members, and themselves. This is pure pornography in print, and a suspect
put-on. Not for libraries but, along with the Linda Lovelace
book (2430), it is noted for the record.

2655   Practical Guide to Classroom Media, by Dolores
        Lindon and David Linton. 118 p. (paperback) illus.
        Dayton, Ohio: Pflaum, 1971.
        Another attractive volume designed to stimulate teach-
ers in the use of media for the classroom. One chapter
deals with film and discusses how film works, choosing a
projector, the nature of film, film criticism, film language,
selecting filmmaking equipment, and student filmmaking. A
list of publishers and distributors completes the chapter.
Other sections of the book deal with radio, recordings, still
photography and television. In addition, there are suggested
procedures for selection, evaluation and administration of
media for the classroom.
        The chapter on film provides a good overview of
film in the classroom. While other books in the Pflaum
series cover the subject in much greater depth, this book
can serve as an introduction for the new teacher. Highly
recommended for all school libraries.

2656.   The Primal Screen, by Andrew Sarris. 337 p.
        New York: Simon and Schuster, 1973.
        Sarris writes with style, wit, intelligence and a
known viewpoint--all of which give him a kind of star quality.
You know well ahead of time what the performance will be.
In this collection, he has gathered writings from Film Cul-
ture, Film Comment, The New York Times, Princeton
Alumni Weekly, Columbia University Forum Moviegoer, The
Drama Review, Mid-Century Arts Magazine, Sight and Sound
and, of course, The Village Voice. He tackles causes (an-
swering Kael and "Raising Kane"), styles (Keaton, James
Stewart, Max Ophuls), genres (The Musical, The Spectacu-
lar), politics (Z, THE BIRTH OF A NATION), tributes (von
Sternberg, Garland, Lloyd), and literary authors (Kerouac,
Orwell). There are nearly 50 articles in all. The book is
indexed. Anyone who enjoys and admires Sarris will delight
in this collection. Since that potential audience is quite
large, the book can be enthusiastically recommended for all
collections.

2657.   A Primer for Film-Making, by Kenneth H. Roberts
         and Win Sharples, Jr. 546 p. (paperback) illus.
         Indianapolis, Inc.: Bobbs-Merrill, 1971.
         The subtitle, "A Complete Guide to 16 and 35mm
Film Production," is modest for this oversized volume.
Not only are all the elements of filmmaking covered thoroughly, but there are several outstanding supporting sections.
Beginning with a discussion of budgets, the authors cover in
succession the following topics: camera, lens, film, lighting, script, lab development, editing, cutting room, opticals,
titles, sound, sound cutting room, sound mix, and printing
the film.
         A long list of recommended films, arranged chrono-
logically by periods and listed under various countries, is
the first appendix. An outline of the items to consider in
preparing a budget follows. A most valuable glossary based
on American standard nomenclature and a short bibliography
complete the text. A detailed index to all the material is
provided.
         The authors' approach to their subject is broad and
one applauds their inclusion and attention to theory, practice,
creativity, technology, and human frailty.   They are interested in telling you "how" but suggest that creativity, imagination and experience must be added to technical proficiency
in order to become a true filmmaker. Evidence of this attitude can be found in the bibliography, which lists no technical books but mostly titles that deal with film aesthetics
and theory. The recommended films again underline this
view.
         By reason of its comprehensive content, treatment,
approach, and arrangement, this volume can be enthusiastically recommended for all collections. The serious filmmaker will probably want to own a personal copy, more as
a continuing reference than as a reading experience.

2658.   A Primer of Visual Literacy, by Donis A. Dondis.
         180 p. illus. Cambridge, Mass.: MIT Press,
         1973.
         According to Ms. Dondis, the invention of the cam-
era has brought about a dramatic new view of communication
and education. This primer is designed to teach students
the interconnected arts of visual communication. The ability
to see and read visual data is one broad definition of visual
literacy. One method of increasing that ability is to make
and design visual messages--art works, craftwork, graphics,
photographs, films, and television programs. The book
gives attention to all these areas in a sound text and, of
course, many visual examples. Noted here as one of the

volumes which has appeared recently on the topic of visual literacy, a topic of importance to film study and filmmaking.

2659.   Princess of Monaco: The Story of Grace Kelly, by
         Gant Gaither. 176 p. illus. New York: Holt,
         1957.
         For approximately 70 pages this book relates Grace Kelly's early life and Hollywood career. The remaining sections are devoted to her life as a princess. Even the short account of her film work consists mostly of brief mentions or surface anecdotes. The Academy Award gets two paragraphs, in which the author explains why she won. It seems she never missed a cue or a day of shooting, indicating a responsibility to her profession. She was cooperative and well-liked. Anyone interested in the validity of the Awards should watch Garland in A STAR IS BORN and Kelly in THE COUNTRY GIRL for a comparison of excellence with competence.
         A positive feature of the book is the three picture sections which total up to 48 pages. There is no index. The content is a surface recital of facts and trivia that sounds all too sticky to believe. Add to that a bland, worshipful writing style and all that is left are the illustrations. They alone make the book merely acceptable.

2660.   Principles of Cinematography, by Leslie Wheeler.
         440 p. illus. Hastings-On-Hudson, N.Y.: Morgan,
         1969.
         Covering the field of cinematography with remarkable thoroughness, this standard work is in its 4th edition. The processes and the apparatus for the production and exhibition of motion pictures are explained, along with a short history of each subject. Chapter topics include: General Principles, Cameras, Emulsions, Processing Equipment, Quality Control, Sensitometry, Printing Film, Reduction Process, Special Effects, Editing, Projectors, Sound, Processing Sound Film, and Sound Reproduction. A bibliography of more than 1,000 entries is especially valuable. One of the outstanding books on cinematography, this volume is highly recommended for all collections.

2661.   Print, Image and Sound: Essays on Media, edited
         by John Gordon Burke. 181 p. Chicago, Ill.:
         American Library Association, 1973.
         A review of five areas of media in the sixties: journalism, educational television, rock music, little magazines, and cinema. A bibliography follows each.

253

Charles T. Samuels is the author of the article on film, "Cinema in the Sixties." This was the decade of "The Director" and Samuels emphasizes that in both the text and the filmography; the latter is arranged by director rather than by national cinema, genre, or film title. As with any such survey, there are omissions (Visconti, Rossen, Frankenheimer, Rohmer) and questionable inclusions (Jessua, Heifetz, Carlsen, Troell). His strong preference for Kubrick's STRANGELOVE over 2001 is never justified in the text, nor is the inclusion of Truffaut's THE BRIDE WORE BLACK with his three early classics (and wasn't THE 400 BLOWS a film of the late fifties?). In any event, the purpose of the article is to give an overview of film in the sixties, and this it accomplishes. Acceptable for all collections.

2662.   The Private Life of Greta Garbo, by Rilla Page
         Palmborg.   282 p.   illus.   Garden City, N.Y.:
         Doubleday, 1931.
         In the introduction of this 1931 biography, the author writes: "This story will reveal the real Greta Garbo, the poor little Greta Garbo in Sweden, the Great Greta Garbo in Hollywood, Greta Garbo as her few intimate friends know her, Greta Garbo in her own home, a most amazing life of a great and most amazing person." The author had some moments with Garbo on a few occasions but the major sources of material are Garbo's cook and butler of this period, Gustaf and Sigrid Norin. John Loder and Wilhelm Sorensen tell a bit more but the rest of the material apparently comes from studio biographies, press releases, and newspaper reports.
         For such an early biography, this one has some virtues. It is flawed by its style and the elusiveness of its subject. Acceptable as supplementary material and suitable only for large collections.

2663.   PSYCHO, by James Naremore.   87 p.   (paperback)
         Bloomington, Ind.: Indiana University Press, 1973.
         One of a new series of filmguides, this short volume is not as immediately impressive as the others. If the reader is willing to accept PSYCHO as "a study of small-town repression that includes cinematic comments on the latent violence and prurience in the viewer himself," the book will be pleasing to him. If this attributing of values and messages to a film statement seems writer-originated rather than director-planned, one may have reservations. Just as there are unsatisfactory portions of the film--the final explanatory scenes which should belong to Norman

254

(Anthony Perkins) but which are given to an unfamiliar psychiatrist--there are some analyses and critical judgments here that will suggest more questions than they answer.

The volume contains the usual elements of this series--cast credits, a plot outline, a short section on Hitchcock, some production notes, an analysis, and a summary critique. The Hitchcock filmography is a selected listing of titles and the bibliography includes reviews, books, interviews and articles from periodicals. The analysis, which is the author's major contribution, leans heavily on the filmscript and the book by Robert Bloch. This section is a combination of straightforward exposition and unconvincing critical comment. Since so much has been written about PSYCHO previously, it may be difficult to do anything except provide a broad overview and summary. The author does this in adequate fashion.

Since the film is quite available via rentals and TV showings, the book should be popular with readers and viewers. It does bring together enough pertinent material to make viewing or re-viewing the film an exciting experience. Acceptable for all collections.

2664.   The Public and the Motion Picture Industry, by
         William Marston Seabury. 340 p. New York:
         Jerome S. Ozer, 1971 (1926).
         Originally published in 1926 by the Macmillan Company, this book is part of a reprint series that Ozer calls "Moving Pictures--Their Impact on Society." In his preface, Seabury states "The purpose of this work is to initiate ... an international movement to fix and establish the status of the motion picture in every nation of the world as a new public utility, and to require the industry without diminishing the popularity of its entertainment, to consecrate its service to the cultivation and preservation of the world's peace and the moral, intellectual and cultural development of all people." Quite an order!

To accomplish this, the author sets out to educate and familiarize the reader with film industry terms, vernacular, and practices. Topics explained include Exhibition, First Run, Block Booking, Circuit Booking, Trade Associations, Film Clubs, Blacklists, Boycotts, Credit Ratings, Raw Stock, Federal and State Statutes, Censorship, etc. The motion picture industry in England, France and other countries is described and the volume ends with a summary of a proposed law reflecting his purpose stated above. Because so much of the material discussed is obsolete and of interest only to the historian or scholar, the book is acceptable only for large collections.

2665.   The Public Relations of the Motion Picture Industry,
         by Dept. of Research & Education, Federal Council
         of Churches of Christ in America. 155 p. New
         York: Jerome S. Ozer, 1971 (1931).
         When this report first appeared, its price was fifty
cents and it was published by the Federal Council of Churches
of Christ in America. It considers the organized relations
of the industry to the public, those maintained largely by the
Hays Office, circa 1931. Data for the report was obtained
by interviews and correspondence. The Hays Office coop-
erated with the researchers and the study, which was begun
in 1930, appeared in 1931. The topic headings indicate the
range of the investigation: The General Situation ... in the
Industry; The Corporate Structure ... in the Industry; Trade
Organizations ... in the Industry; Production Process and
the Public Interest; Distribution Process and the Public Interest; Exhibition and the Public Interest; The National Board
of Review; Legal Censorship; The Committee on Public Relations; The Open Door Policy; Publicity Methods; Organizations Cooperating with the Industry; Organizations Advocating
Legal Regulation; Self Regulation in the Industry.
         A short chapter indicating conclusions is offered and
there is an index to complete the report. Of interest primarily to researchers and historians, this volume is suitable
for inclusion in larger collections.

2666.   Published Screenplays: A Checklist, by Clifford Mc-
         Carty. 127 p. Kent, Ohio: Kent State University
         Press, 1971.
         In this reference book, there are 388 entries listing
published screenplays, the definition of which encompasses
both complete scripts and excerpts. Arranged alphabetically
by title, each entry gives: 1) Title of Script, 2) Production
Company, Date, 3) Director, 4) Script Authorship, 5) Original Source, 6) Title of Book containing script or excerpt,
author, publisher, year, and pages. For anyone interested
in excerpts, the book has some value. The complete script
information is available in other reference works along with
much other material--see Cinema Booklist or Guide Book to
Film.
         This is a rather specialized reference book, suitable
only for very large collections.

2667.   THE PUMPKIN EATER. A script of the 1964 film,
         by Harold Pinter (director: Jack Clayton). 367 p.
         London: Methuen & Co. Ltd., 1971.
         Found in Five Screenplays by Harold Pinter (2291).

2668. Pure Cinema, by William Park. 16 p. (paperback)
Bronxville, N.Y.: Sarah Lawrence College, 1972.
This short essay is noted here for two reasons.
Primarily, it is an interesting statement on types of film--
the movie, the documentary and the avant-garde. The latter
genre receives the most attention, but the concluding paragraph predicts the persistence of all three by stating, "Pure
cinema is any well-made and thoughtful film, regardless of
the quarter from which it appears." Secondly, the publication is the first in a series of occasional pieces designed to
communicate faculty (Sarah Lawrence) thinking to alumnae,
parents and friends--an idea to be applauded.

2669. PYGMALION. A script of the 1938 film, by Bernard
Shaw (directors: Anthony Asquith and Leslie Howard).
125 p. (paperback) illus. Baltimore, Md.: Penguin Books, 1951.

2670. Pyramid Illustrated History of the Movies (A Series),
edited by Ted Sennett. 160 p. each. (paperback)
illus. New York: Pyramid Publications, 1973.
The four initial releases in this series are a sort
of mini-version of the much higher priced Citadel coffee
table books. This is meant to be complimentary; in many
ways, this series equals and surpasses the older one. Included in the first releases are the following titles which
are treated individually elsewhere in this book: Humphrey
Bogart (2077), Bette Davis (2182), Clark Gable (2310),
Katharine Hepburn (2373).
The books are fairly consistent in structure: a
brief introduction is followed by the star's films arranged
into chronological periods. Each has a brief bibliography,
a good filmography with cast and production credits and an
index. The first volumes give the reader some fresh views
of four rather familiar subjects; the quartet is also characterized by a general high quality of writing and production
not found in many higher priced volumes. A most promising series is evident here. Recommended.

2671. QUE VIVA MEXICO, by S. M. Eisenstein. 89 p.
illus. New York: Arno, 1972.
An introduction by Ernest Lindgren and a brief biographical sketch open this outline of the script for QUE
VIVA MEXICO. The script outline consists of six parts:
a prologue, four novels, and an epilogue. The conclusion
tells what happened after the filming was discontinued. Most
of the script portion is devoted to visuals which are very
poorly reproduced. Acceptable for large collections only.

2672. THE QUILLER MEMORANDUM. A script of the 1966 film, by Harold Pinter (director: Michael Anderson). 367 p. London: Methuen & Co. Ltd., 1971.
Found in Five Screenplays by Harold Pinter (2291).

2673. QUO VADIS. 18 p. (paperback) illus. New York: Al Greenstone, 1951.
This older example of a souvenir book is characterized by the unnatural color process used in reproducing the photographs. Attention is given to the story, the filmmaking, the cast, the production personnel, the novel, and the music. One of the titles used in the book describes it best--"Rome Burns Again."

2674. Focus on RASHOMON, edited by Donald Richie. 185 p. (paperback) illus. Englewood Cliffs, N.J.: Prentice-Hall, 1972.
After an introduction to Kurosawa and the film, eight reviews are reprinted. Commentaries and essays on the Japanese film in general and RASHOMON in particular complete the text. Plot outline and synopsis, a script extract, a filmography, a bibliography, and an index support the text articles. The two short stories upon which the film was based are included and there is a good sampling of illustrations in the centerfold. There can be no argument with the material offered. The selection offers a range of writing that will increase the study-viewing of the film immeasurably. The consistent excellence of this series is further reinforced by this fine volume. Highly recommended for all collections.
Note: The importance of RASHOMON is acknowledged, but a "focus on" book for IKIRU would be cause for celebration.

2675. The Real Howard Hughes Story, by Stanton O'Keefe. 251 p. illus. New York: American Affairs Press, 1972.
This paperback was designed to capitalize on the Clifford Irving-Howard Hughes biography fraud. It has one chapter on Hughes' Hollywood activities which reads like an outline rather than a narrative. One surprising element in this quickie book is the quality of the photo reproduction. Printed on pulp paper, the many visuals nevertheless have a clarity lacking in more expensive books. Many of the female film stars who knew Hughes in one way or another are shown. Sexual innuendo and contrived dramatics abound in the rickety narrative. Noted here for the record and for the historian who may write "Howard Hughes in Hollywood."

2676.   The Real Stars, edited by Leonard Maltin.   320 p.
         (paperback) illus. New York: Curtis Books,
         1973.
             As one of the first titles in a new paperback series,
this collection of articles about and interviews with character
actors is most pleasurable.   The book pays tribute to those
supporting players whose faces are usually more familiar
than their names.   The selection includes Sara Allgood, Edgar Buchanan, Joyce Compton, Hans Conried, Bess Flowers,
Gladys George, Billy Gilbert, Dorothy Granger, Rex Ingram,
Rosiland Ivan, Patsy Kelly, Una Merkel, Mabel Paige, Gale
Sondergaard, Hope Summers, Grady Sutton, and Blanche
Yurka.
             Each performer article is accompanied by several
illustrations which are reproduced with consistent clarity and
contrast.   A filmography that gives title, studio, date, director and cast for each film follows the textual portion.   In
the case of Una Merkel, 94 films are listed, while Grady
Sutton has appeared in more than 118.
             Whether for nostalgia, entertainment or reference,
this book has much merit.   Many of the articles have appeared earlier in periodical format and are written by several authors with Maltin as major contributor.   Consistent
in quality with the other books Maltin has brought into being,
this one can be highly recommended for all collections.

2677.   REBECCA'S DAUGHTERS.   An unfilmed script, by
         Dylan Thomas.   144 p.   (paperback) Boston: Little,
         Brown, 1966.

2678.   Reel Plastic Magic, by Laurence Kardish.   297 p.
         illus. Boston: Little, Brown, 1972.
             The subtitle of this book, "A History of Films and
Filmmaking in America," lacks a few adjectives--such as
"short," "repetitive," "flat," or several others.   Purporting
to be "addressed to the young who are without the background
information to ponder more academic texts," the book ignores any new approach and opts for an old-fashioned textbook format.
             Emphasis in the text falls on the silent film and the
early sound films.   Some attention is paid to such current
"in" topics as underground avant-garde films, blacks in
films, video cassettes, etc., but they are not woven into the
text with naturalness or ease.   The book closes with some
suggested programs, distributor addresses, and a poorly selected bibliography.   Several of those more "academic texts"
referred to in the book's rationale are recommended here:
the volumes of Jacobs, McCann, Ramsaye, Powdermaker,

Lillian Ross, Renan and Sarris, to name a few. Picture selection seems to have depended upon the collection at the Museum of Modern Art, where the author is currently employed. This photo availability may have determined the emphasis on the early years of film history.

Some of the information in the film program section is already obsolete (e.g., availability of certain films) and one questions its values to a young reader, or to anyone else. Any teacher worth his salary would find much of the material obvious, condescending, and unnecessary. This is a book surrounded by inconsistencies of approach, rationale, coverage, and style; an inferior re-telling of material that appears in many other more appropriate volumes. Not recommended.

For excellent presentations of similar material, look at Cecile Starr's Discovering the Movies (2199), or Gerald Mast's A Short History of the Movies (1233), or, best of all, William Kuhns' Movies in America (2570).

2679. A Reference Guide to Audiovisual Information, by James Limbacher. 197 p. New York: Bowker, 1972.

Audiovisual in the context of this book means mostly motion pictures, some music, and very little else. Transparencies, filmstrips, study prints, slides, posters, and the many other items that usually are associated with the term are barely mentioned, if at all. A helpful-hints kind of chapter called "The Ready Reference File" opens the book. What follows is a bibliography of reference books with short descriptive annotations; 325 books deal solely or primarily with film and about 60 others are concerned mostly with either recordings, television, or cataloging rules. The books are arranged alphabetically by title.

The periodical section which follows is only slightly more diversified. The books and the periodicals are indexed by subject in the next section. A glossary of audiovisual terms, a listing of publisher addresses and a long "selected" bibliography complete the book. This last section is arranged by subject heading: Moving Pictures--History, Moving Pictures--Editing, etc. So much is attempted here that some major flaws within this overwhelming accumulation of data may be overlooked. But the professional librarian should be concerned about:

The imbalance of film titles over others.

The placement of so many titles in the reference category--e.g., The New Wave, New Cinema in the U.S.A., Movies and Censorship, Mr. Laurel and Mr. Hardy, How to Make Animated Movies. What book about film, then is is not a reference book?

The placement of certain titles in the second selected bibliography which certainly have more reference value than some of those chosen--101 Films for Character Growth, The Rise of the American Film, etc.

The appearance of certain titles in both sections: Cinema, A Pictorial History of the Western Film, etc.

The criteria for placement: The Films of Roman Polanski in the first group and The Films of Otto Preminger in the second. Is an evaluation intended? Can it be justified?

The listing of titles that were not as yet published: The Films of Cary Grant, Best Film Plays 1970-1971.

The incorrect titles for books: Lana Turner for Lana; Classical Movie Shorts for The Great Movie Shorts; Homosexuality in the Movies for Screening the Sexes, etc.

The placement of titles under inappropriate headings: Film Scripts One and Film Scripts Two belong under Moving Picture Plays rather than under Moving Pictures--Production and Direction.

The Cinema as Art is better placed under the General Category, Moving Pictures, than under Moving Pictures --Production and Direction since it deals with film aesthetics.

Film and Its Techniques fits much better into the Production and Direction category than in Documentary. (There are many other questionable placements in this section.)

Careless proofreading: "Lelouche" for "Lelouch," D. W. Griffith" for "Mrs. D. W. Griffith" (Linda Arvidson), etc.

Careless annotation: Audiovisual Resource Guide deals with all audiovisual media, not exclusively with films as suggested here.

With all these reservations this volume cannot be recommended. The fact that some reference questions may be answered with its use qualifies it as merely acceptable. It is, indeed, a disappointing book.

2680.   Reference Guide to Fantastic Films: Volume I,
        A-F, compiled by Walt Lee. 189 p. (paperback)
        illus. Los Angeles: Chelsea-Lee Books, 1972.
The guide to fantastic films covers only titles beginning with A to F, and groups the films into three categories: the largest group which are completely described, a small group of exclusions, and some films which are termed "problems," since they conflict in some way with the defined criteria for a fantastic film. The main section gives much

data. A typical entry shows title, date, company, running time, producer, director, story, screenplay, art director, cameraman, editor, music, cast, plot, and some sources of reviews. The plot outline for FINGERS AT THE WINDOW gives some idea of the tight but valid annotation: "Evil psychiatrist Rathbone uses hypnotized lunatics to murder others with axes." There is so much potential reference value in this first book that one hopes the remaining volumes are issued quickly. Recommended for inclusion in all collections.

2681.   Jean Renoir, by André Bazin. 320 p. illus. New York: Simon and Schuster, 1973.
This translated work of André Bazin is one of the better books on Renoir. It is affectionate and admires Renoir's technical brilliance and compassionate view of his fellow men. Bazin died before the completion of the biography, but several of his disciples such as Truffaut, Godard and Rohmer offer some help. The book is illustrated, indexed, and contains a filmography. Recommended for all collections.

2682.   Jean Renoir, by Pierre Leprohon. 256 p. illus. New York: Crown, 1971.
This translation of the original French volume published in 1967 by Editions Seghers has much to recommend it. A long enthusiastic essay by Leprohon is followed by some short selections from Renoir's writings on film. Five excerpts from Renoir screenplays and a wide sampling of critics' evaluations of Renoir complete the text. There is a filmography, a bibliography, and an index.
The seventies have already seen the almost simultaneous appearance of several books on Renoir. This compact volume is one of the best. The author's rather one-sided essay is balanced by his perceptive selection of Renoir material. The illustrations are acceptable, although some are rather dark. This book provides a portrait of the director, a description of his films, and an evaluation of his place in film history. It is recommended for all collections.

2683.   Jean Renoir: The World of His Films, by Leo Braudy. 286 p. illus. Garden City, N.Y.: Doubleday & Co., 1971.
The 50-year career of Jean Renoir is documented in this thorough, careful and interesting study. All of Renoir's 36 films are examined to determine relationships that pervade the entire body of his work. The two major motifs of nature and theatre are related to both society and to the actor-heroes who must link them. The text is largely

critical and saves the usual biographical sketch for a closing chapter. The appendix has a filmography, a bibliography and an index. Illustrations are plentiful and adequately reproduced. They are mostly one-half page in size which diminishes their effectiveness somewhat. The volume has much to recommend it and deserves a place in most collections.

2684.   The Report of The Commission on Obscenity and
         Pornography, by The Commission on Obscenity and
         Pornography.   700 p.   (paperback)   New York:
         Bantam, 1970.
         The authoritative study by government-appointed experts on the effects of pornography and obscenity on the American Society is reprinted here.   It includes:
    1) Overview of the Findings
    2) Recommendations of the Commission
    3) Reports of the Panels
         A - Traffic and Distribution of Sexually Oriented Materials in the United States
         B - The Impact of Erotica
         C - The Development of Healthy Attitudes Toward Sexuality
         D - Legal Considerations Relating to Erotica
    4) Separate Statements by Commission Members.
         There is no index and the user will have to search for the sections dealing with films.   Much of this material has implication for education, law, filmmaking, codes, censorship, etc.   It is a source study that can be used for reference and citation over and over again.   Essential for all libraries serving mature users.

2685.   The Reproduction of Colour in Photography, Printing,
         and Television, by R. W. G. Hunt.   500 p.   illus.
         New York: John Wiley, 1967.
         Addressed to anyone dealing with color pictures.
The technical chapters are separated from the general text.

2686.   Research Films in Biology, Anthropology, Psychol-
         ogy, and Medicine, by Anthony R. Michaelis.   490 p.
         illus.   New York: Academic Press, 1955.
         Discusses cinematography in the experimental sciences, describing past methods and indicating possibilities. describes use in biology, animal behavior, human record films, anthropology, psychology, psychiatry, X-ray, surgery, and medicine.

2687.   The Revealing Eye: Personalities of the 1920s.

Photos by Nickolas Muray; text by Paul Gallico.
307 p. illus. New York: Atheneum, 1967.

This coffee-table book has many beautiful full-sized portraits, faithfully reproduced in black-and-white, and a pedestrian text. It is not a film star collection, but since it includes so many persons who had a career of one kind or another in films, the book is noted here. The outstanding photographic work consistently captures much more of the subject than does the text. Not essential in any way, this volume is so attractively produced that it will enhance any film collection, nevertheless.

2688.   A Ribbon of Dreams, by Peter Cowie. 262 p. illus.
         New York: Barnes, 1973.

Comparing this "revision" with Cowie's earlier work, The Cinema of Orson Welles (230), we find: 1) it has been retitled, with the original title relegated to sub-status; 2) it is updated to include Welles' three most recent films, CHIMES AT MIDNIGHT, FALSTAFF, and THE IMMORTAL STORY; 3) corrections ("sunrise" for "sunset," 1937 for 1938, etc.), rearrangements, and deletions have been made; 4) bibliographic citations have increased from 120 to 152; 5) it is now indexed; 6) visual content has increased but is not reproduced as well as in the earlier book; 7) new text material amounting to approximately 15 per cent of the original text has been added; 8) the original retail price of the softcover edition has multiplied about six times for this hardcover revision.

Much of the newer text material has probably been suggested by recent writings on Welles by authors such as Kael (2145), Higham (525), Bessy (2872), McBride (2873), and others. Since the original annotation of the book (230) called the book "excellent and recommended for all collections and readers," most of the changes above may be assumed as added values to an already acceptable volume. The high price and poor photo reproduction will give pause.

2689.   THE ROBE. 18 p. (paperback) illus. New York:
         ABC Vending Corp., 1953.

The story of the film is told in several introductory pages of this souvenir book which features pictures spread over a double page, thus simulating a wide-screen image. Since this was the first film in Cinemascope, there is also an article explaining the process. In addition to the cast and production credits, there is an article by Lloyd C. Douglas entitled "Why I Wrote The Robe". One final section takes the reader "Behind the Scenes With the People Who Bring You THE ROBE."

2690. Will Rogers, by Donald Day. 370 p. illus. New
York: David McKay, 1962.
Since Donald Day acted as editor of Will Rogers'
autobiography, it is not surprising to find him mining the
same material for this biography. This volume differs in
that the narrative line here is more distinct. Much use is
made, however, of Rogers' written work. The account of
the silent films is almost negligible and the short chapter on
the sound films, "Playing Himself in the Talkies," takes up
only nine pages and does not deal directly with the filmmaking, but more with personalities like Shirley Temple, Bill
Robinson, Irvin Cobb, and John Ford. The book is indexed
and contains a few illustrations. From a film viewpoint,
this is a disappointing biography, acceptable only for larger
collections.

2691. Will Rogers: Ambassador of Good Will, Prince of
Wit and Wisdom, by P. J. O'Brien. 288 p. illus.
Chicago: John C. Winston, 1936.
This biography arranges its materials in a conven-
ient fashion. Chapter headings such as "Rogers on the
Stage," "Rogers and Politics," "Rogers As Writer," make
specific information easier to obtain. In the chapter on
"Rogers in the Moving Pictures," his film career is traced
from the 1919 film, LAUGHING BILL HYDE, to STEAM-
BOAT 'ROUND THE BEND in 1935. He made 24 silent films
and 19 sound films, with all of the latter becoming financial
successes. Probably his most famous screen roles were in
DAVID HARUM and STATE FAIR.
Other than the chapter indicated, the rest of the
biography is a dated tribute that is fan-magazine-factual
rather than a thoroughly researched portrait. There is no
index. The pictures are effective in recreating the era of
Will Rogers. Acceptable only for very large collections.

2692. Will Rogers: His Wife's Story, by Betty Rogers.
312 p. illus. Indianapolis: Bobbs Merrill, 1941.
A valuable biography. Many of the small trivial
incidents that Betty Rogers relates help to give a portrait
of this beloved entertainer. The portrait is of course, prejudiced and impossibly positive. The film career from the
silents during the twenties to the sound films of the early
thirties is noted, with emphasis on the silents. One would
suspect that with Rogers' increasing celebrity in the 30's,
his wife saw less of him; this may be why that period is
sketched rather than detailed. The book is not indexed and
there are only a few illustrations. This is specialized material of concern mostly to historians and researchers. For
large collections only.

2693. Will Rogers: The Man and His Times, by Richard
       M. Ketchum. 448 p. illus. New York: American
       Heritage, 1973.
       This announced biography of Rogers sounds interest-
ing on several counts. First, more than 400 illustrations
are to be used in the volume, and secondly, a recording entitled "The Voice of Will Rogers" is to be available with the
book. Coverage of the films is probable in both text and
stills.

2694. Eric Rohmer, by Eric Rohmer. (paperback) illus.
       London: Lorrimer, 1972.
       Contains script, cast and production credits for:
CLAIRE'S KNEE, 1972 (2146); MY NIGHT AT MAUD'S, 1970
(2581); LA COLLECTIONEUSE, 1968 (2157A). Announced
for publication in the U.S. by Simon and Schuster.

2695. ROMEO AND JULIET. 34 p. (paperback) illus.
       New York: National Publishers, 1968.
       There are only a few colored stills in the center
section of this souvenir book based on a film which utilized
color photography so well. The black and white photographs
are devoted to the usual topics: stills, cast members, sets,
etc. The production under Franco Zefferelli's direction is
discussed. Other supporting cast and production credits
are noted.

2696. ROMEO AND JULIET. A script of the 1936 film,
       by Talbot Jennings (director: George Cukor).
       290 p. illus. New York: Random House, 1936.
       Found in ROMEO AND JULIET by William Shake-
speare (2697).

2697. ROMEO AND JULIET, by William Shakespeare.
       290 p. illus. New York: Random House, 1936.
       This volume was published simultaneously with the
appearance of the 1936 film version of ROMEO AND JULIET.
It contains chapters written by Nora Shearer (Juliet), Leslie
Howard (Romeo), John Barrymore (Mercutio), Cedric Gib-
bons (Settings), Adrian (Costumes), etc. Shakespeare's play
and the film script are included. Also published in London
by Arthur Barker.

2698. Rossellini: The War Trilogy, by Roberto Rossellini.
       (paperback) illus. New York: Grossman, 1973.
       Announced as containing the following scripts: OPEN
CITY, 1945 (also known as ROME, OPEN CITY); PAISAN,
1946; GERMANY, YEAR ZERO, 1947.

266

2699.   Run Through: A Memoir, by John Houseman.
         507 p. illus. New York: Simon and Schuster,
         1972.
         The memoir runs from 1902 to 1942, with the greatest
attention given to the decade of the thirties. The attraction
for many readers will be the portrait of Orson Welles as a
teen-aged actor, director, producer and radio performer.
The final portion of the book will be of most interest to film
enthusiasts. Houseman went to Hollywood with Welles and
his account of the evolution of CITIZEN KANE is fascinating.
He worked in the film industry with others but those experiences are not covered in this volume. His productions include: THE BLUE DAHLIA, LETTER FROM AN UNKNOWN
WOMAN, JULIUS CAESAR, LUST FOR LIFE, THE BAD
AND THE BEAUTIFUL, among others.
         Houseman's partial biography needs no further en-
dorsement here. A brilliant book, it was given wide critical
praise and was the recipient of several honors. Its contribution to film literature is the reason for its inclusion in this
book. By furnishing the Welles' portrait, the information on
such pre-KANE films as TOO MUCH JOHNSON, and confirm-
ing much of Kael's argument, he helps add to the legend and
importance of Welles and KANE. The book has fine illustrations and is indexed. It belongs in all libraries which serve
a general audience.

2700.   THE RUSSIAN ADVENTURE, by May Okon. 32 p.
         (paperback) illus. New York: Perry Sales, Ltd.,
         1966.
         This is the souvenir book of a travelogue of Russia
that was produced in the Cinerama format and was narrated
by Bing Crosby. Consisting mostly of stills from the film,
the book illustrates a circus, a ballet, a whale hunt, the
Moiseyev dancers, a boar hunt, reindeer races, etc. One
page is devoted to Crosby, another to the producers, and the
center section contains a map of Russia.

2701.   THE SAND PEBBLES, by Bruce Graham. 32 p.
         (paperback) illus. New York: Alsid Distributors,
         1966.
         The problems of reproducing "China in the 20's"
are detailed in this souvenir book. How the production was
begun under the guidance of producer-director Robert Wise
is noted. There are some attractive full-page color portraits
of the stars and other cast credits and production names are
given. One of the more interesting sections pertains to the
building of the gunboat, "The San Pablo," whose name in
jocular form gives the film its title.

2702.   Saturday Afternoon at the Bijou, by David Zinman.
         511 p. illus. New Rochelle, N.Y.: Arlington
         House, 1973.
         One of three recent books that treat similar mate-
rial, the series films which usually occupied half of the
double bills during the 1930's and 1940's. The Great Movie
Series (2342) and A Thousand and One Delights (2804), are
the others. This late entrant in the competition has some
omissions and inconsistencies that lessen its effectiveness.
         The title is somewhat misleading, since Zinman's
concern is more with a survey of series films rather than
with Saturday matinee film material. There is an appreciable difference. Starting with the Tarzan films, he discusses, in turn, the Wolf Man, Frankenstein's monster, the
Invisible Man, The Mummy, Planet of the Apes, Gene Autry,
the Cisco Kid, Hopalong Cassidy, The Three Musketeers,
Sherlock Holmes, the Saint, the Falcon, the Thin Man,
Crime Doctor, Charlie Chan, Mr. Moto, Fu Manchu, James
Bond, Dr. Kildare, Dr. Christian, Doctor in the House,
Andy Hardy, Henry Aldrich, Blondie, Nancy Drew, Mexican
Spitfire, Torchy Blane, The Dead End Kids, Lassie and Our
Gang. Selective, to be sure, but why some of these over
Ma and Pa Kettle, Abbott and Costello, Maisie, Philo Vance,
the East Side Kids, the Bowery Boys, the Carry-On Films,
or the Three Stooges? Why the inclusion of the British doctor series, the James Bond series, or the Planet of the
Apes films, all of which appeared from the mid-50's to late
60's, but none of which was a Saturday matinee series?
         For each series, a single film is described in some
detail to convey the flavor of the series. A complete filmography follows each series chapter and more than 250 photographs aid greatly in the descriptions. The text is chatty,
informative, and full of factual trivia. It makes for enjoyable reading, and that Zinman is a dedicated film buff is obvious on every page. His affection for these old mediocre
films is apparently limitless. The book is indexed and there
is a short selected bibliography.
         While one can appreciate and approve Zinman's ardor
for the series films, this tribute is a little late and a little
less than some earlier volumes. It is, however, an acceptable addition to large collections, and has both reference and
entertainment values for patrons in any type of library.

2703.   SATURDAY MORNING. A script of the 1971 film,
         by Kent Mackenzie and Gary Goldsmith (director:
         Kent Mackenzie). 143 p. (paperback) illus. New
         York: Avon Books, 1971.

Contains cast credits, production credits, and an introduction by the producer-director, Kent Mackenzie.

2704.   SAVAGES. A script of the 1973 film, by George Swift Trow, Michael O'Donoghue and James Ivory (director: James Ivory). 152 p. (paperback) illus. London: Plexus, 1973.
Contains: An introduction by James Ivory; "A Motion Picture Treatment" by Trow, O'Donoghue, and Ivory; cast and credits. Found in SAVAGES, SHAKESPEARE WALLAH (2705).

2705.   SAVAGES, SHAKESPEARE WALLAH, by James Ivory. 152 p. (paperback) illus. London: Plexus, 1973.
Contains scripts and articles for: SAVAGES, 1973 (2704); SHAKESPEARE WALLAH, 1965 (2728).

2706.   SCENT OF MYSTERY, by Dick Williams. 32 p. (paperback) illus. 1959.
This souvenir book was published to accompany showings of a film which used a process called "Scentavision" or "Smell-O-Vision." Presented by Mike Todd, Jr., this was the process which flooded the theatre with synthetic smells correlated to some action or person on the screen. In this film it is the smell of the perfume that the killer wears which proves her undoing. The plot, the process, the cast, and the actual filming are shown and described. A cardboard recording of two musical selections from the film is included with the book. Cast and production credits are noted. If for no other reason, the book is noted here as proof that the process and the film were actually tried out for one brief period. The public rejected the concept of smelling its movies and the film was re-released without the smells and with a new title, HOLIDAY IN SPAIN. The public was consistent --it still ignored the film.

2707.   Focus on The Science Fiction Film, edited by William Johnson. 182 p. (paperback) illus. Englewood Cliffs, N.J.: Prentice-Hall, 1972.
This anthology might also serve as a general history of the science fiction genre since it is arranged chronologically. Following an introduction and a chronology, the book is divided into four sections: Beginnings (1895-1949), The Popular Years (1950-59), Moving On (1960-70), and Taking Stock: Some Issues and Answers. A filmography, bibliography, index and a few stills complete the volume.
The articles vary in their subject matter, dealing

with trends, techniques, directors, scripts, diaries of film-making, etc. The filmography is a short one for a major genre and suggests a scarcity of classic science fiction films. The absence of DEVIL DOLL, BARBARELLA, THE BLOB, BUCK ROGERS, THE FLY, and many others makes the reader wonder what the qualifications were for inclusion. The definition offered in the introduction does not cover the omissions. But this is a very minor matter. The concern should be the quality of the material offered, and it is first-rate here. From Melíes to 2001 the subject is handled in an informative, exciting manner that should please most readers. Recommended for all collections.

2708.   Scoring for Films, by Earle Hagen.   253 p.   illus.
          New York: Criterion Music Corp. , 1971.
          An advanced technical book that still has certain values for the lay person interested in knowing more about the writing of music for films or television. Its stated purpose is "to orient the reader with the problems, possibilities and language of film music composition. A very short history of movie music introduces the text which is divided into three major sections: I) The Mechanics and Vocabulary of Film Composition; II) The Psychology of Creating Music for Films; and III) The Responsibilities of the Composer. A few summary statements and a valuable glossary conclude the book. Throughout there are many illustrations, charts, music pages, script pages, and tables.
          The second (Psychology) section features a sympo-sium which proposes four provocative questions to film com-posers Alfred Newman, Jerrald Goldsmith, Hugo Friedhofer, Quincy Jones, and Lalo Schifrin. Their replies differ as widely as their musical styles. One further bonus is the in-clusion of two 7" recordings which contain musical segments from actual film sound tracks conducted and narrated by Hagen. These are coordinated with the text. The author has provided a service to the musician and the lay person that is soundly based on his teaching and professional ex-perience of scoring more than 2,000 television episodes.
          The stated purpose of the book is more than ac-complished by the logical presentation of his text and the support of the visuals and the recordings. It is a fine teach-ing-learning package presented with efficiency and enthusiasm. Highly recommended for all collections which support courses in filmmaking or film study. It is also a most valid addi-tion to other film collections.

2709.   Screen Greats Series, edited by Millburn Smith.

(paperback) illus. New York: Barven Publications, 1972.

This promising publishing venture made its appearance with ten issues of a periodical which resembled the Citadel Series in many ways. Each issue was devoted a personality or a team and consisted mostly of stills, portraits, and candids. A filmography was given at the end of each volume. The number of pages averaged about 60. Subjects covered were:

1. Screen Greats
2. Humphrey Bogart
3. Clark Gable
4. Marilyn Monroe
5. Spencer Tracy and Katharine Hepburn
6. Gary Cooper
7. Fred Astaire and Ginger Rogers
8. Greta Garbo
9. Mickey Rooney and Judy Garland
10. Errol Flynn.

These volumes were better in many ways than the Primestyle Michael Burrows books or the Cinefax series of the late sixties. The continuance of this series is questionable.

2710. Screening the Sexes: Homosexuality in the Movies, by Parker Tyler. 384 p. (paperback) illus. New York: Holt, Rinehart, Winston, 1972.

The trend of many of our well-known writers to come "out-of-the closet" gets another push forward with this newest Parker Tyler volume. His position is quite similar to that of the gay militants. Combining super-intellectuality with gutter language, analysis with gossip, and criticism with camp, he creates a fascinating book. It is not always easy to comprehend Tyler but here he is clearer than usual. Believing that films reflect behavior, myth, hidden desires, and so on, he analyzes many films to support his sexual freedom thesis and to enlighten filmgoers who may never have realized what they were seeing.

Most of the films are of recent, post-60's vintage and this gives him richer subjects with which to work. Joe Cairo in THE MALTESE FALCON or Franklin Pangborn in any film get some mention, but the strongest guns are saved for the STAIRCASE, THE KILLING OF SISTER GEORGE, BOYS IN THE BAND, PERFORMANCE, FELLINI SATYRICON, MIDNIGHT COWBOY and others. Some unexpected titles also get the critical scalpel from the author--THE WIZARD OF OZ, PERILS OF PAULINE, HUSBANDS, etc. This is a

writing performance that merits attention and applause.
Highly recommended for libraries serving mature audiences.

2711.   The Screen Writer Looks at the Screen Writer, by
         William Froug. 352 p. New York: Macmillan,
         1972.
         The purpose of this volume is to further the recogni-
tion of the screen writer who has a past history of neglect,
abuse and professional oblivion. Putting down the auteur
theory as being almost impossible within the Hollywood structure of filmmaking, Froug makes a strong argument for the
emergence of the writer into the economic mainstream. One
bit of evidence he offers is the current publication of many
modern and classic scripts. The quality of the film is often
found in the script before directorial style is superimposed
upon it: "Style follows content and is meaningless without
it."
         The format of the book is a collection of interviews
by Froug with the following screen writers: Lewis John
Carlino, William Bowers, Walter Brown Newman, Jonathan
Axelrod, Ring Lardner, Jr., I. A. L. Diamond, Buck Henry,
David Giler, Nunnally Johnson, Edward Anhalt, Stirling Silliphant, and Fay Kanin. The mixture of names, semi-names,
and unknowns seems intended to support Froug's argument.
Each interview is preceded with the writer's credits, a
lengthy background article, and a sample script page. Anyone interested in filmmaking is referred to this collection of
views on screen writing. Its importance is argued with intelligence and balance, and the result is a clarification of
questions dealing with theory, aesthetic and process. Highly
recommended.

2712.   Script Writing for Short Films, by James A. Bever-
         idge. 45 p. (paperback) illus. New York:
         UNESCO, 1969.
         A brief discussion of script writing which treats top-
ics such as audience, objectives, sponsors, research, budget,
production crew, dialogue, showmanship, etc. Certain unique
problems of the short film are examined and some solutions
are offered. There are script excerpts from JAI JAWAN,
THE DREAMS OF MAUJIRAM, PHOEBE, and POISONS,
PESTS, AND PEOPLE. Two storyboard outlines are shown
and recent films which illustrate the concepts developed in
the text are listed. As usual with most UNESCO publications,
this one may be difficult to obtain but the effort is worthwhile. It is a most effective, concise summary of scripting
for the short film. Highly recommended.

2713.   SCROOGE, by Elaine Donaldson.   62 p.   (paperback)
        illus. Nashville, Tenn.: Aurora Publishers, 1970.
        All the elements that contribute to the creation of a
musical film are noted in this souvenir book.   There is a
listing of the musical numbers and all the lyrics, special
double pages devoted to the major participants, Albert Finney, Edith Evans, Kenneth More, Alec Guinness, director
Ronald Neame, writer-composer Leslie Bricusse and producer Robert Solo.   There are special sections about the
production, costumes, make-up, and story.   The willingness
of the book producers to offer nearly double the usual number of pages has resulted in a rather complete and impressive coverage of a movie musical.

2714.   SEARCH FOR PARADISE.   20 p.   (paperback) illus.
        New York: Cinerama Publishers, 1957.
        This is a souvenir book of the Cinerama adventure
that featured Lowell Thomas as he explored Ceylon, the
Hunza River and Valley, the Indus River, Kashmir, and
Nepal.   Dimitri Tiomkin's music is acknowledged and the
diagram of the three-projector system of Cinerama is included.   Photography throughout is disappointing.

2715.   Second Sight: Notes on Some Movies, 1965-1970,
        by Richard Schickel.   351 p.   New York: Simon
        and Schuster, 1972.
        Richard Schickel was the film critic for Life Maga-
zine during the years 1965-1970.   The collection of reviews
in this volume represents about half of all he wrote for the
magazine.   The unusual technique of adding a second and
later evaluation to the original adds a provocative dimension
to the reviews: a film critic rereading his first opinions and
judging how well they have stood the test of time.   A lengthy
introduction combines some Schickel career history with the
development of his aesthetic for reviewing films.
        The reader may take exception to Schickel's com-
ments.   Why, for example, does he dislike Fellini so?--
"His is a mind of truly stupefying banality."   But one can
only admire his candid evaluations of his own writing--"Not,
I'm afraid, a very good performance on my part," or "I
overpraised this movie," or "sometimes I feel like cutting
my tongue out."   A critic capable of such introspection can't
be all bad.
        The book reviews many of the important films which
appeared in the latter half of the Sixties, and there is an
index to make the volume more serviceable.   Schickel writes
in a style which avoids obfuscation, intellectual boasting, and

bandwagon-joining. He is clear, economical, and always his own man. This is an entertaining collection of the writings of a critic who has yet to experience the fame and celebrity that lesser critics now enjoy. Because of its uniqueness and the balance it provides to other existing criticism, the book is recommended for inclusion in all film collections.

2716.   Seeing With Feeling, by Richard Lacey. 118 p. (paperback) illus. Philadelphia: W. B. Saunders, 1972.

Lacey's major topic, "Film in the Classroom," is the subtitle of this useful book. He begins with the premise that films by themselves do not "work"--it is the experience provided with the film that either works or does not. While there are no certainties in film study methodologies, the author suggests some as starting points and encourages the development of other unique individual methods by teachers who use films.

A general overview on film use is followed by a provocative section called "What To Do When the Lights Go On." The major portion of the text is devoted to "The Image-Sound Skin" and some related classroom procedures. The "Skin" concept is defined as the basis of a collaborative approach to integrate feeling and intuition with the intellectual concerns of a film. Closing sections of the text anticipate certain problems in gaining acceptance of film study procedures in schools and suggest measures to gain understanding and support. Some appendices on literature, periodicals, and film sources complete the book. Illustrations consist of stills taken mostly from the films mentioned in the text.

Different approaches to film study derived in part from educational research concepts and philosophy are the concern of this book. The pioneer works of Culkin, Mallery, Sullivan, Sohn, Lowndes and others have suggested much of what is offered here. The service provided by Lacey is one of sythesis and justification. The book is certainly essential for all schools and colleges that offer film courses. Any librarian using films will find the suggestions quite valuable for developing programs. Highly recommended.

2717.   Seen Any Good Dirty Movies Lately?, by James Arnold. 118 p. (paperback) illus. Cincinnati, Ohio: St. Anthony Messenger Press, 1972.

The constant search for fresh critical insight in evaluating films may be satisfied for the moment by this modest but rather significant book. Arnold is the movie critic for the Milwaukee Journal, several Catholic newspapers, and St. Anthony Messenger magazine. His approach is based on the issue of morality in films, in addition to the usual aesthetics. As his guide he quotes sociologist Andrew Greeley: "I believe that love is at the core of the universe; that man is estranged essentially because of his inability to respond to love since he is estranged from love; this estrangement is ended by the intervention of Love in the Person of the Son of Man. ... Love and life are proclaimed by celebrating. The most appropriate human relationship is friendship, ...because it mirrors love ... Man's role is to strive so that the world may be pervaded by friendship. Whenever men come together in friendship, the spirit of loving life is present in their midst, inspiring them to break out of the bonds of hesitation, doubt, and distrust in order that they might be for one another."

Films such as Fellini's CABIRIA and 8-1/2 or MID-NIGHT COWBOY are considered moral when applied against the life-friendship-love aesthetic above. Sex and love in films, what films tell our youth, and whether parents should forbid films for their children are other topics discussed with intelligence, wit and sensitivity. The closing section reprints Arnold's reviews of films that caused some moral flurry when they first appeared. His response to them is offered as a guide for laymen to use in coping with films yet to appear.

The book has many fine illustrations and is indexed. How such quality can be placed in an original paperback film book and sold at a very low cost is a lesson for other publishers to study. Highly recommended for inclusion in all collections as a further step in establishing a film aesthetic for our time.

2718.   Mack Sennett's Keystone: The Man, the Myth, and the Comedies, by Kalton C. Lahue. 315 p. illus. New York: Barnes, 1971.

In his ninth trip to the mines of silent film, author Lahue purports to set the record straight on Mack Sennett and the Keystone Film Company. He discounts Sennett's autobiography and several other books and uses instead films made available by both Paul Killiam and Blackhawk Films and a series of interviews with Sennett's business manager, George B. Stout. The opening section on Sennett is followed by chapters dealing with the Keystone Players. Mabel Normand, Fred Mace, Ford Sterling, Roscoe "Fatty" Arbuckle, Chester Conklin, Mack Swain, and Charlie Chaplin are given individual attention, and the careers of many lesser known personalities are described. Certain of the Keystone films are described and illustrated by the use of frame enlargements from the films. Many of the illustrations lack total focus and look rather fuzzy. Others do not have a balanced contrast, with black predominating.

The appendices include a list of the Keystone films indicating the length, working title, final title, director, and the date finished. Three Keystone scripts are reprinted and there is an index of titles and one of names. While one may have some reservation about the author's announced goal and his success in reaching it, the obvious effort spent in creating this volume is laudable. Acceptable for large collections. Smaller libraries may find this duplicates much of what they already own.

2719.   Series, Serials, and Packages. Vol. 12, Issue # 2, edited by Avra Fliegelman. 414 p. New York (51 E. 42nd St., NYC 10017): Broadcast Info. Bureau, 1971.

Another excellent reference book about television programming of filmed material; in this case, the films are series, serials, and packages. The first section is a title index listing series films running from 20 seconds to 120 minutes. They are arranged in time divisions (1 hour, one-half hour, 15 minutes), with appropriate subject headings under each division. Adventure, Documentary, Drama, Mystery, and Interview are some of the subject headings to be found. For each series the following information is offered: title, stars, story line, number of films available or planned, running time, black and white or color, gauge, year produced, leasing fee range, markets open, sponsors, producer, distributor.

A second section lists foreign language series arranged alphabetically by language from Arabic to Yugoslav. Other sections include series available for cable television, a total title index and a listing of film sources. As a reference source on TV serials and series, the book is invaluable. Unfortunately it is only available at this time by a subscription which costs $89.

2720.   THE SERVANT. A script of the 1963 film, by Harold Pinter (director: Joseph Losey). 367 p. London: Methuen & Co. Ltd., 1971. Found in Five Screenplays by Harold Pinter (2291).

2721.   1776. 24 p. (paperback) illus. New York: Souvenir Publications, 1972.

An article entitled "1776--The Way It Was and Is!!!" attempts to provide background to the film by contrasting historical fact with legend and myth. Jack L. Warner, who never misses an opportunity to occupy center stage, receives two pages of profile and tribute. Illustrations are in both black and white and color, with the latter group fuzzy and out of focus. In the centerfold there is a reproduction of The Declaration of Independence with the signers designated. A second article, "The Spirit of 1776," relates the filming of the original play. Capsule biographies of the cast are presented in a unique way with leading players first, followed by groupings of the delegates arranged according to the state they represented. Production credits are also listed.

2722.   Focus on THE SEVENTH SEAL, edited by Birgitta
         Steene. 182 p. (paperback) illus. Englewood
         Cliffs, N.J.: Prentice-Hall, 1972.
         This compilation of articles about Ingmar Bergman
and THE SEVENTH SEAL continues the excellent "focus on" series. Ingmar Bergman is described in the introductory articles, interviews and analyses. Eight reviews of the film are followed by 17 more essays and commentaries. The original play, "Wood Painting," which served as the inspiration for the film, is reprinted. A plot synopsis, an outline, a script excerpt, a filmography, a bibliography and an index complete the book. This wealth of material will assist anyone studying Bergman, THE SEVENTH SEAL, or both, and a viewing of the film will be more rewarding after the use of this resource. The selection, arrangement and concept of this volume is excellent. Highly recommended for all collections.

2723.   THE 7TH VOYAGE OF SINBAD. 12 p. illus.
         1958.
         The emphasis in this short souvenir book is on the
special effects used in the film. They are explained in a section entitled "This is Dynamation" which describes the duel between Sinbad and a skeleton, and other unusual sequences from the film. The story is outlined and cast and production credits are noted. Most of the illustrations are fuzzy and out of focus. It is somewhat ironic that Bernard Herrmann's score, a soundtrack recording rarity at this writing, is merely acknowledged.

2724.   Sex Goddesses of the Silent Screen, by Norman
         Zierold. 207 p. illus. Chicago, Ill.: Henry
         Regnery, 1973.
         The sex goddesses are Theda Bara, Barbara Lamarr,
Pola Negri, Mae Murray, and Clara Bow. An essay which combines biographical and critical elements is given for each, as are separate filmographies. Acceptable for all collections.

2725.   The Shadow of an Airplane Climbs the Empire State
         Building, by Parker Tyler.   248 p.   Garden City,
         N.Y.:   Doubleday, 1972.
         Parker Tyler resembles Marshall McLuhan (whom
he deprecates whenever possible) in that he explores but does
not explain.   In this frustrating collection of intellectual obfuscation, Tyler is supposedly seeking a theory of world
film.   Congratulations are extended to those who can find it
here.   The last few paragraphs contain such world shaking
statements as "So, film makers, I make an envoi: Hold to
the sprocket holes of the images dictated to you by your own
voices, your personal and peculiar voices, and no other
voices.   This is your hope and, of course, my theory."
         Many of the films analyzed or used as arguments by
Tyler are quite obscure.   This becomes a tactic to intimidate
the reader; select the unknown, pontificate about it, and leave
the reader with self-doubt.   There may be those who have the
time, energy, or curiosity to wade through this volume.   May
their effort and patience be rewarded--although it is unlikely.
Not recommended unless it is used as an example of film
criticism which, if it appears with any frequency, will kill
off the art.

2726.   Shakespeare and the Film, by Roger Manvell.   172 p.
         illus.   New York: Praeger, 1971.
         Shakespeare on silent film was covered by Robert
Hamilton Ball (1230), and Manvell concentrates on sound
films in this book.   A short chapter acknowledges the silents
and is quickly followed by analyses of the Pickford-Fairbanks'
THE TAMING OF THE SHREW, Reinhardt's A MIDSUMMER
NIGHT'S DREAM, Cukor's ROMEO AND JULIET and Czin-
ner's AS YOU LIKE IT.   Laurence Olivier, Orson Welles,
and Akira Kurosawa are accorded individual chapters as are
the Russian and Italian Shakespeare films.   Attention is given
to two adaptations of JULIUS CAESAR and to recent transla-
tions of specific stage productions to film.   Peter Brook's
1970 film of KING LEAR is discussed in detail as the most
recent Shakespearian film.   A filmography with extensive
cast credits, a selected bibliography and an index conclude
the book.
         Each of the films is represented by some stills
which are brilliantly reproduced in most cases.   The visuals
here help to interpret much of the text and are an essential
ingredient of the book.   As with all of Manvell's work, the
text is scholarly, readable, thorough, and linear.   Production work, especially with the visuals, is outstanding.   This
is a beautiful book that is essential for all high school and

college libraries, and a valuable addition to any public library collection.

2727.   Focus on Shakespearean films, by Charles W. Eckert. 184 p. (paperback) illus. Englewood Cliffs, N.J.: Prentice-Hall, 1972.

An unusual approach is used by Eckert in this survey of Shakespearean films. After a section of introductory articles, he selects certain films made from the plays, arranges them chronologically, and gives one or two reviews under each. Thus we have Dierterle's A MIDSUMMER NIGHT'S DREAM (1935); Olivier's HENRY V (1944) and HAMLET (1948); Welles' MACBETH (1948) and OTHELLO (1951); Mankiewicz's JULIUS CAESAR (1953); Castellani's ROMEO AND JULIET (1954); the Russian ROMEO AND JULIET BALLET (1954) and OTHELLO (1955); Olivier's RICHARD III (1955); the Russian HAMLET (1964); Burge's OTHELLO (1965); Zeffirelli's THE TAMING OF THE SHREW (1966); and, finally, Welles' CHIMES AT MIDNIGHT (1966). The reviewers include Allardyce Nicoll, James Agee, Bosley Crowther, Mary McCarthy, Dwight MacDonald, John Simon, and others. A filmography, a bibliography, an index, and a few stills complete the book. The filmography indicates many other Shakespearean films that are not mentioned in the text. The question of selection arises again: why, for example, the seldom seen Russian films instead of Cukor's ROMEO AND JULIET (1936) or Zeffirelli's in 1968?

For anyone interested in the topic of "From Shakespearean Play to Film," the book will be most valuable. If used together with Manvell (2726) and Ball (1230), the subject can be covered in considerable depth. Recommended for inclusion in all collections.

2728.   SHAKESPEARE WALLAH. A script of the 1965 film, by R. Prawer Jhabvala and James Ivory (director: James Ivory). 152 p. (paperback) illus. London: Plexus, 1965.

Contains: An introduction by James Ivory; cast and credits. Found in SAVAGES, SHAKESPEARE WALLAH (2705).

2729.   SHAME. A script of the 1968 film, by Ingmar Bergman (director: Ingmar Bergman). 191 p. (paperback) illus. New York: Grossman, 1972.
Found in Bergman: PERSONA and SHAME (2058).

2730.   SHANGHAI EXPRESS. A script of the 1932 film, by Jules Furthman and Harry Hervey (director: Josef

von Sternberg).   (paperback)   illus.   London: Lorrimer, 1972.
Found in MOROCCO, SHANGHAI EXPRESS (2549).

2731.   (Those Scandalous) Sheets of Hollywood, by Ray Lee.
         185 p.   (paperback)   Van Nuys, Calif.:   Venice Pub-
         lishing, 1972.
         The Hollywood scandals appear again for their an-
nual resurrection in this exploitation paperback.   The assort-
ment this round is Flynn, Chaplin, Arbuckle, Lana Turner,
Valentino, William Desmond Taylor, and a pair of less-
abused subjects--Clara Bow and Ramon Novarro.   That readers can still find this material of interest is puzzling.   They
obviously do, based on the number of printed rehashes that
have appeared.   Acceptable only for very large collections.

2732.   THE SHOES OF THE FISHERMAN.   34 p.   (paper-
         back)   illus.   New York: National Publishers, 1968.
         Many photographs, both stills and candids, tell the
story of the film and its production in this souvenir book.
Some attention is given to director Michael Anderson, producer George Englund, and star Anthony Quinn.   The author
of the novel upon which the film is based, Morris West, is
also profiled.   Supporting cast and production credits are
noted.

2733.   Focus on SHOOT THE PIANO PLAYER, edited by
         Leo Braudy.   182 p.   (paperback)   illus.   Engle-
         wood Cliffs, N.J.:   Prentice-Hall, 1972.
         The same format used with the other "focus on"
books is employed here.   An introductory section deals with
Truffaut and SHOOT THE PIANO PLAYER.   Five reprinted
reviews are followed by 13 essays and commentaries.   The
final portion of the book contains a synopsis and outline,
three scenes not used in the final film, an excerpt from the
script, a filmography, a bibliography and an index.   A few
illustrations are included in a center section.   The book can
be used in a variety of ways and should be helpful in most.
It adds to the literature on Truffaut and offers a study guide
for viewing the film.   Recommended for inclusion in all film
collections.

2734.   The Show Business Nobody Knows, by Earl Wilson.
         415 p.   illus.   Chicago: Cowles Book Co., 1971.
         Wilson begins his book with: "Today almost every-
body knows almost everything about show business."   Then
he launches into an uninspired retelling of familiar gossip
column material, treating all aspects of show business--

night clubs, recordings, films, the big bands, the new black stars, television, etc. Because of the predominance of so many film names in the text, the book is considered here.

Extended attention is given to the Burton-Taylor affair, Bergman-Rossellini, Marie MacDonald, Jayne Mansfield, the Barrymores, Bogart-Bacall, Robert Mitchum, Marilyn Monroe, Dean Martin, Lena Horne, and Sammy Davis, Jr. Many other film personalities are mentioned in short humorous anecdotes or narrative examples. The text tends to be snickering hypocrisy, the author pretending shock and surprise at the behavior of his subjects, then betraying his jaded cynicism a few paragraphs later. A picture section provides momentary relief and there is an index that might help scholars or researchers.

Perhaps the most disheartening things about the book are the respectful production and prolonged exploitation given to this tired material. When quickie paperback material is given such full publisher treatment, it is ultimately the purchaser-reader who feels cheated. It is similar to the 42nd Street movie whose inducements and promises outside have no relationship to the quality inside. Not recommended.

2735.   Sight - Sound - Motion, by Herbert Zetti.   400 p.
        illus.   Belmont, Calif.:   Wadsworth, 1973.
        Announced as a five-dimensional approach to image communication: light, space, time, motion and sound. Employing information from the fields of art theory, psychology of perception, film theory, film direction and editing and so on, the book attempts to give an understanding of film and television aesthetics and their use. Almost 1,000 illustrations are promised, with some in color. A glossary, bibliography and index are also included. The book sounds promising.

2736.   Silent Snow, Secret Snow, by Gerald R. Barrett and
        Thomas L. Erskine.   193 p.   (paperback) illus.
        Encino, Cal.:   Dickenson Publish. Co., 1972.
        The first of a new series of books titled "From Fiction to Film" (see also 2612). An introduction by Barrett is followed by Conrad Aiken's short story, "Silent Snow, Secret Snow." The gradual withdrawal of a young boy into his own private world of fantasy is the story's theme. A dozen critical articles about the author and his short story are offered next.

        The second section deals with a 17-minute film made from the story in 1966 by director Gene Kearney. A preface entitled "Shot Analysis" explains shots, transitions, camera movement, camera angles and sound. This information is used throughout the script, which follows. Final sections include five articles about the film and some suggestions for written assignments.

Everything about the series looks promising. This first book is evidence of thoughtful planning combined with intelligent selection and good production. Schools and colleges can use this approach to film and literature study with a predictable success. Highly recommended.

2737. THE SILVER STREAK. A script of the 1934 film, by Roger Whately, Jack O'Donnell and H. W. Hanemann (director: Tommy Atkins). 268 p. illus. Los Angeles: Haskell-Travers, 1935.
The RKO film featured Charles Starrett and was based on an unpublished story by Whately.

2738. SINGIN' IN THE RAIN. A script of the 1951 film, by Betty Comden and Adolph Green (directors: Stanley Donen, Gene Kelly). 75 p. (paperback) illus. New York: Viking, 1972.
Contains: An introductory article by Betty Comden and Adolph Green, cast and credits.

2739. Sirk On Sirk, by Douglas Sirk and Jon Halliday. 176 p. (paperback) illus. New York: Viking, 1972.
Douglas Sirk is a little-known director whose films have been enjoyed by large audiences for many years. They are now appearing with annoying regularity on television and certain titles need a rest. This is, of course, a sort of belated tribute to Sirk. A sampling of his film titles will give the reader some idea of his metier: WRITTEN ON THE WIND, IMITATION OF LIFE, MAGNIFICENT OBSESSION, TARNISHED ANGELS, LURED, TAKE ME TO TOWN. Apparent from this sampling is a Universal-Ross Hunter audience type of film and this was Sirk's kind of operation. After starting with German theater and films, he came to America in 1937 and worked for Columbia (1942-48) and Universal (1950-58). He now lives in Switzerland and this collection of interviews conducted by Halliday took place there in 1970.

The interviews cover, in chronological fashion, the German theatre, German films, France and Holland, the Columbia period, the Universal period, and his retirement. The bio-filmography at the book's end is an interesting article by itself. In outline form, it describes Sirk's films and tells just enough of his life to give a satisfying portrait of a

professional. The structure of the book works very well.
Illustrations are a bit small at times but mostly
acceptable. A non-bibliography is included ("non" because
it includes so little written on Sirk and so much more on
some of the personalities with whom he worked). Very nicely done; recommended for all collections.

2740.   The Slapstick Queens, by James Robert Parish.
          298 p. illus. New York: Barnes, 1973.
          This volume is really a 5-in-1 version of the Citadel
series. In abbreviated form it offers "The Films of ...
Marjorie Main, Martha Raye, Joan Davis, Judy Canova, and
Phyllis Diller." The format is consistent: an introductory
essay which is part biography and part critical review is followed by a picture gallery arranged in chronological fashion.
A filmography with full cast and production credits for each
film follows.
          The text is well-researched and blends reviews,
quotations, comment and straight information to give both a
personal and professional portrait. For the most part,
these portions of the book are successful. The picture sections are surprisingly good and it is hoped that future Barnes
books will offer similar quality. While there are still a few
dark pictures, the majority are clearly reproduced with the
contrast values apparently under control. Occasionally there
is an indication of poor layout policy with a single small illustration taking up an entire page that might accommodate
at least two or three other visuals.
          When one considers the very few slapstick queens of
the screen, it is readily apparent why Parish had to include
such as Phyllis Diller. Lucille Ball and Carol Burnett are
television slapstick artists whose films do not reflect that
facet of their talent.
          In any event, it is a pleasure to see this tribute paid
to at least four great comediennes. In providing coverage on
these few neglected ladies, Parish has provided pleasure, information, and nostalgia that cannot fail to win a large and
appreciative audience. Recommended for inclusion in all collections.

2741.   Sluts, Saints and Superwomen Sinners, by James
          Harvey. 160 p. (paperback) Los Angeles, Calif.:
          Edka Books, 1967.
          Among the women who are discussed and demeaned
by this trashy book are Zsa Zsa Gabor, Ingrid Bergman, and
Elizabeth Taylor. Nothing new is divulged about the facts of
their lives, which are already well recorded. What the author does contribute is the leer and the innuendo, along with

a lot of suggestive wording. A cheap, untalented retelling
that makes scandal in high places a bore. Noted for the
record.

2742.   SOLOMON AND SHEBA. 18 p. (paperback) illus.
1952.
One of the opening sections in this souvenir book,
entitled "Unforgettable Moments," gives the reader some idea
of the film being described.   The large 70mm super Tech-
nirama process, a cast of thousands, Yul Brynner, Gina
Lollobrigida, and King Vidor are some of the elements considered by the book.   Some fuzzy illustrations attempt to
link sequences from the film to biblical sources.

2743.   SONG OF NORWAY. 28 p. (paperback) illus.
New York: A B C Pictures Corp., 1970.
Most of the attention in this souvenir book is focused
on composor Edvard Grieg, whose life and music were the
inspiration of the play upon which the film is based.   Cast
and production credits are given.

2744.   Son of Groucho, by Arthur Marx. 357 p. illus.
New York: David McKay, 1972.
Arthur Marx is a man burdened through his lifetime
with an enormous problem--Groucho.   The relationship between famous fathers and sons has been documented many
times: Keenan-Ed Wynn, Edward G. Robinson, Jr.-Sr.,
Michael-Charles Chaplin, Jr.-Sr., etc.   Some offspring
come to terms with the problem, others go down to defeat
via drugs, alcohol, and public scandal.   Arthur Marx has
accepted his fate as the son of Groucho with a minimum of
self-pity, but uses this volume to make his own claim for
personal recognition.   It is not a persuasive case because
the book's major appeal is still Groucho, not Arthur.
The author provides a revealing and quite objective
portrait of Groucho.   At times, the technique is interesting.
Some negative quality about Groucho is mentioned--almost
externally--and then Arthur comes to Groucho's defense as
a forgiving understanding son.   In this manner Groucho is
depicted as being stingy, foolish, insecure, cynical, and unloving.   His inability to give of himself via affection or understanding to those in his immediate family is emphasized,
as is his constant need for "a victim" for his insult-wit. A
few pictures of father and son appear in the book's center
section.
The final effect of the book is probably not what the
author intended.   Most readers will ignore Arthur Marx, his
story and his achievements, in favor of the larger-than-life

legend that he was blessed/cursed with as a parent. The exorcism of Groucho is an act of which the author seems incapable. Most readers will enjoy this most recent attempt. Recommended for all collections with a small warning for school libraries. Like most of his remarks, Groucho's comments about women and sex are calculated to surprise, insult and shock. At times he is quite a dirty old man.

2745. THE SORROW AND THE PITY. A script of the 1972 film by Marcel Ophuls (director: Marcel Ophuls). 194 p. illus. New York: Outerbridge and Lazard, 1973.
A translation of the French filmscript. Contains: an introduction by Stanley Hoffman, appendix, chronology, glossary, newsreel stills.

2746. THE SOUND OF MUSIC, by Herb Lubalin and Howard Liebling. 48 p. (paperback) illus. New York: National Publishers, 1965.
The first and longer section of this souvenir book is a retelling of the story with accompanying color stills from the film. The second part spotlights the cast, the composers, and the production personnel of the film. The black and white photographs used in this section provide a marked contrast to the earlier color stills. The book, like the film, seems aimed at the emotion rather than the intellect.

2747. SOUTH PACIFIC (The Tale of), by Thana Skouras. 48 p. illus. New York: Lehmann Publishers, 1958.
An unusual feature of this souvenir book is the information contained on the front and back endpapers. It is a listing of all the awards and nominations that the entire personnel, both on screen and behind the cameras, have received. The stage and theatre awards accorded the original New York production are also noted. James Michener discusses his original short story and Brooks Atkinson offers a biographical sketch of Rodgers and Hammerstein, who follow with statements of their own. Buddy Adler, the producer, introduces the center section which is a visualized or storyboard version of the film. Shots are described, notations about lighting, costume design and set decorations are noted, and the pages are supposed to resemble a romantic idea of a film script. The remainder of the volume is devoted to the director, the cast, the score, the color work, set decoration, costume, and dance. A section describing the Todd-AO film process gives a chronology of important dates in the history of motion picture technology.

This volume is so far superior to most of the others in this genre that it merits the detailed discussion above. If a souvenir book is to be published, this is one very fine way of doing it.

2748.   SOUTH SEAS ADVENTURE.   20 p.   (paperback) illus.   New York: Cinerama Publishers, 1958.
In this souvenir book a few miscellaneous articles about the South Seas are accompanied by some rather poor photographs of the locales.   Historical background is given, but most reader interest will probably center on the diagram of the three-projector system of Cinerama.   Producer Carl Dudley and composer Alex North are mentioned.

2749.   Soviet Cinema, by A. Arossev.   326 p.   illus. Moscow: Voks Publishing, 1935.
This scarce volume is noted here because of its historical importance.   It emphasizes a 15-year period of the Soviet film, 1920-1935, combining pictures and text of the films, directors, actors, and other artisans.   The many unusual pictures throughout are fascinating from both an historical and a technical viewpoint.   The text alternates between being quaint, predictable, and amusing.   Cecil B. DeMille's tribute to the Soviet film, for example, appears alongside John Howard Lawson's.   Anyone studying Soviet film should be familiar with this volume.   Recommended highly for university and college libraries.

2750.   SPARTACUS, by Stan Margulies.   30 p.   illus. 1960.
In this souvenir book an opening article entitled "Portrait of a Production" is followed by "Spartacus, Rebel Against Rome" by C. A. Robinson, Jr.   Several pages discuss gladiators and the role they played in ancient Rome. One complete section is devoted to those artisans "On the Other Side of the Camera" and there is a fold-out art section on the individual stars of the film.   Supporting cast and production credits are noted.

2751.   Spellbound in Darkness, by George C. Pratt.   576 p. (paperback) illus.   Greenwich, Conn.:   New York Graphic Soc., 1973.
Originally published in 1966 as a unique two-volume college text, the present version has had 66 photographs added, and the material has been redesigned into a single large volume.   Subtitled "A History of the Silent Film," the book is a collection of readings which cover a variety of actors, directors, and films from 1896 to 1929.   Melíes,

Porter, Griffith, Chaplin, Sennett, DeMille, von Stroheim, Flaherty, Dreyer, and Lubitsch are discussed along with the films and topics that were the major elements of the silent era. The author provides a commentary to many of the articles which explains and enhances their contribution to the historical account being presented. Picture reproduction is excellent and there is a helpful index provided.

While this volume is not a history in the usual sense, it provides much more than the usual straightforward narrative approach. All of the elements combine to create a memorable tribute to the silent screen. Its appearance as a trade book can only be applauded. Highly recommended for all collections.

2752.   SPLENDOR IN THE GRASS. A script of the 1961 film, by William Inge (director: Elia Kazan). 121 p. (paperback) illus. New York: Bantam Books, 1961.

2753.   Split Focus, by Peter Hopkinson. 119 p. illus. London: Rupert Hart-Davis, 1969.
Peter Hopkinson is an English filmmaker who began his career with home movies at a very early age. When he was 16, he began working at the film studios, and later worked with Gracie Fields, George Formby, King Vidor, and Alexander Korda. In World War II he served with distinction as a cameraman through many different campaigns. After the war he worked for the March of Time and has since produced documentaries for television. The self image that Hopkinson presents is a most admirable one. He is a dedicated professional who believes in such rare virtues as integrity of purpose, honesty, modesty, and justice. In addition to presenting himself, he is able to describe the world he is photographing. A specialized book about a little known filmmaker, but a very rewarding reading experience. Recommended.

2754.   STAGECOACH. A script of the 1938 film, by Dudley Nichols (director: John Ford). 152 p. (paperback) illus. New York: Simon & Schuster, 1971.
Includes: Cast, production credits, and "Stage to Lordsburg" by Ernest Haycox (original short story).

2755.   A STAIN ON HIS CONSCIENCE, by Paul A. Schreivogel. 20 p. (paperback) illus. Dayton, Ohio: Pflaum, 1970.
A study guide for the 1968 film directed by Dusan Vukotic. Found in Films in Depth (2274) and also available separately.

2756.   STAR, by Howard Newman. 48 p. (paperback)
        illus. New York: National Publishers, 1968.
        This souvenir book is presented as a scrapbook de-
voted to a female star, Gertrude Lawrence. Using candids,
stills and studio photographs, there is a mixture of the originals with Gertrude Lawrence and the film shots with Julie
Andrews. Old program covers and caricatures are also
used, along with reprints of news articles about the filming
and about Miss Lawrence. This intermingling of the old and
the new is an imaginative and clever approach to a screen
biography. Major cast members are given special attention
and full supporting cast and production personnel are listed.

2757.   Stargazer: Andy Warhol and His Films, by Stephen
        Koch. 216 p. illus. New York: Praeger, 1973.
        An attempt to analyze the Warhol films by relating
them to the development of the underground film movement.
Much meaning is read into the films, and for those enthusiasts who enjoy film without rationale, message, merit or
technique, the book may be rewarding. Others may not have
the patience, as many viewers did not for the films. Acceptable for the larger film collections.

2758.   STATE OF SEIGE. A script of the 1972 film, by
        Franco Solinas (director: Constantine Costa-Gavras).
        214 p. (paperback) illus. New York: Ballantine,
        1973.
        This book is divided into two parts: "Reflections"
(containing various articles about the making of the film including an interview with the director and the scriptwriter)
and "Documents" (containing various articles on internal politics in Chile). Also includes cast and production credits
and bibliography.

2759.   John Steinbeck and His Films, by Michael Burrows.
        36 p. (paperback) illus. London: Primestyle Ltd.,
        1970.
        Using plot outlines, critical blurbs and visuals, the
author gives a chronological history of Steinbeck and the
filming of his novels. Readers may also refer to Schulberg's
account of the writer's career in Hollywood (2302). Acceptable for all collections.

2760.   STOLEN KISSES. A script of the 1968 film, by
        Francois Truffaut (director: Francois Truffaut).
        320 p. illus. New York: Simon and Schuster,
        1971.

288

Contained in The Adventures of Antoine Doinel
(2006). Includes work notes, a first treatment, and the final screenplay.

2761.   Straub, by Richard Roud. 176 p. (paperback)
        illus. New York: Viking, 1972.
        At 38, Jean-Marie Straub has made five films to
date: MACHORKA-MUFF (1963), NOT RECONCILED (1965),
CHRONICLE OF ANNA MAGDELENA BACH (1968), THE
BRIDEGROOM, THE ACTRESS, AND THE PIMP (1968), and
OTHON (1969). Although he is French, he has chosen to
work in Germany and Italy for political reasons. Known as
an underground revolutionary, he uses an almost stationary
camera and non-narrative structures in his films.
        This volume analyzes each of his films critically,
contains quotes from interviews, and includes the entire
script of NOT RECONCILED. A filmography appears at the
book's end and there are sufficient illustrations to suggest
the filmmaker's style.
        This volume, as Roud states, is a bit premature.
It is a fine gesture to introduce new artists to the public
but those selected for this honor should perhaps not be as
obscure as Straub. Far more deserving are other filmmakers whose work is already proven: Saul Bass, Frederick
Wiseman, the Maysles Brothers, etc. The quarrel here is
with subject selection and not with treatment. In all fair-
ness, the book is well done and will interest young filmmakers. Acceptable for all collections.

2762.   A STREETCAR NAMED DESIRE. A script of the
        1951 film, by Tennessee Williams and Oscar Saul
        (director: Elia Kazan). 544 p. (paperback) New
        York: Appleton-Century-Crofts, 1971.
        Included in Film Scripts One (2267).

2763.   Studies in Documentary, by Alan Lovell and Jim
        Hiller. 176 p. (paperback) illus. New York:
        Viking, 1972.
        The title of this book may be adequate but it is also
misleading. The names of John Grierson and Humphrey Jennings should be in the title, or at least in the subtitle, since
the two major essays are devoted to these two personalities,
and they dominate the book. Such associates of Grierson as
Edgar Anstey, Alberto Cavalcanti, Sir Arthur Elton, Stuart
Legg, Paul Rotha, Henry Watt and Basil Wright are given
short biographical sketches.
        Completing the book is a third essay called "Free

Cinema"--a name given to six programs of documentary film given between 1956-59 at the National Film Theatre. It included classic films by directors such as Lindsay Anderson, Tony Richardson, Karel Reisz, Norman McClaren, Georges Franju, Roman Polanski, and others.

This is a critical history of the British documentary film with emphasis on two of its greatest artists. Partial filmographies for Jennings and Grierson are included, as are credits for the films in the Free Cinema program. The accompanying visuals are too dark and lack proper contrast values. This is specialized material that will please a small American audience. Recommended for large collections, although acceptable for others.

2764.   Preston Sturges: An American Dreamer, by James Ursini. 240 p. (paperback) illus. New York: Curtis Books, 1973.

The full title of this book is The Fabulous Life and Times of Preston Sturges, An American Dreamer. That's a lot of words but in this case they are all appropriate. He wrote successful plays and film scripts, and later directed a series of films which were recognized almost immediately as minor film classics. In an attempt to explain the mystery of Sturges and what made him run, author Ursini has made use of interviews, Sturges memorabilia, the films, and persons who knew and wrote about Sturges. What emerges from this research is a much better than usual biography and a critical appreciation of the films.

Each major film is treated separately and is followed by reference notes. In addition, there is a filmography and a bibliography at the book's end which enhance the book's reference value. A short pictorial section makes the reader wish for more, since some of the films are not represented at all. The book, based on work done at UCLA, is readable, enjoyable, and rewarding. The text is respectful and the ultimate portrait of Sturges comes as much from his films as from his actual experiences. What he believed is expressed by his characters, and the Sturges blend of American Horatio Algerism with European cynicism is usually evident.

A fine book in a new series that should find an appreciative and responsive audience. It is recommended for all libraries.

2765.   [No entry]

2766.   SUNDAY BLOODY SUNDAY. A script of the 1971

290

film, by Penelope Gilliatt (director: John Schlesinger).
135 p. New York: Viking, 1972.
Contains cast and production credits.

2767.   SUNDAY LARK, by Paul Schreivogel.   20 p.   (pa-
         perback) illus. Dayton, Ohio: Pflaum, 1970.
         A study guide for the 1964 film directed by Sanford
Semel.   Found in Films in Depth (2274) and also available
separately.

2768.   SUNRISE AT CAMPOBELLO.   24 p.   (paperback)
         illus. New York: David March, 1960.
         Other than a few articles about the backgrounds and
the writing of the play by Dore Schary, the content of this
souvenir book consists of the usual items: major cast acknowledgement to Ralph Bellamy and Greer Garson, major
production credits to producer-writer Dore Schary and director Vincent Donehue, and shorter recognition to the supporting players.   The production, story, and some highlights
of the film are also presented.

2769.   Surrealism and Film, by J. H. Matthews.   198 p.
         illus. Ann Arbor, Mich.: University of Michigan
         Press, 1971.
         A lengthy introductory discussion of the surrealist
viewpoint in general is followed by an enumeration of those
qualities the surrealist looks for and expects in films.   The
body of the book examines, describes, and evaluates films,
scripts, and filmmakers that have pertinence for the surrealist.   A final chapter is devoted to Luis Buñuel.   Included
are many explanatory footnotes and a detailed index.   The illustrations are a distinct disappointment, both because of the
small obvious selection and their reproduction.   The idea of
using a mono-blue color on the visuals may suggest surrealism but it diminishes the value of the photographs.
         The pedantic text is another matter.   It is scholarly,
well-researched, and impressive in its choice and treatment
of topic.   While it may please the artist/scholar, much of
it may be a challenge to the average reader.   It almost de-
mands some prior knowledge of surrealism, many remote
films, and the French school of avant-garde filmmakers of
the twenties.   Recommended only for large collections and
for college and university libraries.

2770.   The Swedish Film Institute, by The Swedish Film
         Institute.   20 p.   (paperback) Stockholm: Svenska
         Film Institutet, 1965.

The Swedish Film Institute is a foundation formed by an 1963 agreement between the government and the film industry. Television, taxes, a limited audience and other factors were killing the film industry when the 1963 Reform was adopted. The details of the agreement as well as its subsequent effects are spelled out in this short booklet. Noted here as an example of governmental cooperation with a threatened film industry.

2771. SWEET CHARITY, by Jay Rothman. 48 p. (paperback) illus. 1969.
Some outstanding color photography is to be found in this souvenir book. After a brief history of the story, from Fellini to Broadway to film, the leading cast members are profiled. In addition there are sections devoted to the songs, dances, set decorations, costume design, and finally to the director, Bob Fosse, and the producer, Robert Arthur. Other cast and production credits are also noted.

2772. Symbolic Leaders: Public Dramas and Public Men, by Orrin E. Klapp. 272 p. Chicago: Aldine Publishing Co., 1964.
According to the publisher, this book "is a probing and provocative analysis of the process of public drama and of the actors who play the leading roles...." A symbolic leader is one who functions primarily through his image or meaning. Film personalities mentioned are Monroe, Bankhead, Mae West, Will Rogers, John Barrymore, Chaplin, Elvis, Sinatra, Valentino and many others. While not a pure film book, the concept of leadership via public image is a challenging question. Not essential but acceptable in any collection.

2773. Take My Life, by Eddie Cantor and Jane Kesner Ardmore. 288 p. illus. Garden City, N.Y.: Doubleday, 1957.
Although this volume is mostly about the stage and is only peripheral to film matters, some insights into the lives of personalities who have worked in both mediums are given. Fanny Brice, Al Jolson, Irving Berlin, Will Rogers, W. C. Fields, Ben Schulberg and Samuel Goldwyn all receive special attention. Surprisingly well written in parts, the book has little pertinence for film collections except as background material.

2774. TAKING OFF. A script of the 1971 film, by Milos Forman, John Klein, John Guare and Jean-Claude Carriere (director: Milos Forman). 220 p. (paperback) illus. New York: Signet, 1971.

Contains cast credits and production credits together with two articles: "How I Came to America to Make a Film and Wound Up Owing Paramount $140,000" (Forman) and "Getting the Great Ten Percent: An Interview with Milos Forman" (Harriet R. Polt).

2775. The Tale of the Tales: The Beatrix Potter Ballet, by Rumer Godden. 208 p. illus. New York: Frederick Warne, 1971.

Rumer Godden was asked to record the making of the movie-ballet that combined five of the Beatrix Potter stories. The result is a report that includes interviews, observations, impressions and many color illustrations. The film, shown here under the title PETER RABBIT AND TALES OF BEATRIX POTTER, featured the Royal Ballet. Everything about this book is first-rate: text (Ms. Godden is an expert on Beatrix Potter), sketches, designs, stills, and production. Highly recommended for school libraries and acceptable for all other collections.

2776. The Talkies, by Richard Griffith. 360 p. (paperback) illus. New York: Dover, 1971.

This collection of 150 articles and hundreds of illustrations from Photoplay Magazine (1928-1940) is a most rewarding film book. Selected, arranged and written by Richard Griffith, the book should surprise no one with its intelligence, its total effect, and its coverage. Griffith places the articles in categories entitled: 1) Stars, Comedians, Child Stars, Support; 2) Living and Working in Movieland; 3) The Fans and Their Magazine; 4) Pictures and Trends.

The text is fan magazine writing of the thirties-- quaint, exaggerated, emotional, and mythical for the most part. Picture quality varies considerably, with many dark reproductions in evidence, yet other illustrations are very clear copies of the original materials. One especially effective feature is the inclusion of feature film advertisements. Adding product advertising is questionable but probably could not be avoided because of production problems. The thoroughness of Griffith is indicated once again in the impressive index.

The book has many values--as history, reference, nostalgia, and as pure entertainment. It is enthusiastically recommended for inclusion in all collections. A joy for all patrons to discover and far superior to the earlier Hollywood and The Great Fan Magazines (682).

2777.　Tallulah, by Brendan Gill.　287 p.　illus.　New
York:　Holt, Rinehart & Winston, 1972.

This oversized book contains much information in
both text and pictures about Tallulah Bankhead's films.
There are stills from a few early silents and large full pictures from her later sound films.　The book begins with a
long biographical essay that is peppered with Bankhead's
"one liners" and bits of scandal and gossip.　In a second
section, an album of personal, professional and news pictures reiterates the life story.　Small illustrations accompany the essay and short explanations identify the visuals in
the second part.　A chronology of her professional activities
(including her films) and an index complete the book.　The
subject is ever-fascinating, the stories are still amusing and
the picture collection is superb.　Recommended for all collections serving mature audiences.　Tallulah was never much
for the kids.

2778.　Tallulah, Darling, by Denis Brian.　285 p.　(paperback) illus.　New York:　Pyramid, 1972.

A paperback biography that captures many of the
anecdotes, stories, and pronouncements of Tallulah.　Based
on 150 interviews of persons acquainted with Bankhead in one
way or another, the text also includes a 1966 interview with
the subject herself.　It is packed with quotations, many of
them taken from Bankhead's 1952 autobiography, Tallulah.
The films are mentioned in some depth and there are two
sections on LIFEBOAT and A ROYAL SCANDAL that will add
to anyone's appreciation of those films.

While the portrait is not always flattering, it is consistently affectionate.　A few pictures and an index are included.　This volume is as enjoyable as some of the other
narrative biographies and is only surpassed by Brendan Gill's
picture-volume (2777).　Recommended for all collections
serving mature audiences.

2779.　Tallulah, Darling of the Gods, by Kiernan Tunney.
228 p.　illus.　New York:　Dutton, 1973.

Another Bankhead book, this one is by an Irish play-
wright and critic.　In 1947 he came to visit Bankhead to
persuade her to perform in one of his comedies.　He writes
of that first instance and others that followed over the next
20 years.　How much of the memoir is valid has been questioned by those who were part of Bankhead's menage.　They
either deny having seen him or only acknowledge his presence
at one or two dinners.

The account is a personal, intimate one and tries to

describe the personality rather than recall the professional triumphs and failures. Acceptable for all collections--with a question about its authenticity.

2780. THE TAMING OF THE SHREW. 32 p. (paperback) illus. 1967.
After a short introductory section on the background of the film, this souvenir book tells the story with a minimum of narrative and a maximum of photographs, some of them full-page illustrations. There are also full-page portraits of Elizabeth Taylor, Richard Burton, and director Franco Zeffirelli. The supporting cast and production personnel are noted, with special attention directed to the designers and scriptwriters.

2781. Teaching Human Beings, by Jeffrey Schrank. 192 p. (paperback) Boston: Beacon Press, 1972.
The subtitle of this timely book is "101 Subversive Activities for the Classroom." Since many of these activities deal with film, the book is considered here. Six major topics make up the book's contents: Sense Education, Hidden Assumptions, Violence and the Violated, Chemicals and the Body (Drugs), Learning About Death, and Subversive Activities. An annotated evaluative filmography follows each of the sections. In addition, there are discussion suggestions, a bibliography, and a sampling of the activities mentioned in the subtitle.
"Subversive" in the context of this book means the use of those simulation games, group encounters, books, and films that seldom appear in a traditional classroom. Any teacher wishing to improve the daily school experience for herself and her students will find stimulating and rewarding material here. Excellent for the professional shelf in all school situations and the college-university crowd could profit from this volume even more.

2782. The Teaching of Film: A Report and Some Recommendations, by Cinema Consultative Committee. 16 p. (paperback) London: British Board of Film Censors, 1959.
An early British report which urged a planned, financially supported approach to film study in England and Scotland. The Committee argued for film study courses in the training colleges and requested that a degree program be established. It was their hope that the film industry would offer support. Noted here for the record, but it may help those teachers and schools who are considering film study for their curriculum.

A similar title, Teaching Film: A Guide to Class-room Method, is worth noting. Written by Grace Greiner, and published by the British Film Institute in 1955, this 32-page book outlines the task of teaching film and considers its implementation in the infants school, the junior school, and the secondary school. The role of the film teacher is outlined in a final chapter. A bit dated but still acceptable in any film collection.

2783. The Technique of Lighting for Television and Mo-
tion Pictures, by Gerald Millerson. 366 p. illus.
New York: Hastings House, 1972.
This book is part of a series which the publishers call The Library of Communication Techniques. A study of the art of creative lighting, it covers introductory topics such as the nature of light, the eye, the camera and the visual world. Basic principles and tools of lighting lead to more advanced chapters on portraiture, still life, persuasive light-ing, and lighting of scenes. Motion picture and television techniques, lighting effects and picture control are discussed in the final sections. Some suggestions for further reading are made and there is an adequate index to the material in the book.
Any book on lighting must contain visuals which il-lustrate techniques and concepts. Not only is this volume rich in such pictures, but the high standard of photo repro-duction which characterizes this series is once again evident. Tables, charts, diagrams, and graphs help support and inter-pret the text also.
This is a specialized technical book that will be of great assistance to the advanced amateur and the professional. It certainly belongs in all college collections as well as other large collections. Smaller public libraries and schools will find it valuable but perhaps not as essential as some of the other titles in this fine series.

2784. The Technique of Screenplay Writing, by Eugene
Vale. 306 p. New York: Grosset & Dunlap, 1972.
An updating of a well known work that appeared originally in 1944. Considered by many to be one of the standard works on writing screenplays, the new volume uses films such as EASY RIDER, MIDNIGHT COWBOY, DOCTOR ZHIVAGO, AIRPORT and BONNIE AND CLYDE to explain various points and techniques.
The author's philosophy is evident in his use of the Delacroix quotation: "First learn to be a craftsman: It won't keep you from being a genius." How applicable that advice is for the would-be filmmakers of today! Vale divides

his text into three major divisions: The Form, The Dramatic Constitution, and The Story. Within each category, he discusses the pertinent elements. For example: under form, such elements as film language, space, picture, time, sound, and information sources are explained. A fascinating diagram comparing the forms of books, plays and films is typical of the provocative and valuable material offered. The other two sections are similar in structure. At all times the text is clear, sequential, and non-pedantic. Frequent references are made to well known films to support statements. The book is not illustrated, but a good index is offered. The logical development, clarity, and practical advice make this volume valuable to anyone interested in writing for the screen. It belongs in all collections which serve college students and adults.

2785. Television, Radio, Film for Churchmen, edited by B. F. Jackson. Nashville, Tenn.: Abingdon Press, 1969.
This is volume #2 in the Communication for Churchmen Series.

2786. Television's Classic Commercials, by Lincoln Diamant. 305 p. illus. New York: Hastings House, 1971.
Written by a man who has had careers in publishing, broadcasting, and advertising, this book looks at 69 classic television commercials which appeared from 1948-1958, the so-called "Golden Years" of television. The awarding of classic status by the American Television Commercials Festival judges basically rests upon three criteria: longevity, memorability, and influence on later techniques. A short historical account of the development of the American commercial is given first. Then the 69 commercials are arranged under subject headings such as Food, Tobacco, Apparel, Cars and Trucks, etc. The description of each film includes a television screen still, the technique used, length, number of words, the air date, advertiser, agency, producer, and other creative personnel involved. Of major importance is the reproduction of the full script with each shot and accompanying audio noted. A final paragraph of background information completes each entry. Three appendices indicate dollar expenditures in advertising and a fourth reproduces the world's first commercial, an audio message broadcast on August 28, 1927 over Radio Station WEAF in New York City. A glossary of more than 500 terms used in broadcasting completes the book.

The importance of this book to film collections is obvious if one considers the social impact the TV commercial has had on our society. Furthermore, since most commercials are shot as film initially and contain the newest filmmaking techniques, the provision of 69 full scripts for filmmakers to study is an offering to be appreciated. Content, arrangement, production and supporting text are all first rate. Many of the Hastings House books are prepared with a publishing longevity in mind and this one is no exception. It should be popular, useful, and in-print for many years to come. Recommended enthusiastically for all libraries including middle schools.

2787.   Television Seminar: NBC, edited by Rochelle Reed.
        24 p. (paperback) illus. Washington, D.C.:
        American Film Institute, 1973.
        Thomas Sarnoff, accompanied by a panel of NBC
executives, discusses the making and use of films for television. A transcript of a meeting held in January 1973. Acceptable for all collections.

2788.   Telling It Again and Again: Repetition in Literature
        and Film, by Bruce F. Kawin. 197 p. Ithaca,
        N.Y.: Cornell University Press, 1972.
        As indicated in the sub-title, this volume concerns
itself with the use of repetition for effect. The literature of Gertrude Stein and Samuel Beckett are obvious examples. Many other examples in literature are cited and if this volume had appeared in the fifties or earlier, it would have concerned itself with literature exclusively. However, now the works of Eisenstein, Buñuel, Bergman, Resnais and other filmmakers are considered. Acceptable for academic libraries.

2789.   THE TEN COMMANDMENTS. 28 p. (paperback)
        illus. New York: Greenstone Co., 1956.
        The emphasis is on director Cecil B. DeMille in
this souvenir book which opens with some excerpts from a DeMille address made in 1956. Full page printings by Arnold Friberg in color are used to tell the story of the film. Although the cast members are grouped three to a page, greater attention is given to biographies of director-producer DeMille, co-producer Henry Wilcoxon, and composer Elmer Bernstein. Some mention is made of the enormous amount of research that was done for the film. See also Moses and Egypt (937a) for more information on the research.

2790.   Ten Years of Films on Ballet and Classical Dance,
        1956-1965, by UNESCO. 105 p. (paperback) illus.
        Paris: UNESCO, 1968.
        This catalogue is a sampling of films on ballet,
classical and modern dance from many countries. It limits
itself to films which are "pure dance" rather than biographies,
how-to-dance films, or folk dance films. After a short introduction by Agnes Bleier-Brody, an alphabetical listing by
country follows. Under each, one or more dance films orig-
inated in that country are described. Included in the description are the names of those responsible for the production, choreography, music, libretto, decor, direction, and
principal roles. Film characteristics of length, gauge, color,
black and white are given along with distributor information.
A last section offers some information about the subject of
the film. Several indexes complete the book: the first lists
the films by country (really a table of contents), the second
is an index of choreographers and the third, an index of
composers.
        Although the book refers to films which are ten or
more years old, they are still pertinent to many persons
concerned with the study of dance, music, and allied arts.
For those libraries catering to such users, this small book
would seem quite valuable.

2791.   Mikis Theodorakis: Music and Social Change, by
        George Giannaris. 320 p. illus. New York:
        Praeger, 1973.
        The biography of the composer of the scores for
ZORBA THE GREEK and Z. His ideas about music and social change are compatible. This is specialized material
suitable only for the larger film collections.

2792.   Theology Through Film, by Neil P. Hurley. 212 p.
        illus. New York: Harper & Row, 1970.
        "The motion picture enjoys a psychological and
pedagogical experience that has as yet not been matched by
a corresponding effectiveness in the modes of religious communication." Today, access to films allows the religous
leader/educator to compare his "message" with that ex-
pounded by others. These statements are taken from the
provocative introduction to this remarkable book.
        In the body of the work, chapters are devoted to
such ideas as man in secular society, inner man, freedom,
conscience, sex, evil, death, grace, sacrificial love, and
the future. In each chapter, films are correlated with the
theme being explored. For example, the chapter on society

uses LILIES OF THE FIELD, A TASTE OF HONEY, MID-
NIGHT COWBOY, CATCH 22, IL SORPASSO, THE ISLAND,
THE APU TRILOGY, RULES OF THE GAME and other films.
A final section deals with the teaching of theology. Chapters
are footnoted and there is an index. Pictorial illustrations
are well chosen and well reproduced.

For those critics who decry the lack of "serious"
writing on cinema, this book is a fine response. It offers
intelligence without conceit, readability without compromise,
and now-ness without faddishness. It is stimulating reading
that will be of value/interest to a wide audience. Highly
recommended for all serious readers and for inclusion in all
collections.

2793.   Theory of Film Practice, by Noel Burch. 172 p.
         172 p. illus. New York: Praeger, 1973.
         This complex series of arguments, opinions, and
derivations on film theory and aesthetics had their first appearance in Cahiers du Cinéma. Burch has arranged them
under headings such as Basic Elements, Dialectics, Perturb-
ing Factors, and Reflections on Film Subjects.

The author attempts to close the gap between the
theory and the practice of filmmaking but the endeavor does
not quite succeed. The difficult writing style is an intellectual hurdle that few will attempt to master. For example:
"Taken in its most elementary sense (which was how Eisenstein certainly took it), 'dialectics' may convey a meaningful
image of the conflictual organization to which these elementary parameters have been subjected by nearly every conse-
quential filmmaker in his or her search for 'unity through
diversity'...." While this verbiage may be fine for the dedicated theoretician, it is probably a bit too concentrated for
the young impatient filmmaker.

The book is indexed and there are a few illustrations. Many of the examples of films in the text are French,
and familiarity with them will help in appreciating the text.
Recommended for large collections and for college libraries.

2794.   THERE'S NO BUSINESS LIKE SHOW BUSINESS.
         16 p. (paperback) illus. 1954.
         After a short plot synopsis, the starring members
of the cast and songwriter Irving Berlin are each given one
page of attention in this souvenir book. Ethel Merman,
Donald O'Connor, Marilyn Monroe, Dan Dailey, Johnny Ray
and Mitzi Gaynor are spotlighted. The supporting cast is
listed but there are no technical or production credits. Photographs are in black and white and the book's inexpensive

appearance suggests that it was a rapidly produced after-thought.

2795.　Thirty Years of Treason, edited by Eric Bentley.
　　　　991 p. (paperback) New York: Viking, 1973.
　　　　This collection of excerpts from hearings held by the House Committee on Un-American Activities covers the period 1938 to 1968. The intention is to show the evolution of HUAC from an investigating panel which operated in a dignified sensitive way into a menacing governmental agency which was a potential threat to every creative person. It is, the publishers say, a warning for the future. The inquiry into Communistic infiltration of the motion picture industry involved Adolph Menjou, Robert Taylor, Ronald Reagan, Gary Cooper, John Howard Lawson, Edward Dmytryk, Emmet Lavery, Ring Lardner, Jr., Larry Parks, Sterling Hayden, Jose Ferrer, Budd Schulberg, Elia Kazan, Edward G. Robinson, Lionel Stander and Lee J. Cobb. An index facilitates access. It is difficult to imagine users reading this large volume as a totality; its greatest use will probably be for reference and as such it can be recommended for inclusion in all collections that serve mature readers.

2796.　THIS IS CINERAMA. 20 p. (paperback) illus.
　　　　New York: Cinerama Publishers, 1954.
　　　　Lowell Thomas narrated much of this first film in the Cinerama process. It began with the well-remembered roller coaster ride which was followed by sequences designed to show the potential of this new process. Four pages of description of the process introduce the program of this pioneer film. The second section (or act) of the film was a flight across the United States.

2797.　THIS IS IT! THE MARIN SHOOT-OUT. An un-
　　　　filmed script, by Michael Goodwin and Greil Marcus.
　　　　128 p. New York: Outerbridge and Lazard, 1972.
　　　　A filmscript-to-be-read, found in DOUBLE FEA-TURE (2206).

2798.　This Was Show Business, by Ira Peck and John
　　　　Springer. 74 p. (paperback) illus. New York:
　　　　Literary Enterprises, 1956.
　　　　Noted here primarily as one of the first picture books combining a literate text by the always dependable John Springer and some excellent visuals. Subjects are divided between films, radio, the stage, etc., but most appeared at some time in films. This volume has been out of

print for years but it would be even more fascinating today if it were reprinted.

2799.   This You Won't Believe, by Corinne Griffith.   115 p. (paperback) New York: Frederick Fell, 1972.
Corinne Griffith has had nine books published.   The outside cover of this, her tenth, suggests that the book is a collection of tales about herself and her circle of celebrity friends.   Well, she does mention Randolph Scott, Dorothy McGuire, Gene Autry, Roy Rogers, John Wayne, Cary Grant, Eva Marie Saint, in sentences such as: "Among my first customers were...." "He directed pictures which starred...." "I ran into...."
The book rambles along chattily, saying very little in a folksy and down-to-earth way.   Most readers will lose interest quickly.   The book offers nothing for film collections--or any other collections for that matter.

2800.   THOROUGHLY MODERN MILLIE.   26 p.   (paperback)   illus.   New York: Universal Pictures, 1967.
The Twenties are discussed by producer Ross Hunter on the inside covers of this short but visually attractive souvenir book.   In an overly cute, and ultimately sickening fashion, using a phone call type of dialogue between two flappers, the plot is related.   Songs from the film provide the opportunity to use full-page photographs in full color as each advances the plot.   The latter section of the book is devoted to full-page cast biographies and some selected production people: director George Roy Hill, arranger Andre Previn and composer Elmer Bernstein, among others.

2801.   Those Endearing Young Charms, by Marc Best. 279 p.   illus.   New York: Barnes, 1971.
In the preface, author Best says, "It seems absurd that out of the countless volumes of film literature that have been published, none whatsoever has given due regard to the youngsters of celluloid."   This statement is indicative of the carelessness that characterizes this volume.   Norman Zierold's The Child Stars, published in 1965, covers some of the same ground and does it much better than Best. There is no definition for the phrase "Child Performer." Many of the subjects continued making films during their teens and into adulthood--e.g., Natalie Wood, Jackie Cooper, Roddy McDowall, Dean Stockwell.
Although it is not stated, the cutoff age for the filmographies appears to be age fourteen.   Fifty of the "most notable child performers" are treated with a short text, a studio portrait, and some film stills.   The subjects are se-

lected in a mysterious manner, with omissions such as Durbin, Garland, the Mauch Twins, Gloria Jean, Elizabeth Taylor, Sabu, Leon Janney, and Bobby Breen. Included are such dubious "notables" as Peter Miles, Philippe De Lacy and Joan Carroll.

The filmographies are very selective lists of only the more widely known films or those for which the author was able to furnish stills. Some inane material about hobbies, schools and civic activities reads like studio publicity. The remainder of the uninspired text is descriptive and never critical. Picture reproduction is adequate.

A comprehensive, carefully researched study on child performers would be a welcome addition to film literature. Zierold (205) is limited in his coverage and lacks illustrations. Best offers an unexplained, haphazard dull approach and some interesting illustrations. A disappointing volume that is acceptable only as a temporary stop-gap.

2802.   Those Great Movie Ads, by Joe Morella, Edward Z. Epstein and Eleanor Clark. 320 p. illus. New Rochelle, N.Y.: Arlington House, 1972.

The popular success of a motion picture depends, according to Judith Crist in her introduction to this book, on "producer's sell" and "word of mouth." Promotion ads figure largely in both factors, and it is the concern of this book to explore the many aspects of film advertising.

Using reprinted ads from a variety of sources--newspapers, magazines, billboards, posters, testimonials, endorsements, press books--the authors have put together a fascinating collection of memorabilia. What is lacking is a general structure that will indicate to the reader some discernible pattern or approach to the collection. The major narrative section, "A Brief Look at Movie Advertising," pops up towards the middle, while "Logos," "Schmeer," and "Critic's Quotes" begin the book and "Walt Disney," "Fan Quiz," and "Turnaround Campaigns" end it. Reproduction of the illustrations and ads varies considerably from excellent to awful (see montages on p. 158, 228, 279). No index is provided.

How important these reservations are to the reader is debatable. The main attraction here is the ads and anything else is icing. Nevertheless, for the serious reader, a bit more quality could have resulted from editor attention to possible reference use, historical arrangement or acknowledgment, and possible improvement of ad reproduction. The potential popularity of this book in any collection is not in question; it is likely to be a great favorite. Recommended for inclusion in all collections.

2803.   THOSE MAGNIFICENT MEN IN THEIR FLYING MA-
         CHINES. 34 p. (paperback) illus. New York:
         20th Century Fox, 1965.
         Produced with much the same spirit and approach as
the film, this souvenir book tells the story in a 1910 gazette
form. Many shots from the film are used as illustrations
and the fashions of the period are given special attention.
An outstanding feature is an art portfolio by artist Ronald
Searle. Cast and production credits are given and there is
a players gallery showing the leading actors in the large
cast.

2804.   A Thousand and One Delights, by Alan G. Barbour.
         177 p. illus. New York: Macmillan, 1971.
         This picture book is in the form of a memoir of the
author's favorite films of the forties. Meant as an entertainment, the book begins with a tribute to Jon Hall and Maria
Montez, then follows with chapters on Abbott and Costello,
reissues of thirties films, horror films, comedies, films
from the Monogram Studio, serials, the B mystery, the B
western, the swashbuckler films, John Wayne, and finally
big budget films. The criterion for inclusion in Barbour's
list is simple--a film that he saw in the forties which he
remembers with great pleasure.
         The brief text is relaxed, chatty and informative.
Picture selection and reproduction are above average. The
book is not indexed. Not essential to any collection, this
volume will provide much reading and browsing pleasure for
patrons. It can be recommended for inclusion in any collection as a supplement, a diversion, or simply an affectionate
remembrance of some films and performers of the past.

2805.   Three Major Screenplays, by Malvin Wald and
         Michael Werner. 394 p. (paperback) illus. New
         York: Globe Book Co., 1973.
         This textbook contains the following: 1) Introduction,
2) "Screenplay Terms"--A Glossary of Moviemaking Terminology, 3) "The Student as Filmmaker"--A Practical Discussion of Some of the Basic Problems in Making Films, 4)
Screenplay of THE OX BOW INCIDENT (2631), 5) Screenplay
of HIGH NOON (2377) 6) Screenplay of LILIES OF THE
FIELD (2484), and 7) A Film Lover's Bibliography. Each
of the three screenplays is preceded by: a) "About the Author," b) "About the Screenplay," and is followed by c)
"What the Critics Said," and d) "To Enrich Your Reading."
A teacher's guide for using the book as a classroom text is
also available.

2806.   THREE SCREENPLAYS, by Robert Rossen.   274 p.
        (paperback) illus. New York: Doubleday, 1972.
        Contains: ALL THE KINGS MEN, 1949 (2016); THE
HUSTLER, 1961 (2413); LILITH, 1963 (2485); a list of the
screenplays written by Rossen; a list of the films directed
by Rossen.

2807.   The Thrill of it All, by Alan G. Barbour.   204 p.
        illus. New York: Macmillan, 1971.
        This pictorial history of the B western disposes of
the first two decades of films in one brief opening chapter.
The cowboy stars of the early thirties--Buck Jones, Tim
McCoy, Hoot Gibson, Tom Tyler, Ken Maynard and Bob
Steele--are introduced next. John Wayne receives one chapter to himself while Gene Autry, Roy Rogers, William Boyd,
and others share sections. The villains, serials, cowboy
trios, singing cowboys, and the eventual demise of the B
western are some of the other topics discussed.
        As with the other Barbour-Macmillan books, the
purpose is primarily entertainment. However, a little more
effort could have increased the overall value of this book.
The addition of some indexes, some expansion of the chapter
introductions and a tighter organization of the material would
have helped a great deal without altering the initial concept
of the book. Picture quality is quite good and the brief text,
emotional at times, is always readable and informative. The
book is not essential to any collection but will please many
readers. Young people will enjoy it especially, and as a
popular volume, it can be recommended for all collections.

2808.   Through Navajo Eyes, by Sol Worth and John Adair.
        28 p. illus. Bloomington, Ind.: Indiana University
        Press, 1972.
        This book is a rarity, and a find. An account of a
study of Navajo Indians using the major fields of anthropology
and film communication may suggest a doctoral thesis made
palatable for publication, but this book is much more than
that. Under grants from the National Science Foundation and
the Annenberg School of Communications, the author's goal
was to teach filmmaking and editing to a group of Navajos.
It was hoped that these abilities would enable them to depict
themselves and their culture via film. Two aspects of the
project emerge: first, the training stage and then the analysis stage. Since both authors have had many similar experiences with other ethnic groups, comparison is frequent
and sometimes surprising.
        The films made are described in detail at the close

of the book and there are frame enlargements to supplement
the written account. A valuable bibliography lists works that
have pertinence to either one or both of the two major dis-
ciplines used. To round out the study completely, a full index is given.

The book should serve as a model for many future
studies which can use film communication with another discipline. Many findings are stated, and yet some new questions or problems are developed. For example, one initial
question raised by an older leader comes to mind: how
would making films help the Navajo? A typical problem for
the authors was the impossibility of translating the film
images into the printed word.

For anyone concerned with teaching or using filmmaking with small groups, the book has much to offer and
suggest. It certainly is an essential for all colleges and for
most schools. Other libraries will find it a unique and interesting addition that shows a use of film not often treated
in other volumes. In summary, this is a book that warrants
placement in all collections.

2809. THUNDERBALL. 34 p. (paperback) illus. New
York: Program Publishing Co., 1965.
A few color photographs are sprinkled in with the
black and white stills which predominate in this souvenir
book. Some background is given but the major emphasis is
on detailing James Bond's exploits in this film. As with the
films, there is much female body exposure. Cast and production credits are barely mentioned.

2810. TILLIE AND GUS. A script of the 1933 film, by
Walter DeLeon, Francis Martin and Rupert Hughes
(director: Francis Martin). 124 p. (paperback)
illus. New York: Simon and Schuster, 1973.
Found in: NEVER GIVE A SUCKER AN EVEN
BREAK (2591).

2811. TIME PIECE, by Paul Schreivogel. 20 p. (paperback) illus. Dayton, Ohio: Pflaum, 1970.
A study guide for the 1966 film directed by Jim
Hensen. Found in Films in Depth (2274) and also available
separately.

2812. To Be Continued, by Ken Weiss and Ed Goodgold.
341 p. illus. New York: Crown, 1972.
Some 220 sound serials of the period 1929 to 1956
are the subject of this attractive volume. Arranged chronologically by individual years, each serial is described by

name, number of episodes, studio, director, cast members, a short synopsis and several stills. The famous serials receive extended annotation and a greater number of illustrations.

The text reflects the enthusiasm and fondness that the authors have for their subject. Pictures are plentiful, nicely chosen, and well-reproduced. The indexes are arranged in two ways: a chronological listing of the titles by year of release, and then a general alphabetical index which includes all the titles.

An example of fascinating subject material treated with knowledge and admiration, and arranged in an attractive usable manner, this volume is pleasant reading and an easy reference tool. Recommended for all collections.

2813. To Encourage the Art of the Film: The Story of the British Film Institute, by Ivan Butler. 208 p. illus. London: Robert Hale, 1971.

The history of the British Film Institute is divided into convenient sections, each dealing with a specific aspect or function. Topics such as The Organization and Administration from 1933 to 1970, Preservation of Films, Education, Film Presentations, Production of Films, Distribution of Films, Publications, and Film Societies are treated individually rather than in a continuing narrative. The appendices include an organization chart, lists of BFI officials, a chronological listing of the film programs given by the Institute, the speakers who have participated in the John Player Lecture Series, and the features shown at the London Film Festival from 1957 to 1970. The book is indexed in detail and many illustrations correlate nicely with the text.

This is a specialized book that will have a limited appeal, but it has implications for even the smallest library that uses film since many of the functions delineated here are repeated in those libraries. This is a volume that is probably more valuable to librarians than to their patrons. Recommended to those libraries which offer films as a part of their service.

2814. Toms, Coons, Mulattos, Mammies and Bucks, by Donald Bogle. 260 p. illus. New York: Viking, 1973.

Subtitled "An Interpretive History of Blacks in American Films," this volume documents the changes in the portrait of the black in film over its 70-year history. Beginning with UNCLE TOM'S CABIN, it covers the silent era to THE BIRTH OF A NATION and the remainder of the twenties when blacks portrayed comic jesters. The black as a servant was

the theme of the thirties, while the forties saw him first as
a musical entertainer and then as a problem personality.
The fifties brought forth the first black film stars, and the
sixties repeated in depth some of the problems which were
merely approached in the forties. Black militants and the
black films are themes for the seventies.

This volume is the most recent and best treatment
of the topic thus far. It repeats some of Noble (1025) and
Mapp (137a) but has much to say in addition. Recommended
for all collections.

2815. TORA! TORA! TORA! 36 p. (paperback) illus.
New York: 20th Century Fox, 1970.
This souvenir book considers the film as two separate stories and two separate films--the American and the
Japanese. The historical background is shown by artwork
and by newspaper headlines. Cast and credits are listed
separately.

2816. The Total Film-Maker, by Jerry Lewis. 208 p.
illus. New York: Random House, 1971.
The term, "total film-maker" may apply to Griffith,
Welles, or Chaplin but to apply that same title to the rather
short presentation of ideas, comments, and ramblings presented here is both immodest and a bit fraudulent. Based
upon lectures given to a group of graduate students at the
University of Southern California, the book is composed of
anecdotes, personal recollections, and observations, practical
advice, and philosophy. In broad terms Lewis considers the
producer, the writer, the actor and the stage crew. Activities such as pre-planning, actual filming, cutting the film,
creating and recording the musical score, and distributing
the film are also treated. The closing portion of the volume
analyzes the art of comedy, with Lewis selecting Chaplin,
Stan Laurel, and Jackie Gleason as his personal "greats."

Since it was based on edited audio tapes of the lectures, the book gives evidence of its origin. It lacks strong
continuity and conciseness, and seems extemporaneous rather
than tightly structured.

As a statement on filmmaking by Jerry Lewis, the
volume is not disagreeable. Lewis writes in the same manner as he speaks on the informal talk shows of television.
He is opinionated, charming, aggressive, and knowledgeable.
As in all his other media appearances, readers will either
love him or loathe him. Libraries can toss a coin on this
one.

2817.   TOYS, by Paul A. Schreivogel.   20 p.   (paperback)
         illus. Dayton, Ohio: Pflaum, 1970.
         A study guide for the 1967 film directed by Grant
Munro.   Found in Films in Depth (2274) and also available
separately.

2818.   Tracy and Hepburn, by Garson Kanin.   307 p.
         New York: Viking, 1971.
         Is there anyone who hasn't seen, heard about or
read this book? It was given a mammoth publicity campaign,
was reviewed in periodicals, newspapers and magazines,
went through several printings in the hardcover version, and
has recently appeared in paperback. In this case, it was
much ado about something; the book is a very good one.
         Based largely on reminiscences of his social and
professional interactions with the pair, Kanin alternates the
spotlight between the two, sometimes allowing them to share
an anecdote.   The author makes no attempt to be objective
and both stars have positive sympathetic roles in his story.
His memory and critical judgment are not always convincing:
for example, "The film (SEA OF GRASS) was a success in
every way"; "The result (STATE OF THE UNION) was a disappointment." In telling a long story about Hepburn and
Cary Grant, the author makes numerous mentions of a film
he calls MEMORY OF LOVE in which Grant appeared with
Carole Lombard.   The film referred to was IN NAME ONLY,
had a different story than that attributed to it here, and was
made the year before PHILADELPHIA STORY; these are some
facts that Kanin has confused in his account.   But this is a
minor matter.   Weakness in their scripts was never a problem
--it was the star quality of the subjects that attracted audiences to their films.   The same condition prevails here.
         No index or illustrations are provided.   This is an
audience book that will be popular in all collections.   Recommended.

2819.   TRANSATLANTIC MERRY-GO-ROUND. A script of
         the 1934 film, by Joseph Moncure March and Harry
         W. Conn (director: Benjamin Stoloff).   342 p.   New
         York: Whittlesey House, 1936.
         Found in The New Technique of Screen Writing, by
Tamar Lane (1037).

2820.   Transcendental Style in Film: Ozu, Bresson,
         Dreyer, by Paul Schrader.   194 p.   illus.   Los
         Angeles: University of California Press, 1972.
         By analyzing examples from the films of three direc-
tors--Yasujiro Ozu, Robert Bresson, and Carl Dreyer--the

author attempts to develop a theory about film style which can express the sacred and the holy. This attempt to create a religious aesthetic for film is admirable but demanding and ultimately exhausting. By using many philosophical, religious and aesthetic concepts and references, the author attempts to define or describe transcendental style.

Each of the three director sections is quite detailed and the reader may wonder how much of what is being discussed was truly the director's intent. Extended footnotes and impressive bibliographies are provided in the appendix. The book is also illustrated and indexed. This is a scholarly attempt to link religion, art, and film by philosophical discussion and conjecture. The text will prove difficult for most readers and the ultimate reaction will probably be frustration or confusion rather than satisfaction.

Larger collections, especially in universities, should find room for this intellectual exercise. Other collections may prefer Butler's Religion in the Cinema (1160), Hurley's Theology Through Film (1346), or Celluloid and Symbols by Cooper and Skrade (178).

2821. TRAPEZE. 16 p. (paperback) illus. 1956.
Attention is focused on personalities in this souvenir book. Burt Lancaster, Tony Curtis, and Gina Lollobrigida each receive several pages for biographical data, and supporting players Katy Jurado and Thomas Gomez are alloted single pages. Director Carol Reed, producer Harold Hecht, and writer James Hill get a page each. Very little of the book is devoted to either background or filmmaking but several scenes from the film are used as illustrations and there is a very short plot outline.

2822. TRISTANA. A script of the 1970 film, by Luis Buñuel (director: Luis Buñuel). 144 p. (paperback) illus. New York: Simon and Schuster, 1971.
Contains: an introductory article by J. Francisco Aranda, cast and credits.

2823. THE TROJAN WOMEN. 22 p. (paperback) illus. New York: Raydell Publishing, 1971.
Reference to the play by Euripides and "A Director's Note" by Michael Cacoyannis are the two leading articles in this souvenir book. The remaining pages are devoted to shots from the film, pages on each of the leading stars-- Katharine Hepburn, Vanessa Redgrave, Irene Papas, Genevieve Bujold--and a biographical sketch of Cacoyannis. Some candid photos made during the filming are also shown and supporting cast and other production credits are noted.

2824.   THE TROJAN WOMEN. A script of the 1971 film,
by Michael Cacoyannis (director: Michael Cacoyannis). 116 p. (paperback) illus. New York: Bantam Books, 1971.
Contains cast credits and is divided into four sections: 1) A Pacifist in Periclean Athens (Edith Hamilton);
2) THE TROJAN WOMEN of Euripides (translated by Edith
Hamilton); 3) Director's Note (Michael Cacoyannis); 4)
Screenplay for THE TROJAN WOMEN (Michael Cacoyannis).

2825.   Francois Truffaut, by C. G. Crisp. 144 p. illus.
New York: Praeger, 1972.
Basing his book on interviews given by Truffaut over
the last decade, Crisp has two goals in mind: to note the
creative activities of Truffaut and to indicate the motives that
shaped them. Thus the films are discussed with a sensitivity
to Truffaut's background and life, and an awareness of the
framework in which the films were conceived and ultimately
made. The introduction is biographical and much attention is
paid to Truffaut's role as a critic for Cahiers. In chronological order, each of the films is described and analyzed.
Few in number, they include THE 400 BLOWS, SHOOT THE
PIANO PLAYER, JULES AND JIM, LOVE AT TWENTY (one
episode), THE SOFT SKIN, FAHRENHEIT 451, THE BRIDE
WORE BLACK, STOLEN KISSES, THE SIREN OF THE MIS-
SISSIPPI, THE WILD CHILD, and BED AND BOARD. Auto-
biographical elements which run through the films are pointed
out.
Illustration quality is above average and the credits
for all the films are given. The bibliography indicates published screenplays, the major interviews, and some of Truffaut's writing for Cahiers.
Like most of the Praeger Film Library Series, this
one is impressive. The writing is authoritative, readable
and informative. Crisp's detection approach is most valid
with Truffaut and worthy of consideration with other auteur
directors. An excellent study of a craftsman-artist, this
book is recommended for all collections. It should prove to
be enormously popular with college students.

2826.   Turn On to Stardom, by Dianne Nicholson. 192 p.
(paperback) New York: Cornerstone Library, 1968.
Directed at those who have an urge to perform professionally, this book includes many interviews with experts
and sets forth some guidelines for action. The qualities
necessary to become a performer are delineated: knowing
yourself, both physically and emotionally, is the most essential requisite. The possibilities for a performer are

listed: theatre, variety, burlesque, opera, concert, television, films, or recordings. How one prepares by training voice, body, and mind is covered, and other sections are devoted to a how-to-do-it approach to getting a job: the places, the trade publications, the photos, resumés, auditions, unions, agents, schools, etc. The final chapter concerns perseverance, timing, existing, and morals.

If the book is rather light on dissuading young people from a career in show business, it is quite thorough in covering the basic elements in preparing for such a career. It is an excellent book for school libraries and is acceptable for all collections.

2827.   TV Feature Film Source Book.   715 p.   (paperback)
         New York: Broadcast Information Bureau, 1972.
         This excellent reference book lists all the feature films which are available for showing on television.   Arranged alphabetically by title, each film entry offers the following information:
    film title
    stars
    type of film
    year of release
    annotation, story line
    running time
    black-and-white or color
    width in mm.
    original producer
    original distributor
    tv distributor.
         As a source for answering many questions on films, the book has much pertinence and value for libraries.   At present, however, it is available only on a yearly subscription basis at a cost of $99.   One master initial volume plus several supplements are the elements of a year's subscription.
         For anyone dealing with film study, film bookings, or simply general reference, this book is a bountiful treasure of information.   It is hoped that some other plan for making it available to all libraries will be forthcoming soon.

2828.   TV "Free" Film Source Book, Vol. 12, Issue 3,
         edited by Aura Fliegelman.   340 p.   (paperback)
         New York: Broadcast Information Bureau, Inc.,
         1971.
         This is indeed a source book.   In the first of three major sections, the reservoir of free television films is subdivided into three categories according to running time--one-

hour films, half-hour films and 15-minute films. The one-hour division, for example, lists films having a running time between 31 minutes and 60 minutes. Major subject headings are provided under each time category--arts, space, sports, religious, travel, etc.--and the individual films are listed under these headings.

The following information is offered for each film:
title
a short annotation
running time
black-and-white or color
charges
markets open
restrictions
underwriter
distributor.

Titles of all the films are arranged in an alphabetical listing in Section II, while the final section lists sources of the films.

Available only on a subscription basis, the book is a most complete and valuable index to free films. With the advent of cable television upon us, librarians are advised to familiarize themselves with this fine reference book as soon as possible.

2829.   TWELVE ANGRY MEN. A script of the 1957 film, by Reginald Rose (director: Sidney Lumet). 548 p. (paperback) New York: Appleton-Century-Crofts, 1971.
Contained in Film Scripts Two (2268).

2830.   20th Century Fox Memorabilia Catalog, by Sotheby, Parke-Bernet Galleries. 275 p. (paperback) illus. Los Angeles: Sotheby, Parke-Bernet, 1971.
The title page reads "Movie Memorabilia--inactive properties including furniture, decorative objects, paintings, posters, set sketches and other decorations, full-size and model boats and ships, airplanes, model trains." This was the catalog required for admission to the auction of the 20th Century Fox props held in February 1971. Not only does it contain illustrations of the properties but many stills from the Fox films are included. Not essential but acceptable for larger collections.

2831.   Twiggy and Justin, by Thomas Whiteside. 136 p. (paperback) illus. New York: Manor Books, 1972.
This paperback is subtitled, "The Inside Story of the Rise to Stardom of the 90-Pound Beauty," and is based on

material which appeared originally in The New Yorker. Its
portrait of the two title characters may be of moderate interest to some, but since it was written before THE BOY
FRIEND it has little pertinence for film collections. Production quality is poor and the book is noted here as a matter
of record.

2832.   TWO-LANE BLACKTOP. A script of the 1971 film,
        by Rudolph Wurlitzer and Will Corry (director:
        Monte Hellman). 160 p. (paperback) illus. New
        York: Award Books, 1971.
        Contains "Cast of Characters"; "Production Staff
Credits"; "Introduction: An Interview with 'Blacktop' Director Monte Hellman"; and "Production Notes."

2833.   Two Russian Screen Classics. 102 p. (paperback)
        illus. New York: Simon & Schuster, 1973.
        Contains: cast, production credits, and introductions
to MOTHER, 1925 (2550); EARTH, 1930 (2210a).

2834.   2001: A SPACE ODYSSEY. 22 p. (paperback)
        illus. New York: National Publishers, 1965.
        This souvenir book is unusual in several ways: it
has been produced in an elongated shape, it has tissues al-
ternating with its pages, and it is quite difficult to handle.
Much of the material in the volume is fine: excellent illustrations, pages devoted to director Stanley Kubrick, original
author Arthur C. Clarke, stars Keir Dullea, Gary Lockwood
and Hal, the computer. Other cast and production credits
are given.

2835.   2001: A SPACE ODYSSEY, by Carolyn Geduld.
        87 p. (paperback) Bloomington, Ind.: Indiana Uni-
        versity Press, 1973.
        One of the first group of film guides, this short
volume contains the following elements: film credits, a plot
outline, a summary of director Kubrick's career, a chronological account of the production, a lengthy analysis and a
summary critique. A brief filmography, an excellent bibliography, and a single rental source form the book's final
pages. The information offered is most impressive. All
aspects of this classic but controversial film are covered,
including critical reception. Any viewing of 2001 will be
greatly enriched by use of this volume before and after the
film experience.
        Two minor reservations might be mentioned. The
Kubrick filmography should have been enlarged to include the
cast and production credits, and rental source information

might have included the rather prohibitive cost of a single showing-- $250 minimum. The book is a most welcome addition to those already published on 2001 and will be an invaluable aid those studying the film in future years. Highly recommended.

2836.   [No entry]

2837.   Liv Ullman, edited by Rochelle Reed. 24 p. (paperback) illus. Washington, D.C.: American Film Institute, 1973.
        While she was making LOST HORIZON in Hollywood, Liv Ullman gave this interview in March, 1972. Much audience interest was expressed about her philosophy of acting and Ingmar Bergman. The responses are as cool as her performances. Acceptable for all collections.

2838.   ULYSSES. 32 p. (paperback) illus. New York: National Publishers, 1967.
        This oversized souvenir book features many full-page illustrations in addition to a rather long synopsis of the film. Author James Joyce receives some attention, as do the actors in the film, Milo O'Shea, Barbara Jefford, Maurice Roeves, T. P. McKenna, and Anna Manahan. Both the executive producer, Walter Reade, Jr., and the director, Joseph Strick, are spotlighted. The book closes with an excerpt from Molly's soliloquy.

2839.   UNDER MILK WOOD. A script of the 1972 film, by Andrew Sinclair and Dylan Thomas (director: Andrew Sinclair). 95 p. (paperback) illus. New York: Simon and Schuster, 1972.
        Contains: "Milk Wood and Magic" by Andrew Sinclair, cast and credits.

2840.   Understanding Movies, by Louis D. Gianetti. 217 p. (paperback) illus. Englewood Cliffs, N.J.: Prentice-Hall, 1972.
        The author's intent is "to help the moviegoer understand some of the complex elements" of film. Individual chapters are devoted to the basic techniques that directors have used to convey meaning--picture, movement, editing, sound, drama, literature and theory. A solid glossary and a detailed index complete the book. Good illustrations and helpful diagrams appear throughout. Under each heading, the author discusses many concepts or ideas. For each he tries to describe or show one film example to illuminate his point.

Books on aesthetics can get overly pedantic or so convoluted that they strain reader patience. Not so here; this readable book is straightforward, intelligent and informative. An example of the book's excellence is the chapter on theories which provides one of the best summaries currently available. Highly recommended for all collections.

2841. Underwater Photography, by Dimitri Rebikoff and Paul Cherney. 144 p. (paperback) illus. New York: Amphoto, 1972.

Addressed to both the professional and the semi-professional, this book explains techniques, equipment, tricks, problems, and materials of underwater photography.

2842. Underworld U.S.A., by Colin McArthur. 176 p. illus. London: Secker & Warburg, 1972.

The re-evaluation of the American cinema begun by the Cahiers critics and then taken up by Movie and Andrew Sarris suggests the presence of auteurs in that cinema. McArthur argues that recent critical attention overlooks far more important elements; for example, the force and function of the genres--western, gangster, musical. This volume addresses itself to the American gangster films, a genre to which he adds a sub-set called Thrillers. His rationale is that the two forms are interrelated by their iconography, personnel, mood, and theme.

A few introductory chapters discuss the elements, the development, and the historical background for the gangster film. To support his thesis, the author analyzes certain films of nine directors, allowing one chapter for each: Fritz Lang, John Huston, Jules Dassin, Robert Siodmak, Elia Kazan, Nicholas Ray, Samuel Fuller, Don Seigel and Jean-Pierre Melville. The inclusion of this latter director is justified as an example of an American genre transferred to Europe. Supporting the text rather well is a fine selection of stills. One may cause some puzzlement--why a full-page still from SINGIN' IN THE RAIN to preface the introduction? An index to film titles and a general index complete the book.

When the author states that there is only the scantiest of material on John Huston, one questions his research. Two full length books come to mind--John Huston, King Rebel (736) and John Huston: A Pictorial Treasury of His Films (735)--in addition to interviews (770) and observations (1106). However, his total theme is provocative and the structure of the book is well designed to support his argument. For the most part it is informative and enjoyable.

The book is not essential, but it is an interesting addition to any collection and will please many readers.

2843.   Unholy Fools, Wits, Comics, Disturbers of the
         Peace, by Penelope Gilliatt. 384 p. illus. New
         York: Viking, 1973.
         A selection of Gilliatt's theatre and film criticism written both here and in England during the last dozen or so years. The range of films is wide, including the work of master directors like Bergman, Kubrick and Renoir, but it is the comedy films that seem to inspire the author. Her method is simple, logical, and effective. Opening portions of the reviews recall the film, the plot, the acting, in an effort to duplicate the viewing experience; she follows with witty, honest, and often profound analysis.
         Gilliatt may be an acquired taste but she is a most rewarding writer for those who appreciate her critical abilities. The theater reviews include works by Shaw, Pirandello, Brecht, Beckett, and Pinter. Recommended for all film collections.

2844.   University Advisory Committee Seminar, edited by
         Rochelle Reed. 24 p. (paperback) illus. Wash-
         ington, D.C.: The American Film Institute, 1972.
         A meeting was held at the AFI Center in Beverly Hills in August 1972 to explore the relationship between the AFI and the academic film community. The transcript published here is of the morning session which was enriched by the participation of Charlton Heston, Alfred Hitchcock, George Seaton, George Stevens, and Robert Wise. A list of suggested films is appended. Acceptable for all collections.

2845.   The Unkindest Cuts: The Scissors and the Cinema,
         by Doug McClelland. 220 p. illus. New York:
         Barnes, 1972.
         The idea of writing a book about the arbitrary cutting of scenes and even entire performances from completed films is intriguing. The author states that he will not consider the usual cutting done by film editors or censors but only that done by directors, producers, leading actors or even exhibitors. This is a dangerous assertion since only the person making the cut knows the true rationale. As a result guidelines are not always followed. He does use the well known examples--GREED, THE MAGNIFICENT AMBERSONS, A STAR IS BORN, and THE RED BADGE OF COURAGE. Other lesser known excisions are also described, but there is always a large difference between the total footage shot and the release print. The author includes here many instances of

what appeared to be normal rearrangement or assessment of primary material. Surely it is not always arbitrary or capricious to try to improve a creative effort by editing, trimming, or shortening. Stories of films which were rescued by post-preview cutting are legion and include such items as LOST HORIZON, THE SIN OF MADELON CLAUDET, and A NIGHT AT THE OPERA. The great unfairness comes about in tampering with a film that has been released and reviewed--i.e., CLEOPATRA, EXODUS, LAWRENCE OF ARABIA, etc.

Another reservation about the volume concerns the constant intrusion of the author's personal opinion of performances--Phyllis Newman is a giddy guts who was mighty lucky to marry Adolph Green, or Eva Marie Saint and Warren Beatty were at the kitchen sink when charm was passed out. The bitchy put-down may be amusing to read but is it appropriate to the subject matter here?

If the author's substitution of hearsay, gossip, and opinion for research and his digressions from the major theme or purpose of the book can be overlooked, the reader will find many fascinating examples of film cuts told with supporting background information. The book is illustrated with scenes that never appeared on the screen. Reproduction quality of these stills varies widely and the size of some diminishes their effect considerably. A lengthy index is provided.

Since most of the previously published material on this topic dealt primarily with official censorship, the broader approach of this book is appreciated. Although it is flawed, non-discriminating readers will appreciate its contents and film buffs will enjoy re-viewing the many legends concerning discarded film treasure. Generally recommended for all collections.

2846. The Uses of Film in the Teaching of English, by English Study Committee, Office of Field Development. Ontario, Canada: Institute for Studies in Education, 1971.

2847. Ustinov in Focus, by Tony Thomas. 192 p. (paperback) illus. New York: Barnes, 1971.
The emphasis in this tribute to Ustinov is on his film work as director, actor and writer. A large introductory section deals with Ustinov as a person--a biographical sketch touching on his early career, his family life, and his attitude towards himself and his work. The second section deals in chronological fashion with those films to which

he has made some contribution.   The appendices include a
listing of his plays, his books, and his recordings.
        Some of the book is based on interviews and visits
with Ustinov and this is the strongest portion.   When the
author gives his personal reaction to the films, the text loses
critical perspective in favor of some gushy tribute.   Illustrations are excellent and the book should please all admirers
of the multi-talented Ustinov.   Recommended.

2848.   VARIETY LIGHTS.   A script of the 1950 film, by
         Federico Fellini, Alberto Lattuada, Tullio Pinelli,
         and Ennio Flaiano (director: Federico Fellini).
         198 p.   (paperback)   illus.   New York: Grossman,
         1971.
         Found in Early Screenplays (2210).

2849.   THE VICTORS.   32 p.   (paperback)   illus.   New
         York: Columbia Pictures, 1963.
         An introduction by director Carl Foreman, in which
he describes the making and the meaning of the film, is
among several interesting articles in this very fine souvenir
book.   "The Blitz--22 Years Later" by Quentin Reynolds,
and "From Book to Box Office" by Alex Baron, author of the
original novel, are two other good features.   The illustrations
are in black and white and some are reproduced on a very
thin paper.   Cast biographies are grouped three to a page and
supporting cast and production credits are given.

2850.   King Vidor on Film Making, by King Vidor.   239 p.
         illus.   New York: David McKay Co. , 1972.
         Combining approximately equal parts of autobiography,
common sense, and how-its-done advice, Vidor has written
a second successful book.   (See A Tree is a Tree, 1373.)
His linking theme is also his major topic, film direction.
All of the elements he believes to be part of that creative
process--acting, lighting, editing, special effects, etc. --are
described in the context of his own experience and observation.   Probably the most unusual aspect of his discussion is
the appreciation and faith he has about 16mm filmmaking.   He
sees much similarity in its use today to the methods employed in the early silent days when creative improvisation by
directors was usual and necessary.
        Vidor's style is both informal and informative.   Al-
though the book is crammed with famous names, the author
is never anything but gentlemanly in their treatment.   Illustrations are reproduced acceptably, but poorly selected.   They
should have complemented the text to a much greater degree.
An index is provided.   The book is a good addition to all

large collections; however, smaller libraries may opt for other less diffuse books on filmmaking.

2851.   Jean Vigo, by P. E. Salles Gomes. 256 p. illus.
        Los Angeles: University of California Press, 1971.
        Jean Vigo's total work--three shorter films and one feature--can be viewed in a single evening. To understand the critical success and the impact of the films may require a more prolonged and deeper examination. This volume will aid greatly in that endeavor. Written with the cooperation of Vigo's family, the original edition of this book appeared in France in 1957. Consisting of five logical sections, it provides a detailed coverage of Vigo's life and work.
        The first section tells about his father, Miguel Alemeyda, an anarchist whose influence on Vigo's films can be traced. Vigo's early life up to the making of A PROPOS DE NICE and TARIS are considered next. Following are lengthy chapters on both ZERO DE CONDUITE and L'ATLAN-TE. The content and the making of the films is told with much detail.
        Vigo's early death at the age of 29 is described in the closing pages. A summarization and analysis of Vigo's influence on later films and directors is made in a final impressive statement. Notes, references, a filmography, and an index are offered. Some of the illustrations are quite rare, coming as they do from Mme. Luce Vigo, while others are stills and frames from the films. Unfortunately, reproduction of the photographs is on the dark and murky side.
        The scholarship, effort, and admiration of the author is apparent throughout. The importance of Vigo is proposed, argued and finally justified in this fine tribute. Recommended for larger collections and college libraries.

2852.   Jean Vigo, by John M. Smith. 144 p. (paperback)
        illus. New York: Praeger, 1972.
        The films of Jean Vigo are given individual attention in this rather special volume. Emphasis is on ZERO DE CONDUITE and L'ATALANTE, but attention is also given to A PROPOS DE NICE and TARIS. The introductory chapter deals with those contributing factors that Vigo used in creating his films. Biographical data is covered in a chronology given at the book's end, along with a bibliography and additional data on the two major films. Many illustrations are murky, probably because they are enlargements of film frames. A viewing of the Vigo films would almost demand a reading of this volume. It is a fine addition to college and large collections but somewhat too specialized for most libraries.

2853.   THE VIKINGS. 18 p. (paperback) illus. New
        York: Progress Lithographers, 1958.
        Opening sections of this souvenir book include the
synopsis of the film and several pages devoted to "Experts
Behind The Vikings." Kirk Douglas contributes an article
entitled "On Making a Movie" and there are the usual full-
page biographies of Douglas, Tony Curtis, Ernest Borgnine,
and Janet Leigh. Stills from the film are included and supporting cast and other production credits are given.

2854.   Violations of the Child Marilyn Monroe, by H. P. S.
        (Anonymous) 159 p. illus. New York: Bridgehead
        Books, 1962.
        If you are willing to believe that this book was writ-
ten by a psychiatrist, and that it was he who called her just
before her death, you may believe the rest of this familiar
narrative. It concentrates on the years from six to 11 in
Monroe's childhood and the emphasis is on the oft-reported
sexual incidents. Mention is made of other times in her
career, of her marriages, affairs, and professional insecu-
rities. The book is illustrated by some vulgar line drawings.
A quick-buck, bad-taste book noted here for the record.

2855.   Violence and the Mass Media, edited by Otto N.
        Larsen. 310 p. (paperback) New York: Harper
        and Row, 1968.
        This volume is a part of the series entitled, "Read-
ers in Social Problems," and it deals with violence as it
exists in all the media. There are several articles pertinent
to film. They include: "Violence in the Cinema" by Philip
French; "The Morality Seekers: A Study of Organized Film
Criticism in the United States" by Jack Schwartz; "New Movie Standards: General Film Code, Not Specific Bans" by Louis
Chapin.
        The general articles are all excellent, and although
the major emphasis is on television and comic books, the
above articles can serve as an introduction to violence in
film. Recommended for all film collections.

2856.   Violent America: The Movies, 1946-1964, by Law-
        rence Alloway. 95 p. illus. New York: The
        Museum of Modern Art, 1971.
        In the spring of 1969, the Museum of Modern Art
presented a series of 35 films, entitling the group, "The
American Action Film 1946-1964." This volume discusses
these films, examining their heroes, villains, females, and
actors. Such topics as The Pleasure of Tragedy/The Appeal
of Violence, Cartharsis Via Film, Film As a Formulaic Art
and others are treated.

As is usual with MOMA publications, the text and production values are excellent. Many full-page stills are used in this slightly oversized volume. A final filmography with accompanying comment is also impressive. Copius footnotes add to the quality of the text. Although it is somewhat specialized and rather expensive, this is a fine addition to all collections.

2857. Visualize, by David R. Anderson, Gary Wilburn, William Kuhns, Robert Stanley and Wayne Jewell. (paperback) illus. Dayton, Ohio: Pflaum, 1971. This kit consists of five components:

1) "Exploring the Film" by William Kuhns and Robert Stanley (380)
2) "Visualize"--Student Manual
3) "Visualize"--Instructor Manual by David Anderson and Gary Wilburn
4) Photo Language--A Collection of 16 Still Pictures--approximately 6" x 9" in size
5) A 3-minute super-8 film called ONE IS THE LONELIEST NUMBER.

The purpose, or use, of the kit is to assist in a course on visual language, the goal of which is improved communication and self expression. It is suggested that culminating activities for the course be a slide presentation and an 8mm film.

The attempt to provide a more effective way of teaching visual skills is most commendable. The proposed course seems both workable and enjoyable by all participants including the teacher. This is a kit to be brought to the attention of teachers in junior and senior high schools.

2858. Visual Thinking, by Rudolph Arnheim. 345 p. illus. Berkeley, Cal.: Univ. of Calif. Press, 1969.

Arnheim's concern here is with visual perception as a cognitive activity. In earlier works, one of his theses was that all artistic activity is a form of reasoning--a combination of perception and thought. This volume is a continuation of that idea with visual perception as the major area of analysis. He draws on philosophy, research, science and art for his arguments. The book is illustrated and indexed. While it is not a film book in the strict sense, it is noted here for its value to educators, filmmakers and researchers.

2859. Von Stroheim, by Thomas Quinn Curtiss. 357 p. illus. New York: Farrar, Straus & Giroux, 1971.

In the introduction to this biography, the author states that he was a close friend and frequent companion of von Stroheim for many years--from about 1940 to 1957. The relationship has not been realized by the author in his book. His straightforward narrative includes some awkward reconstructed conversations but not much personal insight or comment about a friend. Other than a few anecdotes, not much of the book is new information. Peter Noble's 1951 biography, Hollywood Scapegoat (701) and Joel Finler's 1968 Stroheim (1293) covered the same ground.

The production of the book is another matter. The dust jacket is striking, with two eye-catching illustrations of von Stroheim, and there are an attractive inner-cover picture, a most impressive type setting and arrangement, and, finally, many beautifully reproduced stills. The production more than makes up for the disappointing text.

An account of the first screening of the uncut 42-reel version of GREED and a filmography of von Stroheim as director and actor make up the appendix. There is no index. What should have been a definitive work emerges as a re-telling of the familiar, enhanced and saved by superior production values. Recommended for large collections and those which do not have the earlier biographies.

2860.   (hommage a) Erich von Stroheim, by Charlotte Gobeil. 54 p. (paperback) illus. Ottawa: Canadian Film Institute, 1966.

This short anthology on von Stroheim includes articles by Iris Barry, Herman O. Weinberg, Lotte H. Eisner, Gloria Swanson and others. In addition, there are two synopses and one film introduction as originally written/spoken by von Stroheim. Most of the book is written in English but there are three articles in French. A filmography and a bibliography complete the tribute.

Rather special material that may be difficult to obtain, this volume is noted here for students, historians and others who have an in-depth interest in von Stroheim. Acceptable for any collection, if and when it is available at a reasonable price.

2861.   The Wajda Trilogy, by Andrzej Wajda. 239 p. (paperback) illus. New York: Simon and Schuster, 1972.

Contains script, cast and production credits for: ASHES AND DIAMONDS, 1958 (2034); KANAL, 1955 (2453); A GENERATION, 1954 (2315); with an introduction by Boleslaw Sulik.

2862.   WAR AND PEACE, by Harold Stern. 34 p. (paperback) illus. New York: National Publishers, 1968.
    This is a souvenir book of the Russian-made film which
was shown in two parts and had a total running time of more
than 6 hours; it should not be confused with the 1956 film directed by King Vidor which starred Henry Fonda and Audrey
Hepburn.   The plot is described with the help of stills, and
a later section tells about the making of the film.   Author
Leo Tolstoy receives an extended biographical treatment and
there is even one page devoted to the Walter Reade Organization, the distributor responsible for bringing the film to
America.   Cast principals and production personnel are noted.

2863.   Warner Brothers Presents, by Ted Sennett.   428 p.
illus. New Rochelle, N.Y.: Arlington House, 1971.
    The two decades from 1930 to 1950 saw the Warner
Brothers Studios produce an enormous number of films,
many of which have become classic legacies from Hollywood's
Golden Years.   Sennett's book is a tribute to Warner
Brothers, to the stars created there and, ultimately, to the
Warner's stock company--Frank McHugh, Glenda Farrell,
Alan Hale, etc.
    Warners' triumphant gamble with THE JAZZ SINGER
set the stage for the recruitment of the Warners Company
of actors, most of whom are identified by capsule career
sketches.   The films, the obvious focus of the text, are efficiently categorized in individual chapters dealing with the
following genres: crime and social problems, musical comedy, mystery-melodrama, man's work, war, and classic-
biography.   Remaining sections list brief paragraphs for
many of the behind-the-scenes personnel at Warners during
these years--directors, cameramen, composers, etc.   There
is a bibliography, a listing of awards received, and a briefly
annotated filmography of all the Warners and First National
films which appeared during the twenty-year period.   An
index to this massive work is also provided.   The sections
dealing with the films are illustrated with many representative and well chosen stills.   Reproduction quality is uniformly high.
    Aside from the author's great affection for his sub-
ject, other positive qualities of this book include the meticu-
lous coverage, the convenient and thoughtful arrangement,
and the production quality.   The appeal of the book is excep-
tionally wide.   The likely tendency to assign it to reference
would deprive a large potential audience of much reading
pleasure, nostalgia, and background information for today's
television viewing.   With the Warners Film Library a primary

candidate for transfer into video-cassettes, the book can only appreciate in value and importance. This is an outstanding volume, highly recommended for all collections.

2864. WATERLOO. 32 p. (paperback) illus. London: Sackville Publishers, 1970.
 This souvenir book is listed even though it was not published in United States and may be most difficult to obtain. Certain films which are financial and critical disasters in this country are more successful in Europe where they are given reserved seat showings. (PAINT YOUR WAGON is another good example.)
 Most of this volume is given to illustrations of the battle scenes. There is some attention to backgrounds, story, and production including a map of Waterloo as of June 18, 1815. There are some short biographies of the producer and director; cast and other production credits are noted.

2865. The Way I See It, by Eddie Cantor. 204 p. Englewood Cliffs, N.J.: Prentice-Hall, 1959.
 Not a biography but a collection of advice, philosophy, reminiscence, and opinion. The best chapter is the one in which he names those performers he considers the greatest. Not for film collections.

2866. The John Wayne Story, by George Carpozi. 279 p. illus. New Rochelle: Arlington House, 1972.
 "....I'd like to predict regarding this book--my fifteenth--that some reviewers will be as critical as they were about each of my other fourteen tomes, saying that I 'failed to capture the real' ... John Wayne, that this biography is only a 'superficial study' and perhaps even an injustice to the most imposing movie actor of our time." Thus, George Carpozi in a forewarning to this volume. Right on, Mr. Carpozi.
 There are inconsistencies between the closing filmography and the text. For example: 1) The text states HANGMAN'S HOUSE was Wayne's first film; the filmography lists MOTHER MACHREE and FOUR SONS as earlier films. A direct quote in Ricci (524): "The first picture I worked on I remember was MOTHER MACHREE...." 2) No other sources list FOUR SONS as a Wayne film--Weaver (559), Michaels (35), Ricci (524), or Tomkies (328). If true, Carpozi should elaborate in the text. He does not. 3) Ricci lists, with a still and cast credits, WORDS AND MUSIC (1929) and CHEER UP AND SMILE (1930) as Wayne films.

Carpozi omits these. Photographic work is only fair, and the overall selection is poor. An index is provided.

Author Carpozi wrote certain of his other books as paperback originals. This volume seems more appropriate to that format rather than a costly hard-bound book. The drugstore audience may be more appreciative and less critical. Not recommended. Interested parties should look at The Films of John Wayne by Mark Ricci, etc.

2867.　A Way of Seeing, by Alfred T. Barson. 218 p. Amherst, Mass.: University of Massachusetts Press, 1972.

In this study, begun as a doctoral dissertation, Barson attempts to define the sources that influenced Agee's work, and to chart the rise and fall of his work. Since it is a bit easier to deal with the novel, the essay, or similar forms than with film reviews or scripts, the analysis tends toward the former. Let Us Now Praise Famous Men, A Death in the Family, and The Morning Watch receive a good share of the attention. In a final chapter, Barson argues that the film adaptations on which Agee was working at the time of his death represented a decline in his artistry. Be that as it may, Agee is known widely for his writing on film, and it is for that reason the book is considered here. There is enough about Agee's film writing, his beliefs, philosophies, and his life to warrant consideration by film collections. In that context, the book is acceptable for academic libraries and larger collections.

2868.　We Barrymores, by Lionel Barrymore and Cameron Shipp. 311 p. illus. New York: Appleton-Century-Crofts, 1951.

The Barrymores descend from a theatrical family and it is not surprising that Lionel evidences the loyalty they had to the stage. He does give recognition and homage to films --one chapter is called "Don't Sell Movies Short,"--but the appendix is reserved for his stage vehicles and not his films. Emphasis is on Lionel, with John and Ethel finishing in that order. One wishes Lionel had told more about his directing experiences, the many actors with whom he worked, and his 25 years in Hollywood. An early chapter relates his experiences with D. W. Griffith at Biograph. The book is indexed and there are a few photographs. Acceptable for all collections.

2869.　WEEKEND. A script of the 1968 film, by Jean-Luc Godard (director: Jean-Luc Godard). 188 p. (paperback) illus. New York: Simon and Schuster, 1972.

Contains: WEEKEND (1968); WIND FROM THE
EAST (1969); "Godard and WEEKEND" by Robin Wood;
"WIND FROM THE EAST , or Godard and Rocha at the
Crossroads" by James Roy MacBean; casts and credits.

2870.   Weep No More My Lady, by Mickey Deans and Ann
         Pinchot. 247 p. illus. New York: Hawthorn
         Books, 1972.
         The only contribution that Mickey Deans apparently
can make to the Garland Legend is to tell of those last
months of her life. This he attempts to do but with a decided lack of sensitivity, talent, and objectivity. The non-
Deans portions of Garland's life are retold in a researcher
fashion and perhaps this is Ms. Pinchot's portion of the book.
It is not much better. The book covers in flashback format
the many well-known incidents in Garland's career and attempts a reply to Mel Torme's book (1073). Most of the
narrative is about the last months with Deans. The illustrations tell a stronger story than the authors'.
         This book resembles many of the later personal ap-
pearances of Garland. Late again, finally she's there, but
surrounded by "takers" pushing her on stage against her will;
and this is not the Garland the audience paid to see. Not
recommended.

2871.   We Have Come for Your Daughters; What Went Down
         on the Great Medicine Ball Caravan, by John Gris-
         som, Jr. illus. New York: William Morrow,
         1972.
         The caravan of hippies, supported by Warner Broth-
ers, traveled across the United States and then flew to England. The idea was to film the tour and come up with a
SON OF WOODSTOCK. Unfortunately, talent was minimal
and drugs were abundant. This volume covers pretty much
the same ground as Forcade's book (2100). Grissom traveled with the group and reports first-hand the debacle, with
the Warner executives getting a very negative notice. It
happened only once and probably never will again. For that
reason, it may interest some readers. Acceptable for all
collections which serve a mature audience.

2872.   Orson Welles, by Maurice Bessy. 195 p. (paper-
         back) illus. New York: Crown, 1971.
         Another book on Welles may seem superfluous or
redundant but, thank goodness, this one is different. Rather
than analyzing the films one-by-one, Bessy is content to offer his own critical-biographical essay and then follow it up

with some articles and documents relating to Welles. Interviews, quotations, an unpublished screenplay of Salome, film reviews and appreciations are some of the forms in this section. The book is completed by a filmography, a bibliography and an index. Visuals used are selected with intelligence and reproduced with care.

The volume more than justifies its subtitle, "An Investigation into His Films and Philosophy." While the author essay tends to get heavy at times, it is nevertheless a satisfying blend of information, opinion, and analysis. The volume is a translation from The Cinema d'Aujourd'hui Directors Series. Highly recommended for all collections.

2873.   Orson Welles, by Joseph McBride. 192 p. (paperback) illus. New York: Viking, 1972.
Another book on Welles? While it may seem unnecessary, McBride does offer some new material. He discusses the "Raising Kane" issue and describes an interview with Welles that took place while they filmed test shots for a proposed film. Several times he mentions the cooperation of Peter Bogdanovich, whose long promised book with Welles is now called "This is Orson Welles." When he comes to the critical evaluations of the films, he treats them all except THE STRANGER. Several short pre-KANE films made by Welles in the 30's are described in much detail. A print of one, THE HEARTS OF AGE, exists and several frame enlargements are shown.

The careers of Orson Welles--as director, actor, radio performer, writer, and recording artist--are catalogued in the appendix. The book is not indexed and the visuals are quite disappointing, being mostly too small and/or too dark. Because of the charisma or mystique of the subject, no book about him can be without some interest. Much of what is related here is familiar but there are some new insights and information offered. Acceptable for all collections.

2874.   We're In the Money: Depression America and Its Films, by Andrew Bergman. 200 p. illus. New York: New York University Press, 1971.
This adaptation of a doctoral study treats the films of the depression decade in two parts. The years 1930-1933 spotlight gangsters, shyster lawyers and politicians, the Marx Brothers, W. C. Fields, "anarchy" films, the worldly women, the street woman, and the musicals. The second and longer part dealing with 1933 to 1939 treats King Kong, the G-man, the cowboy, the social themes of Warner films, Frank Capra, screwball comedy, the mob, and the juvenile delinquent. References and notes are given for each

of these sub-sections in the book's appendix in addition to a listing of the films discussed and a general bibliography.

As a different approach to the study of film, the book is most welcome. The author makes a strong case for using films to explain or identify an era in American history and indicates the service they performed for a distressed nation. Because of its origins certain portions of the book may be a bit intellectual for the reader in search of a nostalgic look at some films of the 30's, but there is more than enough entertainment value here to make the book a valuable addition to all collections. Recommended.

2875. West Coast Theatrical Directory, 1972. 324 p. (paperback) illus. San Jose, Cal.: Gousha/Times Mirror, 1972.

This directory covers not only Los Angeles and San Francisco, but also Nevada, Hawaii and has some large company representation for Chicago, Nashville, and New York City. It contains listings of firms and individuals from all entertainment areas--agents, production companies, distributors, public relations firms, schools, etc. An acceptable film reference.

2876. WEST SIDE STORY. 40 p. (paperback) illus. New York: Program Publishing Co., 1961.

Because of the many creative talents involved in the film, much information about personalities is offered in this souvenir book. In addition to the usual sections on the story, its origin and the filmmaking, there is a short article by Hollis Alpert. Individual pages are presented for Natalie Wood, Richard Beymer, Russ Tamblyn, Rita Moreno, and George Chakiris as well as for directors Robert Wise and Jerome Robbins, writer Ernest Lehman, and composer Leonard Bernstein. The stills are mostly in black and white although there is an attractive centerfold in full color. The Sharks and the Jets get individual pages and other cast and production credits are noted.

2877. What is a City? (paperback) Boston, Mass.: Boston Public Library, 1972.

An example of the kind of work that libraries might consider, this bibliography and filmography is about urban life. It uses headings such as Victims of the City, A Place to Earn a Living, Cities of the Future, etc.

2878. What Is Cinema? Volume II, by André Bazin. 200 p. Berkeley: University of California Press, 1971.

Another collection of the writings of the highly regarded French critic André Bazin, this volume deals with
specifics rather than the aesthetics theory of the first book.
Italian neo-realism, certain films of Italy (LA TERRA TREMA,
BICYCLE THIEF, UMBERTO D, CABIRIA), and some Italian
directors--Visconti, De Sica, Fellini, and Rossellini are discussed. Another section analyzes the work of Chaplin, emphasizing two films, LIMELIGHT and MONSIEUR VERDOUX.
Final sections treat the American western and the pin-up
girl, the book, Eroticism in the Cinema, and Jean Gabin.
The book is indexed.
    As with Volume One, the text is informative, pro-
vocative, readable and ultimately rewarding. It is an excellent collection of cinema criticism that is highly recommended
for all collections.

2879. What's Wrong With the Movies?, by Tamar Lane.
       254 p. New York: Jerome S. Ozer, 1971 (1923).
       Tamar Lane is the author of The New Technique of
Screen Writing (1037) which appeared some 13 years after
this volume was published by the Waverly Company in Los
Angeles. It is a book of criticism and comment about all
aspects of motion pictures, encompassing producers, authors,
critics, morals, players, the church, etc. Most of it is
quite enjoyable to read, although Lane was not the most perceptive of critics. Acceptable for all collections.

2880. When Movies Began to Speak, by Frank Manchel.
       76 p. illus. Englewood Cliffs, N.J.: Prentice-
       Hall, 1969.
       Dr. Manchel continues to write non-comprehensive
but informative and entertaining surveys of film topics. In
this instance, he continues his history by taking the films
from the introduction of sound to the late sixties. Included
are such topics as the development of sound, some pioneers
(Lee De Forest and his audio amplifier, for example), directors, and films. Unionization, war films, the end of the
Star system, the McCarthy era, the invasion of foreign films,
and the effect of television on the film industry are also
treated. The book is illustrated by James Caraway. This
is another in the series that Dr. Manchel has created for a
young audience. Recommended for elementary and junior
high school libraries.

2881. When Pictures Began to Move, by Frank Manchel.
       76 p. illus. Englewood Cliffs, N.J.: Prentice-
       Hall, 1969.

The title may be somewhat misleading, since the book covers film history from pre-screen days up to the middle twenties. Perhaps because the subject is technical, the text here lacks the sparkle of other Manchel books. The author does not receive much assistance from the production either, several of the illustrations being far too dark and murky. Line drawings by James Caraway are few and rather uninspired.

The first half includes the pre-screen gadgets, the early projectors and cameras, pioneers, the Trust, early companies and films. In the second half, the emphasis is on people, with Fairbanks, Pickford, Sennett, Chaplin and Griffith predominating. The post-World War I film schools of German impressionism and Russian realism are described and the book ends with the French avant-gardists, Garbo, von Stroheim, von Sternberg and Flaherty. A bibliography and an index are added.

Because of the scope of the book, it may be unfair to carp about emphases, omissions, treatment. Certainly, if the intention is to create an appetite for further inquiry into film history, the book is most adequate. Acceptable for middle grades to junior high school libraries.

2882. White Russian, Red Face, by Monja Danischewsky. 192 p. illus. London: Victor Gollancz, Ltd., 1966.
This is the biography of a Russian writer-producer who began his British film career in the early thirties. His early responsibility was publicity work for various British studios; later he was a producer of such films as WHISKY GALORE (1948), THE GALLOPING MAJOR (1950), THE BAT-TLE OF THE SEXES (1961), TWO AND TWO MAKE SIX (1961). In 1964 he wrote the screenplay of TOPKAPI. Al-though many famous British film names appear in the latter portion of the volume, the period of the author's major film activity, 1948 to 1964, is covered in only a few pages. The photographs are of the author's family and there is an index.

Since the film-related content is minimal, the style is self-congratulatory, and there are no pertinent illustrations or indexes, the book has very little importance for film col-lections. Not recommended.

2883. THE WHITE SHEIK. A script of the 1952 film, by Federico Fellini, Michelangelo Antonioni and Tullio Pinelli (director: Federico Fellini). 198 p. (pa-perback) illus. New York: Grossman, 1971. Contained in Early Screenplays (2210).

2884.   Who Could Ask for Anything More?, by Ethel Mer-
          man and Pete Martin.   252 p.   Garden City, N.Y.:
          Doubleday, 1955.
          Merman has never had the success in films that she
enjoyed on the musical comedy stage.   In this brisk, flippant
autobiography she does give sufficient attention to her films
to warrant some notice here.   The first film she made was
a short for Warners in 1929.   WE'RE NOT DRESSING,
ALEXANDER'S RAGTIME BAND, ANYTHING GOES, CALL
ME MADAM and THERE'S NO BUSINESS LIKE SHOW BUSI-
NESS are films she talks about.   Since she was a supporting player in the early films, much of her material landed
on the cutting room floor.   Her big number, "The Animal
in Me," in WE'RE NOT DRESSING took weeks to film, included 40 elephants, kangaroos and sundry other animals.
It did not appear in the final print.
          This is flashy, surface autobiography typical of the
early fifties Pete Martin school of writing.   No index, no
illustration, no filmography--just Merman and Martin.   It is
harmless, occasionally informative (as above), and acceptable for any film collection.

2885.   Who's on First, by Richard Anobile.   256 p.   illus.
          New York: Darien House, 1972.
          This is one of what is apparently a series--"Verbal
and Visual Gems From the Films of...."   First, the
Marxes (2887), then W. C. Fields (2291), and now Abbott
and Costello.
          After a preface by Howard Thompson and an intro-
duction by Carol Burnett (who believes that the boys will be
rediscovered), Anobile presents his compilation of frame
blow-ups and accompanying dialogue.   Probably the most
famous bit is the "Who's on First" routine that the team
used in burlesque, on Broadway, radio, and finally in films.
The films are selected from the Universal group, and the
excerpts indicate the kind of slapstick and verbal humor that
amused audiences in the forties.
          Not essential by any means but sure to please most
readers.   Acceptable for all collections, and school libraries
may score a few points by including this one.

2886.   Who's Who in Show Business.   542 p.   illus.   Rye,
          N.Y.: B. Klein Publications, 1971.
          A directory of the entertainment world, this volume
contains a listing of performers along with the names and addresses of their agents or representatives.   All fields of
entertainment are covered and the range of personalities is
world-wide.   An acceptable film reference.

2887.　Why A Duck?　Visual and Verbal Gems from the
　　　　Marx Brothers' Movies, edited by Richard J. Ano-
　　　　bile.　288 p.　(paperback)　illus.　New York:
　　　　Darien House, 1971.
　　　　The subtitle tells it all.　This book uses photographs
and dialogue excerpts from the nine early Marx Brothers
films--COCONUTS, 1929, to THE BIG STORE, 1941.　Stills
and frame enlargements make up the more than 600 visuals
which attempt to simulate the classic moments in these films.
While the book is a pleasant entertainment, it is not important to any film collection.

2888.　THE WILD CHILD.　A script of the 1970 film, by
　　　　Francois Truffaut and Jean Gruault (director:　Fran-
　　　　cois Truffaut).　189 p.　(paperback)　illus.　New
　　　　York:　Pocket Books, 1973.
　　　　Contains an article entitled "About Truffaut" by
Linda Lewin and "How I Made THE WILD CHILD" by Truffaut;
also cast and production credits.

2889.　Paul Williams, edited by Bruce Henstell.　31 p.　(pa-
　　　　perback)　Washington, D.C.:　American Film Insti-
　　　　tute, 1972.
　　　　Paul Williams is the director of OUT OF IT, THE
REVOLUTIONARY, and DEALING:　OR THE BERKELEY-TO-
BOSTON FORTY BRICK LOST-BAG BLUES.　The first two
films had been made and he was preparing the third when
this interview was held in November of 1970.　The focus is
filmmaking and how one gets into it.　A bibliography and a
three-item filmography are included.　Acceptable for all collections.

2890.　Will There Really Be A Morning?, by Frances Farm-
　　　　er.　318 p.　illus.　New York:　G. P. Putnam's
　　　　Sons, 1972.
　　　　This autobiography lingers in the mind long after it
has been set aside.　Much of what it relates is not pleasant
or attractive.　Farmer's family life, her early professional
career, her stay in mental institutions and her final rehabilitation are the substance of the book.　These major threads
of Miss Farmer's life are interwoven with honesty and artistry.　Much of the book is shocking:　the author's descriptions of the behavior of her fellow steerage passengers, of
the inhabitants and life within a mental institution, and of a
lesbian rape make strong reading.
　　　　The author describes her career in Hollywood in
some detail and that aspect makes the book a fine addition
to all film collections.　Only four photographs are included

but they are carefully selected to supplement the story. This
is very powerful writing that will appeal to mature readers.
Highly recommended for all collections but may be very controversial for high school libraries.

2891.   WIND FROM THE EAST. A script of the 1969 film,
         by Jean Luc-Godard (director: Jean Luc-Godard).
         188 p. (paperback) illus. New York: Simon and
         Schuster, 1972.
         Contained in WEEKEND (2869).

2892.   WINDJAMMER, by James W. Hardiman.   62 p.
         illus. New York: Random House, 1958.
         This souvenir book describes a film-travelogue that
was done in the Cinemiracle process and was directed by
documentary filmmaker, Louis de Rochemont.   The story of
the cruise is related by the participants, the cadets and the
captain, and is supplemented by maps and illustrations.   An
interesting section deals with the superstitions which surround
any sailing of the seas.   Director de Rochemont is profiled
and other cast and production credits are noted.   The book
creates the same feeling in the reader that the film did--a
pleasant, visually rewarding trip, but lacking any great excitement.

2893.   With A Hays Nonny Nonny, by Elliot Paul and Luis
         Quintanilla.   188 p.   illus.   New York: Random
         House, 1942.
         An early diatribe about the Hays Code and Hollywood
censorship, this book considers the stories of the Old Testament as potential screen material.   One by one they are
eliminated because of their unacceptance by the Code, or
their unsuitability for a mass entertainment audience.   There
is a wealth of comment about motion picture writing/making
circa 1940.   Since many of the author's suggestions are now
standard procedures, the book has a certain historical value
but it is not very pertinent to filmmaking today.   The argument is made with humor and some fine line sketches accompany the text.   The book will have appeal for anyone interested in censorship.   Acceptable for large collections.

2894.   David Wolper, Leni Riefenstahl, edited by Rochelle
         Reed.   24 p.   (paperback) illus.   Washington, D.C.:
         American Film Institute, 1972.
         The format change of this series presents a new
problem in its indication of titles.   One would expect this to
be another double interview, but it is not.   Only David

334

Wolper is the subject and the title seems to refer to the cover illustration. Wolper's specific topic is the 1972 Olympic Games, although he deals more generally with the film of today--documentary, commercial, or television. Three staff members from his organization contribute to the discussion. Acceptable for all collections.

2895. The Woman at the Well, by Dale Evans Rogers.
191 p. illus. Old Tappan, N.J.: Fleming Revell Co., 1970.

According to the publisher, there are over 150,000 copies of this book in print. In addition, this is the tenth book written by Dale Evans Rogers, known as an entertainer via films, radio, television and personal appearances. It is an autobiography told with many references to her religious beliefs.

After a short career as a singer, she arrived in Hollywood at the age of 28. In a short section she discusses her early career, the westerns made at Republic with Roy Rogers, Gabby Hayes, and the Sons of the Pioneers. Her divorce and subsequent marriage to Rogers finishes the film section. The remaining portion of the book is concerned with family, church, religion and patriotism. It is hard to go too far wrong with that quartet and author Evans apparently knows it.

There is apparently an audience for this kind of book. Its value to film collections is minimal, but it is easy to understand its appeal to a segment of the reading public. A picture book autobiography, Dale (2176), covers almost the same material. The author's style is folksy and she stresses honesty and objectivity in viewing her life. However, the continual sermonizing negates the warm effect of her narrative skill. A few illustrations are provided.

2895a. Womanhood Media, by Helen Wheeler. 335 p.
Metuchen, N.J.: Scarecrow Press, 1972.

This volume is noted here as a reference for films on or about topics of concern for the Woman's Liberation Movement. In a section entitled "Non-Books: Audio-Visual," the reader will find both short films and feature films listed along with other materials such as posters, filmstrips, and recordings. The list is very selective and anyone familiar with films might find argument with both selections and omissions. However, all the titles are of interest in that they explore a wide range of topics, problems, and history.

There is much other material in the volume with attention to the films being rather minor. For instance the

basic book collection is an annotated list of 318 volumes.
Certainly there are enough films to warrant individual attention. This is a minor reservation to a volume that will assist many persons in locating materials on womanhood.

Perhaps a volume on "Woman in Films" will be
forthcoming. Certainly the currently prevalent image of
women in the popular "X" and "R" rated films of today needs
examination. A very large audience is being conditioned to
a degrading image of women as a device for man's sexual
gratification.

2896. THE WONDERFUL WORLD OF THE BROTHERS
       GRIMM. 32 p. illus. New York: Metro Goldwyn
       Mayer Co., 1962.
       This souvenir book is devoted to the first film pro-
duced in the 3-camera Cinerama process by a major studio,
Metro-Goldwyn-Mayer. The Cinerama process is discussed
in an introductory article which is followed by some water-
color portraits of the many stars who appear in the film.
The story is related with a short narrative and many colored
stills from the film, some taking a double page. The background of the Grimm stories and their adaptation to film
form is related. Producer George Pal and director Henry
Levin are given special attention and the remaining cast and
production credits are noted.

2897. WOODSTOCK. 48 p. (paperback) illus. New York:
       Concert Hall Publications, 1971.
       The influence of McLuhan can be detected in this
souvenir book which consists almost exclusively of pictures
of the artists and audience at the Woodstock Concert. The
illustrations are fascinating, well chosen, and nicely reproduced. A short list of performer and production credits is
included.

2898. The Work of the Motion Picture Cameraman, by
       Freddie Young and Paul Petzold. 245 p. illus.
       New York: Hastings House, 1972.
       Here is a technical book that is also a pleasure to
read as a leisure activity. Written via audio tapes by
Freddie Young, it is unusual in several ways. Some biographical information and a filmography for Young appears
at the book's opening, introducing the author and establishing
his credentials. His expertise is given further reinforcement
by the selection of visuals, which include both film stills and
production shots.

       The rest is also praiseworthy, a blend of technical
information, observation, and advice based upon experience.

Diagrams are used constantly to help explain positions, movements, or concepts. The topics covered are filmmakers, cameras, lenses, lighting, preliminaries to filming, camera techniques, studio and location filming, artificial backgrounds, marine sequences, etc. A glossary and an index complete the book.

This is another volume of high quality in the Hastings House series. All the elements combine to create what will inevitably become a standard work going through many printings and subsequent editions. Highly recommended for filmmaking situations, but many general readers will find it rewarding, too.

2899. The Work of the Science Film Maker, by Alex Strasser. 306 p. illus. New York: Hastings House, 1973.

Strasser is an experienced professional whose concern here is to indicate how specific equipment and certain techniques may be used in the making of specialized films. The range of possibilities he discusses is wide and includes both the scientific film and the industrial-technological film. As in all of the Hastings House series, the illustrations are outstanding and supplement the excellent text in fine fashion. An appendix, "glossary," bibliography and an index are included. Highly recommended for academic libraries and selected special libraries, and most acceptable for others.

2900. World Dictionary of Stockshot and Film Production Libraries, by J. Chittock. 72 p. Elsford, N.Y.: Pergamon Publications.

2901. World Encyclopedia of the Film, edited by Tim Cawkwell and John M. Smith. illus. New York: World, 1973.

There are two main elements in this encyclopedia: the cast and credits for about 20,000 films, and an international biographical dictionary with about 2,000 entries. The book goes up to 1971 and offers rather complete filmographies for selected directors. Silent film is somewhat neglected and the directors may be a bit overemphasized, but these are minor faults. The volume is an excellent reference work, easy and pleasureable to use. Highly recommended for all collections.

2902. The World of Film, by Bruce Stewart. 75 p. illus. Richmond, Va.: John Knox Press, 1972.

Intended as an introduction to film, this short volume

contains abbreviated and superficial accounts of film history, filmmaking, film sociology, aesthetics, and film content. The few chapters are written in a concise, literate style that almost conceals some of the questionable content: e.g., 1) "3-D soon enough will become as normal to films as sound and color"; 2) "Film will have flopped over into propaganda which is always fatal"; 3) "The barbed wit of PASSPORT TO PIMLICO, THE LAVENDER HILL MOB, THE LADY KILLERS ... puzzled the Americans."

Much of the presentation is supported by citing film examples and, when Stewart writes about them subjectively, the text improves considerably.   The illustrations appear in four groupings and are interesting and well reproduced.   Nothing about this volume is sufficiently outstanding to warrant immediate acquisition.   The topics are covered in greater depth in many other earlier works and the author's style is not individualistic enough to make the book unique.   Acceptable as a supplementary volume in all collections.

2903.   The World Viewed: Reflections on the Ontology of Film, by Stanley Cavell. 174 p. (paperback) New York: Viking Press, 1971.

For 25 years, going to the movies was a weekly experience for Stanley Cavell.   Around 1960 his attendance habit and his relation to films changed.   His desire "to come to terms with movies" has resulted in the philosophical-aesthetic explorations of this unusual book.   It poses questions such as "Why are films important?", "What happens to reality when it is projected and screened?", "What does the silver screen screen?", "What is the cinema's way of satisfying the myth?"

The author is a professor of aesthetics and philosophy at Harvard, and his frequent references to Bazin, Wittgenstein, Baudelaire, Nietzsche, Heidegger, Rousseau and others presuppose a background on the part of the reader.   An extended section of footnotes follows the text and will assist or rescue some readers.   For the intellectuals who can partake of this philosophical smorgasbord with ease and pleasure, the book is a publishing rarity today.   Others will find the going quite heavy but may be rewarded with sufficient prodding and provocation toward a possible re-examination of their own views about film.   Acceptable for those collections serving mature audiences.

2904.   WR: Mysteries of the Organism. A script of the 1971 film, by Dušan Makavejev (director: Dušan Makavejev). 144 p. (paperback) illus. New York: Avon Books, 1972.

Contains: Cast and production credits; Film Festivals entered and awards won; An interview with Makavejev by Phillip Lopate and Bill Zavatsky.

2905. Young Soviet Film Makers, by Jeanne Vronskaya. 127 p. illus. London: George Allen & Unwin, 1972.

This survey covers the period from about 1955 to 1970, and chronicles the rise of Soviet film artists in the post-Stalin era. The films discussed are unfamiliar to Western audiences. Beginning with a short history, the book quickly enters on a discussion of the new filmmakers. Vronskaya considers them as controversial young intellectuals and describes the departure from social realism and the appearance of comedies. The popular actors and films are indicated. Filmmaking by national minority groups, such as those in Georgia, Armenia, Azerbaidzhan, Lithuania, Moldavia and the Steppes, is described.

The appendices which support this broad survey are well chosen: a list of Soviet studios, a chronological list of the important films (1956-1972), filmographies, a short bibliography, and an index. There are many stills and most are adequately reproduced. This small volume apparently offers both quality and quantity. This is stated with reservation since judgment of the validity of the author's work would require an unusual expertise in modern Soviet film. It does bring to the attention of the Western world, however, artists whose works deserve a greater audience. Recommended for all collections.

2906. YOUNG WINSTON. 22 p. (paperback) illus. New York: Columbia Pictures, 1972.

An article by Barry Norman introduces the film in this souvenir book which features some very attractive color photography. The remaining pages are devoted to actors Robert Shaw, Anne Bancroft, and Simon Ward and to the characters they portray. Producer Carl Foreman and director Richard Attenborough are profiled and supporting cast and production credits are listed.

2907. YOUNG WINSTON. A script of the 1972 film, by Carl Foreman (director: Richard Attenborough). 157 p. (paperback) illus. New York: Ballantine Books, 1972.

Contains cast credits and an introduction by the director, Richard Attenborough.

2908.   Z.   14 p.   (paperback) illus. 1970.
>This short souvenir book furnishes some background for the film by discussing the Lambrakis Affair which served as original source material. Characters from the film are shown, some press comments are quoted, and some stills from the film presented. Cast and production credits complete the book.

2909.   Z is for Zagreb, by Ronald Holloway. 128 p.   illus. New York: Barnes, 1972.
>The artists who are the foundation of the Zagreb Studios--such as Dusan Vukotic, Boris Kolar, or Ante Zaninovic--are a relatively unfamiliar group in America. Their cartoons which emanate from the Zagreb Cartoon Studio in Yugoslavia are more widely known. This book is about both. It starts with a short history of the studio which had its beginning in the late forties. Short biographies consist of factual/statistical data rather than narrative, but it is the final section which will have the most value and appeal. Entitled "A Guide to Zagreb Cartoons (1956-70)," it is a chronological listing of the Zagreb output, with individual films arranged each year in a preferential ranking. Credits and a brief story annotation are given for each. The ranking via position in each year's listing serves as the only evaluation. The distributors of the Zagreb films in countries all over the world are listed on a closing page. The drawings used in the book are all reproduced in black and white and probably lose a great deal in the absence of color. The book jacket has some color illustrations which are most effective. An index is provided.
>This is special material that will appeal to those familiar with the excellence of the cartoons. It is difficult to generate a great deal of enthusiasm for the films with the sparse evaluations and the visual representation given here. Acceptable for all collections.

Appendix A

FILM SCRIPTS

341

LA PASSION DE JEANNE
D'ARC (Dreyer) 566
PERSONA (Bergman) 2640
PETER PAN (Unfilmed) 2642
LE PETIT SOLDAT (Godard)
1092
PIERRE LE FOU (Godard) 1111
POINT OF ORDER (De Antonio)
1115
POTEMKIN (Eisenstein) 355,
1121
THE PRINCE AND THE SHOW-
GIRL (Olivier) 1126
THE PRIVATE LIFE OF HENRY
VIII (Korda) 1129
THE PUMPKIN EATER (Clay-
ton) 2667
PYGMALION (Asquith/Howard)
2669

QUARTET (Various) 1141
QUE VIVA MEXICO (Eisenstein)
1143, 2671
THE QUILLER MEMORANDUM
(Anderson) 2672

RASHOMON (Kurosawa) 1146
REBECCA'S DAUGHTERS (Un-
filmed) 2677
ROCCO AND HIS BROTHERS
(Visconti) 1427
ROMEO AND JULIET (Cukor)
2696
THE RULES OF THE GAME
(Renoir) 1178, 1939

SALESMAN (Maysles) 1185
SALT OF THE EARTH (Biber-
man) 1186
SATURDAY MORNING (Mac-
Kenzie) 2703
SATYRICON (Fellini) 409
SAVAGES (Ivory) 2704
SCOTT OF THE ANTARCTIC
(Frend) 1358
SENSO (Visconti) 1397
THE SERVANT (Losey) 2720
SEVEN SAMURAI (Kurosawa)
1221
THE SEVENTH SEAL (Berg-
man) 567, 1224
SHAKESPEARE WALLAH (Ivory)
2728

SHAME (Bergman) 2729
SHANGHAI EXPRESS (von Stern-
berg) 2730
THE SILENCE (Bergman) 534,
1360
LE SILENCE EST D'OR (Clair)
565
SILENT SNOW, SECRET SNOW
(Kearney) 2736
THE SILVER STREAK (Atkins)
2737
SIMON OF THE DESERT (Buñuel)
1361
SINGIN' IN THE RAIN (Donen,
Kelly) 2738
SMILES OF A SUMMER NIGHT
(Bergman) 567
SOME LIKE IT HOT (Wilder)
1255a
THE SORROW AND THE PITY
(Ophuls) 2745
SPLENDOR IN THE GRASS (Kazan)
2752
THE SPY (Vidor) 2612
STAGECOACH (Ford) 2754
STATE OF SIEGE (Costa-Gavras)
2758
STOLEN KISSES (Truffaut) 2760
STORM IN THE WEST (Unfilmed)
1286
A STREETCAR NAMED DESIRE
(Kazan) 2762
SUNDAY BLOODY SUNDAY
(Schlesinger) 2766
SWEET SWEETBACK'S BAADASSSSS
SONG (Van Peebles) 1311

TAKING OFF (Forman) 2774
THE TEMPTATIONS OF DR. AN-
TONIO (Fellini) 1362
LA TERRA TREMA (Visconti)
1397
THE TESTAMENT OF ORPHEUS
(Cocteau) 1396
THINGS TO COME (Menzies) 1351
THE THIRD MAN (Reed) 1352
THIS IS IT! THE MARIN SHOOT-
OUT! (Unfilmed) 2797
THROUGH A GLASS DARKLY
(Bergman) 534, 1360
TILLIE AND GUS (Martin) 2810
TO KILL A MOCKINGBIRD (Mul-
ligan) 1202

344

TOM JONES (Richardson) 1367
TRANSATLANTIC MERRY-GO-
ROUND (Stoloff) 2819
THE TRIAL (Welles) 1374
TRIO (Various) 1376
TRISTANA (Buñuel) 2822
THE TROJAN WOMEN (Cacoyan-
nis) 2823
TWELVE ANGRY MEN (Lumet)
2829
TWO FOR THE ROAD (Donen)
1391
TWO-LANE BLACKTOP (Hell-
man) 2832

UNDER MILK WOOD (Sinclair)
2839

VARIETY LIGHTS (Fellini) 2848
THE VIRGIN SPRING (Bergman)
1424
VIRIDIANA (Buñuel) 1361
I VITELLONI (Fellini) 1362
VREDENS DAG (Dreyer) 566

A WALK IN THE SPRING RAIN
(Green) 410
THE WAR GAME (Watkins)
1436
WEEKEND (Godard) 2869
WHITE NIGHTS (Visconti) 1427
THE WHITE SHEIK (Fellini)
2883
WHO IS HARRY KELLERMAN...
(Grosbard) 1459a
THE WILD CHILD (Truffaut)
2888
WILD STRAWBERRIES (Berg-
man) 567, 1466
WIND FROM THE EAST (Godard)
2891
WINTER LIGHT (Bergman) 534,
1360
WOMAN IN THE DUNES (Teshi-
gahara) 1481
THE WORD (Dreyer) 566
WR: MYSTERIES OF THE
ORGANISM (Makavejev) 2904

YOUNG WINSTON (Attenborough)
2907

SOUVENIR BOOKS

The souvenir books listed below emphasize mostly films of the fifties and sixties when reserved-seat showings of films were quite prevalent. Not examined but listed in various catalogs are the following souvenir books (the release date of the film is indicated in parentheses):

THE BENNY GOODMAN STORY (1955)
CAN-CAN (1960)
CAROUSEL (1956)
CAT BALLOU (1965)
FANTASIA (1940)
A FAREWELL TO ARMS (1957)
FOR WHOM THE BELL TOLLS (1943)
THE GREAT DICTATOR (1940)
GUYS AND DOLLS (1955)

HANS CHRISTIAN ANDERSEN (1952)
LIMELIGHT (1952)
MOULIN ROUGE (1952)
RAINTREE COUNTY (1957)
THE RIVER (1951)
SINCE YOU WENT AWAY (1944)
SONG OF THE SOUTH (1946)
A SONG TO REMEMBER (1945)
THE TALES OF HOFFMAN (1951)
THAT DARN CAT (1965)

A few souvenir books annotated in the first volume of Cinema Booklist included:

AROUND THE WORLD IN 80 DAYS (1956)
BEN HUR (1959)
THE BIG FISHERMAN (1959)

THE AGONY AND THE ECSTASY 2010
THE ALAMO 2011
ANNE OF THE THOUSAND DAYS 2025
ARIZONA 2031
AROUND THE WORLD IN 80 DAYS 63

BARABBAS 2043
BATTLE OF BRITAIN 2049
BATTLE OF THE BULGE 2050

BECKET 2053
BEN HUR 112
THE BIBLE 2063
THE BIG FISHERMAN 132
THE BLUE MAX 2074
THE BRIDGE ON THE RIVER KWAI 2089

CABARET 2093
CAMELOT 2096
THE CARDINAL 2101
THE CHARGE OF THE LIGHT BRIGADE 2115

Appendix C

INTERVIEWS WITH FILMMAKERS

The word, "filmmakers," is considered in the broad sense in the following listing and includes:

director	(d)	producer	(p)
actor	(a)	executive	(e)
cameraman	(c)	writer	(w)
musician	(m)	studio personnel	(s)

349

Carlino, John Lewis (w) 2711
Carné, Marcel (d) 202
Caron, Leslie (a) 265, 2506
Carradine, John (a) 714
Carson, Johnny (a) 2337
Cassavetes, John (d) 451, 2105
Cawston, Richard (d) 1030, 2204
Chabrol, Claude (d) 770
Chambers, Marilyn (a) 2169
Chaplin, Charles (a) 770, 1081
Chaplin, Geraldine (a) 319, 349, 1222
Chaplin, Saul (m) 2506
Chase, Borden (w) 2392
Chevalier, Maurice (a) 1091, 2337
Christie, Julie (a) 1222
Clair, René (d) 2139, 2215
Clark, Jim (d) 2194
Cocteau, Jean (d) 244, 427, 473, 2154
Cohn, Joe (e) 2506
Cole, Sid (d) 2194
Connery, Sean (a) 349
Conried, Hans (a) 2676
Cooper, Gary (a) 1091, 1212
Coppola, Francis Ford (d) 451
Corman, Roger (d) 451
Cort, David (d) 2204
Cortez, Stanley (c) 685
Costa-Gavras, Constantine (d) 2758
Crabbe, Buster (a) 264
Crawford, Michael (a) 319
Crichton, Charles (d) 2194
Cukor, George (d) 180, 301, 770, 2394, 2618
Curtis, Tony (a) 1222
Curtiz, Michael (d) 714

Daniels, William (c) 685
Davis, Bette (a) 241, 265
Day, Doris (a) 1378
DeBroca, Philippe (d) 106
DeMille, Cecil B. (d) 1081
Dennis, Sandy (a) 319
Denny, Reginald (d) 1081
DePalma, Bryan (d) 451
DeSica, Vittorio (d) 2215
Diamond, I. A. L. (w) 2711
Dietrich, Marlene (a) 319
Diller, Phyllis (a) 2337

Donner, Clive (d) 770
Downey, Robert (d) 451
Dreyer, Carl (d) 770
Duke, Patty (a) 265
Durante, Jimmy (a) 2337
Duryea, Dan (a) 714
Dwan, Allan (d) 329, 1081

Eisenstein, Sergei (d) 770
Emshwiller, Ed (d) 2082
Evans, Dame Edith (a) 319

Falk, Peter (a) 264, 2105
Farmes, Lee (c) 685
Farrar, Geraldine (a) 1081
Farrow, Mia (a) 1222
Fazan, Adrienne (s) 2506
Fellini, Federico (d) 106, 241, 349, 406, 409, 426, 442, 770, 809, 2216, 2231
Finney, Albert (a) 265
Foch, Nina (a) 2506
Fonda, Henry (a) 264
Fonda, Jane (a) 1222
Fonda, Peter (d) 319, 335, 2021, 2416, 2647
Ford, Glenn (a) 2441
Ford, John (d) 553, 770
Forman, Milos (d) 451, 2299, 2774
Franju, Georges (d) 2204
Frankenheimer, John (d) 180, 220
Freed, Arthur (p) 2506
Friedhofer, Hugo (m) 2708
Friedman, Dave (p) 2169
Fuller, Samuel (d) 302
Funt, Allen (d) 1030

Gable, Clark (a) 1091
Gabor, Zsa Zsa (a) 1091, 2441
Gance, Abel (d) 1081
Gardner, Ava (a) 319, 714
Garland, Judy (a) 241
Garner, James (a) 1222
Garnett, Tony (d) 2204
Garson, Greer (a) 714
Giallelis, Stathis (a) 1222
Gibson, George (s) 2506
Gilbert, Lewis (d) 886
Giler, David (w) 2711
Gilks, Alfred (c) 2506
Gilliatt, Penelope (w) 2392

350

Gleason, Jackie (a) 1091
Gleason, Keogh (s) 2506
Godard, Jean-Luc (d) 607, 608, 770, 904, 1111, 2206, 2322, 2323
Godowsky, Dagmar (a) 1151
Goldsmith, Jarrald (m) 2708
Gordon, Ruth (a) 265
Gorin, Jean-Pierre (d) 2206
Granger, Dorothy (a) 2676
Green, John (m) 2506
Gregory, Dick (a) 2337
Griffith, D. W. (d) 2349

Haddock, William (d) 1151
Hall, Conrad (c) 2055
Harrison, Rex (a) 714
Hawks, Howard (d) 221, 770, 2367
Hayes, Helen (a) 1091
Hayworth, Rita (a) 1378
Hellinger, Mark (p) 714
Hellman, Monte (d) 2832
Hemmings, David (a) 1222
Henry, Buck (w) 2711
Heston, Charlton (a) 264, 2375
Hitchcock, Alfred (d) 180, 222, 349, 473, 679, 770, 1091, 2216, 2382, 2383
Hoffman, Dustin (a) 1222
Holden, William (a) 1091
Hope, Bob (a) 1222, 2337
Hopper, Dennis (d) 335, 1222, 2021
Hornbeck, William (s) 1081
Horton, Edward Everett (a) 1151
Howe, James Wong (c) 685
Hudson, Fred (d) 531a
Hudson, Rock (a) 1222
Hurt, John (a) 1222
Hussey, Olivia (a) 265, 1222
Huston, John (d) 443, 770, 2394

Jansco, Miklos (d) 2416
Jay, Antony (d) 1030
Jessel, George (a) 2337
Jewison, Norman (d) 301
Jires, Jaromil (d) 2416
Jodorowsky, Alexandro (d) 2215
Johnson, Nunnally (w) 714, 1091, 2711
Jones, Quincy (m) 2708

Kanin, Fay (w) 2711
Karloff, Boris (a) 2454, 2455
Karsh, Ed (w) 2169
Kaye, Danny (a) 1091
Kazin, Elia (d) 301, 1212
Keaton, Buster (a) 319, 770, 1081
Keeler, Ruby (a) 241
Kelly, Gene (a) 2506
Kelly, Grace (a) 1091
Kelly, Patsy (a) 2676
Keyes, Johnnie (a) 2169
King, Allen (d) 1030
King, Henry (d) 1081
King Brothers (p) 714
Kluge, Alexander (d) 767
Knight, Shirley (a) 319
Kramer, Stanley (d) 301
Kubrick, Stanley (d) 451, 885
Kuney, Jack (d) 1030
Kurosawa, Akira (d) 770, 2674

Lancaster, Burt (a) 714, 1091
Lang, Fritz (d) 180, 770, 832, 1151
Lansbury, Angela (a) 319
Lardner, Ring Jr. (w) 2392, 2711
La Rocque, Rod (a) 1151
Leacock, Richard (d) 426, 2204
Lean, David (d) 770
Leigh, Vivien (a) 241
Leiterman, Richard (d) 1030
Lemmon, Jack (a) 1091
Lerner, Alan Jay (m) 2506
Lesser, Sol (e) 1151
Lester, Richard (d) 301, 451
Lewin, Albert (e) 1151
Lewis, Jerry (a) 301, 1222, 2337
Lloyd, Harold (a) 1081
Loach, Kenneth (d) 2204
London, Julie (a) 1091
Loos, Anita (w) 1151
Loren, Sophia (a) 1222
Losey, Joseph (d) 224, 241, 265, 770, 870, 2194, 2394
Loy, Myrna (a) 265
Lubitsch, Ernst (d) 770, 873
Lupino, Ida (a) 2441
Lumière, Louis (d) 473

McBride, Jim (d) 451
McCarey, Leo (d) 714

351

McCord, Clay (d) 2169
MacLaine, Shirley (a) 1091
McLaren, Norman (d) 443,
1030
McQueen, Steve (a) 1222, 2505
Magnani, Anna (a) 349
Mailer, Norman (w) 451
Makavejev, Dusan (d) 2904
Malden, Karl (a) 264
Mamoulian, Rouben (d) 180,
770, 2394, 2515
Mankiewicz, Joseph (d) 2546
Margolin, Janet (a) 1222
Marsh, Mae (a) 1151
Martin, Dean (a) 349, 1091
Marx, Groucho (a) 1091
Mason, James (a) 319
Maysles, Albert (d) 1030,
2204
Maysles, David (d) 2204
Melville, Jean-Pierre (d) 2531
Mercouri, Melina (a) 319
Merkel, Una (a) 2676
Milestone, Lewis (d) 180,
2441
Miller, Arthur C. (c) 685,
2055
Mills, Hayley (a) 319, 1222
Minnelli, Vincente (d) 180,
2506
Mitchell, Artie (p) 2169
Mitchell, Jim (p) 2169
Mohr, Hal (c) 1151, 2055
Monroe, Marilyn (a) 1091
Montagu, Ivor (d) 2449
Montand, Yves (a) 1222
Montez, Maria (a) 714
Montez, Mario (a) 241
Moreau, Jeanne (a) 349

Nagel, Conrad (a) 1151
Neal, Patricia (a) 265
Negulesco, Jean (d) 180
Newman, Alfred (m) 2708
Newman, Paul (a) 265,
1378
Newman, Walter Brown (w)
2711
Nichols, Mike (d) 319
Nicholson, Jack (a) 2375
Niven, David (a) 1222
Norton, Bill (d) 2143
Novak, Kim (a) 1378

Olivier, Laurence (a) 1222
Olmi, Ermanno (d) 2216
Ophuls, Max (d) 770
O'Toole, Peter (a) 1222

Parks, Michael (a) 1222
Pasolini, Pier Paolo (d) 770,
1083
Peck, Gregory (a) 264, 714
Peckinpah, Sam (d) 770
Penn, Arthur (d) 302, 2079,
2080
Pennebaker, Don Allen (d) 426,
1030, 2204
Peppard, George (a) 319
Perry, Eleanor (w) 2392
Pickett, Lowell (p) 2169
Pickford, Mary (a) 1081
Pincus, Ed (d) 2204
Poe, James (w) 2392
Poitier, Sidney (a) 1222
Polanski, Roman (d) 451, 1222
Pollard, Michael J. (a) 1222
Polonsky, Abraham (d) 302,
1387, 2394, 2416
Preminger, Otto (d) 226, 319,
770, 2129, 2394
Prevert, Jacques (w) 202

Rapper, Irving (d) 180
Ray, Nicholas (d) 770, 2394
Ray, Satyajit (d) 770
Redford, Robert (a) 1222
Redgrave, Lynn (a) 319, 1222
Reed, Carol (d) 2216
Reed, Oliver (a) 265
Reid, Beryl (a) 319
Reisch, Walter (d) 873
Remick, Lee (a) 1222
Renoir, Jean (d) 770, 1178,
2216, 2416
Resnais, Alain (d) 241, 443,
473, 770, 1178
Reynolds, Debbie (a) 1222
Richardson, Tony (d) 106, 2194
Riefenstahl, Leni (d) 770
Roach, Hal (d) 518, 1151
Robinson, Edward G. (a) 264
Robson, Mark (d) 180
Rock, Joe (e) 1151
Rosson, Hal (c) 2055
Rouch, Jean (d) 2204
Rudolph, Ken (d) 531a

Sanders, George (a) 265, 1091
Schary, Dore (p) 1151, 2441,
2506
Schell, Maria (a) 1222
Schifrin, Lalo (m) 2708
Schlesinger, John (d) 106,
2194
Schneemann, Carolee (d) 377
Seberg, Jean (a) 265, 1222
Sellers, Peter (a) 1222
Shamberg, Michael (d) 2204
Shamroy, Leon (c) 685
Sharaff, Irene (s) 2506
Sharif, Omar (a) 265, 1222
Shaw, Wini (a) 1151
Shiffrin, Saul (e) 2107
Siegel, Don (d) 2707
Signoret, Simone (a) 241,
265
Silliphant, Stirling (w) 2711
Silvers, Phil (a) 1091
Silverstein, Elliot (d) 301
Sirk, Douglas (d) 2739
Skolimowski, Jerzy (d) 2194
Sloman, Edward (d) 1081
Smith, Emily (a) 2169
Sondergaard, Gale (a) 2676
Stanwyck, Barbara (a) 2441
Stehura, John (d) 377
Steiger, Rod (a) 264
Steiner, Max (m) 1151
Stewart, James (a) 1091
Stoney, George (d) 1030
Storck, Henri (d) 2204
Straub, Jean-Marie (d) 2761
Streisand, Barbra (a) 319, 1222,
1378
Strickling, Howard (s) 2506
Strohm, Walter (s) 2506
Struss, Karl (c) 685
Sturges, Preston (d) 770,
2394
Sutton, Grady (a) 2676
Swanson, Gloria (a) 1081
Sweet, Blanche (a) 1151

Thomas, Danny (a) 1091, 2337
Thulin, Ingrid (a) 2299
Tourneur, Jacques (d) 180
Truffaut, Francois (d) 426,
564, 770, 1039, 2216,
2733, 2825
Trumbo, Dalton (w) 2392

Ullman, Liv (a) 2837
Umeki, Miyoshi (a) 1222
Ustinov, Peter (a) 2847

Van Dyke, William (d) 2204
Vidor, King (d) 180
Voight, Jon (a) 265, 1222, 2021
von Sternberg, Josef (d) 770,
1081
von Stroheim, Erich (d) 770

Wanger, Walter (p) 1151
Warhol, Andy (d) 451, 1378
Watkins, Peter (d) 1030
Wayne, John (a) 1091, 1212,
2441
Welch, Raquel (a) 1378, 2021
Weld, Tuesday (a) 1222
Welles, Orson (d) 229, 473,
548, 770, 2021, 2394, 2872,
2873
Wellman, William (d) 1081
Werner, Oskar (a) 265, 1222
West, Mae (a) 2441
White, Carol (a) 265
Whiting, Leonard (a) 265, 1222
Whitney, James (d) 377
Whitney, John (d) 377
Whitney Brothers (d) 377
Wilde, Larry (a) 2337
Wilder, Billy (d) 180
Williams, Paul (d) 2889
Winters, Shelley (a) 241, 1091
Wise, Robert (d) 301
Wiseman, Frederick (d) 1030,
2204
Wolper, David (d) 2894
Woodward, Joanne (a) 265, 1378
Wright, Basil (d) 2204
Wyler, William (d) 301
Wyman, Jane (a) 265
Wynn, Ed (a) 2337

Zukor, Adolph (p) 1151

Aylesworth, Thomas G. 2543

Babin, Pierre 2036
Babitsky, Paul 1262
Baddeley, W. Hugh 1323
Baechlin, Peter 471, 1036
Baer, D. Richard 2241
Bahrenburg, Bruce 2255
Bailey, David 2331
Bain, Donald 1419
Bainbridge, John 588a
Bakeless, Katherine 772
Baker, Fred 374, 2564
Balaban, Carrie 263
Balázs, Béla 1348
Balcon, Michael 851, 1388
Ball, Robert Hamilton 1230
Balshofer, Fred J. 1063
Barber, Rowland 658
Barbour, Alan 282, 810, 2077,
  2804, 2807
Bardeche, Maurice 673, 676
Bare, Richard L. 450
Barkas, Natalie 1354
Barker, Felix 2617
Barnet, Sylvan 2192
Barnett, Lincoln 1492
Barnouw, Erik 756
Barr, Charles 839
Barrett, Gerald R. 2307, 2612,
  2736
Barrie, James M. 2642
Barry, Iris 634, 843
Barrymore, Diana 1367a
Barrymore, Lionel 2868
Barsam, Richard M. 2607
Barson, Alfred T. 2867
Bartlett, Richard 2062
Bartolini, Elio 86, 87, 337,
  632
Bassotto, Camillo 454
Bast, William 282a
Battcock, Gregory 1028
Battison, John 984
Baxter, John 587, 691, 1193,
  2038, 2126, 2132, 2386
Bayer, William 2087
Bazelon, David T. 1115
Bazin, Andre 1451, 1452,
  2681, 2878
Beal, J. D. 2406
Beaton, Cecil 395, 2051
Beaumont, Charles 1162

Beck, Reginald 2372
Beckett, Samuel 421
Behlmer, Rudy 504, 2532
Behm, Marc 2114
Bell, Mary Hayley 1453
Bellocchio, Marco 206
Bellone, Julius 1136
Beman, Lamar T. 2110
Bendick, Jeanne 887, 2256
Bendick, Robert 2256
Benet, Stephen Vincent 21
Benner, Ralph 1498
Bennett, Joan 113
Benoit-Levy, Jean 74
Bentley, Eric 2030, 2795
Benton, Robert 2078
Berg, R. D. 917
Bergman, Andrew 2874
Bergman, Ingmar 534, 567,
  878, 1223, 1224, 1239, 1251,
  1360, 1363, 1424, 1466, 1467,
  1474, 2058, 2640, 2729
Bergsten, Bebe 2338
Berman, Morton 2192
Bernard, Matt 2468
Bertsch, Marguerite 2411
Bessie, Alvah 763
Bessy, Maurice 2872
Best, Marc 2801
Betts, Ernest 764, 800, 1129
Beveridge, James A. 2712
Beylie, Claude 1164
Biberman, Herbert 1186
Bickford, Charles 164
Bierce, Ambrose 2612
Billings, Pat 710
Billquist, Fritiof 591
Bird, John H. 232
Biro, Lajos 1129
Bishop, Jim 666
Bitzer, G. W. (Billy) 2071
Blacker, Irwin 301
Blakeston, Oswell 1484
Blesh, Rudi 812
Blinn, William 2088
Blistein, E. M. 248
Bluem, A. William 2561
Bluestone, George 1056
Blum, Daniel 1103, 1104, 1204
Blum, Eleanor 2047
Blumer, Herbert 976, 982
Bobker, Lee R. 358, 2511
Bodeen, DeWitt 501

355

Bogdanovich, Peter 221, 222, 229, 329, 553, 832, 1442
Bogle, Donald 2814
Bolt, Robert 311
Bonomo, Joe 1294
Booker, Floyde E. 1295
Boorstin, Daniel J. 748
Boost, C. 452
Booth, John Erlanger 9
Bordwell, David 2636
Bower, Dallas 1111a
Bowman, William Dodgson 192
Bowser, Eileen 478
Box, Kathleen 210
Boyarsky, Bill 1171
Boyer, Deena 1392
Boyum, Joy Gould 2240
Brackett, Charles 872, 2606
Brackett, Leigh 2065
Brakhage, Stan 2083
Brasillach, Robert 673, 676
Braudy, Leo 2683, 2733
Brewer, Terry 824
Brian, Denis 2778
British Film Institute 160, 415, 476, 799, 905
British Universities Film Council 2272
Brodbeck, Emil E. 654, 963
Brodsky, Jack 240, 2309
Brogger, F. 278
Brosnan, John 2443
Brough, James 2220
Brown, James 1421
Brown, Joe E. 835
Brown, Roland G. 2081
Brown, Royal S. 2322
Brown, Wm. 837
Brown, William O. 2501
Brown, William R. 2418
Browning, Norma Lee 2536
Brownlow, Kevin 722, 1081
Broz, Jaroslav 1086, 2637
Brule, Claude 845
Brunel, Adrian 447, 485a, 1042a
Bruno, Michael 1418
Brusendorff, Ove 370
Bryher, Winifred 480a, 2151
Bryne-Daniel, J. 618
Buache, Freddy 2125
Buchanan, Andrew 435, 474, 528a, 555a, 2254

Bucher, Felix 597
Buchman, Herman 2236
Buchman, Sidney 668, 1077
Buckle, Fort Gerard 921
Bucquet, Harold S. 320
Budgen, Suzanne 406
Bukalski, Peter J. 2263
Bull, Clarence 390
Bulleid, H. A. V. 1264
Buñuel, Luis 14, 198, 382, 1245, 1361, 1425, 2056, 2224, 2225, 2496, 2588, 2822
Buranelli, Prosper 1114
Burch, Noël 2793
Burder, John 1324
Burke, John Gordon 2661
Burnett, Linda R. 2590
Burrows, Michael 2297, 2456, 2469, 2471, 2589, 2759
Burto, Wm. 2192
Burton, Alexis L. 2136
Burton, Jack 141
Burton, Richard 2530
Butler, Frank 610, 908
Butler, Ivan 225, 718, 884, 1160, 2121, 2813
Byars, Mel 2440
Byrne, Richard B. 522

Cacoyannis, Michael 2823
Cady, Jerome 1139
Cahn, William 616, 834, 866, 1101
Cain, James M. 317
Cairn, James 663
Calder-Marshall, Arthur 762
Callenbach, Ernest 1074
Cameron, Elizabeth 277, 665
Cameron, Ian 53, 277, 495, 507, 665, 1208, 2566
Cameron, James R. 171, 366, 943, 2221, 2555
Cameron, Ken 1258
Campanile, Pasquale Fest 1173
Campbell, Russell 1094, 1123
Canfield, Alyce 789, 2327
Canham, Kinsley 2391
Cannom, Robert C. 1416
Cannon, Doran Wm. 153
Cantor, Eddie 76, 2061, 2773, 2865
Capote, Truman 1375
Capra, Frank 173, 787, 788,

827, 1003
Carey, Gary 275, 871, 2084, 2546
Carlson, Sylvia 1133
Carlson, Verne 1133
Carmen, Ira H. 980
Carne, Marcel 202, 805
Carothers, A. J. 655
Carpozi, George Jr. 94, 266, 583, 933, 2866
Carr, Larry 562
Carr, William H. A. 711
Carrick, Edward 64, 288, 289
Carrico, J. Paul 2170
Carrier, Rick 2003
Carriere, Jean-Claude 934, 2056, 2774
Carroll, David 2003, 2526
Carson, L. M. Kit 279
Carter, Huntley 1034, 1035, 1038
Cashin, Fergus 2091
Cassady, Ralph Jr. 930
Cassavetes, John 389, 2537
Casty, Alan 321, 519, 2187
Cates, Gilbert 760
Caunter, Julien 2407
Cavell, Stanley 2903
Cavett, Frank 610
Cawelti, John G. 2079
Cawkwell, Tim 2901
Cayrol, Jean 1043
Ceram, C. W. 60
Chabot, Jean 1208
Chaplin, Charles 195, 1007, 1019
Chaplin, Charles Jr. 1008
Chaplin, Lita Grey 1013
Chaplin, Michael 740
Chaplin, Prescott 2591
Charters, W. W. 954
Chayefsky, Paddy 90, 609, 900
Chermayeff, Clair 2623
Chermayeff, Peter 2623
Cherney, Paul 2841
Chevalier, Maurice 781, 892
Chicorel, Marietta 1399
Chittock, J. 2900
Chodorov, Edward 1496
Churchill, Hugh B. 2246
Cifre, Joseph S. 943
Ciment, Michel 1208
Cinema Commission of Inquiry 218

Cinema Consultative Committee 2782
Cinémathèque Canadienne 906
Cirker, Hayward 2569
Citadel Series 2280
Clair, René 101, 110, 368, 565, 599, 620, 1054, 1158, 1240, 2139
Clarens, Carlos 274, 746
Clark, Eleanor 2802
Clark, Frank P. 1265
Clark, Henry 2
Clark, Joan E. 2196
Clarke, Charles 1132
Clarke, T. 363
Clason, W. E. 292
Clayton, Jack 2667
Clements, Mary Jo 1498
Cline, Edward 2591
Cocteau, Jean 102, 139, 244, 291, 1339, 1396, 2052, 2154, 2157, 2219, 2627
Cogley, John 1165
Cohn, Art 63, 1045
Collet, Jean 608
Collier, John 2634
Collings, Pierre 1289
Colman, Hila 883
Colpi, Henri 672
Combs, Carl 2096
Comden, Betty 2738
Commission on Obscenity and Pornography 2684
Committee on Community Use of Film, The 2510
Conant, Michael 52
Conn, Harry W. 2819
Connell, Brian 823
Conrad, Earl 376, 1020
Conway, Jack 320
Conway, Michael 497, 506, 509, 515
Cook, Olive 962
Cook, Raymond Allen 539
Cooke, Alistair 394, 592
Cooke, David C. 105
Cooke, Inez 283
Coombs, P. H. 1032
Cooper, John 178
Cooper, Morton 1013
Coorey, Philip 867a
Coplans, John 1437
Copyright Office, U.S. 2538
Corbett, D. J. 2551

357

Corliss, Richard 2392
Cormack, Bartlett 582
Corneau, Ernest N. 653
Corry, Will 2832
Costa-Gavras, Constantine 2758
Costello, Donald P. 1218
Cotes, Peter 861
Cottrell, John 43a, 2091
Couffer, Jack 1256, 2489
Coulter, Catherine 855
Council for Cultural Cooperation 268a, 1345a
Courtney, Winifred F. 1147
Coward, Noel 155
Cowie, Peter 56, 230, 255, 767, 1225, 1307, 1308, 1309, 2688
Cox, Alva I. 82
Coynik, David 2262
Crabtree, A. 1141
Crawford, Joan 1120, 2584
Cressey, Paul G. 152
Crichton, Kyle 901
Crisp, C. G. 1377, 2825
Crist, Judith 1128
Croce, Arlene 78
Cromwell, John 609
Crone, Rainer 1438
Crosby, Bing 169
Crosland, Margaret 2155
Cross, Brenda 464
Crow, Jeanne 2529
Crowther, Bosley 628, 699, 854
Croy, Homer 723, 1277, 2629
Cukor, George 862, 1480, 2005, 2696
Culkin, John 487
Currie, Hector 2247
Curry, George 267
Curti, Carlo 1250
Curtis, David 377a, 2223
Curtiss, Thomas Quinn 1432, 2859
Curtiz, Michael 174, 2103
Cushing, Jane 1062
Cushman, George 2563
Cushman, Robert B. 2019
Cussler, Margaret 1049
Czeszko, Bodhan 2315

Dadci, Younes 2013
Daglish, William A. 910

Daisne, Johan 2260
Dale, Edgar 203, 261, 725, 941, 957
Dali, Salvador 14, 198
d'Amico, Suso Cocchi 802, 1173, 1216, 1337, 1457
Dancigers, Oscar 2496
Dandridge, Dorothy 374
Danischewsky, Monja 2882
Daudelin, Robert 1208
Davidson, Bill 1150
Davis, Bette 868
Davis, Frank 1372
Davy, Charles 551
Day, Beth 1356
Day, Donald 2040, 2690
DeAcosta, Mercedes 669
Deans, Marjorie 911
Deans, Mickey 2870
De Beauvoir, Simone 93
Debrix, Jean 212
De Concini, Ennio 632
De Coulteray, Georges 1182
Deer, Harrieta 2652
Deer, Irving 2652
De Havilland, Olivia 375
Delannoy, Jean 2219
De La Roche, Catherine 235, 922, 1261
DeLeon, Walter 2810, 2591
Delluc, Louis 189
Delmar, Viña 880
De Mille, Cecil B. 84
De Mille, W. C. 700
Deming, Barbara 1179
Denby, David 2271
Densham, D. H. 258
Dent, Alan 841
Deren, Maya 2033
Deschner, Donald 503, 508, 521
De Sica, Vittorio 130, 923
de Vecchi, Mario 2464
Dewey, Langdon 1076
De Witt, Jack 1131
Diamant, Lincoln 2786
Diamond, I. A. L. 57, 782, 1255a, 2028
Dick, Esme J. 2248
Dickens, Homer 498, 502, 510, 2283
Dickinson, Thorold 1261, 2200
Dickson, Antonia 677
Dickson, W. K. L. 677

358

Dieterle, William 21, 806, 849, 1289
Dietrich, Marlene 298
Dietrich, Noah 2401
Diffor, John W. 347
Dimmitt, Richard B. 8, 1364
Dixon, Campbell 766
Doak, Wesley A. 2264
Dody, Sanford 868
Donaldson, Elaine 2713
Donchin, Fannie 785
Dondis, Donis A. 2658
Donen, Stanley 2114, 2738
Donner, Jörn 1090, 2281
Dorfles, Gillo 822
Dougall, Lucy 1439a
Douglas, Drake 717
Douglas, Nathan E. 2185
Douglas-Home, Robin 1246
Dovzhenko, Alexander 2210a
Downey, Robert 188
Doyle, G. R. 1386a
Dressler, Marie 850, 1016
Dreyer, Carl 281, 566, 1084, 1415, 1482, 2446
Drinkwater, John 849
Dufty, William 1009
Dukore, Bernard F. 1184
Dunbar, Janet 1172a
Dunn, Fannie 957
Dunn, Maxwell 723a
Dunne, John Gregory 1297
Dunne, Philip 721
Durant, Will 2228
Duras, Marguerite 671, 672
Durgnat, Raymond 165, 270, 369, 482, 570, 589, 926, 1055
Dwiggins, Don 569a, 698
Dworkin, Martin S. 858, 2490
Dyssegaard, Soren 2207
Dysinger, Wendell S. 362

Eastman, Charles 860, 2014
Eastman Kodak 2048, 2427
Eby, Lois 1335a
Eckert, Charles W. 2727
Edelson, Edward 2340
Edelstein, Robert 80, 2504
Edmonds, I. G. 699a
Educational Film Library Association 456
Educational Media Council 344

Edwards, Lee 1149
Eels, George 2368, 2481
Eisenstein, Sergei 39, 455, 461, 462, 488, 791, 792, 842, 1050, 1121, 1143, 1305, 2671
Eisler, Hanns 253
Eisner, Lotte 659
Eliot, T. S. 480, 1004
Elisofon, Eliot 703
Elliott, Godfrey 428
El-Mazzaovi, Farid 2124
Endore, Guy 1288
Engel, Andi 1208
Englander, David A. 732, 1100
Englander, James 2396
English Study Committee 2846
Enrico, Robert 2611, 2612
Enser, A. G. S. 453
Epstein, Edward Z. 807, 1153, 2086, 2465, 2502, 2802
Epstein, Julius J. 174, 2103
Epstein, Philip G. 174, 2103
Ernst, Morris L. 183, 184, 186, 540
Erskine, Thomas L. 2307, 2612, 2736
Essoe, Gabe 286, 505, 585, 1318
European Committee on Crime Problems 209a
Evans, Bergen 2230
Evans, Charles 1169
Evans, Dale 2176, 2895
Evans, Jon 2300
Evans, Peter 1214, 2045, 2331
Evans, Ralph M. 383
Everson, William K. 34, 71, 91, 513, 518, 1105, 1447, 2186
Ewers, Carolyn H. 1116
Eyles, Allen 31, 710, 903, 1446

Fadiman, William 2389
Fairbanks, Letitia 393
Fairweather, Virginia 1061
Falk, Irving A. 1500
Fallaci, Oriana 349
Faragoh, Francis 859
Farber, Donald 2004
Farber, Manny 1024
Farber, Stephen 2565
Farnum, Dorothy 800
Farrell, Barry 1085
Fast, Howard 670
Faulkner, William 2066

359

Faure, Elie 1200
Fawcett, Marion 2423, 2424
Federation Council of Churches 2665
Feiffer, Jules 2102, 2492
Feild, Robert D. 70
Feininger, Andreas 2047
Feldman, Harry 331
Feldman, Joseph 331
Fellig, Arthur 2586
Fellini, Federico 131, 314, 409, 809, 1336, 1362, 1429, 2210, 2848, 2883
Fenin, George N. 1447
Fensch, Thomas 526
Fenton, Robert W. 134
Ferguson, Helen 1350
Ferguson, Robert 731
Fernett, Gene 1042, 1278
Feyen, Sharon 1199
Field, Alice Evans 713
Field, Mary 151, 555a, 613
Fielding, Raymond 1329, 1333, 2020
Fields, Ronald J. 2233
Fields, W. C. 322, 412, 759, 2233, 2591
Film Centre 466, 1404
Film Daily 2245
Films Incorporated 290a, 652
Findlater, Richard 1154
Finler, Joel H. 1293
Firestone, Ross 2564
Fischer, Edward 1196
Fisher, J. David 269
Fisk, Margaret 364
Flaherty, Frances Hubbard 359, 1059
Flaherty, Robert 2587
Flaiano, Ennio 1053, 1336, 1429, 2210, 2848
Fletcher, John G. 1201
Fliegelman, Aura 2719, 2828
Flint, R. W. 2521
Floherty, John J. 968
Flora, Paul 1430
Florescu, Radu 2429
Flournoy, Richard 936
Flynn, Errol 1020
Focal Press 2475
Fonda, Peter 335
Foort, Reginald 231
Foote, Horton 1202

Forcade, Thomas King 2100
Ford, Glenn 552
Ford, John 622, 721, 1273, 2754
Ford, Richard 201
Foreman, Carl 2376, 2377, 2651, 2907
Foreschel, George 1002
Forman, Evan 2431
Forman, Henry James 1075
Forman, Milos 2290, 2298, 2498, 2774
Foster, Lewis 937
Fowler, Gene 401, 919, 1190, 2333
Fowler, Roy Alexander 466a, 1443
Fraenkel, Heinrich 596, 2317
Franciosa, Massimo 1173
François, Camille 1778
Frank, Gerold 1367a
Frank, Robert 1138
Franklin, Joe 239, 934
Franklin, Sidney 614
Frazier, George 1064
Fredrik, Nathalie 681, 1031
Freeburg, Victor Oscar 72, 1099
Freedland, Michael 2447
Freiman, Ray 2230, 2653
French, Harold 363, 1141, 1376
French, Philip 970
French, Warren 2336
Frend, Charles 1195
Freulich, Roman 2301
Frewin, Leslie 138, 299
Friar, Natasha 2621
Friar, Ralph 2621
Friedlander, Madeline S. 2473
Friedman, Leon 1057
Frost, David 2021
Froug, William 2711
Fry, Christopher 128
Fülop-Miller, Rene 38, 944
Fulton, Albert R. 958
Funke, Lewis 9
Furhammer, Leif 1117, 2649
Furie, Sidney 860
Furthman, Jules 2066, 2548 2730

Gable, Kathleen 586
Gaither, Gant 2659

Gale, Arthur L. 733
Gallico, Paul 1168, 2687
Garceau, Jean 283
Gardiner, H. C. 989
Gardner, Herb 1459a
Gardner, Hy 2111
Gargan, William 1463
Garnett, Tay 2483
Garnham, Nicholas 2308
Garrett, George P. 2267, 2268, 2269
Gaskill, Arthur L. 732, 1100
Gassner, John 120, 121, 627, 1385
Geduld, Carolyn 2835
Geduld, Harry M. 354, 473, 2039, 2252, 2294, 2349, 2353
Gehman, Richard 143, 1343
Geis, Bernard 1110
Geisler, Jerry 695
Gelfman, Jane R. 2267, 2268, 2269, 2270
Gelman, Barbara 1097, 2643
Gelmis, Joseph 451
Gerber, Albert 96
Gertner, Richard 489
Gessner, Robert 998
Getlein, Frank 989
Gianetti, Louis D. 2840
Giannaris, George 2791
Giardino, Thomas F. 103a
Gibbon, Monk 1156, 1313
Gibney, Sheridan 1289
Gibson, Arthur 1241
Gidal, Peter 1439
Gifford, Denis 157, 971, 1192, 2455, 2644
Gill, Brendan 2777
Gill, Jerry 116
Gill, Sam 242
Gill, Theodore H. 300
Gilliatt, Penelope 2766
Gilson, Rene 243
Ginsberg, Milton Moses 249
Gipson, Henry Clay 489a
Gish, Lillian 990
Glut, Donald Frank 2305, 2341
Gobeil, Charlotte 2860
Godard, Jean-Luc 25, 876, 899, 904, 1092, 1111, 2323, 2869, 2892

Godden, Rumer 2775
Goldblatt, Burt 962, 2131
Golden, Milton M. 694
Goldman, Frederick 2590
Goldman, James 2488
Goldman, William 168
Goldsmith, Gary 2703
Goldwyn, Samuel 107
Goode, James 1292
Goodgold, Ed 1366, 2812
Goodman, Ezra 147, 416
Goodwin, Michael 2206, 2797
Goodwin, Nancy 2500
Gordon, Bernard 1200
Gordon, Cora 1276
Gordon, George 1500
Gordon, Jan 1276
Gordon, Ruth 2005, 2582
Gottesman, Ronald 354, 548, 2252, 2294, 2353
Govoni, Albert 2335
Gow, Gordon 689, 1304, 2385
Graham, Bruce 2701
Graham, Peter 294, 1039
Graham, Sheilah 257, 593, 1167
Grant, Elspeth 179
Grau, Robert 1344a, 2092
Green, Abel 1235
Green, Adolph 2738
Green, F. L. 1058
Green, Fitzhugh 2250
Green, Guy 1433
Green, Roger Lancelyn 2642
Greenberg, Joel 180, 690
Greene, Graham 1352, 2348
Greensfelder, Linda B. 640a
Gregory, Carl Louis 2554
Greiner, Grace 2782
Grey, Elizabeth 104
Grierson, John 633
Griffith, Corinne 2799
Griffith, D. W. 1170, 2069
Griffith, Linda 1454
Griffith, Richard 40, 172a, 297, 533, 612, 974, 993, 1489, 1504, 2127, 2776
Grissom, John Jr. 2871
Gromo, Marco 418
Grosbard, Ulu 1459a
Grosset, Philip 2164
Grove, Martin A. 2107
Groves, Peter D. 467
Gruault, Jean 2888

361

Grubbs, Eloyse 1407
Gruen, John 241, 2592
Guare, John 2774
Guarner, Jose Luis 1176
Guback, Thomas H. 768
Guerra, Tonino 86, 87, 337, 1053, 2072
Guild, Leo 1501a
Guiles, Fred L. 1047, 2181
Gussow, Mel 316
Guthrie, Tyrone 2631

Haas, Kenneth B. 441
Hackl, Alfons 76a
Hagen, Earle 2708
Hagner, John G. 396
Haining, Peter 601, 2318
Halas, John 69, 290, 726, 1326, 2032, 2238
Hale, Bryant 1102
Hale, William Storm 967, 2435
Hall, Alex 668
Hall, Ben M. 124
Hall, Hal 2135
Hall, Stuart 530, 1118, 2652
Halliwell, Leslie 463
Hallowell, John 1378
Hamblett, Charles 684
Hamill, Pete 309
Hammett, Dashiell 1440
Hammond, Ion 1357
Hampton, Benjamin B. 674, 678
Hancock, Margaret 2300
Hancock, Ralph 393, 835
Handel, Leo A. 696
Haneman, H. W. 2737
Hanna, David 85
Hannon, William M. 1201
Happe, I. Bernard 97
Harcourt, Peter 530
Hardiman, James 132, 2892
Hardison, O. B. Jr. 2267, 2268, 2269, 2270
Harding, James 650
Hardwicke, Sir Cedric 1421
Hardy, Forsyth 633, 1189
Hardy, Phil 579
Harley, John Eugene 1491
Harmon, Bob 2390
Harmon, Francis S. 249a
Harmon, Jim 2341

Harmon, Sidney 2360
Harper, Donald 84
Harrington, Mildred 1016
Harris, Mel 2586
Harrison, Joan 1152
Hart, H. H. 2109
Hart, Henry 2275
Hart, James 2519
Hart, William S. 1011
Hartley, Wm. H. 2409
Harvey, Anthony 2488
Harvey, James 2741,
Harwood, Ronald 2512, 2619
Hashimoto, Shinobu 1146, 1221
Hastings House 2475
Hatch, Eric 1015
Hausen, Ray Harry 2249
Hauser, Philip M. 982
Hawks, Howard 2066
Hayakawa, Sessue 1503
Hayden, Nicola 2080
Hayden, Sterling 1435
Hayman, Edward 2319
Haymes, Nora Eddington Flynn 371
Hayne, Donald 84
Hays, Will 916, 1201, 1209
Head, Edith 325
Heath, Eric 385
Hecht, Ben 199, 1267, 1493
Heerman, Victor 862
Helfman, Harry 888, 2514
Hellman, Monte 2832
Hellmann, Lillian 1048
Henderson, Robert M. 636, 2350
Henderson, Ron 2416
Hendricks, Gordon 103, 340, 816, 2625
Henie, Sonja 1472
Henningsen, Paul 370
Henrey, Robert 528
Hensen, Jim 2811
Henstell, Bruce 2012, 2094, 2105, 2299, 2375, 2382, 2889
Hepworth, Cecil M. 47, 172
Herald, Heinz 849
Herczeg, Geza 849
Herdeg, Walter 2238
Herling, Michele 2354
Herman, Lewis 343, 1122
Herndon, Venable 17
Herrington, Eugene H. 1295
Hervey, Harry 2730

Heyer, Robert   304
Hibbin, Nina   334
Hift, Fred   2494
Higham, Charles   180, 525, 685, 690, 2384
Hill, George Roy   168
Hill, Jonathan   148
Hill, Norman   867b
Hiller, Jim   2763
Hilton, James   1002
Hirsch, Phil   687, 712
Hirschberg, Jack   2370
Hitchcock, Alfred   1152, 1267, 2609
Hoadley, Ray   724
Hoban, Charles   765, 957, 994
Hodgkinson, Anthony   1197
Hoellering, George   480
Hoffman, William   1236
Hofmann, Charles   1259
Holaday, Perry W.   598
Holloway, Ronald   2909
Holloway, Stanley   1479
Holstius, E. Nils   709
Hope, Bob   660
Hopkins, Jerry   360
Hopkinson, Peter   2753
Hopper, Dennis   335
Hopper, Hedda   461, 578
Hopwood, Henry V.   864
Horkheimer, Mary Foley   347
Hornby, Clifford   1232
Hornby, George   1157
Horne, Lena   841a
Houseman, John   2699
Houston, Beverle   2152
Howard, Leslie   2669
Howard, Leslie Ruth   1144
Hoyt, Edwin P.   897
Hrabal, Bohumil   2150
Huaco, George   1255
Hubler, Richard G.   1455
Hudgins, Morgan   2577
Hudson, James A.   2583
Hudson, Richard   1306
Huettig, Mae D.   338
Huff, Theodore   190, 333, 774, 2069
Hughes, Eileen Lanouette   1067
Hughes, Elinor   399, 400
Hughes, Langston   137
Hughes, Robert   442, 443, 844

Hughes, Rupert   2591, 2810
Hulfish, David Sherill   961
Hull, David Stewart   470
Hunnings, Neville March   444
Hunt, R. W. G.   2685
Hunter, William   1205
Huntley, John   161, 163, 1145, 1328, 2402
Hurley, Neil P.   1346, 2792
Huss, Roy   457, 2073, 2398
Huston, John   12, 128, 806, 844, 2478, 2538, 2539
Huston, Penelope   259
Hutchins, Robert M.   1505
Hutton, Clayton   875
Hyams, Joe   149, 1010

Inge, William   2752
Inglis, Ruth A.   571
Irwin, Will   720
Isaacs, Neil P.   410
Isaksson, Folke   1117, 2649
Isaksson, Ulla   1424
Israeli, Lee   2540
Issari, M. Ali   2138
Ivens, Joris   170
Ivory, James   2704, 2705, 2728

Jackson, Arthur   2388
Jackson, B. F.   2785
Jackson, Pat   363
Jacobs, Lewis   313, 361, 378, 538, 777, 979, 1172
James, David   1194
Jarratt, Vernon   783
Jarrott, Charles   2045
Jarvie, I. C.   977, 1369
Jeavons, Clyde   2645
Jenkins, Charles Francis   48
Jennings, Dean   1010
Jennings, Gary   964
Jennings, Talbot   614, 2696
Jensen, Paul M.   223
Jewell, Wayne   2857
Jinks, William   178a
Jobes, Gertrude   942
Jodorowsky, Alexandro   2215
Joels, Merrill E.   727
John, Errol   2201, 2295, 2296, 2364
Johnson, Nunnally   622
Johnson, William   2707
Johnston, Alva   630

Johnston, Winifred 916a
Johnstone, Will B. 2542
Jones, Emily 2158
Jones, G. William 290a, 1302, 2466
Jones, Ken D. 520, 2374
Jones, Lon 92
Jordan, Rene 2310
Jordan, Thurston C., Jr. 605
Jul, Christen 1415

Kabir, Alamgir 217
Kael, Pauline 234, 611, 747, 821, 2145, 2184
Kagan, Norman 2128
Kahle, Roger 2650
Kahn, Gordon 697
Kahnert, F. 1032
Kalmar, Bert 2208, 2542
Kane, Thomas J. 2011
Kanfer, Stefan 493, 2448
Kanin, Garson 2005, 2818
Kantor, Bernard R. 301
Kaplan, Mike 2450
Kaplan, Richard 356
Kardish, Laurence 2678
Karpf, Steven Louis 2311
Karr, Kathleen 2018
Katz, John Stuart 2641
Kauffmann, Stanley 420, 1490, 2017
Kaufman, George S. 2603
Kawin, Bruce F. 2788
Kazan, Elia 26, 89, 387, 1372, 2752, 2762
Kearney, Gene 2736
Keaton, Buster 1021
Keats, John 734
Keene, Ralph 1444
Kehoe, Vincent J-R 1325
Keliher, Alice 997
Kelley, Kevin J. 2218
Kelly, Gene 2738
Kelly, Terence 250
Kennedy, Donald 1263
Kennedy, Joseph P. 1291
Kennedy, Keith 2259
Keown, Eric 1181
Kepes, Gyorgy 1023
Kerbel, Michael 80, 2504
Kernan, Margot 2242
Kernodle, George R. 780
Kerouac, Jack 1138

Kerr, Laura 667
Ketchum, Richard M. 2693
Khan, M. 778
Kibbee, Lois 113
Kiesling, Barrett C. 1317
Kihm, Jean-Jacques 2156
Kinder, Marsha 2152
King, Henry 1470, 2428
Kingery, R. A. 917
Kinsey, Anthony 46, 729
Kirschner, Allen 2261
Kirschner, Linda 2261
Kitses, Jim 716, 1316
Klapp, Orrin E. 2772
Klapper, Joseph T. 348
Klein, John 2774
Kleiner, Dick 372, 600
Kline, Herbert 556
Klingender, F. D. 929
Kloepfel, Don V. 949
Knef, Hildegard 602
Knight, Arthur 703, 863, 1112, 2648
Knight, Derrick 867
Knight, Frank R. 715
Knox, Donald 2506
Kobal, John 296, 589, 617
Koch, Howard 174, 2103, 2104
Koch, Karl 1178
Koch, Kenneth 2112
Koch, Stephen 2757
Kodak Co. 730
Koenigil, Mark 986
Kone, Grace Ann 350
Konzelman, Robert G. 2523
Korda, Alexander 1129
Korty, John 2467
Koury, Phil 1395, 1497
Kracauer, Siegfried 577, 1347
Krahn, Frederic A. 342
Kramer, Anne 301
Kramer, Stanley 2185, 2451
Kraus, Robert 2587
Kreuger, Miles 37
Kriegsman, Sali-Ann 2019
Krishnaswamy, S. 756
Kronhausen, Eberhard 2306
Kronhausen, Phyllis 2306
Krows, A. E. 1314
Kubrick, Stanley 2149
Kuhns, William 103a, 380, 1345b, 2570, 2857
Kula, Sam 2064

Kulick, Buzz 2088
Kurosawa, Akira 744, 1146, 1221, 2168
Kurtz, Alice S. 2218
Kyrou, Ado 166

La Bau, Tom 2359
La Cava, Gregory 1015
Lacey, Richard A. 2716
Lahue, Kalton C. 150, 242, 245, 262, 324a, 824, 826, 1473, 1488, 2718, 2316
Lake, Veronica 1419
Lamarr, Hedy 339
Lamb, Harold 2213
Lambert, Gavin 2618
Lambert, R. S. 555a
Lamparski, Richard 1449
Lanchester, Elsa 836
Landau, Jacob M. 1296
Landers Film Review 830
Lane, Tamar 1037, 2879
Lang, Edith 1005
Lang, Fritz 582, 874, 2533
Lang, Walter 919
Langley, Noel 1376
Lanier, Vincent 750
Larsen, Egon 1270
Larsen, Otto N. 2855
Larson, Rodger 640, 1499
Lasky, Jesse L. 739
Lasky, Victor 1188
Latham, Aaron 271
Latham, G. C. 11
Lattuada, Alberto 2210, 2848
Laughton, Charles 1044
Laurie, Joe Jr. 1235
Lauritzen, Einar 1310
La Valley, Albert J. 2383
Lawson, John Howard 468, 532
Lawton, Richard 2417
Leahy, James 224, 1154a
Lean, David 155
Leavitt, Hart Day 1285
Lebel, J. P. 813
Lecouvette, Guy 252
Lee, Laurie 1444
Lee, Ray 2731
Lee, Raymond 286, 390, 517, 542, 585, 588, 1051, 1306, 1458
Lee, Robert E. A. 2650
Lee, Walt 2680

Legg, Stuart 929
Leglise, Paul 1345a
Le Harivel, J. P. 549
Lehman, Ernest 2609
Leites, Nathan 978
Lejeune, Caroline A. 197, 207, 555a, 1341
Lelouch, Claude 890
Lennig, Arthur 237, 479, 1244
Leonard, Harold 465
Leprohon, Pierre 55, 786, 2438, 2682
LeRoy, Mervyn 789, 859, 1353
Leslie, Al 1138
Lester, Richard 2363
Lester, Sandra 2425
Levant, Oscar 913, 1402
Levien, Sonya 2428
Levin, G. Roy 2204
Levin, Martin 682
Levitan, Eli L. 24, 49
Levy, Alan 1068
Lewin, William 1096
Lewis, Arthur H. 2441
Lewis, Howard T. 945
Lewis, Jerry 2816
Lewis, Leon 831
Lewis, Richard 430
Lewis, Sinclair 1286
Leyda, Jay 455, 485, 820, 2189
Library of Congress 846, 847, 949, 950, 951, 955
Lidstone, John 200
Liebling, Howard 2010, 2063, 2074, 2746
Likeness, George 1072
Lillie, Beatrice 2220
Limbacher, James 403, 404, 561, 1161, 1408, 2679
Linden, George W. 1159
Lindey, Alexander 184
Lindgren, Ernest 73, 1108
Lindsay, Cynthia 938, 1022
Lindsay, Vachel 75
Linton, David 2655
Linton, Dolores 2655
Lipton, Lenny 2412
Livingston, Don 434
Lloyd, Harold C. 30
Lods, Jean 1134
London Film Society 2279
London, Kurt 477
Lonstein, Albert I. 2163

365

Look (magazine) editors 967a
Loos, Anita 604, 1480
Lorentz, Pare 183, 419
Lorenz, Denis 1299
Losey, Joseph 2002, 2321, 2720
Lounsbury, Myron Osborn 2626
Lovan, Nora G. 2026
Lovelace, Linda 2430
Lovell, Alan 2763
Low, John B. 2559
Low, Rachel 675, 2380
Lowndes, Douglas 475
Lubalin, Herb 2063, 2746
Lubitsch, Ernst 2606
Lubovski, Git 215
Lumet, Sidney 2829
Lumsdaine, Arthur A. 840
Lutz, Edwin George 2552
Lyle, J. 1032
Lynch, William F. 749

McAnany, Emile 535
MacArthur, Charles 1493
McArthur, Colin 2842
Macaulay, Richard 123
McBride, Jim 279
McBride, Joseph 1089, 2367, 2873
McCabe, John 1000
McCaffrey, Donald W. 563, 2113
McCaffrey, Patrick J. 648a
McCallum, John 1342
McCambridge, Mercedes 1394
MacCann, Richard Dyer 426, 431, 693
McCarey, Leo 610, 880, 2208, 2542
McCarty, Clifford 146, 445, 504, 2288, 2666
McClelland, C. Kirk 1065
McClelland, Doug 2845
McClure, Arthur F. 520, 975, 1420, 2374
McClure, Twomey 1420
McCrae, Arthur 363
McCrindle, Joseph F. 106
MacDonald, Dwight 330, 345
McDonald, Gerald D. 497, 1107
MacDonnell, Kevin 2578
McDowall, Roddy 316a

MacGowan, Kenneth 109
McGregor, Dion 506
McGuiness, James 2603
McGuire, Jeremiah C. 211
McIntosh, Don 200
McKenna, Virginia 1066
MacKenzie, Aeneas 806
MacKenzie, Kent 2703
McKowen, Clark 2440
McLaglen, Victor 381
MacLaine, Shirley 315
MacLeish, Archibald 356, 1175
McLeod, Norman 2542
MacLiammoir, Michael 1140
McNally, Raymond 2429
MacPherson, Kenneth 2151
McVay, Douglas 1006
Maddux, Rachel 410
Madsen, Axel 1465
Madsen, Roy P. 45
Maelstaf, R. 2024
Magny, Claude-Edmonds 2009
Mailer, Norman 2507, 2520
Mainds, Roger 1198
Makavejev, Dusan 2904
Malkiewicz, J. Kris 2137
Mallery, David 469, 1191
Maltin, Leonard 966, 1384, 2055, 2343, 2676
Manchel, Frank 1338, 2097, 2880, 2881, 2567
Mancia, Adrienne 1434
Manfull, Helen 10
Manilla, James N. 2509
Mank, Chaw 1411
Mankiewicz, Herman 234, 2144
Mankiewicz, Joseph L. 18, 2546
Mann, Abby 2451
Mann, Delbert 90, 278, 900
Mann, May 2518
Manoogian, Haig P. 472
Manvell, Roger 44, 69, 290, 379, 422, 437, 596, 865, 972, 1027, 1028, 1029, 1207, 1326, 1328, 1358, 1450, 2032, 2317, 2432, 2726
Mapp, Edward 137a
March, Joseph Moncure 2819
Marcus, Fred 2235
Marcus, Greil 2206, 2797
Marey, Etienne Jules 2560
Margadonna, Ettore 418
Margrave, Seton 1301

366

Margulies, Stan 2750
Marill, Alvin 273, 810, 2130, 2373
Marinas, Louise 2511
Marino, Vito 2163
Marion, Francis 2410, 2614
Markopoulos, Gregory J. 1142
Marlowe, Don 705
Marner, Terence St. John 2194
Marquis, Dorothy P. 204
Marshall, Herbert 791
Martin, Francis 2810, 2591
Martin, Marcel 252, 569
Martin, Olga J. 702
Martin, Pete 169, 660, 696, 714, 1091, 1287, 1468, 2884
Marx, Arthur 852, 2744
Marx, Groucho 637, 638, 912
Marx, Harpo 658
Mascelli, Joseph V. 543
Mason, Paul 759
Mason, Sarah 862
Mast, Gerald 1233, 2159
Mattfeld, Julius 1417
Matthews, J. H. 2769
Matzkin, Myron 126, 2572
Mauerhofer, Hugo 2033
Maugham, W. Somerset 363, 1141, 1376
May, Mark A. 840, 1252
Mayer, Arthur 918, 974
Mayer, David 355
Mayer, J. P. 158, 1254
Mayer, Michael F. 554
Mayersberg, Paul 707
Maynard, Richard A. 2106
Maysles, Albert 1185
Maysles, David 1185
Meade, Ellen 1499
Meade, Walter 1195
Medoli, Enrico 1173
Meeker, David 2445
Mekas, Jonas 2562
Mellor, G. J. 2646
Meltzer, Milton 137
Mendes, Lothar 800
Mendez, Jiri 2150
Menjou, Adolphe 790
Mercer, John 775, 2434
Mercouri, Melina 2442
Meredyth, Bess 919
Merman, Ethel 2884
Meyer, Anthony 304

Meyer, Nicholas 2500
Meyers, Warren B. 1460
MGM Library of Film Scripts 2534
Michael, Paul 3, 35, 145
Michaelis, Anthony R. 2686
Michalek, Bosilaw 2133
Milestone, Lewis 1048, 1139
Milius, John 2478
Millar, Gavin 1327
Miller, Ann 2536
Miller, Arthur 2538, 2539
Miller, Arthur C. 1063
Miller, Diane Disney 1287
Miller, Don 2076
Miller, Edwin 1222
Miller, Maud 151
Miller, Max 557
Miller, Patricia George 2174
Miller, Seton 668
Miller, Tony 2174
Miller, Vernon L. 204
Miller, Virgil E. 1269
Millerson, Gerald 2783
Mills, Earl 2178
Milne, Tom 219, 870, 889, 2323
Milner, Michael 1227
Minney, R. J. 196, 2257
Minus, Johnny 967, 2435
Mirwis, Allan 2198
Mitchell, Alice Miller 2116
Mix, Olive Stokes 385
Mix, Paul E. 2477
Modern Times Booksellers 405
Moholy-Nagy, Laszlo 1079, 1428
Moley, Raymond 61, 662
Monier, Pierre 251
Montagu, Ivor 39, 537, 791, 1195, 1305, 1478
Montgomery, John 247
Monti, Carlotta 411
Moore, Colleen 1243
Moore, Grace 1501
Morella, Joe 807, 1153, 2086, 2465, 2502, 2802
Morgan, Diana 2360
Morgan, Guy 1155
Morgan, Thomas B. 1212
Morgenstern, Joseph 493
Morin, Edgar 1279
Morley, Robert 936
Morris, Lloyd 1052

367

Morris, Peter 2098, 2191
Morrison, John 941
Mosel, Tad 22
Moshier, W. Franklin 2285
Mosley, Leonard 98
Moussinac, Leon 353
Moving Picture World 2574
Mullen, Pat 894
Muller-Strauss, Maurice 1036
Mungo, Raymond 2062
Munro, Grant 2817
Münsterberg, Hugo 439, 1095
Muray, Nickolas 1168, 2687
Murfin, Jane 320, 1480
Murphy, George 1188
Murray, Edward 2134
Murray, Ken 2328
Museum of Modern Art 423,
959, 1284
Musselman, M. M. 790
Mussman, Toby 607
Musun, Dr. Chris 898

Naremore, James 2663
National Archives and Records
Service 2355
National Audiovisual Center
1406
National Conference on Motion
Pictures 2160
National Information Center for
Educational Materials 754,
755
Naumburg, Nancy 1445
Neergaard, Ebbe 326, 1290
Negri, Pola 915
Nelson, Al P. 136
Nelson, Ralph 2484
Nemcek, Paul L. 496
Nemeskurty, Istvan 1483
Neville, John T. 2591
Newman, David 2078
Newman, Howard 2756
Newman, Jeffrey 2117
Newquist, Roy 1266
New York Library Association
2273
New York Times 1040, 1041,
2426, 2598, 2599
Nichols, Dudley 120, 121,
1273, 1355, 1385, 2754
Nichols, Mike 2102
Nicholson, Dianne 2826

Nicklaus, Thelma 861
Nicoll, Allardyce 433
Nilsen, Vladimir 213
Nisbett, Alec 1332
Niven, David 2544
Niver, Kemp R. 541, 771, 956,
1098, 2067, 2351
Nizer, Louis 1012, 2595
Nizhny, Vladimir 842
Noble, Lorraine 568
Noble, Peter 162, 280, 386,
701, 1025, 1109a
Noerdlinger, Henry S. 937a
Nogueira, Rui 2531
Nolan, William 736, 1248,
2505
North, Joseph H. 2209
Norton, Bill L. 2143
Norton, Graham 250
Notcutt, L. A. 11
Nowell-Smith, Geoffrey 1426
Nuetzel, Charles 1459

Oakley, C. A. 1456
Oberfirst, Robert 1414
Oberholtzer, Ellis Paxson 2545
O'Brien, P. J. 2691
O'Brien, Pat 1471
O'Dell, Paul 635
Odets, Clifford 1046
O'Donnell, Jack 2737
O'Donoghue, Michael 2704
Offen, Ron 2085, 2095
Offenhauser, William H. 1249
Oguni, Hideo 1221
O'Keefe, Stanton 2675
Okon, May 2700
O'Konor, Louise 2211
O'Laoghaire, Liam 779
O'Leary, Liam 1242
Olivier, Laurence 1126, 2372
Ommanney, Katherine A. 1272
Ommanney, Pierce C. 1272
Ophuls, Marcel 2745
Oppenheimer, George 1422, 2183
Orrom, Michael 1124
Ortman, Marguerite G. 409a
Osborne, John 1367
Osborne, Robert 4, 118, 119,
560, 1071
Otis Art Institute 686
Ott, Frederick W. 2286
Ott, John 2580

Ottieri, Ottiero 337
Owen, Alun 2363

Palmborg, Rilla Page 2662
Palmer, Charles 176
Palmer, Laurie 934
Palmieri, E. Ferdinando 418
Papousek, Jaroslav 2290, 2498
Papst, G. W. 2633
Parish, James R. 545, 810,
2130, 2303, 2342, 2635,
2740
Park, William 2668
Parker, Norton S. 83
Parkinson, Michael 2645
Parks, Gordon 2293
Parrish, Robert 773
Parsons, Christopher 2513
Parsons, Louella 595, 1335
Partridge, Helen 828
Pascal, Gabriel 2508
Pascal, John 657
Pascal, Valerie 303
Pasolini, Pier Paolo 2613
Passer, Ivan 2290, 2498
Pasternak, Joseph 336
Pate, Michael 425
Paul, Elliott 460, 2893
Payne, Robert 625
Pearl, Ralph 2470
Pearson, George 544
Pechter, William S. 1387
Peck, Ira 2798
Peetz-Schou, Morten 2122
Pelissier, Anthony 363
Penn, Arthur 17, 2078
Pennebaker, D. A. 2205
Pensel, Hans 1206
Pepper, Beverly 1017
Perelman, S. J. 2542
Perkins, V. F. 2239
Perlman, William J. 991
Perry, Eleanor 1312, 1375
Perry, Frank 309, 1375
Perry, George 250, 511
Peters, Charles C. 952
Peters, J. M. L. 1321
Peterson, Marcelene 1102
Peterson, Ruth C. 953
Petrie, Graham 228
Petzold, Paul 19, 2898
Pfragner, Julius 384
Philip, John 2220

Phillips, Henry A. 1093
Photoplay Research Society 1070
Pichel, Irving 908
Pickard, R. A. E. 295, 2161,
2193
Pickford, Mary 1303
Pinchot, Ann 990, 2870
Pincus, Edward 641
Pinelli, Tullio 809, 1336, 1429,
2210, 2848, 2883
Pinter, Harold 2002, 2046, 2291,
2321, 2667, 2672, 2720
Pirosh, Robert 2183
Pittaro, Ernest M. 1379
Platt, Frank C. 631a
Playboy 2647
Poe, James 2484
Political and Economic Planning
159
Pollack, Sydney 1349
Porter, Vincent 867
Poteet, G. Howard 2162
Powdermaker, Hortense 706
Powell, Dilys 627
Powell, Michael 1393
Pratley, Gerald 220, 226, 2129
Pratt, George C. 1268, 2751
Prawer, Jhabvala R. 2728
Prevert, Jacques 202, 805
Price, Vincent 745
Privett, Bob 726
Provisor, Henry 351
Pudovkin, Vladimir I. 531, 2550
Pulman, Jack 278
Puzo, Mario 2326

Quigley, Isabel 191
Quigley, Martin 284, 879, 1033
Quigley, Martin, Jr. 489
Quinn, Anthony 2624
Quinn, James 432
Quint, Beverly 2101
Quintanilla, Luis 2893
Quirk, John 2359
Quirk, Lawrence J. 494, 499,
514, 516, 2287

Racheva, Maria 1124a
Raine, Norman 849
Ramsaye, Terry 920
Rand, Helene 430
Randall, Richard S. 185
Ransen, Mort 2608

Rapee, Erno 365, 946
Raphael, Frederic 1391, 2179
Rathbone, Basil 753
Rattigan, Terence 1126
Rau, M. 1008
Rau, N. 1008
Rawlinson, Arthur R. 800
Read, Herbert 2033
Reagan, Ronald 1455
Rebel, Erique J. 624
Rebikoff, Dimitri 2841
Redi, Riccardo 2314
Redfield, Margaret 552
Reed, Carol 1058, 1352
Reed, Rex 133, 265, 319
Reed, Rochelle 2035, 2082,
    2787, 2837, 2844, 2894
Reed, Stanley 208, 645, 2119,
    2402
Reeves, Leonard 2493
Regnier, George 2572
Reid, Alastair 1365
Reid, Seerley 1407
Reille, Louis 490
Reilly, Adam 2172
Reinhardt, Wolfgang 806
Reiniger, Lotte 1229
Reisch, Walter 2606
Reisman, Philip 22
Reisz, Karel 1327
Renan, Sheldon 776
Renoir, Jean 621, 1178,
    1260, 1355
Renshaw, Samuel 204
Resnais, Alain 639, 671, 672,
    833, 1043, 2602
Reynertson, Jean 1485
Reynolds, Burt 2399
Rhode, Eric 1370
Ricci, Mark 497, 506, 509,
    515, 524
Rice, Susan 2276
Richards, Dick 603, 1479
Richardson, Robert 857
Richardson, Tony 1367
Richie, Donald 512, 796, 797,
    798, 1283, 2444
Rideout, Eric H. 32
Rilla, Wolf 88
Rimberg, John 1262, 2553
Ringgold, Gene 500, 501, 2288
Riskin, Robert 787, 788, 827,
    1003

Ritchie, Donald 2674
Rivkin, Allen 667
Robbe-Grillet, Alain 833, 2419
Roberts, James R. 2001
Roberts, Kenneth H. 2657
Roberts, Marguerite 320
Robinson, David 629, 692, 814,
    2381
Robinson, Edward G., Jr. 1009
Robinson, Gerda 458
Robinson, W. R. 891
Robson, E. W. 438, 1486
Robson, M. M. 438, 1486
Robyns, Gwen 853, 2482
Roeburt, John 597a
Rogers, Betty 2692
Rogers, Dale Evans 2176, 2895
Rogers, Robert E. 2137
Rohdie, Sam 2449
Rohmer, Eric 2146, 2157a, 2581,
    2694
Rollins, Charlemae 398
Rondi, Brunello 809
Rondi, Gian 785
Rooney, Mickey 742
Rose, Reginald 2829
Rose, Tony 2166
Rosenberg, Bernard 1151
Rosenstein, Jaik 2387
Rosenthal, Alan 1030
Rosmond, Babette 111
Ross, Frank 937
Ross, Helen 1113
Ross, Lillian 1106, 1113
Ross, Murray 1281
Ross, T. J. 436, 2398
Ross, Wallace 125
Rossellini, Roberto 2698
Rossen, Robert 2016, 2413,
    2485, 2806
Rosten, Leo 708
Rotha, Paul 182, 312, 533,
    555a, 972, 1177
Rothman, Jay 2771
Rotsler, William 2169
Roud, Richard 606, 1069, 2761
Routt, William D. 1154a
Rubin, Martin 302
Rubin, William S. 2107
Rubinstein, E. 2313
Ruby, Harry 2208, 2542
Rucknick, Christian A. 362
Ruddy, Jonah 148

370

Rudman, Jack 2221
Russel, Robert 937
Russell, Tina 2654
Rutherford, Margaret 2040
Ryan, Tom 2222
Rynew, Arden 2258
Ryskind, Morrie 1015, 2396, 2603

Sadoul, Georges 575, 2123, 2190, 2191
St. Johns, Adela Rogers 631a
Salachas, Gilbert 407
Salem, James M. 640b
Salles-Gomes, P. E. 2851
Samuels, Charles 817, 1021
Samuels, Charles T. 175, 2216
Sanders, George 914
Sands, Pierre Norman 2379
Sarris, Andrew 28, 256, 424, 492, 523, 770, 2394, 2656
Sartre, Jean-Paul 2433
Saul, Oscar 2762
Saunders, Marvin 2499
Savary, Louis M. 2170
Saxe, Raymond F. 2378
Schaffner, Franklin 2060
Schary, Dore 176, 1286
Scheed, Wilfred 2547
Scherer, Kees 459
Scheuer, Steven 992, 1381, 1382, 1383
Schickel, Richard 307, 491, 841a, 995, 1280, 2715
Schillaci, Anthony 487, 2568
Schlesinger, John 2179, 2766
Schmalenbach, Werner 471
Schmidt, Georg 471
Schneider, Alan 421
Schneider, Etta 957
Schrader, Paul 2820
Schramm, Wilbur 1032
Schrank, Jeffrey 909, 2781
Schreivogel, Paul A. 2274, 2293, 2467, 2491, 2602, 2608, 2611, 2623, 2630, 2755, 2767, 2811, 2817
Schulberg, Budd 6, 387, 2302
Schultz, Dodi 2045
Schultz, Ed 2045
Schumach, Murray 388
Schuster, Mel 946a, 2552a

Schwartz, Alan 186
Scotland, John 1315
Scott, Adrienne 2240
Scott, Audrey 793
Scott, Evelyn F. 2395
Scrymgeour, J. O. 844
Seabury, William Marston 2664
Sears, M. E. 373
Seaton, George 2183
Segal, Abraham 252
Segal, Alex 22
Seldes, Gilbert 623, 719, 981, 983, 1136, 1220
Seltz, George B. 1496
Semel, Sanford 2767
Semprun, Jorge 639
Sennett, Mack 819, 2670
Sennett, Ted 2863
Serina Press 642, 643, 644, 646, 647
Seton, Marie 352, 1119
Shah, Panna 757
Shakespeare, William 2697
Sharp, Dennis 1109
Sharples, Win Jr. 2657
Sharps, Wallace S. 293
Shavelson, Melville 728
Shaw, Arnold 109a, 1247
Shaw, Bernard 1184, 2669, 2508
Shaw, Irwin 773
Shaw, M. 373
Shay, Don 264
Sheekman, Arthur 2542
Shelley, Frank 1271
Sheridan, Marion 940
Sherman, Eric 302
Sherman, William David 831
Sherriff, R. C. 1058, 1141, 1376
Sherwin, David 743
Sherwood, Robert E. 599, 1152, 2007
Shillinger, E. H. 917
Shinde, M. K. 1231
Shipman, David 631, 2344
Shipp, Cameron 819, 2868
Shulman, Irving 656, 1410
Shumlin, Herman 1440
Shuttleworth, Frank 1252
Siegel, Joel E. 2474
Silke, James A. 2099, 2231, 2515
Silliphant, Stirling 410, 1433

373

1275, 2461
Walker, Kathrine Sorley 2177
Walker, Michael 187, 1208,
1377
Wall, C. Edward 2575
Wall, James M. 2118
Wallace, Carlton 2140
Walls, Howard Lamarr 948
Walter, Ernest 1330
Wanger, Walter 1014
Ward, John 1166
Warhol, Andy 142
Warman, Eric 1448
Warner, Jack L. 1010
Warshow, Robert 751
Wasserman, Paul 2041
Waterbury, Ruth 167, 1319
Watkins, Peter 1436
Watts, Stephen 108
Wayne, Jane Ellen 2479
Weaver, John T. 559, 1390a
Weber, David O. 2605
Weber, Olga S. 81
Weegee 2586
Weinberg, Herman G. 873,
1183, 1431, 2167
Weiner, Janet 2408
Weintraub, Joseph 1476
Weiss, Ken 1366, 2812
Weiss, Nathan 240, 2437,
2616
Weldon, Don 739
Welles, Orson 234, 1374, 2144
Wellman, William 1078, 1288,
2631
Wells, H. G. 896, 1351
Weltman, Manuel 1458
Werner, Michael 2805
West, Claudine 614, 1002
West, George 1005
West, Jessamyn 1368
West, Mae 615, 1476
Wexler, Norman 803
Whannel, Paddy 530, 1118,
2652
Whately, Roger 2737
Wheeler, Helen 2895a
Wheeler, Leslie James 1127,
2060
Whitaker, Rod 832a
White, David M. 1237, 2108,
2651
White, Eric W. 1200

Whiteside, Thomas 2831
Whyte, Alistair 2593
Wiese, E. 2217
Wilburn, Gary 2857
Wilcox, Herbert 1386
Wilde, Larry 2337
Wilder, Billy 57, 317, 782, 872,
1255a, 2028, 2606
Wilk, Max 100, 1475
Will, David 268, 580
Willans, Geoffrey 1409
Willemen, Paul 268
Williams, Chester 584
Williams, Dick 2706
Williams, Raymond 1124
Williams, Richard 2491
Williams, Robert 535
Williams, T. M. 2197
Williams, Tennessee 89, 2762
Willis, Donald C. 2397
Willis, John 1204
Wilner, Norman 246
Wilson, Earl 2734, 2414
Wilson, Harold 2639
Wilson, Robert 2243
Wilson, William H. 441
Wimperis, Arthur 1002, 1129
Wincor, Richard 856
Windeler, Robert 43
Windust, Bretaigne 154
Winnington, Richard 323
Winter, David 2596
Wiseman, Thomas 209, 1219
Wlaschin, Ken 784, 2075
Wolfe, Glenn Joseph 2486
Wolfe, Maynard Frank 886
Wolfenstein, Martha 978
Wollen, Peter 580, 1238
Wollenberg, H. H. 41, 417
Wood, Alan 1001
Wood, James 2603
Wood, Leslie 924, 1174
Wood, Robin 53, 58, 115, 187,
661, 680, 1087, 1208, 2029
Wood, Sam 2183
Wood, Tom 156
Woolfenden, John R. 2472
Worth, Sol 2808
Wurlitzer, Rudolph 2832
Wrede, Casper 2619
Wright, Basil 895, 1405
Wright, Edward A. 1125
Writers Guild of America 1462

Wyler, William 1002, 1493
Wynn, Keenan 1494
Wysotsky, Michael Z. 1464

Yoakem, Lola Goelet 1380
Young, Colin 844
Young, Donald Ramsey 2557
Young, Freddie 2898
Young, Loretta 1350
Young, Vernon 214, 2033,
  2620
Young, William C. 2022
Youngblood, Gene 377
Yulsman, Jerry 2165

Zalman, Jan 483
Zarkhi, N. 2550
Zavattini, Cesare 923, 1502
Zelmer, A. C. Lynn 2160a
Zetti, Herbert 2735
Zierold, Norman J. 205,
  590, 928, 2724
Zimet, Julian 1200
Zimmer, Jill Schary 1477
Zimmerman, Paul D. 902
Zinman, David 414, 2702
Zinnemann, Fred 2376, 2377
Zinsser, William K. 1210
Zmijewsky, Boris 524
Zmijewsky, Steve 524
Zolotow, Maurice 931
Zuckerman, Ira 2325
Zugsmith, Albert 2404
Zukor, Adolph 1137
Zwerdling, Shirley 2237
Zwerlin, Charlotte 844

SUBJECT INDEX

Bara, Theda 2303, 2724, 2751
BARABBAS 92
Bardem, J. A. 473
Bardot, Brigitte 93, 94, 2044
Barrie, James M. 2235
Barron, Arthur 2204
Barrymore, Diana 867b, 1367a, 2734
Barrymore, Ethel 95, 2734, 2868
Barrymore, Lionel 95, 108, 2734, 2868
Barrymore, John 95, 631a, 1367a, 2316, 2333, 2526, 2734, 2868
Barthelmess, Richard 2316
Bartholomew, Freddie 205
Baseball, in films 2393
THE BATTLE AT ELDERBUSH GULCH 2351
THE BATTLE OF BRITAIN 98
Baxter, Anne 2303
Bazin, Andre 1039
Beatles, The 100
Beaton, Cecil 2051
Beatty, Warren 257, 319
BEAUTY AND THE BEAST 102, 291, 2131
Becker, Jacques 572
Belafonte, Harry 109a
Belgian films, animated 2024
BELLE DE JOUR 2147
Bellocchio, Marco 206
Belmondo, Jean Paul 319
Benchley, Robert 111, 1157, 2343
BEN HUR 112
Bennett, Constance 113
Bennett, Joan 113
Bennett, Richard 113
Bergen, Candice 241
Bergman, Ingmar 56, 114, 115, 116, 214, 216, 473, 534, 770, 891, 1090, 1241, 1298, 1360, 1424, 2057, 2216, 2281, 2416, 2722, 2837
Bergman, Ingrid 117, 265, 349, 494, 1150, 1492, 2734, 2741
Berkeley, Busby 241
Bernhardt, Curtis 180

Bernhardt, Sarah 2059
Bertolucci, Bernardo 451
Betts, Ernest 764
Bible, as film material 2893
Bibliographies
    audio visual information 2679
    communications 2046
    directors, periodicals 2552a
    film as art 465
    film history (Italian) 454
    film in education 941
    film librarianship 2064
    film literature 1147, 2046, 2172, 2263, 2314, 2432
    film reviews 640b, 2277, 2575
    magazines 2046
    mass media 2046
    motion picture discrimination 941
    multi media reviews 2575
    newspapers 2046
    performers 946a
    periodicals 2046, 2172
    "What is a City?" 2877
Bickford, Charles 164
THE BICYCLE THIEF 2147, 2638
THE BIG FISHERMAN 132
Biograph camera 103
Biographies, index to film 135
Biograph Studios
    Bulletins (1896 to 1908) 2067
    Bulletins (1908 to 1912) 2068
    general 103, 636, 1098, 2351
Biography, collective 35, 76, 205, 242, 246, 277, 318, 398, 399, 400, 631, 631a, 653, 665, 687, 712, 752, 772, 928, 993, 1064, 1091, 1113, 1150, 1151, 1168, 1212, 1248, 1280, 1492, 2303, 2316, 2344, 2432, 2901
Biology films, making of 2136
THE BIRTH OF A NATION 136, 539, 1170, 2070, 2071
Bitzer, Billy 2071
THE BLACK CAT 2131
Blacklisting 10, 697, 763, 1165, 1186, 2448, 2622, 2795
Blacks
    actors in films 137, 137a,

378

Blacks (cont.)
398, 1025, 2070, 2118, 2814
  image in films 2070, 2118, 2814
Blackwell, Carlyle 2316
Bletcher, Billy 1151
Blom, August 2338
Blondie films 2342, 2702
BLOW UP 175, 2073
B Movies 2076
Boetticher, Budd 302, 716
Bogart, Humphrey 143, 144, 145, 146, 147, 148, 149, 1064, 2077, 2734
Bogdanovich, Peter 302
Bomba films 2342
Bonhoeffer, Dietrich 300
BONNIE AND CLYDE 175, 2079, 2080
Bonomo, Joe 1294
Books see Literature
BORN FREE 1066
Borzage, Frank 132
Boston Blackie films 2342
Bow, Clara 2635, 2724
Bowery Boys films 2342
Boy Friends films 2343
Brackett, Charles 1492
Brakhage, Stan 2082, 2083
Brando, Marlon 257, 1091, 1248, 2084, 2085, 2086, 2282, 2325, 2326
Breaking into films 727, 789, 1070, 1498, 1500, 2404, 2826
Bresson, Robert 424, 495, 572, 770, 2216, 2820
BREWSTER McCLOUD 1065
Brice, Fannie 2773
THE BRIDE OF FRANKENSTEIN 2131
British Film Institute
  archive catalogs 160
  work of 2813
British films
  actors, directors 157
  actors, monographs 1181
  audience 158, 201
  British Film Institute 2813
  color films 163
  documentary films 2753, 2763
  film design 64

history
  (1895 to 1971) 2121
  (1896 to 1918) 675
  (1896 to 1971) 2646
  (1903 to 1944) 1270
  (1918 to 1929) 2380
  (1925 to 1945) 1388
  (1939 to 1945) 527
  (1945 to 1970) 1027
  industry 159, 250, 285, 549, 764, 825, 851, 1001, 1177, 1405, 1456, 2882
  John Player Lectures 2813
  music 161
  pioneers 2646
  short films 867
  survey of films (1895 to 1971) 2121
  war films (1939 to 1945) 2753
Broads, in films 91, 277
Brook, Peter 770
Brooks, Richard 301
Brown, James 801
Brown, Joe E. 835
Brunel, Adrian 1042a
Brynner, Yul 1091
Bulgarian films 334, 1124a, 2593
Bulldog Drummond films 2186
Buñuel, Luis 14, 165, 166, 198, 216, 473, 770, 1361, 2125, 2769
Burns and Allen 966
Burroughs, Edgar Rice 134
Burton, Phillip 2091
Burton, Richard 167, 240, 1014, 2091, 2530, 2734
Burton, Sybil 2091
Bushman, Francis X. 714, 2316, 2526
Business films 441, 489a, 758

THE CABINET OF DR. CALIGARI 522, 2147
Cable TV 2094
CAESAR AND CLEOPATRA 303, 911, 1218
Cagney, James 276, 2095, 2283
Cahiers du Cinema 2825
Camera, motion picture 1331
Camera angles 543
Cameramen
  alphabetical guide to 624
  interviews with 685, 2055

379

work of 2898
Cameron's Encyclopedia 171
Canadian films, feature 2098
Cannes Film Festival 459
Cannon, Dyan 2335
Canova, Judy 2740
Cantor, Eddie 2061, 2773, 2865
Capra, Frank 172a, 173, 2099
CARAVAN OF LOVE 2100, 2871
Careers in cinema 727, 789, 1070, 1498, 1500, 2404, 2826
Caricatures, film actors 2390
Carné, Marcel 202, 805
Caron, Leslie 265
Carradine, John 714
Carroll, Nancy 496
Cartoons see Animated films
Cartridges, film, index to 754
CASABLANCA 2104
Cassavetes, John 389, 451, 2105
CAST A GIANT SHADOW 728
Catalog, Library of Congress see Library of Congress; Copyright records; Catalogs
Cataloging, cinema literature 177
Catalogs
  copyright entries 846, 847, 948, 949, 950, 951, 2558
  film 80, 423, 652, 1154a, 2090, 2158, 2212, 2504
  film literature 215, 2120
  memorabilia 2830
Cates, Gilbert 760
Caulfield, Joan 2635
Cawston, Richard 2204
Censorship
  film 183, 184, 185, 186, 209a, 284, 388, 540, 571, 662, 693, 702, 916, 980, 986, 991, 1057, 1170, 1211, 1491, 2107, 2109, 2110, 2118, 2665, 2893
  film, British 444
Center, Media, for community 2160a

Ceylon, films of 867a
Chabrol, Claude 187, 573, 770, 1039, 2566
Chaney, Lon 2227, 2316
Chaney, Lon, Jr. 2340
Chaplin, Charles 65, 189, 190, 191, 192, 193, 194, 195, 196, 333, 497, 563, 597a, 625, 631a, 719, 740, 770, 861, 1007, 1008, 1013, 1019, 1107, 2113, 2393, 2718, 2751
Chaplin, Charles, Jr. 1008
Chaplin, Geraldine 319, 349
Chaplin, Lita Grey 1013
Chaplin, Michael 740
Character actors 1420, 1460, 2676
Charlie Chan films 2186, 2342, 2702
Chase, Charlie 2343
Chauvel, Charles 2038
Chevalier, Maurice 781, 892
Children
  as actors 205, 528, 742, 1335a, 2801
  Entertainment Film Movement 614
  films for 151, 614, 2276
  research on, re: films 2116
Chinese films 2189
A CHRISTMAS MEMORY 1375
Churches, film use in see Religion
Cinemascope 2459
Cinematic literacy 998
Cinematography see also Filmmaking
  biology films 2136, 2686
  books on 2023
  color films 383, 2047, 2685
  early techniques 47, 48, 2135
  8mm 2003, 2165, 2421
  experimental sciences films 2136, 2686
  high speed 2373
  medicine, films about 2136, 2686
  pre-1900 history 48
  special effects 1264, 1265, 2249, 2407, 2723
  techniques 29, 543, 775, 1123, 1127, 1132, 1133, 2135, 2136, 2137, 2140, 2164,

380

382

Davis, Joan 2740
Davis, Sammy Jr. 2734
De Acosta, Mercedes 669
Dead End Kids films 2702
Dean, James 282a
De Broca, Philippe 106
DeHavilland, Olivia 375
DeLaurentis, Dino 92
Delinquency and film 982
DeMille, Cecil B. 84, 286, 501, 700, 928, 1497, 2395, 2751
DeMille, William 700, 2395
Demy, Jacques 573
Dennis, Sandy 319
DePalma, Brian 451
Depression, films during the 2108, 2311, 2874
DeRenzy, Alex 2107
DeSica, Vittorio 130, 923, 2216
Detective films 2186
De Villeneuve, Nigel 2831
Dictionary see also Encyclopedia and Yearbook
  actors 631, 2344, 2432, 2901
  cameramen 624
  cinema 292, 294, 605, 1231, 2191, 2193, 2432, 2901
  cinematic terms 2192
  cinematography 293
  cinematography, Russian-English 1180
  fantastic films 2680
  film, four languages 536
  filmmakers 2190
  film names, humorous 2075
  films 2191, 2193, 2432, 2901
  literature into films 2260
  music 292
  1,000 films 295, 2193
  production libraries 2900
  sound 293
  stock shots 2900
Dietrich, Marlene 138, 296, 297, 298, 299, 319, 502, 562, 2635
Diller, Phyllis 2740
Direction
  film 450, 1485, 2194, 2816, 2850

  problems 442
Directors see also individual name listings
  American 28, 35, 180
  articles in periodicals 2552a
  biography, collective 216, 2190
  comedy 31
  documentary films 1030, 2204
  experimental films 776, 2138
  filmographies 28, 35, 2190, 2432, 2901
  Guild of America, members 2195
  interviews, collective 106, 180, 241, 301, 302, 349, 451, 473, 714, 770, 1151, 1222
  problems of 442
Discussions, film, leading 2473
Disney, Walt 70, 306, 307, 1287
Disney Studios
  general 70, 305
  wild life films 1256
Distribution
  American films 2160, 2665
  films 898
  monopoly 930
  pornographic films 2684
Distributors, film 81, 82, 855, 2559, 2875
Dix, Beulah Marie 2395
Dix, Richard 2316
Dixon, Thomas 539
Dr. Christian films 2342, 2702
Doctor-in-the-House films 2702
Dr. Kildare films 2342, 2702
Doctors, in films 2393
Documentary films see also Educational films
  British 392, 1177
  filmmakers 1030, 2204
  general 312, 313, 633, 2607, 2894
  history 2204
  production 1049, 1323
  sound in 1258
  U.S. Government 1082
Donat, Robert 314a
Donner, Clive 770
Douglas, Kirk 2284
Downey, Robert 188, 451
Dracula legends 2429

Drake, Betsy 2335
Dreams, reflected in film 1179
Dressler, Marie 850, 1016
Dreyer, Carl 219, 326, 473,
566, 770, 2083, 2207,
2636, 2751, 2820
Drugs, films on 2605
Duke, Patty 265
Durante, Jimmy 616, 1190
Durbin, Deanna 205
Duryea, Dan 714
Dutch Films 452
Dwan, Alan 329
Dynamation 2249, 2723
Dziga Vertov Group 2206

East European film, guide to
334, 2593
Ecology films 2218
Economics, film 51, 52, 159,
250, 285, 338, 471, 537,
693, 856, 898, 929, 930,
942, 945, 1291
THE EDGE OF THE WORLD
1393
Edison, Thomas 1395
Edison laboratory, early work
340, 2625
Editing see also Filmmaking
film 531, 2246
techniques 1324, 1327
Editor, film, exam for 2221
Education
adult 82, 535, 741, 761,
909, 910, 1074, 1199,
1408
bibliography, film in education 941
filmmaking by students 200,
475, 476, 526, 618, 640,
731, 881, 883, 1272, 1295,
1322, 1499, 2258, 2259
general 428, 530, 741, 765,
840, 994, 1032, 1074,
1199, 1404, 1408, 2106
higher 82, 446, 467, 526,
529, 530, 535, 909, 910,
1074
natives, African 11
religious 82, 304, 909, 910,
1062, 1302, 1346
summary of the literature
957

use of films in 2081, 2106,
2214, 2254, 2590, 2655,
2716, 2781, 2782, 2846
vans, mobile, in education
1404
yearbook, British 1198
youth 82, 304, 380, 424,
430, 469, 487, 535, 909,
910, 940, 996, 1062, 1074,
1096, 1191, 1197, 1199,
1272, 1316, 1321, 1404,
1469
Educational films
British 392, 2272
cartridges 754
college, university, films for
2158, 2272
directing 343, 531a
discussion guides 648a, 1062,
1345b, 2274
distribution 81, 1345a
drugs, films on 2605
ecology, films on 2218
environment, films on 2218
European 268a, 341
evaluations of 82, 430, 456,
648a, 830, 909, 910, 1062,
2037, 2248, 2272, 2273,
2276, 2277, 2575
general 81, 392, 428, 441,
531a, 1032, 2254
guide to free films 347
index to 344, 350, 755, 2037,
2198, 2248, 2272, 2273,
2276, 2277
in libraries 345
producers 81
producing 343
publications about 346
older 342
research 765
reviews, index to 2264, 2575
use of 441, 530, 648a, 840,
994, 2106, 2254, 2716,
2781, 2782, 2846
writing of 343
young adults, films for 2273
Effect of film
erotic 2684
general 348, 422, 431, 432,
623, 708, 891, 969, 1254,
1486, 1491, 2261, 2573
on literature 287, 857, 2134

384

Effect of film (cont.)
 on plays 2134
 on writers 2134
 on youth 61, 65, 152, 201,
  203, 204, 209a, 261,
  362, 367, 598, 952, 953,
  954, 976, 982, 1075,
  1252, 1254, 2116
Eggeling, Viking 2211
Egyptian films 778, 2124
8 1/2 1392
8mm films
 filmmaking 2003, 2165,
  2421
 films 350, 754
Eisenstein, Sergei 39, 252,
  352, 353, 354, 355,
  455, 473, 480a, 770,
  791, 792, 842, 1050,
  1121, 1478, 2083
Eldridge, Florence 2287
ELEPHANT BOY 359
Ellery Queen films 2342
Elsevier's Dictionary 292
Emotions, children's response
  to films 362
Emshwiller, Ed 2082
Encyclopedia see also Dictionary and Yearbook
 actors 2264, 2432, 2598,
  2901
 American musical films 36,
  2388
 Associations, film 364
 awards 2264, 2598
 British actors, directors
  157
 cinema 463, 2432
 companies 2264, 2598
 credits, 18, 000 films 2264,
  2598
 Eastern European actors,
  directors, films 334
 film information 2353, 2432,
  2901
 film production 24, 2432
 films, general 2241, 2432,
  2598, 2901
 film techniques 24, 546
 film technology 943
 French actors, directors,
  films 569
 gangster films, actors, di-

 rectors 587
 genres 2161
 German actors, directors,
  films 597
 Hollywood actors, directors,
  recent 710
 international actors, directors,
  film titles 294, 2161
 Japanese actors, directors,
  films 795
 photography 547
 sound motion pictures 171,
  2432, 2901
 Swedish actors, directors,
  films 1307
 TV films see Films on TV
English, teaching of, with films
  940, 2162, 2846
Environment films 2218
Erikson, Leif 2890
Erotic content in films see
  Pornography
Errol, Leon 2343
Etaix, Pierre 573
European films since 1946 1028
Evaluations, film
 college, university films 2158
 educational see Educational
  films
 entertainment features 648,
  985, 992, 1040, 1041, 1381,
  1382, 1383, 1384, 2598
 environment films 2218
 short films 82, 430, 456,
  648a, 830, 909, 910, 1062,
  2037, 2248, 2272, 2273,
  2276, 2277, 2575
Evans, Charles 1169
Evans, Dale 2176, 2895
Exams for film jobs 2221
Exhibition
 American films 2160
 British films 232
 new techniques 561, 1033,
  1464
Experimental films
 American 776, 1026, 2592,
  2757
 general 67, 377, 448, 1142,
  1400, 2223, 2562, 2592,
  2757
 international 377a, 379, 2223
 periodicals about 378, 448

Expressionism in films 522, 659, 1255

Factual films see Documentary films and Educational films
Fairbanks, Douglas 393, 394, 2316, 2526
Fairbanks, Douglas, Jr. 823
Falcon films 2342
Falk, Peter 264, 2105
THE FALLEN IDOL 528
Famous people in films 642
Famous Players Company 720
Fan magazines 682, 1097, 2643, 2776
Fantasy, films of 2131, 2249, 2680
Farmer, Frances 2890
Farnum, William 2316
Farrow, Mia 257
Faye, Alice 2285, 2303
Featured players 1420, 1460, 2374, 2676
Feature films
    American, 1892 to 1970 33
    index to 8mm, 16mm 403, 404
    reviews, index to 2264, 2426
    source book 405
    use in adult education 535, 1074, 1199
    use in schools 380, 446, 469, 487, 940, 1191, 1272, 1469, 2081, 2106, 2214, 2590, 2655, 2716, 2781, 2782, 2846
Fellini, Federico 106, 216, 241, 314, 349, 406, 407, 408, 409, 424, 770, 809, 891, 1362, 1392, 2216, 2231
FELLINI SATYRICON 1067
Festivals, film 459, 1389, 2237
Fiction see Literature
Fields, W. C. 71, 276, 322, 411, 412, 413, 503, 759, 2233, 2293, 2343, 2773
Film

as art 73, 74, 75, 213, 2253
as mass media 623, 749, 1118, 1136, 1220
general 422, 426, 427, 436, 440, 537, 777, 780, 895, 979, 989, 2239, 2247, 2253, 2261, 2262
periodicals 68, 1399, 2172, p. 413-421 in Cinema Booklist
Film collections 2196, 2198
Film collectors 2431
Film Daily's 10 Best Awards 35
Film design, British 64
Film librarianship, bibliography of 2064
Film libraries 2196, 2198
Filmmaking see also Production and Directing, and Script Writing and Cinematography
advice on 2087
amateur 715, 730, 2003, 2396, 2405, 2407, 2657
animation 20, 24, 45, 46, 49, 69, 70, 305, 726, 729, 881, 1322, 1326, 2024, 2032, 2048
anthropology 2048, 2808
by students 103a, 200, 475, 476, 526, 618, 640, 731, 881, 883, 1295, 1322, 1499, 2165, 2166, 2256, 2258, 2259, 2405, 2406
careers in 1500, 2404
color photography 383, 2047
early techniques 47, 48, 723, 999, 2554
8mm 2003, 2165, 2421
general 19, 73, 74, 88, 104, 105, 108, 358, 447, 474, 528a, 551, 619, 667, 707, 713, 724, 865, 882, 884, 887, 888, 968, 997, 1088, 1207, 1256, 1270, 1317, 1323, 1450, 2137, 2165, 2166, 2253, 2257, 2359, 2396, 2402, 2404, 2406, 2509, 2554, 2567, 2816, 2850, 2898
glossary 2174
handbook of 641, 2164, 2165, 2166, 2359, 2657
how to books 726
industrial films 2899

SCOTT OF THE ANTARCTIC
1194, 1195
THE SECRET PEOPLE   882
SONS OF MATTHEW   723a
TRILOGY   1375
2001: A SPACE ODYSSEY
885, 2461, 2835
A WALK IN THE SPRING
RAIN   410
Filmography
African   2008
Automation   2026
Computer Science   2026
Data Processing   2026
Drugs   2605
Ecology   2218
Environment   2218
Film Reviews, index to   2264
Films
American sound, guide to
35, 489, 652
and the stage   1124, 1125,
2651
classics   237, 238, 239,
414, 415, 628, 1225
early paper print   956
for children   2276
for colleges, universities
2158
for TV use   984, 2197,
2719, 2827
in the sixties   2661
non-royalty, for TV   2197
N.Y. Times reviews   1040
on TV, guide to   648, 985
992, 1041, 1381, 1382,
1383, 1384
16mm sound   1249
surrealist   2769
war and peace, guide to
1439a
Warner Brothers   2863
womanhood   2895a
young adults, films for
2273
Films in Review
indexes to   2423, 2424
2425
periodical   2275
Film societies
organizing   2278, 2300,
2408
programmes   2279

Film Study
BIRTH OF A NATION   2070
BLOW UP   2073
BONNIE AND CLYDE   2079
Chaplin, Charles   2113
Children   2199
CITIZEN KANE   548
course outlines   2242
criticism   424
discussion guides   290a, 304,
648a, 909, 1062, 1074,
1199, 1345a, 2252, 2274,
2294, 2307
films, catalog of   2212
FLAVIO   2293
general   380, 446, 468a, 487,
1074, 1199, 1316, 1321,
2162, 2199, 2641, 2782
THE GENERAL   2313
THE GRAPES OF WRATH
2336
Griffith, D. W.   2349
guides, to films   2252, 2274,
2294, 2307
Hawks, Howard   2367
Hitchcock, Alfred   2383
Horror films   2398
in colleges   526, 529, 640a,
2354, 2844
in schools   2081, 2590
THE LANGUAGE OF FACES
2467
THE LITTLE ISLAND   2491
NIGHT AND FOG   2602
NO REASON TO STAY   2608
AN OCCURRENCE AT OWL
CREEK BRIDGE   2611, 2612
ORANGE AND BLUE   2623
OVERTURE   2630
OVERTURE/NYITANY   2630
LA PASSION DE JEANNE
D'ARC   2636
perspectives on   2641
PSYCHO   2663
RASHOMON   2674
Science Fiction films   2707
THE SEVENTH SEAL   2722
Shakespearean films   2727
SHOOT THE PIANO PLAYER
2733
Silent Snow, Secret Snow   2736
A STAIN ON HIS CONSCIENCE
2755

Film Study (cont.)
  stills, for study 2247
  SUNDAY LARK 2767
  TIME PIECE 2811
  TOYS 2817
  2001: A SPACE ODYSSEY
    2835
Finance, film 929, 942
Finney, Albert 265
Fitzgerald, F. Scott 271,
  2302
Flaherty, Robert 359, 473,
  762, 894, 1059, 1489,
  2138, 2751
FLASH GORDON 2131
FLAVIO 2293
Flebbe, Beulah Dix 2395
Fleisher, Richard 92
Florey, Robert 2393
Flynn, Errol 371, 504,
  545, 597a, 1020, 1064,
  2065
Fonda, Henry 264, 550
Fonda, Jane 550
Fonda, Peter 319, 550, 2021,
  2416, 2647
FORBIDDEN PLANET 2131
Ford, Glenn 552
Ford, John 553, 770, 2126,
  2297, 2336
Ford Film Collection 2355
Foreign films
  general 238
  in America 554
Foreign governments, films
  of 643
Forman, Milos 451, 2299
Form and function 1159
Forties, films of the 2804
THE 400 BLOWS 2006
Fox, William 626, 928, 1403
Francis-the-Mule films 2342
Franju, Georges 570, 573,
  2204
Frankenheimer, John 180,
  220
FRANKENSTEIN 2304, 2305
Frankenstein films 2305,
  2702
FREAKS 2131
Freedom of the screen 1186
Free films 347, 644, 2197
French film

alphabetical guide 569
general 466a, 572, 573, 574,
  575
World War II 466a
THE FRIENDLY PERSUASION
  1368
Friese-Greene, William 576
Fuller, Samuel 302, 579, 580,
  2308, 2842
Fu Manchu films 2702

Gable, Clark 283, 505, 583,
  584, 585, 586, 817, 1091,
  1150, 2310
Gabor, Zsa Zsa 2741
Gallery portraits 316a, 390,
  562, 2301, 2331, 2417,
  2687
Gangster films 91, 587, 665,
  2311, 2842, 2874
Garbo, Greta 276, 506, 562,
  588a, 589, 590, 591, 631a,
  2051, 2312, 2662
Garden of Allah Hotel 593
Gardner, Ava 85, 319, 714
Gargan, William 1463
Garland, Judy 205, 241, 594,
  807, 867b, 1073, 2870
Garnett, Tay 2483
Garnett, Tony 2204
Garson, Greer 714
Gaynor, Janet 2303
Geisler, Jerry 1492
Gene Autry films 2702
THE GENERAL 2313
Genres of film 645, 891, 2262,
  2668
Georgian films 2905
German films
  alphabetical guide 597
  East Germany 334, 2593
  expressionism 522, 659, 1255
  general 417, 596
  history
    1895 to 1970 2317
    1895 to 1945 417
    1918 to 1933 577
    1918 to 1929 659
    1933 to 1945 470
GERMANY, YEAR ZERO 2638
Gielgud, John 2319
Gilbert, John 2316, 2526
Ginsberg, Milton M. 249

389

390

History (cont.)
1291, 1344, 1344a
2092, 2209, 2625,
2751
sound 35, 416, 489, 652,
689, 690, 691, 1029,
1104, 2385, 2386
European film 1028
International film
history, general 109,
151, 208, 209, 255,
361, 384, 427, 438,
533, 777, 780, 924,
958, 964, 965, 972
995, 1108, 1225,
1450, 2119, 2187,
2200, 2253, 2275,
2381, 2432, 2881
history, 1895 to 1927
2881
history, 1932 to 1952
1389
history, to 1935 676
history, to 1955 863
history, post-war II 259
history, to 1968 1225
history, to 1970 1233,
2381
silent films 1242
pre-screen 60, 864, 879,
962
technical developments 103,
384
technological, inventions, etc.
1333
Warner Brothers 1930 to
1950 2863
Hitchcock, Alfred 180, 216,
222, 349, 473, 511, 679,
680, 770, 891, 1091,
2216, 2382, 2383, 2566,
2663
Holden, William 1091
Holland see Dutch
Holloway, Stanley 1479
Hollywood
authors in 2302
decline of 416, 693, 707,
2384, 2441, 2628
defined 667
glamour 682, 2417, 2643,
2776
gossip columnists 257,

578, 593, 595, 1167, 1335,
1461, 2111, 2368, 2387,
2414, 2470
history
1920 to 1929 692
1930 to 1939 691
1940 to 1949 690
1950 to 1959 2385
1960 to 1969 2386
homes 703
Hollywood today 710, 815,
2384, 2389, 2441, 2628
impressions of 460, 557, 669,
684, 705, 707, 709, 828,
938, 1022, 1169, 1276,
1356, 1422, 1477, 1478,
2301, 2384, 2387, 2441,
2586, 2614
police 127
religion in 2327
scandals 597a, 683, 699a,
704, 711, 712, 1459, 2476,
2731
social structure 706, 708
Ten 10, 697, 763, 2030,
2448, 2795
wit and wisdom 1475
Holographic films 377
Holt, Jack 2316
Homosexuality, in films 2710
Honors, film 2042
Hoodlums in films 91, 587, 665,
2311, 2842, 2874
Hopalong Cassidy films 2342,
2702
Hope, Bob 660
Hopkins, Miriam 2635
Hopkinson, Peter 2753
Hopper, Dennis 335, 2021
Hopper, Hedda 578, 1461, 2368,
2387
Horne, Lena 841a, 2734
Horror Films see also Monsters
717, 718, 746, 1338, 2319,
2397, 2398, 2474, 2644
Horton, Edward Everett 1151
Houdini, Harry 2316
Houghton, Katharine 1266
Houseman, John 2699
House Un-American Activities
Committee 10, 697, 763,
2030, 2448, 2622, 2795
Howard, Leslie 108, 1144

HUAC see House Un-Amer-
ican Activities Committee
Hughes, Howard 96, 734, 2401,
2675
Humanities, film in 1253
Humor, Hollywood 1475
Hungarian films 334, 1483,
2593
Hussey, Olivia 265
Huston, John 735, 736, 770,
1106, 2394, 2842
Hutton, Betty 2635

I AM CURIOUS (BLUE) 737,
794
I AM CURIOUS (YELLOW) 738,
794
Image
America, in comedy films
270
American society, in films
1179
artist in film 750
blacks in film 2814
British, in films 926
created by film 748
Indians, in films 2393,
2621
public 2772
Ince, Thomas 324a, 2751
Indexes
Film Culture 2422
Film Reviews 2264
Films in Review (1950 to
1959) 2423
Films in Review (1960 to
1964) 2424
Films in Review (1965 to
1969) 2425
Multi-Media Reviews 2575
N.Y. Times Film Reviews
2426
India, films of 756, 757, 867a,
Indians in films 2374, 2393,
2621
Industrial films 441, 489a,
758, 1131, 2427, 2899
Industry, film
American 51, 52, 249a,
338, 674, 707, 768, 898,
918, 929, 930, 942, 945,
961, 967, 967a, 977,
1042, 1070, 1291, 2092,

2160, 2561, 2664, 2665,
British 159, 929, 1456, 1484,
2664
European 466, 768, 2664
opportunities (1922) 1070
Russian 1262
Influence of films see Effect
Influence of stage on film 1274
Informational films see Educational films
Instructional films see Educational films
Intermedia 377
Interviews, collective
cameramen 685, 1123, 1151
directors 106, 180, 241,
301, 302, 349, 451, 473,
714, 770, 1030, 1151, 1222,
2188
executives 1151
personalities 241, 264, 265,
319, 349, 684, 714, 1091,
1113, 1141, 1219, 1222,
1378, 1492, 2778
INTOLERANCE 308, 2147
INVASION OF THE BODY
SNATCHERS 2131
Invisible Man films 2702
Irish film - 1940 779
Italian film
festival, Venice 1389
filmmakers 2438
history
1895 to 1969 2438
1904 to 1954 418
1907 to 1950 783
1952 to 1965 785
neo-realism 1255, 2638
overview 786, 2438
IT HAPPENED HERE 722
Ivens, Joris 170

James Bond films 2342, 2443,
2702
Jansco, Miklos 2416
Japanese film
alphabetical guide 795
analysis 798, 2444
art of 796, 2444
directors 2444
general 795, 796, 797, 798,
2444, 2674
history 797, 2444

Libraries
  film, in North America
    2196
  film use in 345, 761
Library collections, film
  materials 1299, 2022
Library of Congress catalogs
  846, 847, 948, 949,
  950, 951, 955, 2558
Lighting, for films 1080,
  2783
Lillie, Beatrice 2220
Lincoln, Elmo 2316
Linder, Max 2393
Lindsay, Vachel 2486
Literature
  and films 178a, 409a, 410,
    436, 453, 857, 2235,
    2307, 2612, 2736, 2835
  books, novels into films
    409a, 453, 1056, 2235,
    2307, 2336, 2512, 2663,
    2759, 2835
  cinema 177, 215, 858,
    2120, 2490
  denatured novel 287
  dictionary, literature into
    film 2260
  effect upon film 857, 2009
  plays into films 409a, 453,
    2722, 2727
  short stories into films
    2307, 2318, 2612, 2674,
    2736
The Literature of Cinema
  Series 858, 2490
Lithuanian films 2905
THE LITTLE ISLAND 2491
Lloyd, Harold 30, 563, 866
Loach, Kenneth 2204
Locomotion studies 2560,
  2578
Logan, Josh 1150
"Lolita" syndrome 93
Lombard, Carole 631a, 2286,
  2635
London Film Festival 2813
Lone Wolf films 2342
Longford, Raymond 2038
Loops, film index to 754
Loos, Anita 604, 1151
Lorentz, Pare 1082
Lorre, Peter 1064

Losey, Joseph 224, 241, 265,
  770, 870, 2394, 2566
Lost films 871
THE LOVED ONE 804
THE LOVERS, court case
  1057
LOVE STORY 2500
Low budget films 2160a, 2501
Loy, Myrna 265
Lubitsch, Ernst 770, 873, 2751
Lugosi, Bela 2340
Lumiere, Louis 473
Lynn, Diana 2635

M 2147
Ma and Pa Kettle films 2342
MACBETH 875
McBride, Jim 451
McCambridge, Mercedes 1394
McCarey, Leo 714
MacDonald, Marie 2734
Mace, Fred 2718
McLaglen, Andrew 2297
McLaglen, Victor 381
MacLaine, Shirley 315, 1091,
  2635
McLaren, Norman 875a
MacLiammoir, Michael 1140
McQueen, Steve 2505
MAD LOVE 2131
Magazines see also Periodicals
  articles on film performers
    946a
  current film periodicals 1399,
    2172
  film 682, 1399, 2172, 2643,
    2776
Magnani, Anna 349
Mailer, Norman 451, 2507
Main, Marjorie 2740
Maisie films 2342
Makavejev, Dusan 1208
Make-up techniques 1325, 2227,
  2236
Malden, Karl 264
Malle, Louis 573
THE MALTESE FALCON 2186
Mamoulian, Rouben 180, 770,
  889, 2394, 2515
Mankiewicz, Herman 2145
Mankiewicz, Joseph 240, 893,
  2546
Mann, Anthony 716

MAN OF ARAN 894
Mansfield, Jayne 2518, 2734
Mantz, Paul 698
Marais, Jean 2153, 2154,
2155, 2156, 2420
March, Frederic 514, 2287,
2471
Marion, Frances 2614
MARIN COUNTY SHOOT OUT
2206
Marinetti, Filippo 2521
Marker, Chris 573, 2138
Marketing films 898
Markets for film writing,
criticism 2172
Markopoulos, Gregory J.
1142
Marsh, Mae 1151
Martin, Dean 349, 966, 1091,
1248, 2734
Martin and Lewis 966
Marx, Groucho 637, 638, 852,
901, 902, 903, 912, 966
1091, 2352, 2744
Marx, Harpo 658, 901, 902,
903, 966, 2352
Marx Brothers 901, 902, 903,
966, 2352, 2887
Mascot Studios 1042
Mason, James 319
Massingham, Richard 905
Mass media, film as 2525,
2529
Matt Helm films 2342
Mayer, Arthur 918, 1151
Mayer, Louis B. 699, 854,
928, 1012
Maysles, Albert 2138, 2204
Maysles, David 2204
Media center, community
2160a
Medical films, making of
2136
MEDICINE BALL CARAVAN
2100, 2871
Meighan, Thomas 2316
Melies, Georges 2083, 2751
Melville, Jean Pierre 573,
2531, 2842
Menjou, Adolphe 790
Mercouri, Melina 319, 2442
Mercury Players 2699
Merman, Ethel 2884
Metro-Goldwyn-Mayer 699,

854, 1012, 1340, 2506,
2535
METROPOLIS 2131
Metzger, Randy 2107
Mexican Spitfire films 2702
Meyer, Russ 2107
Microfilm, Film Daily on 2245
Milestone, Lewis 180
Military films 647
Miller, Ann 2356
Miller, Arthur C. 1063, 2055
Miller, Virgil 1269
Mills, Hayley 319, 1453
Mills, John 1453
Minnelli, Vincent 180, 922
MIRACLE IN MILAN 2638
Miranda, Carmen 2303
MIRIAM 1375
THE MISFITS 1292
Mr. Moto films 2186, 2342,
2702
Mitchum, Robert 597a, 2541,
2734
Mix, Tom 385, 2477, 2526
Modern film scripts see p. 409
MODERN TIMES 592
Moguls, film 928, 970
Mohr, Hal 1151, 2055
Moldavian film 2905
Monogram Studio 2804
Monograph, screen 1200, 1201
Monopoly, film 930
Monroe, Marilyn 257, 515,
867b, 897, 931, 932, 933,
934, 1047, 1091, 1250,
1468, 2303, 2520, 2583,
2734, 2854
MONSIEUR HULOT'S HOLIDAY
935
Monsters, film 91, 122, 397,
601, 717, 718, 746, 971,
1257, 1338, 2340, 2398,
2543, 2644
Montez, Maria 714, 2804
Montez, Mario 241
Monti, Carlotta 411
Moore, Colleen 1243, 2393
Moore, Grace 1510
Morality in films 218, 952, 989,
2545, 2717
Moreau, Jeanne 349
Moreno, Antony 2316
Morley, Robert 936
Motion, art of 1023

Psychological thrillers 2398
Psychology of vision 383
Publicity, film 308, 2802
Public Library Inquiry 761
Pudovkin, Vsevolod 480a

QUE VIVA MEXICO 354, 1143, 2671
Quinn, Anthony 2624
Quiz, film topics 973, 1263, 2569

Racial problems
  of actors 376, 841a, 1116, 1236, 1266
  in films 137a, 1025, 1266, 2118, 2621, 2814
  slurs, in films 2265
Racism 2242
Radical Voices 2242
Railroads, in films 1145
Ralston, Vera Hruba 1219
Ranier, Prince 2659
Rank, J. Arthur 1001
Rapper, Irving 180
RASHOMON 2674
Rathbone, Basil 753
Ratings of films see Evaluations
  G, PG, R, X classifications 2565
Rawlinson, Herbert 2316
Ray, Charles 2316
Ray, Nicholas 770, 2394, 2566, 2842
Ray, Satyajit 58, 473, 770, 1119, 2029
Raye, Martha 2740
Reagan, Ronald 257, 1149, 1171, 1455
Realism, Soviet 1255
REBECCA 2532
Rebel hero in films 1153
THE RED BADGE OF COURAGE 1106
RED DESERT 2147
Redgrave, Lynn 319
Redgrave, Michael 1154
Reed, Sir Carol 2216
Reed, Oliver 265
Reid, Wallace 2316
Religion
  and films 178, 1346, 2036, 2118, 2568, 2650, 2785, 2792
  themes in films 648a, 1160, 2118, 2568, 2650, 2792
  use of films in 82, 304, 909, 910, 1302, 2036, 2523, 2650, 2792
Remakes of films 1161
Renoir, Jean 473, 572, 621, 770, 1164, 2216, 2416, 2681, 2682, 2683
Repetition in films 2788
Research
  film 348, 696, 765, 2116, 2808
  for a film 937a
  use of films in 258, 467
Residual rights 1300
Resnais, Alain 56, 216, 227, 241, 473, 573, 671, 770, 833, 1166
Reviews see also Evaluations
  film 1040, 2598, 2599, 2600
  index to 2264, 2425, 2575
Reynolds, Burt 2399
Rhetoric and film 436
RHODES OF AFRICA 1232, 1354
Richards, Cliff 2596
Richardson, Tony 106, 473
Richter, Hans 2211
Riefenstahl, Leni 770
Ritz Brothers 966
Rivette, Jacques 573
Roach, Hal 518, 1151
Robbe-Grillet, Alain 473, 573
Robinson, Edward G. 264, 1009, 2130
Robinson, Edward G., Jr. 597a, 1009
Robson, Flora 1172a
Robson, Mark 180
Rocha, Glauber 1208
Rock, Joe 1151
Rogers, Ginger 78, 603
Rogers, Roy 2176, 2895
Rogers, Will 2041, 2316, 2418, 2629, 2690, 2691, 2692, 2693, 2773
Romanian films 334, 2593
Room, Abram 480a
Rooney, Mickey 205, 742
Roosevelt, Eleanor 356, 1175

Rossellini, Roberto 117, 770, 1176
Rossen, Hal 2055
Rossen, Robert 519
Rouch, Jean 573, 2138, 2204
Rouquier, Georges 572
Rozier, Jacques 2138
THE RULES OF THE GAME 2147
Ruspoli, Mario 2138
Russian film
  an alphabetical guide 334
  filmmakers, 1956 to 1972 2905
  history
    1896 to 1947 820, 1038, 1261
    1917 to 1928 480a, 1035, 1038
    1918 to 1952 2553
    1920 to 1935 2749
    1956 to 1972 2905
  industry 1262
  realism in 1255
  sociology of 2533
Rutherford, Margaret 1181, 2040

Sadism in films 1182
Saif, Salah Abu 778
The Saint films 2342, 2702
SALT OF THE EARTH 1186
Sanders, George 265, 914, 1091
San Simeon 2328
SARABAND FOR DEAD LOVERS 1187
Saroyan, William 2302
SATYRICON 2147
SAWDUST AND TINSEL 2057
Scandals see Hollywood Scandals
Scandinavian film 1189
Scentavision 2706
Schary, Dore 1151, 1477
Schenck, Joseph 928
Schlesinger, John 106
Schneider, Alan 421
Schools, use of film in 469, 487, 1272, 2081, 2106, 2162, 2214, 2254, 2590, 2641, 2655, 2716, 2781,
2782, 2846
Schulberg, B. P. 928, 2773
Science Fiction films 160, 1192, 1193, 2397, 2707
Science films, making of 2899
Scott, Audrey 793
Scott, Lizabeth 2635
SCOTT OF THE ANTARCTIC 1194, 1195
Screen
  credits, actors 35, 559, 1040, 1364, 1390a, 2344, 2426, 2432, 2901
  size 561, 1033, 1464
  writers, a guide to 1462, 2392
  writers, female 604, 669, 815, 2614
Screen Snapshots 2343
Scripts see also Collections and individual titles
  as literary property 856
  checklist of 2666
  for amateur films 888, 2396, 2509
  surrealist 2769
  TV commercials 2786
  unfilmed 39, 99, 310, 670, 907, 1184, 1286, 1305, 2062, 2201, 2295, 2364, 2433, 2446, 2634, 2642, 2677, 2797
Script Writing
  amateur films 888, 2396, 2509
  and The Code 702
  forms 538
  general techniques 83, 485a, 486, 733, 1037, 1122, 1301, 1334, 1380, 2392, 2410, 2411, 2711, 2712, 2784
  short films 2712
  silent films 604, 1093
  terms used 2805
Seastrom, Victor 1206
Seberg, Jean 265
Second features 2076
THE SECRET PEOPLE 882
Sellers, Peter 257, 1214, 1248
Selznick, David O. 928, 1215, 2532
Selznick, Lewis 928, 1215

Selznick, Myron 928, 1215
Semiology in film 1238
Sennett, Mack 324a, 401, 473, 819, 2718, 2751
Sequels to films 1161, 2186, 2342, 2702, 2719
Serials
  film 1217
  silent 150, 262, 826
  sound 282, 1366, 2341, 2812
  TV films 2719
Series, books in a
  cinema literature 858, 2490
  fiction to film 2307
  films 2294, 2342
  guides 2252
  impact on society 2573
  MGM scripts 2534
  personalities 2294, 2670, 2709
  picture books 2280
  scripts 2266
  techniques 2475
Series, films in a 1161, 2186, 2342, 2702, 2719
Service films 2427
Set design 395
THE SEVENTH SEAL 2147
Sex
  in films 181, 986, 1112, 1227, 2118, 2648, 2684
  in 1970 films 1112
  in 1971 films 2648
Sex ritual in films 1228
Sexuality in films 181, 2118
Shadow films 1229
Shahin, Youssef 778
Shakespearean films
  silent 1230
  sound 2726, 2727
Shamberg, Michael 2204
Sharif, Omar 265, 778
Shaw, George Bernard 303, 911, 1218
Shearer, Douglas 108, 1151
Shelley, Mary 2305
Sherlock Holmes films 2186, 2342, 2702
Shinde's Dictionary 1231
SHOE SHINE 2638
SHOOT THE PIANO PLAYER 2733

Short films
  American 1893 to 1970 33
  comedies 1488, 2343
  evaluations 82, 430, 456, 648a, 830, 909, 910, 1062, 2037, 2248, 2272, 2273, 2276, 2277, 2575
  reviews, index to 2264, 2575
Sidney, Sylvia 2635
Siegel, Don 2842
Signoret, Simone 241, 265
Silent film see also History and Comedy, etc.
  articles about 1268, 2751
  classics 239
  comedians 242, 2718
  general 1242, 2751
  heroes 2316
  heroines 826
  history 1103, 2751
  screen credits 1390a
  serials 150, 262
  short films 541
SILENT SNOW, SECRET SNOW 2736
Sills, Milton 2316
Silverstein, Elliot 301
Sinatra, Frank 257, 569a, 1150, 1246, 1247, 2163, 2288
Sinkala cinema 867a
Siodmak, Robert 2842
Sirk, Douglas 2739
Sixties, films in the 2386, 2661
Size, screen 561, 1033, 1464
Sjoman, Vilgot 737, 738
Skolimowski, Jerzy 1208
Skouras, Spyros 928, 1250
Sleep, effect of motion pictures upon 204
Slides, film 252
Smell-o-vision 2706
Smith, Albert E. 1395
SMILES OF A SUMMER NIGHT 2057
Social
  attitudes and films 953
  commentary, films 427, 2108
  conduct of filmgoers 1252
  effect of film 1052 see also Effect of Film
  history, films 975
  institutions and film 1237
  legislation 2557
  problems, films on 471

Unfilmed scripts (cont.)
2677, 2797
Unions, Hollywood 1281
University film collections
2198
Using films, suggestions for
304, 535, 741, 940,
1074, 1191, 1199,
1408, 2081, 2106,
2162, 2274, 2409,
2466, 2473, 2510,
2523, 2568, 2590,
2650, 2655, 2716,
2781, 2782, 2846
Ustinov, Peter 1409, 2847

Vadim, Roger 93, 94, 573,
845
Valentino, Rudolf 631a, 1410,
1414, 2316, 2526
Value philosophy and film
211
Vampires 2429
Vamps 1430
Van Dyke, W. S. 1416
Van Dyke, Willard 2204
Vans, mobile for films
1404
Varda, Agnes 573
Venice Film Festival 1389
Vertov, Dziga 473, 2138
Vertov Group 2206
Vidor, King 180, 1373,
2850
Viertel, Salka 815
Vigo, Jean 1423, 2851,
2852
Villains 91, 665
Violence in films 2855,
2856
Visconti, Luchino 891, 1397,
1426, 1427
Visual arts and film 436
Visual literacy
exercises 1285, 2658
general 2036, 2658,
2855, 2857
need for 2590, 2658
perception 66
teaching 2857
thinking visually 2855
Vitagraph Pictures 1395
Vizzard, Jack 1211
Vocabulary, film 1, 536

Voice animation 1151
Voight, Jon 265, 2021
von Sternberg, Josef 140, 473,
523, 581, 770, 1431, 2132,
2566
von Stroheim, Erich 701, 770,
1293, 1432, 2167, 2347,
2751, 2859, 2860

Wajda, Andrej 473, 2133
A WALK IN THE SPRING RAIN
410
Wallis, Hal 1434
Walsh, Raoul 2391
Walthall, Henry B. 2316
Wanger, Walter 113, 1014, 1151
War
activities, motion picture indus-
try 249a, 916a, 967a
filmmaking in WW II 2753
films 443, 1439a, 2649
movie theatres during, British
1155
WAR AND PEACE 1110
Warhol, Andy 142, 451, 1437,
1438, 1439, 2757
Warner, Harry 928
Warner, Jack 928, 1010
Warner Brothers 928, 1010,
2250, 2863
Washburn, Bryant 2316
Wayne, John 328, 524, 1091,
1212, 1278, 2804, 2807,
2866
Welch, Raquel 2021, 2303
Welles, Orson 229, 230, 386,
473, 525, 770, 1140, 1248,
1374, 1442, 1443, 2021,
2145, 2394, 2688, 2699,
2872, 2873
Werner, Oscar 265
West, Mae 615, 1476, 2635
West, Jessamyn 1368
West, Nathanael 2302
Western films
actors in 653, 2374, 2645,
2807
directors of 2645
general 716, 1105, 1446,
1447, 1448, 2097, 2374,
2477, 2645, 2807
heroes 1473, 2477, 2645,
2807
outlaws 91, 2374

Western Films (cont.)
  serials, silent 2807
  stars, biographies 653,
    2374, 2807
Wheeler and Woolsey 966
White, Carol 265
White, Pearl 1458
Whiting, Leonard 265
Wide screen 561, 1033,
  1464
Wilcox, Herbert 1386
Wilder, Billy 156, 180, 1465,
  1492
Wildlife, filming 2513
Williams, Paul 2889
Wilson, Ben 2316
WINTER LIGHT 2057
Winters, Shelley 241, 1091
Wise, Robert 301
Wiseman, Frederick 2138,
  2204
Wit, Hollywood 1475
Withers, Jane 205
The Wolf Man films 2702
Wolper, David 2894
Womanhood, films on 2895a
Woodward, Joan 265
THE WORLD OF APU 2029
World War I, in films 2393
Wright, Basil 2204
Wyler, William 112, 301
Wyman, Jane 265
Wynn, Ed 1494
Wynn, Keenan 1494

Yearbook, film
  American, 1938 555
  British, 1946-47 162,
    760a, 1357
Yearbooks, film see also
  Dictionary and Encyclo-
  pedia
  Academy Players Directory
  2001
  American - Film Daily
    1918 to 1970 449
    1918 to 1969 2245
    1918 to 1922 2244
  British 2090
  Guide to College Courses in
  Film and Television
  2354
  International

1929 to 1970 481, 760a,
  769, 1109a
1957 to 1959 766
1964 to 1973 767
International film releases
  1949 to 1971 1204
Motion Picture, TV, and
  Theatre Directory 2559
Screen education, British
  1967 to 1969 1198
West Coast Theatrical Direc-
  tory 2875
Yellow Ball Workshop 881
YELLOW SUBMARINE 100
Young, Loretta 1350, 2303
YOUNG WINSTON 2035
Yugoslavian film 334, 2593

Zagreb Studios 2909
Zanuck, Darryl F. 316, 928,
  1501a
Zavattini, Cesare 1502
ZERO DE CONDUITE 2851, 2852
Zimmer, Jill Schary 1477
Zinnemann, Fred 1504
Zoopraxiscope 2578
Zukor, Adolph 720, 928, 1137,
  1151

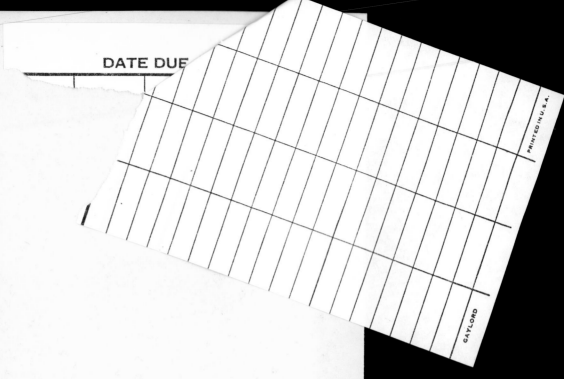